EVERYDAY SPORTS INJURIES

EVERYDAY SPORTS INJURIES

LONDON, NEW YORK, MUNICH,
MELBOURNE, DELHI

Senior Editors	Gareth Jones, Ed Wilson
Editors	Marcus Hardy, David Summers, Joanna Edwards, Nicola Munro
Medical Editor	Martyn Page
US Editor	Jill Hamilton
US Medical Consultant	Eric N. Dubrow, MD
Senior Art Editors	Gillian Andrews, Phil Gamble
Senior Designer	Keith Davis
Designers	Joanne Clark, Tim Lane
Production Controller	Ben Marcus
Jacket Designer	Mark Cavanagh
Managing Editor	Stephanie Farrow
Managing Art Editor	Lee Griffiths
Illustrators	Philip Wilson, Debbie Maizels, Richard Tibbitts, Mike Garland, Mark Walker, Darren R. Awuah, Debajyoti Dutta, Phil Gamble

First American Edition, 2010
Published in the United States by
DK Publishing
375 Hudson Street
New York, New York 10014

11 12 13   10 9 8 7 6 5 4 3 2 1

176375–Nov/2010

The information in this book is designed to help
you make informed decisions about your health and
fitness, and exercise/rehabilitation program. It is not
intended as a substitute for professional advice from
doctors and/or physical therapists. If you suspect you
have an injury or other medical problem you should
seek the approval of your physician and physical
therapist before beginning any form of exercise.
The publisher, nor the author, nor anyone else
involved in the preparation of this book are engaged
in rendering professional advice or services to the
individual reader. For further safety advice (>>p.272).

Published in Great Britain by
Dorling Kindersley Limited.
A catalog record for this book is available
from the Library of Congress
ISBN 978-0-7566-5737-6
Printed and bound in Singapore by
Tien Wah Press Ltd.
Discover more at www.dk.com

CONTENTS

TREATMENT & REHABILITATION

BMA MEDICAL EDITOR

Dr. Michael Peters is Consulting Medical Editor to the British Medical Association (BMA) and Director of the Doctors for Doctors Unit at the BMA, having previously worked as a General Practitioner.

CONSULTANT EDITORS

Prof. Nicola Maffulli is the Center Lead and Professor at the Centre for Sports and Exercise Medicine at Queen Mary, University of London, Barts and The London School of Medicine and Dentistry, and was appointed as an Orthopedic Consultant in 1996. He chairs the Scientific Committee of the English Football Association, and is an editorial board member of 10 sports medicine journals.

Dr. Stephen Motto is a Sports and Musculo-skeletal Physician at London Bridge Hospital, Honorary Lecturer at the Centre for Sports and Exercise Medicine, Queen Mary, University of London, and Clinical Tutor for the MSc in Sports and Exercise Medicine, University College, London. In his 20-year career, he has worked with the British International Rowing Team and was on the 1996 Olympics medical team.

Mr. Panos Thomas is a Consultant Orthopedic Surgeon at the Whittington Hospital, London, Director of the MSc in Sports and Exercise Medicine at University College, London, and on the Executive of the British Orthopedic Sports Trauma and Arthroscopy Association. He advises several professional soccer clubs and sports associations, and is editor of the sports orthopedic section of the electronic NHS Library.

Scott Tindal is a physiotherapist with 10 years' experience of working with private clients and elite athletes, across a range of sports, including rowing, cricket, and rugby union at both club and national level. Scott holds an MSc in Sports and Exercise Medicine from Queen Mary, University of London, and a BSc in Physiotherapy from the University of Sydney, Australia.

WHAT IS A SPORTS INJURY?

Whether you are keen to boost your fitness, play competitively, or simply increase your general wellbeing, there are many good reasons to take part in sports. While the benefits of any form of exercise should outweigh the risks, at some point most people will experience an injury of some kind, ranging from minor strains and sprains to more serious injuries, such as dislocations and fractures.

Identifying the problem

Many minor injuries can be treated simply and effectively at home, while more serious injuries may require professional help. Learning how to recognize the symptoms and identify your injury will guide you toward the most appropriate treatment, and, in turn, help you return to your chosen activity more quickly.

MOST COMMON SPORTS INJURIES

- Groin strains
- Shin splints
- Neck strain
- Lower back injury
- Pulled muscles
- Fractured bones
- Rotator cuff tendinopathy
- Tennis elbow
- Ankle sprain
- Runner's knee
- Achilles tendinopathy
- Knee ligament rupture

What is a sports injury?

A sports injury is any form of stress placed upon your body during athletic activity that prevents it from functioning to the full, and which requires a period of recovery to allow your body to heal. It usually affects your musculoskeletal system—your bones, muscles, tendons, and cartilage— and often results in pain, swelling, tenderness, and the inability to use, or place weight on, the affected area.

Sports injuries can be divided into two types: acute, or "traumatic," injuries, which occur as the result of a specific impact or traumatic event; and chronic, or "overuse," injuries, which result from wear and tear on the body and occur over an extended period of time. Acute injuries include bone fractures, muscle and tendon strains, ligament sprains, and bruising. They are common among players of collision or contact sports, such as rugby, soccer, and ice hockey. Chronic injuries include tendinopathy, bursitis, and stress fractures; they are more common among participants in endurance sports, such as long-distance running, and in people who play individual sports involving repetitive movements, such as swimming, tennis, gymnastics, and weight lifting.

Understanding the causes

There are a number of common risk factors that can lead to sports injuries, ranging from the continual repetition of an action using a poor technique to wearing inappropriate footwear. While accidents do happen, there are numerous ways that you can reduce your risk of sustaining an injury.

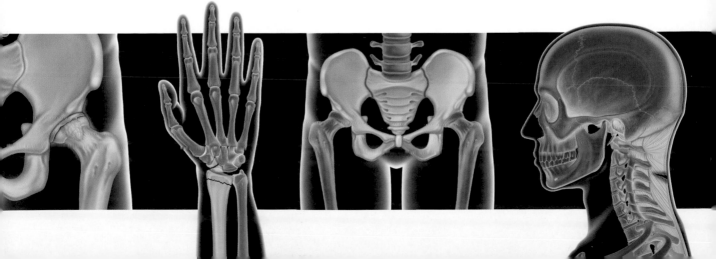

MOST COMMON CAUSES OF INJURY

- **Failure to warm up**, resulting in your muscles being less responsive and prone to strain.

- **Overtraining**, which increases the risk of chronic injury by putting continuous pressure on your body.

- **Excessive loading on the body**, which applies forces to your tissues for which they are unprepared.

- **Not taking safety precautions**, or ignoring the rules of a sporting activity, increasing the risk of an accident.

- **An accident**, often the result of an impact or collision, and usually occuring suddenly.

- **Inappropriate equipment**, so your body may not be adequately supported or protected from shock.

- **Poor exercise technique**, leading to overloading on body tissues—especially if carried out repeatedly.

- **Recurring injury**, which can weaken your body and make it more susceptible to other injuries.

- **Genetic factors**, which are intrinsic (belonging to you) and influence the shape and structure of your joints.

- **Muscle weakness or imbalance**, which can lead to a loss of strength in your body.

- **Lack of flexibility**, which will decrease your range of motion and limit some of your body's capabilities.

- **Joint laxity** (a condition which, if you have it, you should already be aware of), which can make it difficult for you to control and stabilize your joints.

ANATOMY OF A SPORTS INJURY

Muscles are tissues that can be contracted to produce force and create motion. The skeletal muscle, which is attached to and covers the skeleton, is prone to being strained or "pulled"—an injury that involves the tearing of the muscle fibers.

Bones protect your internal organs and are connected together by ligaments to form the skeleton. Bone fractures and breakages often damage surrounding soft tissue.

Joints are capsules—made of cartilage, bursae, ligaments, and tendons—that hold together two or more bones and facilitate movement. Partial or full dislocation of the joints can occur.

Cartilage is a fibrous connective tissue that forms smooth surfaces over the ends of bones where they meet the joints, allowing movement and absorbing impact and friction. Worn or torn cartilage is a common side effect of joint injuries, and is commonly caused by trauma.

Bursae are small sacs of fluid that reduce friction within some joints, and are usually located where muscles and tendons slide across bones. Bursitis is inflammation due to overuse or infection.

Ligaments are fibrous, connective tissues that connect bones, providing stability within joints and limiting movement of the limbs. An overstretched or torn ligament is known as a sprain.

Tendons are fibrous, connective tissues that connect muscles to bones, and help produce movement by enabling force to be exerted on the bones. Tendons can be strained or ruptured, and tendinopathy is pain caused by overuse or repetitive motion.

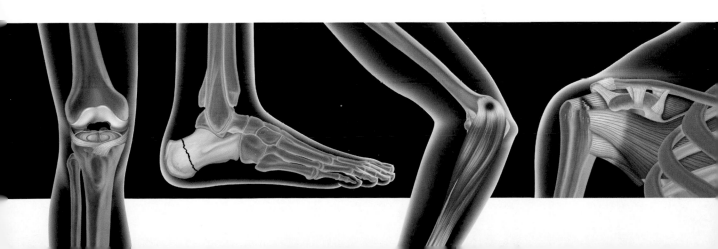

AVOIDING INJURY

Depending on your age, and basic level of health, you should be able to enjoy exercise and sports to a fun and rewarding degree. The benefits of exercise are well documented: improved cardiovascular health leads to a greater sense of psychological well-being and reduces the risk of heart disease, high blood pressure, and high cholesterol. However, regular exercise does carry the risk of injury, so take steps to reduce the chances of suffering one in the first place, and familiarize yourself with first aid in case injury strikes you or your teammates.

Assessing your fitness and tailoring your exercise

You should always visit a physician for a medical check-up to assess how fit you are before you begin playing a new sport. Starting from a low level of fitness, being overweight for your height, or having a preexisting medical condition or injury all increase the likelihood of your injuring yourself. Get in shape before starting a new sport and talk to a professional about the appropriate intensity, duration, and frequency of activity for your level of fitness.

To maximize your performance, formulate a training regimen suited to the demands of your chosen sport. Each sport calls for certain fitness requirements—for example, long-distance running requires stamina and endurance, while weight lifting necessitates a high level of muscle

CHOOSING THE RIGHT GEAR

Ill-fitting or unsuitable equipment increases the chances of injury. Consider the following tips when buying your gear:

Footwear should be suited to your chosen sport and must provide sufficient support and cushioning for your feet and ankles. Seek specialist advice regarding footwear that is specific to your sport, and always try before you buy.

Clothing should be constructed from a material suited to the purpose, such as breathable fabric for warm-weather sports or insulated fabric for cold- and wet-weather sports.

Sport-specific equipment, such as rackets, skis, and bicycles, should be custom-fitted to your body's dimensions and weight, and suited to your level of ability.

strength—so different physiques and attributes may be suited to different sports. Seek professional advice on the best activities for your sport, such as strength training, plyometric exercises, and circuit training, and learn the correct technique for each exercise. Build up your strength and stamina gradually.

Resting and fueling your body

Allowing time for rest and recovery in your training program is just as important as the exercise itself. Any type of strenuous activity places physical stress upon the body, leading to minor tissue damage. When sufficient time is allowed for your body's natural repair processes to take place, these stresses actually stimulate the body to adapt and recover, resulting in increased fitness. However, training too often prevents your body from recovering sufficiently, impairing your fitness and increasing the likelihood of injury. Avoid exercise altogether if you are already injured, or unwell or tired—or you may in fact delay your recovery.

The final element of an effective exercise regimen is diet and nutrition, which should be tailored to the requirements of your training program. Glycogen is the fuel that your body burns during exercise, so you should eat food rich in complex carbohydrates, such as whole grain bread and pasta, in the hours prior to exercise. Small quantities of

KEY TRAINING TERMS

Weight: The weight to be lifted.

Set: Groups of repetitions are organized into sets. You could, for example, perform three sets of ten repetitions.

One-rep max (one-repetition maximum): The most weight you can lift in a single repetition of a given exercise.

% one-rep max: The percentage of your one-rep max that a weight represents if the maximum weight you can lift in one repetition is 220 lb (100 kg), a weight of 175 lb (80 kg) represents 80% of one-rep max.

ROM (range of motion): The distance and angle a joint can be moved to reach its full potential.

food rich in simple carbohydrates, such as nuts, dried fruit, and energy bars, are ideal for providing fast-release energy during exercise, while a recovery meal of protein and carbohydrates should be eaten within two hours of finishing exercise. Hydration is equally important: drink enough water during exercise to keep from becoming thirsty, and continue your intake of fluids after exercise by drinking water or a specially formulated recovery drink.

Preparing your body for exercise

Warming up is an essential aspect of exercise that not only prepares your body for energetic activity and reduces the risk of injury, but also improves your potential performance and maximizes the health benefits of your chosen sport. The purpose of warming up is to ease both your mind and body from a state of rest into a state of strenuous activity. A warm-up routine consisting of gentle loosening exercises, dynamic stretching, and sport specific exercises will increase your core and muscle temperature, which helps make your muscles loose, supple, and pliable. You will also increase your heart and respiratory rate, boosting blood flow and the supply of oxygen and nutrients to your muscles, which helps prepare your muscles, tendons, and joints for action. Your cooling-down period involves gentle stretches and activity that helps dissipate lactic acid buildup in your muscles, return your heart rate to a resting pace, and prevent light-headedness, cramps, and shortness of breath.

When injury strikes

Pain is your body's way of telling you that something is wrong. Sharp pain is likely to accompany an acute injury, while dull, nagging pain is usually a sign of the onset of a chronic injury. In either case you need to identify the injury and determine what treatment is necessary. Soft tissue injuries—including damage to muscles, tendons, joints, and ligaments—are accompanied by swelling due to internal bleeding from ruptured blood vessels in the affected area, so immediate stabilization of the injury, such as the RICE procedure (»p.170), is essential for stemming the bleeding and reducing the swelling. For acute injuries, especially those involving collisions or head injuries, first aid (»pp.164–73) or medical attention may be necessary.

WARM-UP

A good warm-up prepares your body for exercise and reduces the risk of injury. Including a sport-specific activity in your warm-up can help you familiarize your body with the movements and techniques of your chosen sport. Every warm-up should include the following routines:

Cardio work, such as skipping, jogging, running, or working on a cross-trainer, will increase your heart rate and blood flow and warm up your muscles. You should begin your warm-up with up to 10 minutes of cardio work.

Gentle loosening exercises help loosen up your body if you have been in a sedentary state, and may include rotations of the ankles, hips, wrists, and shoulders, and gentle jogging on the spot. The duration and intensity of the exercises depends on your level of fitness, but should last between 5 and 10 minutes, and produce a light sweat.

Dynamic stretching contributes to muscular conditioning as well as flexibility. It is best suited to high-level athletes and should only be performed once your body has reached a high degree of flexibility.

Sport-specific exercises consist of activities and exercises related to your chosen sport, and should be performed at a more vigorous level of exertion than the first stages of your warm-up routine.

COOL-DOWN

Cooling down after exercise is equally as important as warming up. Cooling-down restores your body to a preexercise state in a controlled manner, helps your body repair itself, and can lessen muscle soreness the following day. You should never skip your cool-down altogether. Your cool-down should consist of the following components:

Gentle jogging or walking allows your heart rate to slow down and recover its resting rate, decreases your body temperature, and aids in the removal of waste products (such as lactic acid) from your muscles. You should spend between 5 and 10 minutes jogging or walking.

Static stretching helps relax your muscles and tendons and allows them to reestablish their normal range of movement. Perform only one or two stretches per muscle group, and hold each position for 20–30 seconds. Take care not to overstretch because this may inadvertently injure the muscle.

YOUR PATH TO RECOVERY

There are a number of things you can do to reduce your chances of getting injured, but no matter how careful you are, and how much you prepare for your chosen sport, injuries can still occur. The good news is that sustaining an injury doesn't have to dent your dreams of athletic success, or blow a hole in your training program. While it is essential to give your body sufficient time to heal—and you must accept that your level of activity will be disrupted to a certain degree—there are plenty of professionals who can advise you on the best form of treatment, and can design a recovery program that is specifically suited your needs.

Initial treatment

Acute injuries that involve some form of trauma or accident will usually require immediate first aid and stabilization (**»pp.164–73**), and possibly even hospital treatment, depending on the severity of the injury. In the case of serious injuries, a program of treatment will be instigated by the hospital's emergency room. For injuries such as bone fractures, this treatment program may involve a surgeon setting the bone in a cast, a follow-up appointment at an orthopedic clinic, and then a program of physical therapy.

For chronic injuries and those that do not require emergency treatment, your should schedule an appointment with your physician. After taking into account your injury history and conducting a clinical examination, your physician may be able to diagnose and treat some minor injuries. However, if your physician feels that further treatment is appropriate, you will be referred to an appropriate specialis

Consulting a specialist

Most sporting injuries affect your musculoskeletal system—your bones, ligaments, muscles, nerves, and tendons. The treatment of such injuries belongs to the realm of orthopedic surgeons and sports and exercise medicine physicians, who are sports physicians and surgeons with specialist training in this field. Rheumatologists with sports medicine experience and qualifications can also provide musculoskeletal assessments. These specialists use a range of surgical, medical, and physical means to investigate and restore function to the musculoskeletal system. After an initial examination, they may use X-rays or scans to help them diagnose the specific nature of your injury before deciding on an appropriate course of treatment. In more serious cases, they may be called upon to mend broken bones, remove torn cartilage, or operate on damaged joints using a minimally invasive procedure known as arthroscopic surgery.

Many of these physicians, including orthopedic surgeons, specialize in specific areas of the body, such as the back, knees, or ankles and feet. Podiatrists are nonmedical practitioners who can provide an assessment of foot

problems and biomechanics of your running and walking. They can perform foot surgery, prescribe orthotics, and may correct underlying problems with customized insoles for your shoes.

Physical therapy

In some cases your physician may refer you directly to a physical therapist, although referral commonly follows consultation and treatment from a sports medicine physician or orthopedic surgeon. Physical therapists specialize in maximizing physical movement and mobility, restoring physical function, and alleviating pain caused by injury, disease, and illness. After drawing up a treatment program based on your physician's prescription and suited to your needs, they use a range of methods—including deep-tissue massage, electrical stimulation, ultrasound, cold compresses and hot packs, and therapeutic exercises—to stimulate your recovery from injury (»pp.12–13).

Complementary treatments

Alongside any clinical and surgical treatment that you require, you may consider seeking further advice from specialists in a wide range of complementary therapies, including osteopaths and acupuncturists (see right). The therapies offered by these healthcare professionals may help speed up your recovery. Additionally, sports psychologists can help you deal with the emotional aspect of injury, while nutritionists can offer advice on modifying your diet to suit any changes in your activity levels due to injury.

ALTERNATIVE THERAPIES

There are a range of healthcare professionals working outside the field of conventional medicine who can help with the treatment of sports injuries. You can refer yourself to these practitioners, but remember to check their professional qualifications and whether they are accredited with the relevant association in your country. Therapists include:

Osteopaths (DO) work on the principle that overall well-being depends on the smooth functioning of the musculoskeletal system, and use osteopathic manipulative therapy (OBT) in addition to conventional methods. They have the same license to practice medicine and surgery as physicians (MD).

Chiropractors follow a holistic approach using manual manipulation of the joints, soft tissues, and particularly the spine to remedy injuries, ailments, and diseases in other areas of the body.

Acupuncturists specialize in the relief of pain through the insertion of sharp needles into a network of pressure points across the body—a method based on Chinese practices that date back more than 2,000 years. Scientific studies into the effectiveness of acupuncture have been inconclusive.

Homeopaths use small doses of homeopathic remedies, which are produced by diluting an herb or mineral multiple times. Remedies are available to assist the healing of a range of injuries such as sprains, bruising, tendinopathy, cuts and abrasions, and fractures. While there is little scientific evidence of its effectiveness, many still believe that homeopathy works if used appropriately.

PHYSICAL THERAPY AND REHABILITATION

While your sports injury may be treated by a variety of healthcare specialists, the leading role in your rehabilitation is likely to be played by your physiotherapist. From making an initial assessment to guiding you through a programme of treatment, your physiotherapist will oversee your rehabilitation, ensuring that your injury is fully healed and that your body is conditioned to prevent it from recurring.

Initial consultation

An accurate initial assessment and diagnosis of your injury is critical to the effectiveness of your treatment and rehabilitation. Depending on the type of sports injury you have suffered, your referral to a physical therapist may come either directly from your physician or follow treatment by an orthopedic surgeon (»pp.10–11). In the case of a serious injury, or following surgery, your

CHOOSING A PHYSICAL THERAPIST

When seeking treatment for a sports injury, aim to find a physical therapist who specializes in the relevant area of the body. Next, make sure they are fully accredited with the relevant organization in your country. Accreditation ensures that your physical therapist is qualified to practice at the highest standards of care, has undertaken the necessary training to maintain accredited status, and is up-to-date with the latest developments in the profession. The American Physical Therapy Association (APTA) is the membership body for physical therapists in the US, while the equivalent in the UK is the Chartered Society of Physiotherapy (CSP).

physical therapist will be provided with a detailed medical history of how the injury occurred, how the treatment has progressed, and the outcome of any surgical procedures. Whether it is an acute or a chronic injury, your physical therapist will test the injured area to assess its power and mobility, and possibly perform a complete posture, gait, and biomechanical assessment, before planning a full program of treatment.

Assessing your injury

Initially, your physical therapist will assess the degree of function—including movement, rotation, and load-bearing capability—of the affected area. The therapist may ask you to attempt normal movement to the best of your ability, and may perform a manual manipulation of the area.

Joint range of motion (ROM) is a good indication of the condition of joints and muscles. Each joint moves a defined amount—measured in degrees—and in certain directions. Your physical therapist will assess whether the joint can move through its full range of movement to determine whether further mobility and strengthening exercises are necessary.

Your physical therapist may also test the muscles in and around the injured part of your body to determine which of them, if any, require strengthening. A guide such as the Oxford Scale (see left) is generally used to grade the muscles in question. Once your physical therapist has made these assessments, an appropriate course of treatment will be determined.

ASSESSING MUSCLE STRENGTH

Physical therapists gauge the strength of a damaged muscle against an established scale, such as the Oxford Scale below. Scores are allocated on a scale from 0/5 to 5/5, with the addition of a plus (+) or minus (–) designating a stronger or weaker performance than expected for each stage.

0/5: There is no discernable muscle movement when the patient attempts to use the muscle.

1/5: The patient's muscle twitches, but the patient is unable to move it through any of its normal range of motion.

2/5: Normal joint movement is possible, but only when the patient's muscle is positioned so that it is not acting against gravity.

3/5: Normal joint movement is possible against gravity, but no manual resistance is applied.

4/5: The patient's muscle can move its joint through the full range of motion, against gravity, and with the application of some resistance.

5/5: There is unimpaired movement of the patient's muscle against gravity and increased resistance (as determined by the physical therapist, according to the patient's age and fitness).

Physical therapy techniques

Physical therapists use a variety of techniques to treat sports injuries. Through massage and manipulation they can relieve inflammation, reduce muscle pain and joint stiffness, and encourage blood flow to and fluid drainage from the affected area. They may also use a combination of electrotherapy, ultrasound, and the application of heat and cold to stimulate the nervous and circulatory systems to reduce pain and accelerate healing. However, in most cases the most important factor in the rehabilitation process is a comprehensive program of remedial exercises.

Your rehabilitation program

The exercises featured in the treatment and rehabilitation chapter of this book (»pp.162–261) have been devised to improve the mobility, flexibility, or strength of various parts of the body. Your physical therapist will use exercises such as these to put together a program of exercises that become progressively more challenging. A critical aspect of recovery and progression is gauging when the injured area is strong enough for you to move on to the next stage of the program. The physical therapist will perform ongoing assessments using "baseline" objective markers that assess whether you can complete a movement or exercise for a specified duration, intensity, or number of repetitions.

The rehabilitation guidelines outlined in the sports injuries chapter of this book (»pp.48–161) are broken up into early, intermediate, and advanced levels of treatment, complete with a final level of markers indicating whether you are ready to return to full engagement in your chosen sport or exercise. However, you should only follow a rehabilitation program that has been tailored to your specific needs and training history under the guidance of an accredited physical therapist.

A successful recovery

Key to your successful and speedy recovery from any sports injury is making sure you are using the correct technique when performing every exercise, and diligently following the guidance given to you by your physical therapist. It is important that you never exceed the number of repetitions or levels of intensity that are recommended, and that you follow the step-by-step instructions given with each exercise closely. Effective communication between you and your physical therapist will also ensure that at every stage of your rehabilitation you are receiving the very best treatment.

There is one crucial component to your recovery from injury that health specialists, despite their high levels of expertise, cannot provide: the will to succeed. If you apply the same determination for success in your chosen sport to practicing the exercises in your rehabilitation program, you will have every chance of making a full recovery in as short a time as possible.

GETTING THE BEST FROM REHABILITATION

- **Get in shape** before starting a new activity or sport.
- Always **stick to the exercises** that have been recommended for your training program.
- Wear the right **protective gear**.
- Always **warm up** and **cool down**.
- Make sure you use the **correct technique**.
- **Keep hydrated**.
- Vary your **routine**.
- **Build up gradually**—don't try to do too much, too soon.
- **Don't exceed** the recommended number of repetitions or level of intensity.
- **Don't overwork your body**—know your limits.
- Immediately **stop** what you are doing **if you feel pain**.
- Make sure you have **adequate rest** between sessions.
- **Avoid exercise** if you are already injured, or if you are unwell or tired.
- **Continue** your program until you have **finished it**.
- **Maintain a positive attitude** and keep your spirits up.

SPORTS
IN PROFILE

Understanding the physical demands of your chosen sport is key to staying injury-free. This chapter examines the areas of your body that are particularly vulnerable to injury across different sports, the kinds of injuries that are most likely to occur, and gives examples of exercises you can use to condition your body to help prevent them.

COLLISION TEAM SPORTS

Collision team sports, such as football, rugby, ice hockey, and lacrosse, all involve high-impact blows to the body, which can cause serious injuries. Contact can lead to head or spinal injuries, while constant dodging movements can result in damage to the ankles, knees, and hips.

SPORTS SUCH AS...

- Football
- Aussie rules football
- Rugby league
- Rugby union
- Ice hockey
- Gaelic football
- Lacrosse
- Hurling

Wrist, hand, and fingers

1

2

3

4

5

6 Thigh

7 Knee

8 Leg

9 Ankle, foot, and toes

INJURY HOTSPOTS

1 **Head and face** High-impact blows and collisions with other players are a common cause of blood injuries (»p.166) and concussion (»p.52).

2 **Neck, spine, and back** Intense pressure is placed on the neck and spine during scrums or tackling, and this can lead to problems such as disk injuries (»p.60) or even fractures (»p.170).

3 **Shoulder and chest** Heavy impact and falls can lead to dislocations or fractures of the collarbone (»p.66) and separation of the collarbone joints (»p.68). Wrenching of the arm into awkward positions can cause rotator cuff tears (»p.70).

4 **Wrist, hand, and fingers** Contact with other players, and falling on the wrist and hand, can cause dislocations (»p.86 and »p.94) or fractures (»p.84 and »p.94).

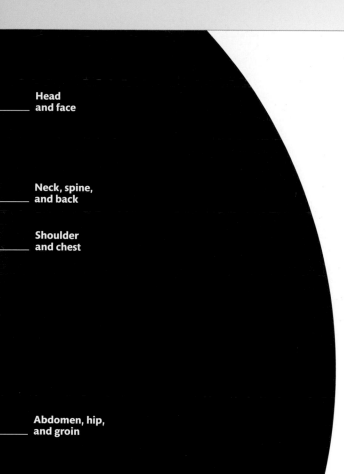

Head
and face

Neck, spine,
and back

Shoulder
and chest

Abdomen, hip,
and groin

5 Abdomen, hip, and groin Rapid changes of direction can lead to strains of the groin (»p.104). Hernias may also occur (»p.106).

6 Thigh Short sprints can strain the hamstrings (»p.108) and quadriceps (»p.110).

7 Knee Turning quickly, or sustaining a strong blow to the knee, can cause damage to the ligaments (»pp.124–29) and meniscal injuries (»p.130).

8 Leg High-impact contact can lead to fractures of the tibia and fibula (»p.134). Pushing off to sprint can cause strains to the calf and the toes, while sudden changes in pace or direction can tear the Achilles tendon (»p.140).

9 Ankle, foot, and toes Rolling over on the ankle while changing direction is a common cause of ankle ligament sprains (»p.144) and, in severe instances, can also cause fractures (»p.142).

STAYING FREE OF INJURY

In addition to using the right protective equipment, such as helmets and mouth guards, a high level of cardiovascular and muscular fitness is also important for avoiding injury. A good warm-up and cool-down procedure on game days, and a training program that offers excellent preparation for games, is essential.

WARM-UP AND COOL-DOWN
Warm-ups for collision sports need to include dynamic stretches and cardiovascular work, such as shuttle runs, to raise the temperature of the body, preparing it for exercise. Cool-downs should include gentle jogging and stretching to prevent muscles from seizing up.

MAINTENANCE TRAINING
Training programs for collision sports should be based around total fitness; a good way to achieve this is by combining strength-training circuits to develop power with interval training to improve cardiovascular fitness.

■ **Flexibility**
The high-impact nature of collision sports makes the joints susceptible to strains and sprains. Flexibility exercises, such as wall sit presses (»p.185), can help prevent this.

■ **Strengthening**
Many collision sports rely on explosive power. Strength-training exercises, such as power cleans (»p.238), are a good way of developing this.

■ **Power and stability**
Twisting and turning leaves the joints susceptible to injury. Stability exercises, such as box jumps (»p.259), help boost acceleration, and also improve hip, knee, and ankle stability.

CONTACT TEAM SPORTS

Although contact team sports, such as soccer and field hockey, do not carry the same risks as collision sports, the fast pace at which they are played, along with the potential for contact between players, result in a relatively high probability of injury.

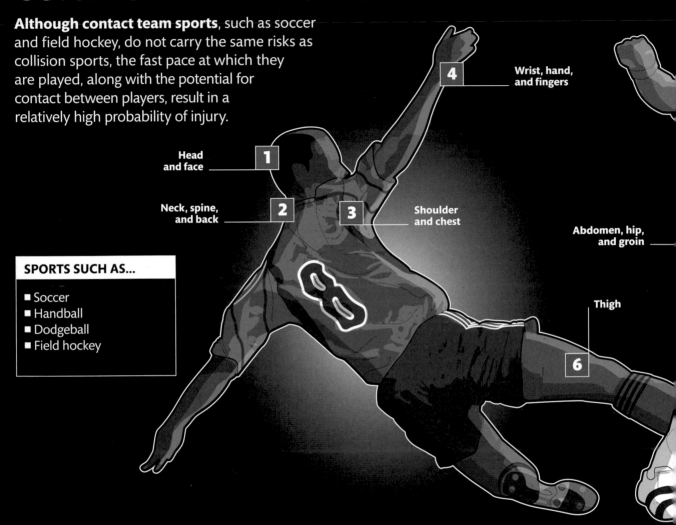

Head and face

Neck, spine, and back

Shoulder and chest

Wrist, hand, and fingers

Abdomen, hip, and groin

Thigh

SPORTS SUCH AS...

- Soccer
- Handball
- Dodgeball
- Field hockey

INJURY HOTSPOTS

1 **Head and face** Collisions between players may cause blood injuries (»p.166) or concussion (»p.52).

2 **Neck, spine, and back** Sustained postures in some sports, such as bending forward in hockey, can lead to pain and stiffness in the neck (»p.56) and lower back. These positions may eventually lead to a slipped disk and sciatica (»p.60).

3 **Shoulder and chest** Falling onto an outstretched hand or arm is common in many contact sports, and may cause dislocation of the shoulder (»p.74) or injuries to the joints of the collarbone (»p.68).

4 **Wrist, hand, and fingers** Using the hand to break a fall can cause dislocations or fractures of the wrist (»p.86 and »p.84), and fingers and thumb (»p.94).

5 **Abdomen, hip, and groin** Constant changes of direction when playing these sports mean that adductor strains (»p.104) are common. The repeated kicking movement required in soccer can lead to overuse injuries, including osteitis pubis (»p.102).

6 **Thigh** Rapid acceleration and deceleration mean that strains of the hamstrings (»p.108) and quadriceps (»p.110) often occur.

Knee

Leg

Ankle, foot,
and toes

STAYING FREE OF INJURY

In contact sports, long-term training as well as pre-game preparation are crucial for preventing injury. They demand high levels of cardiovascular and muscular fitness—and so a training program should take this into account. Protective gear, such as shin guards, may also be worn.

WARM-UP AND COOL-DOWN

A thorough warm-up and cool-down on game days is essential. Warm-ups should include dynamic stretches and cardiovascular work to raise the body's temperature to prepare it for exercise. Gentle jogging and stretches help cool-down, and ice baths aid muscle recovery.

TRAINING

Training programs for contact sports should focus on total fitness. Circuit training with weights (to improve strength and power) alongside interval training (for the cardiovascular system) works very well.

■ **Flexibility**

Contact sports require good flexibility. Exercises such as stride stretches (»p.244) help increase range of movement as well as promote good posture, which may reduce pressure in the lower back.

■ **Strengthening**

Strength is essential for contact sports. Strengthening the legs and lower back with exercises, such as straight-leg deadlifts (»p.197), can improve performance and prevent injury.

■ **Power and stability**

Training for contact sports should include the development of explosive power. Exercises such as kneeling supermen (»pp.228–29) help by strengthening core muscles in the back.

7 **Knee** Twists, turns, or awkward falls put a lot of strain on the knees, and this can lead to ligament injuries (»pp.124–29) or dislocations (»p.114).

8 **Leg** Impact from tackles can result in fractures of the tibia and fibula (»p.134). Sudden acceleration from standing can lead to tendinopathy or Achilles tendon tears (»p.140).

9 **Ankle, foot, and toes** Metatarsal fractures (»p.158) can result from the foot being stood on, and rolling over on the ankle may sprain the ligaments (»p.144). Toe strains are also common (»p.156).

NET-BASED SPORTS

The frequent jumping and landing involved in net–based team sports, such as basketball, netball, and volleyball, puts a great deal of stress on the hips, knees, and ankles. As a result of these repeated actions, injuries to the lower limbs are common. The large amount of throwing involved can also cause problems in the shoulder, elbow, and wrist.

INJURY HOTSPOTS

1 **Neck, spine, and back** Looking up at the basket repeatedly can cause inflammation and pain in the neck (»pp.56–59). It can also give rise to poor posture, again leading to neck pain.

2 **Shoulder and chest** Repetitive overhead movements stress the muscles of the shoulder joints, and may cause rotator cuff inflammation (»p.70), and shoulder bursitis and impingement (»p.72).

3 **Arm and elbow** Repeated extension movements while shooting can lead to pain and inflammation in the tendons around the elbow (»p.78).

4 **Wrist, hand, and fingers** Falls and contact with other players can cause dislocations or fractures of the wrist (»pp.84–87). Repetitive actions, such as overhead shooting, may lead to strain injuries of the wrist (»p.88).

5 **Abdomen, hip, and groin** Sharp changes of movement when dodging past players may cause groin strains (»p.104) or hernias (»p.106).

6 **Thigh** The sprints and jumping that are involved in net-based sports place stress on the thigh—tears of the hamstrings (»p.108) and quadriceps (»p.110) are a risk.

7 **Knee** Repeated jumping and landing can lead to overuse injuries, such as patellar tendinopathy (»p.122).

8 **Leg** Jumping or accelerating quickly from standing may strain the calf muscle, causing injuries to the Achillies tendon, such as tendinopathies or ruptures (»p.140).

9 **Ankle, foot, and toes** Landing on the ankle in a position where it rolls inward can cause ligament sprains (»p.144).

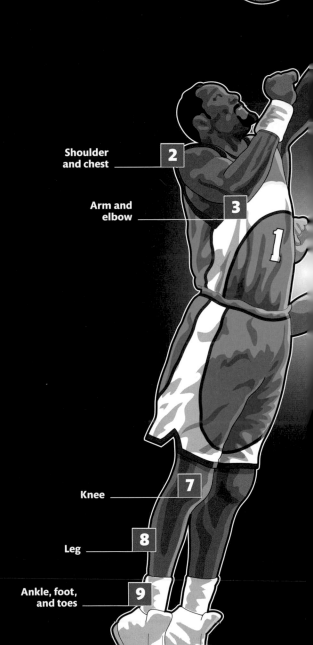

Shoulder and chest **2**

Arm and elbow **3**

1

Knee **7**

Leg **8**

Ankle, foot, and toes **9**

4 Wrist, hand, and fingers

1 Neck, spine, and back

SPORTS SUCH AS...

- Basketball
- Netball
- Korfball
- Volleyball

5 Abdomen, hip, and groin

6 Thigh

STAYING FREE OF INJURY

In addition to the muscular strains that can be caused by rapid acceleration and deceleration, the jumping and landing in net-based sports require good stability in the ankles and knees to reduce stress on the joints. Supportive footwear can help with this.

WARM-UP AND COOL-DOWN
Warm-ups should include shuttle runs to increase body temperature, and jumping drills or shooting practice to ready the ankles and knees for the game ahead. Perform dynamic stretches prior to a game and jog gently to cool down afterward.

TRAINING
Players of net-based sports require stamina as well as quick bursts of power. A training program incorporating plyometric exercises—which use explosive movements to develop power in the muscles—is key to achieving optimum performance and preventing injury.

■ Flexibility
Running on hard surfaces places stress on the lower body. Stretching exercises, such as rotational walking lunges (»p.181), are a good way of preventing overuse injuries.

■ Strengthening
Power in the shoulders helps prevent injury and improves performance. Exercises, such as medicine ball throws (»p.216), assist in developing this.

■ Power and stability
Jumping effectively for the ball requires power. Exercises, such as box step-ups (»p.203), develop this, as well as increasing ankle and knee stability.

BAT- AND CLUB-BASED SPORTS

Bat- and club-based sports, such as baseball, cricket, and golf, put a lot of stress on the upper limbs, particularly the shoulders, elbows, and hands. Repetitive strain injuries often develop as a result of repeated actions, such as swinging a club or bat over and over.

SPORTS SUCH AS...

- Baseball
- Softball
- Rounders
- Cricket
- Golf

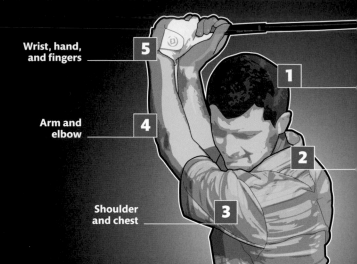

Wrist, hand, and fingers **5**

1

Arm and elbow **4**

2

Shoulder and chest **3**

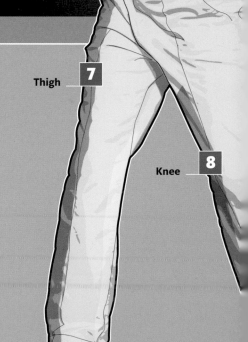

6

Thigh **7**

Knee **8**

INJURY HOTSPOTS

1 **Head and face** Head injuries, such as skull fractures or concussion (»p.52), are a risk when standing in close proximity to the ball striker, or facing a quickly delivered ball when batting.

2 **Neck, spine, and back** Abrupt spinal twists can cause degeneration of the disks (»p.60), lower back pain, and damage to the nerves in the neck (»p.58).

3 **Shoulder and chest** Lack of stability in the shoulder, or bad technique when bowling or batting, can lead to rotator cuff injuries (»p.70), shoulder bursitis (»p.72), or even subluxation (»p.74).

4 **Arm and elbow** Overuse of the forearm muscles, which attach to the inside of the elbow, can cause inflammation of the elbow tendons, or tennis elbow (»p.78).

5 **Wrist, hand, and fingers** Fractures to the thumb (»p.94) are a frequent result of being hit by a ball when batting in sports like baseball.

6 **Abdomen, hip, and groin** Contact between the hip and a ball thrown at high speed can cause inflammation of the bursa around the hip, a condition known as trochanteric bursitis (»p.98). Frequent rotation of the hip when batting, bowling, or swinging a golf club can result in wear and tear of the hip joint.

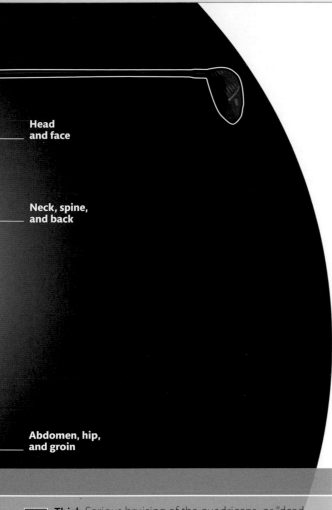

Head
and face

Neck, spine,
and back

Abdomen, hip,
and groin

7 **Thigh** Serious bruising of the quadriceps, or "dead legs" (»p.110), are a common injury if a fast-moving ball makes contact with the thigh. This is a relatively common occurrence in sports such as baseball and cricket.

8 **Knee** Frequent changes in direction when fielding put a large amount of pressure on the knees; twisting the knee can tear the ligaments (»pp.124–29) or cause meniscal injuries (»p.130).

9 **Ankle, foot, and toes** Heavy and constant pressure on the foot when bowling in cricket can lead to inflammation on the underside of the foot, a condition known as plantar fasciitis (»p.160).

9 Ankle, foot, and toes

STAYING FREE OF INJURY

Although cardiovascular fitness is important for staying injury-free in all sports, bat- and club-based sports rely on good technique. Correct posture and alignment are important in making sure technique does not suffer as a result of injury.

WARM-UP AND COOL-DOWN
Short warm-ups such as dynamic stretches and sport-specific drills are important, particularly just before batting or bowling, because players are often inactive before this, making them more susceptible to injury.

TRAINING
A training regimen that concentrates on strengthening the stabilizing muscles in the shoulder will help limit shoulder problems, which can be a frequent occurrence in these sports. Stretching the chest can help prevent shoulder pain arising as a result of repeated throwing or swinging motions.

■ **Flexibility**
Exercises to reduce tightness in the shoulder muscles, such as pec stretches (»p.240), will decrease the risk of tears to the rotator cuff when batting or throwing.

■ **Strengthening**
Strengthening the muscles that stabilize the shoulder joint will improve performance and reduce the risk of injury—exercises such as standing Ys (»p.215) can help with this.

■ **Power and stability**
Exercises such as pulley chops (»pp.230–31) build core power, enabling a more explosive batting action or golf swing.

RACKET-BASED SPORTS

Racket-based sports, such as badminton, squash, and tennis, require excellent endurance of both the cardiovascular and muscular systems. The knees and the ankles are put under stress during accelerating movements and quick changes of direction. Repeated overhead movements of the arms during serves and smashes also put considerable strain on the upper limbs.

SPORTS SUCH AS...

- Tennis
- Badminton
- Squash
- Raquetball
- Table tennis

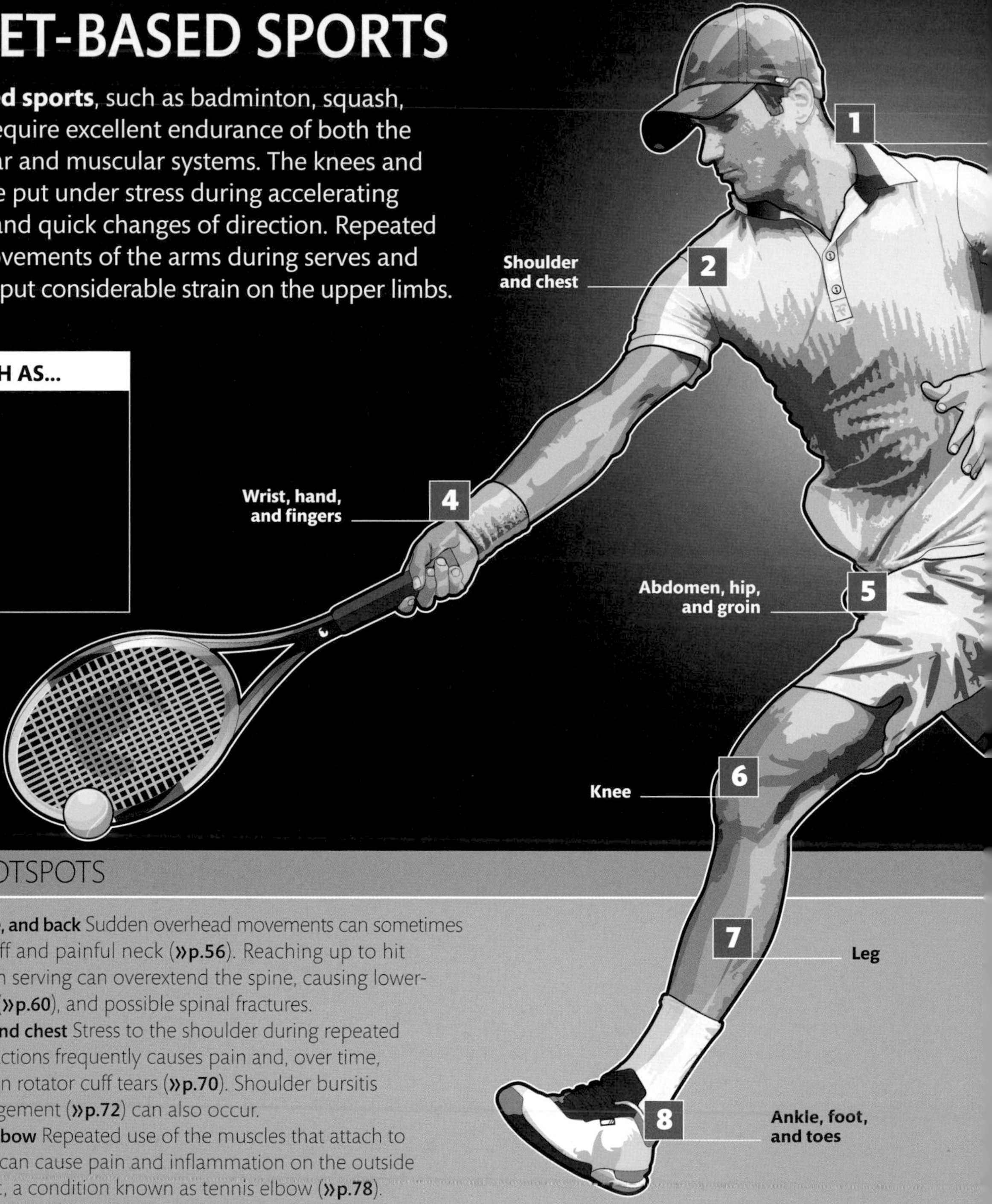

1

Shoulder and chest **2**

Wrist, hand, and fingers **4**

Abdomen, hip, and groin **5**

Knee **6**

7   Leg

8   Ankle, foot, and toes

INJURY HOTSPOTS

1 **Neck, spine, and back** Sudden overhead movements can sometimes cause a stiff and painful neck (»p.56). Reaching up to hit a ball when serving can overextend the spine, causing lower-back pain (»p.60), and possible spinal fractures.

2 **Shoulder and chest** Stress to the shoulder during repeated overhead actions frequently causes pain and, over time, can result in rotator cuff tears (»p.70). Shoulder bursitis and impingement (»p.72) can also occur.

3 **Arm and elbow** Repeated use of the muscles that attach to the elbow can cause pain and inflammation on the outside of the joint, a condition known as tennis elbow (»p.78).

4 **Wrist, hand, and fingers** The repetitive movements of the wrist common in racket sports may cause carpal tunnel syndrome (»p.90).

5 **Abdomen, hip, and groin** Quick changes of direction are a common cause of adductor strain (»p.104).

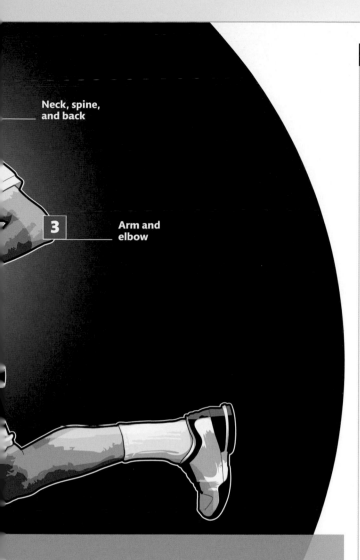

Neck, spine, and back

3 Arm and elbow

STAYING FREE OF INJURY

Racket sports rely on excellent stability around the outer limbs in order for a player to change direction quickly and retrieve difficult shots. The body must also be accustomed to powerful movements when hitting overhead shots—it is therefore essential to have a good core stability for the transference of power through the body.

WARM-UP AND COOL-DOWN
Warm-ups should involve raising the body temperature with light cardiovascular work and practicing movements needed during the game. Practicing all the required shots or elements used in the sport helps accustom the body to activity. Thorough stretching is vital to cool down.

TRAINING
Training programs for racket sports need to focus on power and cardiovascular fitness. Interval training for the cardiovascular system combined with plyometric exercises for developing power should help with this.

■ **Flexibility**
Stretches that improve the flexibility of the shoulder, such as sleeper stretches (**»p.245**), reduce stiffness and decrease the risk of injury.

■ **Strengthening**
Strengthening exercises, such as lawnmowers (**»p.190**), that mimic the movements used in racket sports, are important for improving performance and reducing the risk of injury.

■ **Power and stability**
Strengthening the lower body through exercises, such as sideways hops and jumps (**»p.257**), increases core stability and develops the power needed for quick changes in direction.

6 **Knee** Lunging and bending movements of the knee may cause inflammation of the patellar tendon (**»p.122**) or the patellofemoral joint (**»p.116**). In younger athletes, this may also lead to Osgood-Schlatter Syndrome (**»p.122**).

7 **Leg** Rapid changes of pace exert the back of the leg and can cause calf strains or tears (**»p.136**). Very occasionally, repeated use of the lower-leg muscles can cause a buildup of pressure in the limb, leading to a more serious condition called compartment syndrome (**»p.139**).

8 **Ankle, foot, and toes** Rolling onto an ankle while changing direction can result in severe ligament sprains (**»p.144**), and toe strains (**»p.156**).

RUNNING

The strain placed on the lower limbs by running means that short-, middle-, and long-distance runners frequently suffer injury. Unsuitable footwear, as well as poor posture and technique, often lead to overuse injuries, such as shin splints and tendinopathies.

INJURY HOTSPOTS

1 **Neck, spine, and back** Repeatedly running on hard surfaces places stress on the spine, and may lead to herniated disks and sciatica (**»p.60**). Weak core-stabilizing muscles can also lead to a possible dysfunction of the sacroiliac joint (**»p.62**), resulting in pain in the pelvic area.

2 **Abdomen, hip, and groin** Tightness around the hips when running long distances can put stress on the outside of the joint, leading to trochanteric bursitis (**»p.98**). Rapid contraction of the thigh muscles during sprinting can also lead to acute groin injuries (**»p.104**). Hernias (**»p.106**) are also quite common in sprinters.

3 **Thigh** Sprinting or running without an adequate warm-up beforehand may cause strains or even tears of both the hamstrings (**»p.108**) and the quadriceps (**»p.110**).

4 **Knee** Running long distances, especially on hard surfaces, puts a lot of stress on the knee joint. Tightness in the iliotibial band (**»p.132**) can cause pain on the outside of the knee while running. Patellar tendinopathy (**»p.122**) causes pain in the front of the knee, and is often the result of the body being unable to cope with an increase in mileage.

5 **Leg** The repetitive action of lifting the toes while running puts strain on the front of the shins, and can cause medial tibial stress syndrome, or shin splints (**»p.138**).

6 **Ankle, foot, and toes** Pushing off from the toes may cause tibialis posterior tendinopathy (**»p.152**), resulting in pain on the inside of the ankle, and toe strain (**»p.156**). It can also lead to flat feet, which puts more stress on the lower limbs when running.

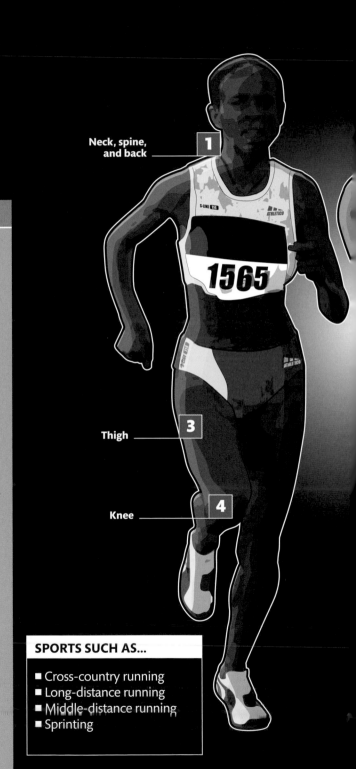

Neck, spine, and back   **1**

Thigh   **3**

Knee   **4**

SPORTS SUCH AS...

- Cross-country running
- Long-distance running
- Middle-distance running
- Sprinting

2 Abdomen, hip, and groin

5

6 Ankle, foot, and toes

STAYING FREE OF INJURY

Runners should concentrate on three key areas during their training: increasing distance gradually (10 percent each week as a guide); wearing appropriate footwear that maintains optimal foot position, in order to put as little stress as possible on the lower limbs; and following a comprehensive strengthening and stretching program in addition to running.

WARM-UP AND COOL-DOWN

Ensure that warm-ups and cool-downs include thorough stretches in order to maintain optimum muscle length. Allowing the muscles to relax in this way helps reduce stress on the lower limbs.

TRAINING

Obviously, cardiovascular fitness is a priority for runners. However, following a core-strengthening program will provide support for the lower back, reducing the risk of herniated disks and sciatica.

■ **Flexibility**
Running on a hard surface can damage the knees. Foam roller exercises (»p.191), or a sports massage, are a good way of mobilizing the tissue on the outside of the leg to help reduce knee pain.

■ **Strengthening**
Performance can be improved, and the risk of injury reduced, by performing leg-strengthening exercises, such as barbell squats (»p.192).

■ **Power and stability**
Stabilizing exercises, such as single-leg squats (»p.193), ensure that the body is well supported when running.

WEIGHTLIFTING AND POWERLIFTING

Weightlifting and powerlifting put huge amounts of stress on the joints throughout the body, and work the muscles to a point of near failure, sometimes resulting in tears and ruptures of the muscles and ligaments. Failure to employ a good technique when lifting heavy weights can also result in injury.

INJURY HOTSPOTS

1 **Neck, spine, and back** Overstraining during weight training may cause spasms of the neck muscles (»p.56). The spine becomes heavily compressed, which, when combined with inadequate spinal stability and poor lifting technique, can cause muscle strains (»p.56), joint fractures, or problems with the spinal disks, such as a prolapsed disk (»p.60).

2 **Shoulder and chest** The shoulders are a frequent area of injury for weightlifters. Overexertion can lead to rotator cuff injuries (»p.70) and shoulder bursitis and impingement (»p.72).

3 **Arm and elbow** The tendons around the elbow joint can become inflamed from overuse, leading to tennis elbow (»p.78).

4 **Abdomen, hip, and groin** Repeatedly flexing the hip under the strain of heavy weights can result in muscle strain or labral tears (»p.100). Hernias can also occur (»p.106).

5 **Knee** Lifting weights using poor technique places great stress on the joints, and may lead to patellofemoral joint pain (»p.116) or patellar tendon rupture.

Arm and elbow

Knee

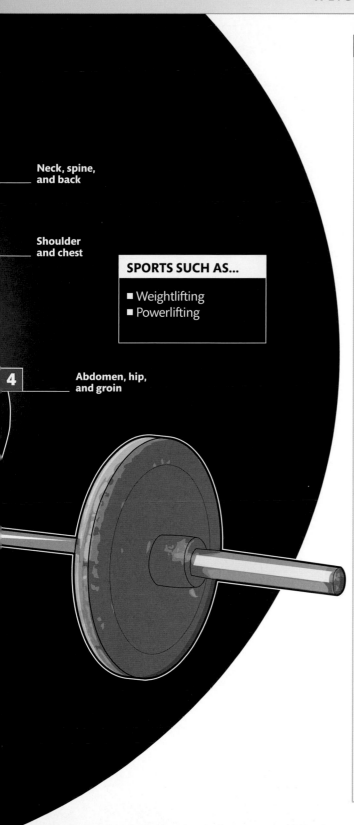

Neck, spine,
and back

Shoulder
and chest

SPORTS SUCH AS...

- Weightlifting
- Powerlifting

4   Abdomen, hip,
and groin

STAYING FREE OF INJURY

Weightlifting and powerlifting place huge strain on the lower back—a supportive belt may help prevent injury to this area. Good lifting technique is also important in reducing risk; weights should not be excessively heavy, and, when lifting from a lying position, there should always be somebody to help in case of difficulties.

WARM-UP AND COOL-DOWN

Warm-ups should consist of cardiovascular work to raise body temperature, dynamic stretches to engage the muscles, and lifting light weights to prepare the body to perform lifts with heavier weights. Cool-downs should involve gentle jogging and static stretches.

MAINTENANCE TRAINING

Training should concentrate on developing explosive power and cardiovascular fitness to maximize performance, along with core strength and flexibility of the joints in order to prevent injury.

■ Flexibility
Lifting weights places stress on the thigh. Stretches that increase mobility in that area, such as hamstring lowers (»p.187), reduce the risk of straining the hamstrings.

■ Strengthening
The legs generate much of the power needed for lifting weights. Exercises such as Romanian deadlifts (»p.196) are excellent for developing strength.

■ Power and stability
Core stability is essential for preventing injuries to the lower back. Torsional exercises, such as chops and lifts (»pp.230–33), can help improve this.

COMBAT SPORTS

Combat sports, such as boxing, judo, and karate make tough demands on the body; training is intense, and participation requires good all-round fitness. Regardless of the fitness of the participants, however, the aggressive blows traded between opponents mean that these sports always carry a serious risk of injury.

INJURY HOTSPOTS

1 **Head and face** High-impact strikes to the head can cause injuries such as concussion (»p.52) and jaw fractures (»p.54).

2 **Neck, spine, and back** Fractures to the cervical spine (»p.170) can be sustained by being thrown onto the neck. Rapid twisting movements of the neck during contact can result in neck strain (»p.56), causing stiffness and pain.

3 **Shoulder and chest** Shoulders undergo stress when wrestling opponents, and landing badly after being thrown can result in posterior or anterior dislocations (»p.74), and sternoclavicular joint injuries (»p.68). Direct blows to the ribs can cause bruising or fractures (»p.76).

4 **Arm and elbow** Falling on an elbow or an outstretched arm may cause fractures of the upper arm, radius, or ulna (»pp.80–83).

5 **Wrist, hand, and fingers** The wrist (»pp.84–87) and fingers (»p.94) are all vulnerable to dislocation or fracture, either from a fall or a blow from an opponent.

6 **Abdomen, hip, and groin** Falls on the pelvis may cause a dislocation or, more seriously, a fracture of the neck of the femur (»p.96).

7 **Knee** The twisting movements involved in grappling place a lot of stress on the knees, and can cause ligament injuries (»pp.124–29) and cartilage damage (»p.120). Falling directly on the knee may result in dislocation of the patella (»p.114).

8 **Leg** Direct blows to the shin from a kick may result in fractures to the tibia or fibula (»p.134).

9 **Ankle, foot, and toes** Ankle fractures can result from direct impact to the joint, while ligament sprains as a result of the ankle being twisted are a reasonably common occurrence (»p.144).

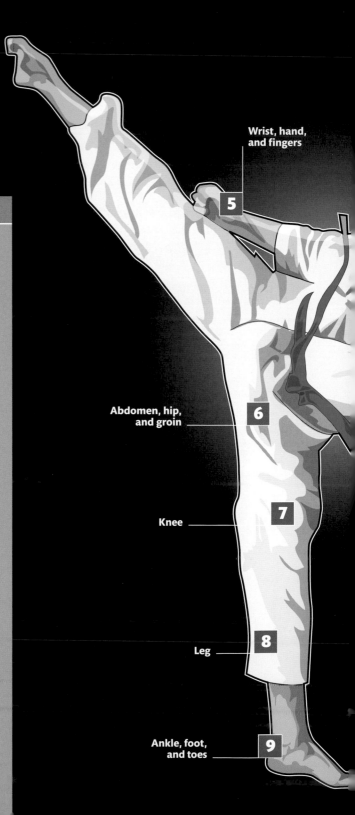

Wrist, hand, and fingers **5**

Abdomen, hip, and groin **6**

Knee **7**

Leg **8**

Ankle, foot, and toes **9**

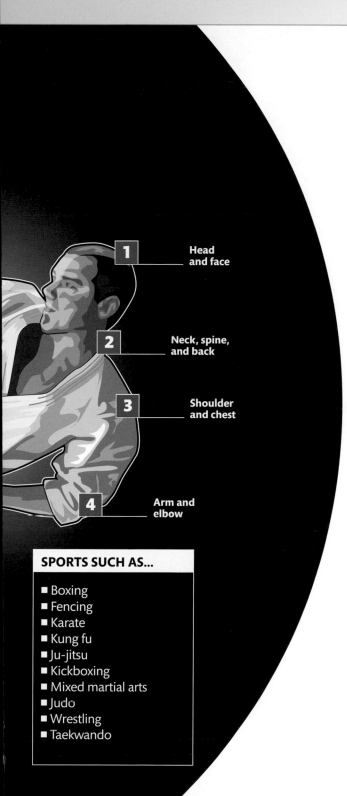

1	**Head and face**
2	**Neck, spine, and back**
3	**Shoulder and chest**
4	**Arm and elbow**

SPORTS SUCH AS...

- Boxing
- Fencing
- Karate
- Kung fu
- Ju-jitsu
- Kickboxing
- Mixed martial arts
- Judo
- Wrestling
- Taekwando

STAYING FREE OF INJURY

In addition to having the right protective equipment, such as a groin guard, participants in combat sports need to follow a training regimen that develops flexibility and power, allowing them to cope with the blows they receive from opponents, and the twisting actions and potential strains.

WARM-UP AND COOL-DOWN
Warm-ups for combat sports should involve dynamic stretches that imitate the movement required to prepare the body for strenuous activity. Cool down using static stretches to prevent tight muscles.

TRAINING
The joints are extremely vulnerable during combat sports, so exercises to promote strength and flexibility are an essential part of any training regimen. Interval training to improve cardiovascular fitness is also important.

■ **Flexibility**
Exercises that improve mobility of the hip, such as walking kick-outs (»p.185), are an effective way of reducing the risk of muscle strain.

■ **Strengthening**
Exercises such as push presses (»p.238) are good for increasing all-round strength, which is essential in combat sports, both in terms of improving performance and avoiding injury.

■ **Power and stability**
Grappling and punching puts strain on the shoulder joint. Exercises such as side-lying Ls (»p.214) help increase stability in the shoulder region, and reduce the risk of dislocation or tears.

BOARD-BASED SPORTS

Board-based sports, such as skateboarding, snowboarding, and windsurfing require balance, core strength, and stability of the knees, hips, and ankles to help prevent injury. A heavy landing from a jump carries a risk of damage to the lower limbs, and fractures and dislocations, resulting from the frequent number of high-velocity falls, are not uncommon.

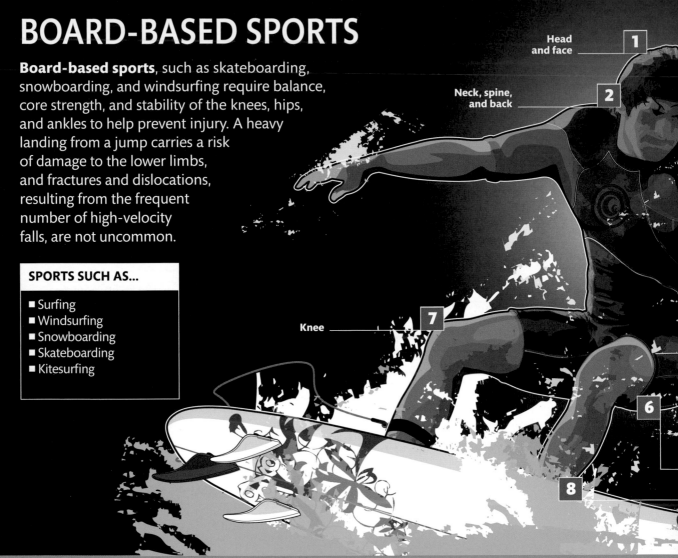

Head and face **1**

Neck, spine, and back **2**

Knee   **7**

6

8

SPORTS SUCH AS...

- Surfing
- Windsurfing
- Snowboarding
- Skateboarding
- Kitesurfing

INJURY HOTSPOTS

1 Head and face High-speed falls from a board onto the head can cause concussion and possibly a fractured skull (»p.52).

2 Neck, spine, and back Falling directly onto the head can put massive pressure on the spine; in severe cases, this may lead to neck fractures, while neck strain and whiplash (»p.56) may result from less serious falls.

3 Shoulder and chest Falling directly onto an outstretched arm can result in shoulder dislocation (»p.74), and falls onto the hand can cause the acromioclavicular joint at the top of the shoulder to separate from the collarbone (»p.68).

4 Arm and elbow Fractures of the lower arm are common due to the impact of high-speed falls (»p.82).

5 Wrist, hand, and fingers Attempting to absorb the impact of a high-speed fall with an outstretched hand can lead to wrist sprains and fractures (»pp.84–87).

6 Abdomen, hip, and groin Direct trauma to the hips caused by repeated falls may lead to bursitis and inflammation (»p.98).

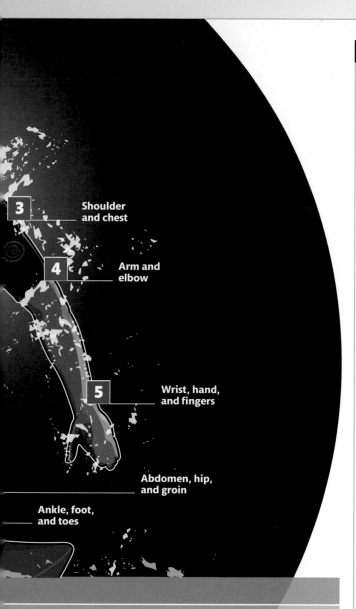

3 Shoulder and chest

4 Arm and elbow

5 Wrist, hand, and fingers

Abdomen, hip, and groin

Ankle, foot, and toes

7 **Knee** Repeated jumping movements put a lot of strain on the knee joints—pain felt in the front of the knee as a result of numerous hard landings is a common condition known as patellar tendinopathy, or jumpers' knee (»p.122). Injuries to the anterior cruciate ligament may also occur as a result of twisting (»p.124).

8 **Ankle, foot, and toes** Falls frequently cause twisting motions of the ankle, leading to sprains or even ruptures of the tendons (»p.144) if the force is strong enough. This causes pain and swelling on the outside of the ankle.

STAYING FREE OF INJURY

The high-speed nature of board-based sports makes protective clothing essential in reducing the risk of direct injury—consult a qualified instructor for the equipment needed for specific sports. However, training that promotes core stability also helps to minimize injuries.

WARM-UP AND COOL-DOWN
Prepare the body for exercise with gentle jogging and dynamic stretches. Cool down with some static stretches to lengthen the muscles because there is a risk of seizing up on leaving the water.

MAINTENANCE TRAINING
Training should promote stability, particularly in the core muscles. This will reduce the amount of stress on the lower back and lower limbs, especially the knee and ankle joints, which absorb much of the impact from jumping and landing.

■ **Flexibility**
Calf stretches, such as Lancelot stretches (»p.244), help minimize the damage done to the lower leg by repeated jumping and landing.

■ **Strengthening**
In board sports, the ankle absorbs much of the impact from jumping and landing, as well as from controlling the board. Stability exercises, such as hopping (»pp.256–58), help develop strength and improve jumping actions.

■ **Power and stability**
Maintaining a stable body position on the board requires good knee and ankle stability. Stability exercises, such as hand clock drills (»p.248), help promote this.

SKI-BASED SPORTS

Ski-based sports frequently result in injury because falls tend to occur at high speeds, and potentially from a height. These sports put tremendous strain on the knees, ankles, and hips and therefore require good stability in the lower limbs.

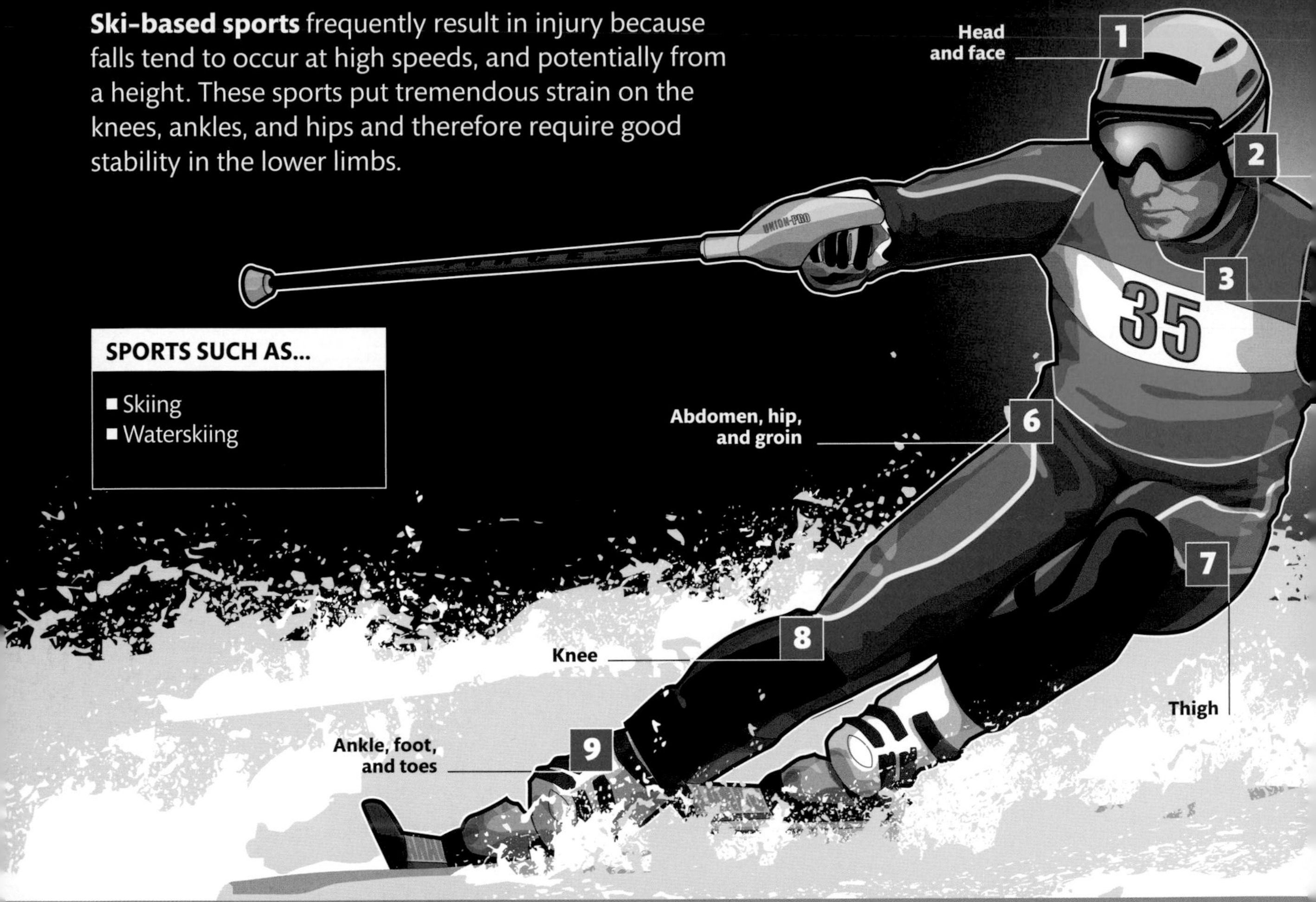

SPORTS SUCH AS...

- Skiing
- Waterskiing

Head and face **1**

2

3

Abdomen, hip, and groin **6**

7

8

Knee

Thigh

Ankle, foot, and toes **9**

INJURY HOTSPOTS

1 **Head and face** High-speed falls can lead to direct trauma to the head. Collisions with other skiers, or obstacles, can result in skull fractures (»p.52), concussion (»p.52), and jaw injuries (»p.54).

2 **Neck, spine, and back** Falling at high speeds can result in direct impact to or twisting of the neck. This can lead to neck strain (»p.56) or even fractures of the neck (»p.170).

3 **Shoulder and chest** Falling awkwardly on the upper arm can cause both anterior and posterior dislocations of the collarbone (»p.68), and shoulder dislocations (»p.74). More serious falls may result in collarbone fractures (»p.66).

4 **Elbow and arm** Collisions with obstacles, or even other skiers, can result in fractures to the upper (»p.80) and lower arm bones (»p.82).

5 **Wrist, hand, and fingers** Fractures of the wrist and hand (»p.84 and »p.94), as the result of a fall, are common injuries for skiers. Sprains to the finger ligaments (»p.92) can occur if the ski pole, or tow-rope in waterskiing, pulls against the hand.

6 **Abdomen, hip, and groin** Adductor strains (»p.104) may occur during turns, when the thigh muscles exert pressure on the outer ski to keep it in the correct position.

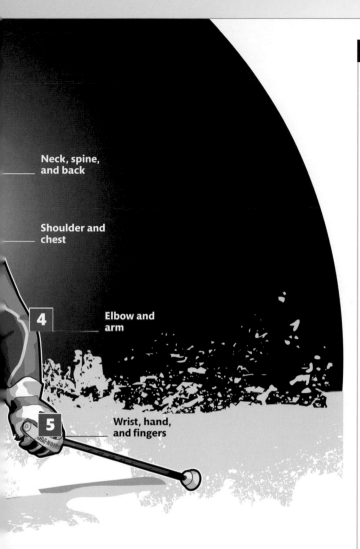

Neck, spine, and back

Shoulder and chest

4

Elbow and arm

5

Wrist, hand, and fingers

7 **Thigh** A bent-knee position puts huge stress on the quadriceps, and can cause tendinopathies or strains of these muscles (»p.110).

8 **Knee** Frequent twisting and turning places stress on the knee ligaments, leading to tears or even ruptures (»pp.124–29). If this happens at high speed, damage may be sustained by more than one ligament. Inflammation of the knee tendons may also occur as a result of repeated twisting (»pp.124–29).

9 **Ankle, foot, and toes** Twisting the ankle when turning can cause sprains (»p.144) and even fractures (»p.142).

STAYING FREE OF INJURY

Ankle injuries are a common problem in ski-based sports: if the ankle is turned, and the bindings that hold the foot in place fail to release, severe ligament damage can occur. For this reason, the right equipment, along with a training regimen that promotes good lower-limb stability, is essential for avoiding injury.

WARM-UP AND COOL-DOWN

Ski-based sports work muscles throughout the body, so a cardiovascular warm-up involving gentle jogging is key. Joint injuries from twisting motions are common, so flexibility stretches are important. Jog and stretch to cool down.

MAINTENANCE TRAINING

Skiing requires total body fitness, interval training is a good way of developing cardiovascular fitness. Mobility exercises are important for avoiding sprains and strains.

■ **Flexibility**
The bent-knee position used in skiing places a lot of stress on the thigh. Stretches, such as quad stretches (»p.243), keep the muscles flexible, and limit the risk of overuse injuries of the knee.

■ **Strengthening**
Hamstring strength is crucial in controlling the skis. Exercises such as Nordic hamstring lowers (»p.202) can help develop this, reducing the chance of straining or tearing the muscles when turning.

■ **Power and stability**
Side-to-side movements are common in skiing. Exercises that mimic this movement, such as sideways floor jumps (»p.257), can improve stability of the hips, knees, and ankles.

SKATE-STYLE SPORTS

Skate-style sports, such as ice-skating and roller-blading, put a large amount of stress on the lower limbs, and falls, especially when skating at high speeds, can cause serious injuries. Maintaining good stability and strength throughout the entire body is an important factor in limiting injury.

Head and face

1

2

3

6

Abdomen, hip, and groin

INJURY HOTSPOTS

1 **Head and face** A blow to the head as the result of a fall is a frequent cause of concussion (»p.52), and may result in fractures to the skull (»p.52) and jaw (»p.54).

2 **Neck, spine, and back** Impact to the head, as the result of a fall or a collision, may put strain on the neck, leading to whiplash (»p.56) and possible fractures (»p.170).

3 **Shoulder and chest** Falling on an arm stresses the shoulder joint—this can cause dislocations (»p.74) and tears of the rotator cuff (»p.70).

4 **Arm and elbow** High-speed falls onto an outstreched arm can cause fractures of the radius and ulna (»p.82).

5 **Wrist, hand, and fingers** Using the hand to break a fall can lead to fractures (»p.84), dislocations (»p.86), or ligament sprains (»p.88) of the wrist, or the hand and fingers (»pp.92-95).

6 **Abdomen, hip, and groin** Repeated exertion of the groin muscles when skating can lead to strains of the adductors (»p.104) or pelvic inflammation, such as osteitis pubis (»p.102). Hernias are also a common injury among skaters (»p.106).

7 **Knee** Falling on the knee or twisting it can often lead to cartilage and ligament injuries (»p.120 and »pp.124–29). Jumping also puts pressure on the knee, and may cause tendon inflammation (»p.122).

8 **Ankle, foot, and toes** Falls can cause the ankle to roll, and may lead to ligament injuries (»p.144) and ankle bone fractures (»p.142).

SPORTS SUCH AS...

- Ice-skating
- Speed-skating
- Roller-skating
- Roller-blading

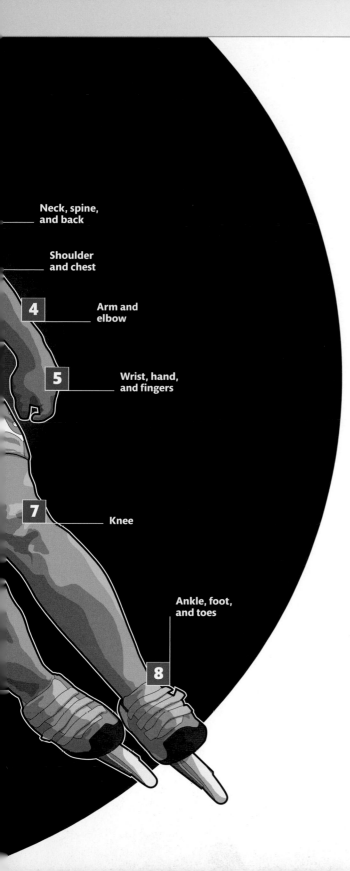

Neck, spine,
and back

Shoulder
and chest

4 Arm and
elbow

5 Wrist, hand,
and fingers

7 Knee

Ankle, foot,
and toes

8

STAYING FREE OF INJURY

The risk of falling at speed means protective clothing—particularly a helmet—is essential when participating in skate-style sports. However, a training program that emphasizes core stability will also reduce the risk of injury and improve performance.

WARM-UP AND COOL-DOWN

Rapid changes of pace are frequent in skate-style sports; a cardiovascular warm-up is needed to prevent muscle strain. Stretching the muscles after exercise stops them from tightening, reducing the risk of overuse injuries.

MAINTENANCE TRAINING

Training should concentrate on strengthening the muscles of the lower limbs and pelvis, reducing the risk of groin injuries. Core stability is also important in allowing the pelvis to transfer power to the lower limbs without placing too much strain on the body.

■ **Flexibility**
The pelvis transfers power through the body during skating. Mobility in this area, which can be helped with stretches such as standing gluteals (**»p.243**), is essential for avoiding muscle strains.

■ **Strengthening**
Targeting the groin muscles with strengthening exercises, such as long-lever adductor drops (**»p.199**), helps limit the risk of strain to these muscles.

■ **Power and stability**
Stretching the groin muscles and strengthening the knees, with exercises such as multi-directional lunges (**»p.249**), helps improve stability.

WATER SPORTS

Water sports, such as kayaking and canoeing, put strain on the shoulders, forearms, and wrists due to repeated arm movements. Back pain is also a danger if good technique and posture are not maintained.

SPORTS SUCH AS...

- Kayaking
- Canoeing
- Dinghy sailing
- Whitewater rafting
- Rowing
- Sculling

Neck, spine, and back **1**

Arm and elbow **3**

S-LINE 114

INJURY HOTSPOTS

1 **Neck, spine, and back** Incorrect posture can lead to muscle imbalance in the neck, causing pain and stiffness (»p.56). Back pain is also a common occurrence when good posture is not maintained—problems such as disk damage and nerve irritation (»pp.58–61) can arise. This can be a particular problem if core strength is weak.

2 **Shoulder and chest** The positions adopted in water sports put a large amount of stress on the shoulders, and this can make the tendons vulnerable to inflammation and overuse injuries (»pp.72–75). Weakness in the muscles that stabilize the shoulders, as well as poor posture, may exacerbate this.

3 **Arm and elbow** Pain due to overuse injuries, such as tennis elbow (»p.78), can arise in the tendons of the forearm and wrist, due to the repeated exertion involved in paddling or rope work.

4 **Wrist, hand, and fingers** Controlling an oar or paddle for long periods of time can place huge stress on the hands and wrists, making ligament and tendon sprains common (»p.88 and »p.92). Severe cases may result in carpal tunnel syndrome (»p.90).

5 **Abdomen, hip, and groin** Repetitive movement of the hips and thighs can cause groin strains (»p.104), and labral tears and femoroacetabular impingement (FAI) in the hip (»p.98 and »p.100).

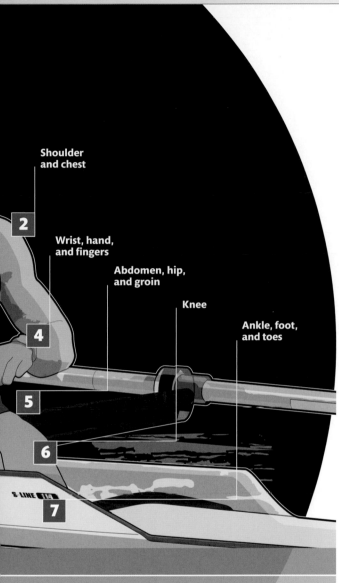

Shoulder and chest

2

Wrist, hand, and fingers

4

Abdomen, hip, and groin

Knee

Ankle, foot, and toes

5

6

S-LINE

7

6 Knee The repeated bending and driving motions performed by the legs place strain on the knee joints. This can cause patella problems such as patellofemoral joint pain (»p.116).

7 Ankle, foot, and toes Rowing for long distances puts strain on the Achilles tendon. This can lead to long-term overuse problems, such as inflammation of the Achilles tendon (»p.140).

STAYING FREE OF INJURY

These sports require good posture in order to limit pressure and stress on the back, which can lead to long-term problems. Excellent muscular endurance is also needed to sustain activity in the upper and lower limbs for long periods of time.

WARM-UP AND COOL-DOWN
A light warm-up should incorporate cardiovascular work, such as gentle jogging, and some stretches that imitate the movements used in water sports. To cool down, alternate between jogging and walking until the heart rate is normal.

MAINTENANCE TRAINING
Due to the strain placed on the back, core-strengthening exercises should be incorporated into a training program to reduce the risk of injury.

■ **Flexibility**
The repeated movement of the hips and thighs during water sports can cause tension in the buttocks, leading to pain in the legs. Stretches, such as those for the piriformis (»p.241), can help prevent this.

■ **Strengthening**
All water sports require strength in the arms. Exercises such as chin-ups (»p.207), which mimic the movements used in these sports, are a good way of developing this.

■ **Power and stability**
Core-muscle strength is essential for developing power and reducing the risk of damage to the back. Exercises such as Swiss Ball jack-knives (»p.223) can help develop this.

SWIMMING-BASED SPORTS

Despite carrying a comparatively low risk of injury, swimming-based sports do place significant strain on the muscles, particularly the back and shoulders. A flexible spine and good stability in the shoulder joints is essential in avoiding injury.

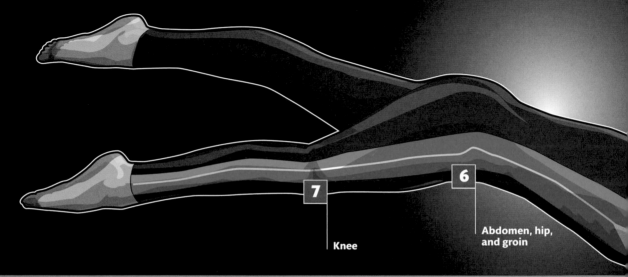

7 Knee

6 Abdomen, hip, and groin

INJURY HOTSPOTS

1 **Head and face** Heavy contact between players during water polo may cause concussion (»p.52) or cuts to the face (»p.166). Due to the fast-paced nature of water polo, there is also a risk of the eyes being struck or gouged by another player (»p.166).

2 **Neck, spine, and back** Twisting or turning the head abruptly can cause neck strain (»p.56), and sudden movements may result in a herniated disk around the lower spine (»p.60). Long-term strain placed on the back by swimming may also result in wear and tear to the disks (»p.60).

3 **Shoulder and chest** Collisions when throwing the ball in water polo—if they impact the shoulder in a vulnerable position—can cause serious injuries, such as dislocation (»p.74). Overuse injuries of the shoulder can arise due to sustained pressure on the joint from the repeated action of swimming strokes. This may cause problems with the rotator cuffs, such as partial or complete tears (»p.70), or impingement of the shoulder joint (»p.72).

4 **Arm and elbow** The repeated strain placed on the muscles in the arm by swimming strokes can cause inflammation in the tendons of the elbow joint (»p.78).

5 **Wrist, hand, and fingers** Blocking shots in water polo can lead to dislocation of the fingers (»p.94) if they are pushed back beyond the point that the joint can tolerate.

6 **Abdomen, hip, and groin** Repeated kicking actions during swimming exert the muscles of the groin; as a result, inflammation of the tendons around these muscles is a common condition in swimmers (»p.98). Femoroacetabular impingement (FAI) (»p.100) is also a relatively common problem.

7 **Knee** Pain on the inside of the knee often occurs due to the stress placed on this region by kicking actions. Degeneration of the joint can occur, and tendon damage due to overuse is a frequent problem (»p.122).

SPORTS SUCH AS...

- Swimming
- Diving
- Water polo

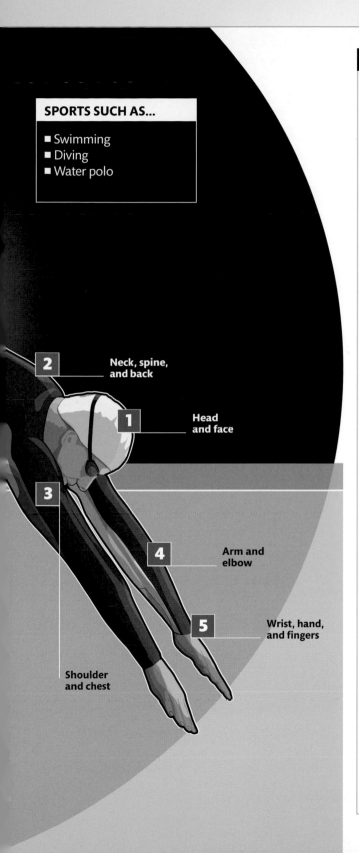

2 Neck, spine, and back

1 Head and face

3

4 Arm and elbow

5 Wrist, hand, and fingers

Shoulder and chest

STAYING FREE OF INJURY

Training programs for swimming should concentrate on reducing the risk of muscular injury. Developing strength in the shoulder joint is essential for shoulder-blade stability.

WARM-UP AND COOL-DOWN

Warm-ups should include shoulder stretches, ideally with movements that mimic those in swimming, to develop joint mobility. Slow laps and stretches help the body cool down.

MAINTENANCE TRAINING

Exercises that promote strength and endurance of the back muscles, along with stretches for the chest and neck, are vital components of a swimmer's training program.

- **Flexibility**
Mobility in the back is key in avoiding muscle strain; exercises such as lat stretches (»p.240) are a good way of developing this.

- **Strengthening**
Much of the power in swimming strokes is generated through work done by the shoulders. Exercises like side-lying Ls (»p.214) help develop rotator-cuff strength, reducing the risk of shoulder impingement or tears to the rotator cuff itself.

- **Power and stability**
Strengthening the core helps prevent back strains. Practicing exercises such as four-point kneels (»p.247) is a good way of achieving this.

BICYCLING

Long-distance bicycling, sprinting, and stunt bicycling, such as BMX biking, all make different demands on the body. Injuries can arise as the result of a fall, or the overexertion of muscles. The different terrains on which bicycling is performed also have an impact on the type of injuries sustained.

INJURY HOTSPOTS

1 **Head and face** High-speed falls can cause head injuries, such as concussion (**»p.52**) and facial abrasions (**»p.165**).

2 **Neck, spine, and back** Falls onto the head and injuries that twist the neck can cause spinal compression and may lead to whiplash (**»p.56**) or even fractures (**»p.170**). Strain is placed on the back when hunched over the bike for long periods, and may lead to degeneration of the disks in the spine (**»p.60**).

3 **Shoulder and chest** Falls may cause shoulder dislocations (**»p.74**) and collarbone fractures (**»p.66**), and can also result in rotator cuff tears (**»p.70**).

4 **Arm and elbow** Gripping the handlebars in a straight-arm position for long periods can cause pain and inflammation of the tendons around the outside of the elbow (**»p.78**).

5 **Wrist, hand, and fingers** Attempting to break a high-speed fall with an outstretched hand may lead to wrist dislocations or fractures (**»pp.84–87**).

6 **Thigh** Sprint starts place heavy strain on the thigh muscles, so injuries to the quadriceps are a common problem among track cyclists (**»p.110**).

7 **Knee** Overuse of the leg in pedaling may lead to patellofemoral pain syndrome (**»p.116**).

8 **Leg** Sprint finishes stress the calf muscles, and can cause strains (**»p.136**).

9 **Ankle, foot, and toes** Overuse of the calf muscles may damage the Achilles tendon (**»p.140**).

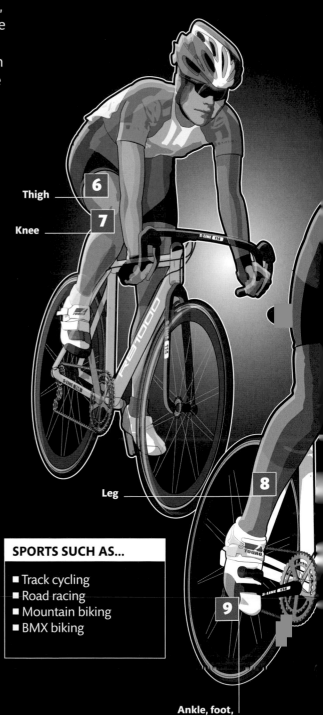

Thigh — 6
Knee — 7
Leg — 8
Ankle, foot, and toes — 9

SPORTS SUCH AS...

- Track cycling
- Road racing
- Mountain biking
- BMX biking

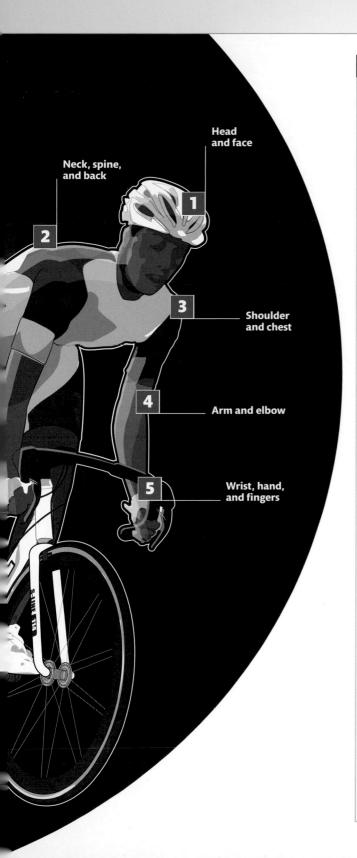

Head
and face
1

Neck, spine,
and back
2

3

Shoulder
and chest

4

Arm and elbow

5

Wrist, hand,
and fingers

STAYING FREE OF INJURY

A helmet is an essential piece of equipment for bicyclists, whatever their discipline. Training to stay free of injury is dependent on distance: for long-distance events, muscular endurance is crucial, while sprint events require power and strength. A bicyclist's training program should prepare the body for the specific demands made on it.

WARM-UP AND COOL-DOWN
Warm-ups and cool-downs should include light bicycling and stretches to prepare the body for the event ahead.

MAINTENANCE TRAINING
Stretches for the legs and back limit the risk of overuse injuries to the muscles. Good posture—supported by a strong pelvis—helps minimize back pain.

■ **Flexibility**
Tightness in the iliotibial band is a frequent problem for bicyclists. Foam roller exercises (»p.191), or a sports massage, are a good way of mobilizing the tissue on the outside of the leg to help reduce knee pain.

■ **Strengthening**
Strong legs are essential for improving bicycling performance and avoiding injury. Exercises such as good mornings (»p.208) are excellent for developing leg strength.

■ **Power and stability**
Core-stability exercises, such as kneeling supermen (»pp.228–29), are important for bicyclists wanting to avoid injury to the spine.

EQUESTRIAN SPORTS

The speed at which many equestrian sports, such as show-jumping and polo, are played means that the risk of serious injury is high. While a helmet offers some protection when falling on the skull, the height from which riders fall makes the limbs and spine vulnerable to fracture.

SPORTS SUCH AS...

- Dressage
- Show-jumping
- Polo
- Eventing
- Horse-racing
- Steeplechase

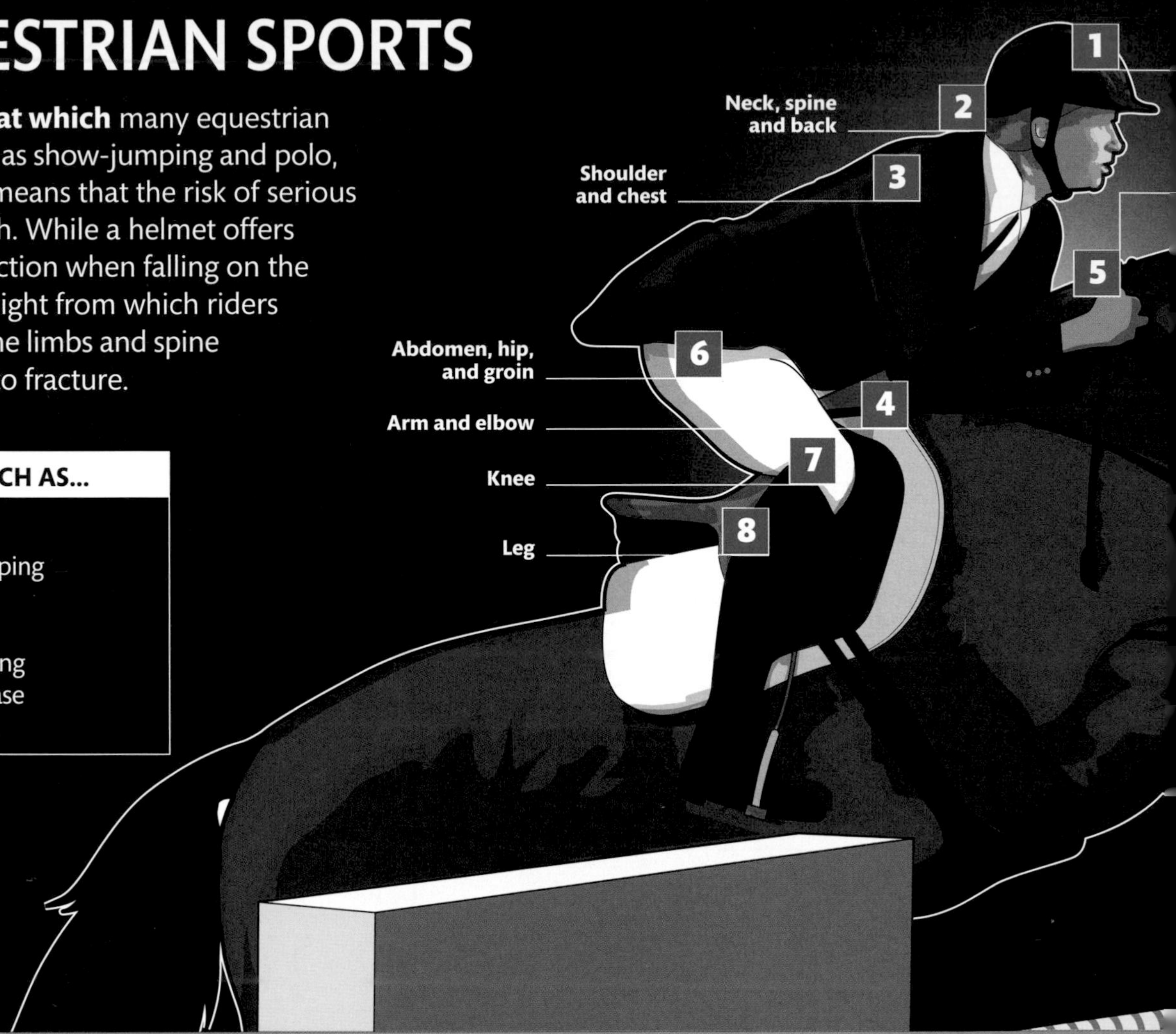

Neck, spine and back

Shoulder and chest

Abdomen, hip, and groin

Arm and elbow

Knee

Leg

INJURY HOTSPOTS

1 **Head and face** Falling from a horse is common, and can cause head injuries and concussion (»p.52). In polo, contact with the ball, or other players, may lead to lacerations of the face (»p.166).

2 **Neck, spine, and back** Failed jumps that lead to falls onto the head and neck can result in damage to the spinal cord (»p.171). High-impact falls may result in whiplash (»p.56), while falling on the back can cause damage to the joints and disks of the spine (»p.60). Riding for long periods can lead to back pain if there is a weakness in the core muscles, due to compression of the spine. This may eventually lead to degeneration of the spinal disks (»p.60).

3 **Shoulder and chest** Falls onto an outstretched hand can fracture the collarbone or the acromioclavicular joint in the shoulder (»pp.66–69), and cause shoulder dislocations (»p.74). A rider falling onto an obstacle, such as a jump, may suffer fractured ribs (»p.76), or even a punctured lung (although this is uncommon).

4 **Arm and elbow** Falling, especially at high speed during a race, can result in injuries such as fractures of the arm and elbow (»pp.80–84).

5 **Wrist, hand, and fingers** Repeatedly gripping the reins firmly may lead to muscle strains of the wrist and thumb becoming strained (»p.88).

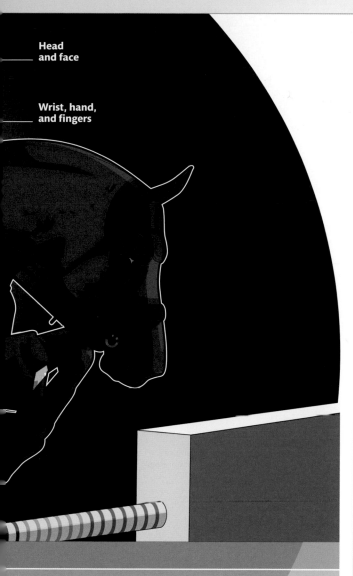

Head and face

Wrist, hand, and fingers

6 **Abdomen, hip, and groin** The groin muscles are instrumental in stabilizing the rider on the horse. For this reason, they can become inflamed; strains to these muscles are also a risk (**»p.104**). The strain placed on the hips may also lead to labral tears or femoroacetabular impingement (**»p.100**).

7 **Knee** Falling directly onto the knee can lead to dislocations, or even fractures, of the patella (**»pp.112–15**).

8 **Lower leg** Colliding with other horses during a polo match may lead to crushing injuries, such as fractures of the leg (**»p.134**).

STAYING FREE OF INJURY

A protective helmet is an essential piece of equipment for preventing riding-related head and neck injuries. However, a training program that emphasizes flexibility is also an important factor in staying free of injury.

WARM-UP AND COOL-DOWN
Cardiovascular warm-ups are not essential for horse-riders, but some gentle stretching, particularly of the lower limbs, may prevent muscle strain. Equally, light stretches after activity may reduce the risk of overuse injuries.

MAINTENANCE TRAINING
In equestrian sports, training programs should concentrate on core strength and spinal stability. Stretches to loosen the joints of the knees, hips, and back are also important, because of long periods spent in a seated position.

■ **Flexibility**
Keeping the trunk and hips flexible is key because maintaining good posture and enduring impact when riding places strain on these areas. Stretches such as Lancelot stretches (**»p.244**) are good for this.

■ **Strengthening**
The muscles to the sides of the torso can be strengthened with exercises such as side planks (**»pp.226–27**). These muscles help maintain good posture, reducing the risk of back problems.

■ **Power and stability**
Core strength is crucial for taking strain from the lower back while riding. Exercises such as prone planks (**»p.225**) help develop this.

EXTREME SPORTS

Extreme sports, such as rockclimbing, parkour, and skydiving, exert the joints and muscles throughout the body, and carry a high risk of falls. Consequently, participation in such activities can give rise to a variety of injuries, including strains, sprains, and fractures.

INJURY HOTSPOTS

1 **Head and face** Head injuries can be serious and may cause concussion (»**p.52**), or fractures to the face, skull, and jaw (»**pp.52–54**).

2 **Neck, spine, and back** Twisting falls can cause neck injuries, from fractures (»**p.170**) to whiplash (»**p.56**), and a stretched neck (»**p.58**). They can also lead to trapped or herniated disks in the spine (»**p.60**).

3 **Shoulder and chest** Using the arm to break a fall may result in dislocation of the shoulder, separation of the acromioclavicular joint in the shoulder (»**p.74 and **»**p.68**), or collarbone fractures (»**p.66**).

4 **Wrist, hand, and fingers** Falls may lead to wrist sprains (»**p.86**), or even wrist fractures (»**p.84**). Climbing relies on grip strength, which may result in overuse of the hand and wrist muscles, leading to strains and inflammation (»**p.88**).

5 **Abdomen, hip, and groin** Falling directly onto the hip can fracture the bone (»**p.96**), and may lead to inflammation of the soft tissue of the joint, a condition known as trochanteric bursitis (»**p.98**).

6 **Thigh** Falls that result in heavy impact to the top of the leg can cause fractures to the thigh bone (»**p.170**).

7 **Knee** Repeated jumps can cause inflammation and pain in the knee, due to overuse of the patellar tendon (»**p.122**) or the patellofemoral joint (»**p.116**). The ligaments of the knee are also susceptible to injury (»**p.124–29**).

8 **Ankle, foot, and toes** Hard landings put pressure on the ankle and foot, and may lead to plantar fasciitis (»**p.160**) an inflammation of the underside of the foot. Twisting of the ankle can cause ligament sprains (»**p.144**) and even fractures (»**p.142**).

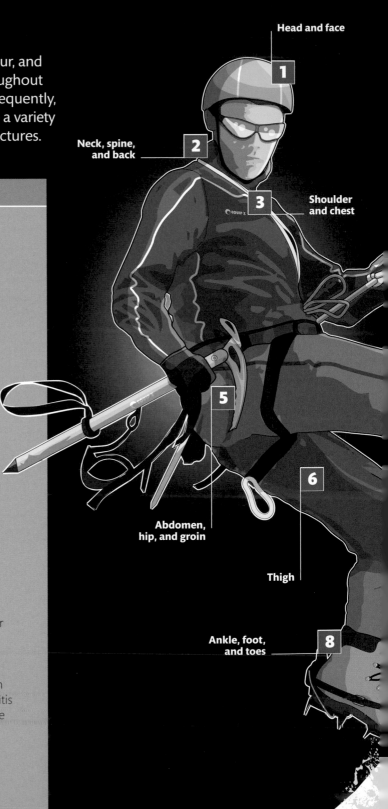

Head and face **1**

Neck, spine, and back **2**

Shoulder and chest **3**

5

Abdomen, hip, and groin

6

Thigh

Ankle, foot, and toes **8**

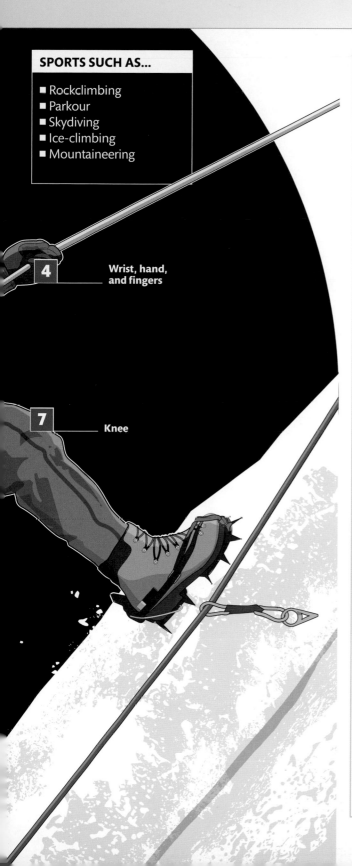

SPORTS SUCH AS...

- Rockclimbing
- Parkour
- Skydiving
- Ice-climbing
- Mountaineering

4 Wrist, hand, and fingers

7 Knee

STAYING FREE OF INJURY

The amount of protective equipment available for extreme sports is extensive; an instructor will advise individuals about their sport-specific requirements. However, total-body muscular conditioning is also important to optimize performance and limit injuries.

WARM-UP AND COOL-DOWN

Warm-ups should involve dynamic stretches that take the joints through their full range of motion to fully prepare the body. Also stretch thoroughly to cool down.

MAINTENANCE TRAINING

Training should focus on improving the joints involved in jumping and landing—principally the knees and ankles, because these areas carry a high risk of injury. General muscular endurance and power are also vital.

■ Flexibility

Mobility in the leg helps minimize the stress from jumping and landing. Exercises such as pike walks (»p.177) are a good way of developing this.

■ Strengthening

Exercises that strengthen the lower back, such as chin-ups (»p.207), are a great way of guarding against injury in extreme sports that require gripping actions.

■ Power and stability

Squat jumps (»p.239) exercise the quadriceps and build stability in the hips, knees, and ankles, reducing the risk of injury when jumping and landing.

SPORTS INJURIES

This chapter profiles the most common sports injuries affecting each area of your body, with detailed information on causes, symptoms, prognoses, and therapy options, and timelines for treatment and rehabilitation.

INJURY LOCATOR

FRONT

HEAD AND FACE

- Concussion (》p.52)
- Cheekbone fracture (》p.53)
- Jaw fracture and dislocation (》p.54)
- Bitten or swallowed tongue (》p.55)

ABDOMEN, HIP, AND GROIN

- Hip fractures (》p.96)
- Trochanteric bursitis (》p.98)
- Hip labral tears and FAI (》p.100)
- Osteitis pubis (》p.102)
- Groin strain (》p.104)
- Hernias (》p.106)

ANKLE, FOOT, AND TOES

- Foot tendon injuries (》p.154)
- Foot ligament sprains (》p.156)
- Morton's neuroma (》p.157)
- Metatarsal fracture (》p.158)
- Toe fracture (》p.159)
- Plantar fasciitis (》p.160)

SHOULDER AND CHEST

- Collarbone fracture (》p.66)
- Collarbone joint injuries (》p.68)
- Rotator cuff injuries (》p.70)
- Shoulder joint inflammation (》p.72)
- Shoulder joint injuries (》p.74)
- Simple rib fracture (》p.76)

THIGH

- Quadriceps injuries (》p.110)

KNEE

- Patella fracture (》p.112)
- Patellar dislocation (》p.114)
- Patellofemoral pain syndrome (》p.116)
- Patellar bursitis (》p.118)
- Osteochondritis dissecans (》p.120)
- Knee tendon injuries (》p.122)
- Anterior cruciate ligament injury (》p.124)
- Meniscus tear (》p.130)

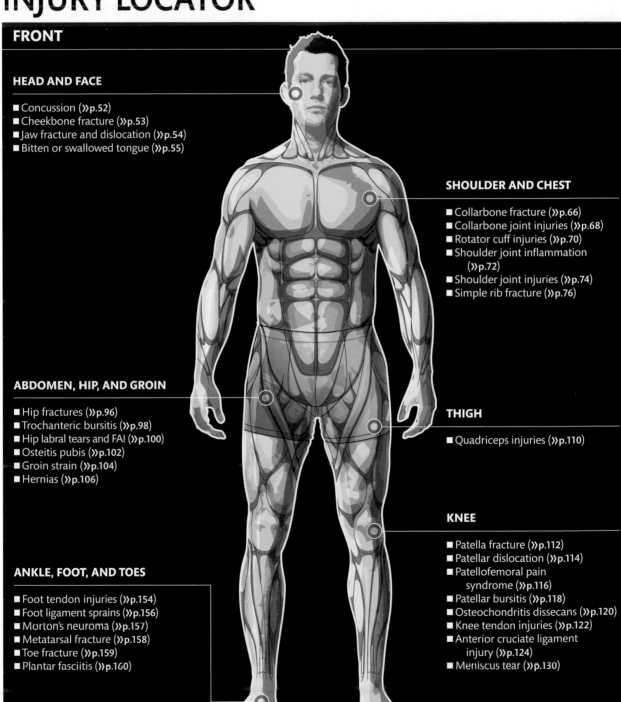

BACK

NECK, SPINE, AND BACK

- Neck strain and whiplash (»p.56)
- Neck nerve injuries (»p.58)
- Low back pain and sciatica (»p.60)
- Sacroiliac joint inflammation (»p.62)
- Piriformis syndrome (»p.64)

ELBOW AND ARM

- Elbow bursitis (»p.77)
- Elbow tendon injuries (»p.78)
- Humerus fracture (»p.80)
- Forearm fractures (»p.82)

WRIST, HAND, AND FINGERS

- Wrist fractures (»p.84)
- Wrist dislocation and sprain (»p.86)
- Wrist and hand tendon disorders (»p.88)
- Carpal tunnel syndrome (»p.90)
- Metacarpal fracture (»p.91)
- Hand and finger tendon injuries (»p.92)
- Finger fracture and dislocation (»p.94)

THIGH

- Hamstring injuries (»p.108)

KNEE

- Collateral ligament injuries (»p.126)
- Posterior cruciate ligament injury (»p.128)
- Iliotibial band syndrome (»p.132)

ANKLE, FOOT, AND TOES

- Achilles tendon rupture (»p.140)
- Achilles tendinopathy (»p.142)
- Ankle fracture (»p.144)
- Ankle sprain (»p.146)
- Heel bone fracture (»p.148)
- Retrocalcaneal bursitis (»p.150)
- Tibialis posterior tendinopathy (»p.152)
- Sinus tarsi syndrome (»p.153)

LOWER LEG

- Lower leg fracture (»p.134)
- Calf injuries (»p.136)
- Shin splints (»p.138)
- Compartment syndrome (»p.139)

CONCUSSION

A forceful blow to the head can cause concussion: temporary disturbance of the brain's normal function. Even though there may be no obvious sign of injury, early medical attention is important to rule out serious underlying damage to the brain or skull.

CAUSES

Concussion is a risk in sports, such as rugby, that involve forceful contact with other players, and those in which the head is vulnerable to high-speed falls, such as bicycling. Impact from a blow can jar the head, possibly bruising the brain as it is shaken around within the skull.

SYMPTOMS AND DIAGNOSIS

Concussion can cause headache, dizziness, vomiting, tinnitus (ringing in the ears), and sometimes a state of confusion. If the blow was especially powerful, you may also experience a brief loss of consciousness. Your physician will make a diagnosis via a physical examination and will ask you questions to establish whether you feel confused or are affected by memory loss. You may also have a CT scan or an X-ray of your head.

RISKS AND COMPLICATIONS

In severe concussion, blood leaking from damaged tissues may build up within your brain, a condition that needs immediate treatment in the hospital. Even in mild cases of concussion, if you receive a further blow to your head before you have fully recovered from the first incident, there is risk of a life-threatening complication known as "second-impact syndrome," in which your brain swells rapidly.

WHEN WILL I BE FULLY FIT?

After mild concussion, you should not resume any sport for at least a week or until your symptoms have disappeared completely. If you have been severely concussed, a month or more may be needed for recovery. In all cases, you should ask your physician for advice on how soon you can safely return to your sport. If you have had repeated concussion, your physician may suggest that you choose a sport with a lower risk of head impact.

CONCUSSION

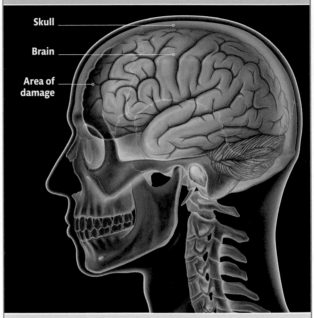

Skull

Brain

Area of damage

The brain is surrounded and protected by the skull. In concussion, damage is caused by the brain hitting the hard inner surface of the skull.

TREATMENT

⊕ SEEK IMMEDIATE MEDICAL ATTENTION

IMMEDIATE

■ If you think you may be concussed, you should: ▶ stop activity. ▶ seek medical attention. ■ If you are unconscious: ▶ a first aider should give you a Basic Life Support AVPU evaluation (**≫p.172**).

SHORT TERM

■ If you are diagnosed with concussion, your physician may: ▶ give you a test to check brain function. ▶ suggest an X-ray or a CT scan of your head. ▶ advise you to rest for a few days.

MEDIUM TERM

■ If your symptoms fail to respond to rest, your physician may: ▶ recommend further tests or scans to investigate possible brain damage.

LONG TERM

■ If you continue to experience symptoms for weeks or months you may: ▶ need to have further medical tests.

MEDICAL

CHEEKBONE FRACTURE

Due to their prominent position, the cheekbones are vulnerable to injury from direct contact. In combat sports, for example, the head is an object of attack, making cheekbone fractures a relatively common occurrence.

CAUSES
Fractures of the cheekbone are most frequently encountered in contact sports such as rugby and football, and combat sports such as boxing or martial arts, in which direct, forceful contact with other participants is inevitable. Sports in which hard objects, such as a ball in baseball or cricket, or a stick or puck in ice hockey, may connect with the face also carry a risk of cheekbone fracture.

SYMPTOMS AND DIAGNOSIS
You will feel pain over the side of your face and you may have bruising and swelling. In more severe fractures, the side of your face may be flattened, giving you a slightly "lopsided" look. If your eye socket is affected, you may have double vision and, possibly, bleeding in the white of your eye. This is known as subconjunctival hemorrhage. Your physician will diagnose your injury through physical examination, followed by an X-ray.

RISKS AND COMPLICATIONS
In a few rare cases, the nerves of your cheekbone may be damaged, causing tingling or numbness on the side of your face. This should subside within about 3 months. Very rarely, some time after the injury you may have bleeding around your eye socket, and altered vision or pain in your eye. If this happens, you should get medical help immediately.

WHEN WILL I BE FULLY FIT?
If you have fractured your cheekbone, you should not take part in contact sports for a minimum of 6 weeks—although you should be able to resume lighter sports activities, such as going to the gym or bicycling, after about 2 weeks.

CHEEKBONE FRACTURE

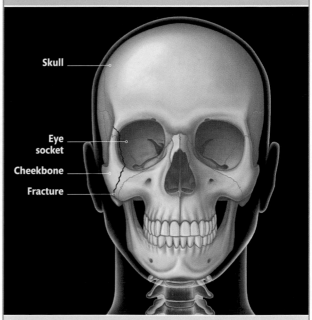

Skull

Eye socket

Cheekbone

Fracture

Because of the proximity of the cheekbone to the eye socket, a cheekbone fracture may also involve a fracture of the eye socket and impaired vision.

TREATMENT

⊕ SEEK IMMEDIATE MEDICAL ATTENTION

MEDICAL

IMMEDIATE
■ If you think you may have a cheekbone fracture, you should: ▶ seek medical attention.

SHORT TERM
■ If you have a simple fracture, your physician may: ▶ prescribe analgesic medication. ▶ manipulate your cheekbone back into the right position. ■ If you have a more complex fracture, your physician may: ▶ recommend surgery to insert a small metal plate and screws.

MEDIUM TERM
■ After surgery, your physician may advise you to: ▶ regularly apply a cold compress to your cheek to reduce swelling and bruising. ▶ sleep propped up in bed.

LONG TERM
■ Until your cheekbone is fully healed, your physician may: ▶ advise you to avoid activities that could result in reinjury.

JAW FRACTURE AND DISLOCATION

The upper and lower jawbones attach at the temporomandibular joint. Jaw fractures usually occur in the lower jaw. Dislocations involve separation from the temporomandibular joint.

CAUSES
These injuries are usually caused by a direct blow to the jaw or face, or a heavy fall. They are most common in sports such as bicycling, motor sports, or boxing.

SYMPTOMS AND DIAGNOSIS
Your jaw may feel painful, and be bruised, swollen, and difficult to move. Your lower lip may feel numb. Your physician will make a diagnosis through physical examination and an X-ray.

RISKS AND COMPLICATIONS
You may have difficulty breathing and there is a risk of inhaling blood or saliva. These complications are serious and require immediate medical attention. Left untreated, both injuries may result in chronic pain and a misaligned jaw.

WHEN WILL I BE FULLY FIT?
It may be several weeks before you are able to resume noncontact sports. It is advisable to wait at least 8–12 weeks before returning to contact, collision, or motor sports.

TREATMENT

 SEEK IMMEDIATE MEDICAL ATTENTION

MEDICAL

IMMEDIATE
■ If you think you may have fractured or dislocated your jaw, you should: ▶ seek medical attention.

SHORT TERM
■ For a dislocation, your physician may: ▶ give you muscle relaxants to aid relocation. ▶ bandage your jaw. ■ For a minor fracture, your physician may: ▶ advise rest, analgesics, and a soft-food diet. ■ For a severe fracture, your physician may: ▶ recommend surgery to fix your jaw with wires and plates.

MEDIUM TERM
■ After surgery, your physician may: ▶ leave the wires in place for 6–8 weeks.

LONG TERM
■ After surgery, your physician may: ▶ monitor your progress for several months to ensure your jaw is healing as expected.

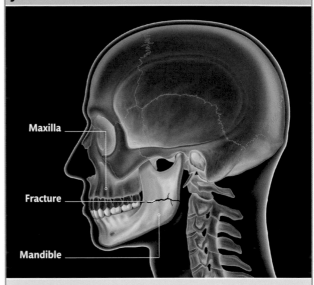

JAW FRACTURE

Maxilla

Fracture

Mandible

The jaw is comprised of the maxilla (the upper jaw) and the mandible (the lower, movable jaw). Most jaw fractures occur in the lower jaw.

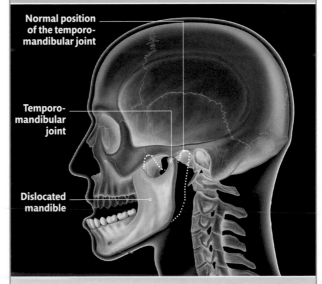

JAW DISLOCATION

Normal position of the temporo-mandibular joint

Temporo-mandibular joint

Dislocated mandible

The mandible (lower jaw) is connected to the rest of the skull by the temporomandibular joint. In a dislocation, the mandible is unseated on one or both sides.

BITTEN OR SWALLOWED TONGUE

The tongue has a large blood supply, so it bleeds profusely if bitten. A "swallowed" tongue is one that has fallen back and blocked the airway.

CAUSES
In high-impact sports, such as boxing and rugby, a blow to the chin can cause the teeth to bite through the tongue. If a player is knocked unconscious, the muscles of the body, including the tongue, relax. The tongue may then flop backward and obstruct the top of the airway, preventing breathing.

SYMPTOMS AND DIAGNOSIS
If you bite your tongue it will bleed heavily. Bites longer than 1 in (2 cm) are serious. A swallowed tongue will make breathing difficult and needs urgent medical attention.

RISKS AND COMPLICATIONS
Untreated, a bitten tongue may not heal, and could become infected. A swallowed tongue can be life-threatening if it blocks the airway completely.

WHEN WILL I BE FULLY FIT?
If you have bitten your tongue, and the wound has healed, you can return to sports immediately. If you have swallowed your tongue, get clearance from a physician before going back.

TREATMENT

MEDICAL

IMMEDIATE
■ If you have bitten your tongue, you should: ▶ wash the bite and press your tongue against the roof of your mouth to stem the bleeding. ▶ apply ice to the wound. ▶ clean the wound with antiseptic until fully healed. ■ If the bite is over 1 in (2 cm), you should: ▶ seek medical attention. ■ If a person's tongue is obstructing his or her airway, you should: ▶ pull the lower jaw forward to release the tongue. ▶ use a finger to sweep the tongue away from the back of the mouth. ■ If a person is unconscious and has swallowed his or her tongue, you should: ▶ seek immediate medical attention.

SHORT TERM
■ If you have bitten your tongue, your physician may: ▶ prescribe analgesic medication. ▶ prescribe antibiotics to prevent infection. ▶ suture the wound.

MEDIUM TERM
■ If you have had stitches for a bitten tongue, your physician may: ▶ advise you to stick to a soft-food diet for 6–10 days, until the stitches dissolve or are removed.

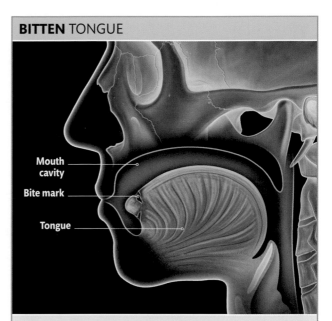

BITTEN TONGUE

Mouth cavity

Bite mark

Tongue

If the teeth bite down on the tongue, they may cause severe laceration, in which part of the upper surface of the tongue is removed.

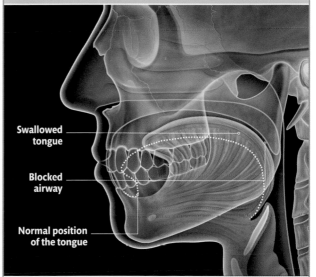

SWALLOWED TONGUE

Swallowed tongue

Blocked airway

Normal position of the tongue

In a swallowed tongue, loss of consciousness may cause the muscles to relax, leading to the tongue flopping backward and blocking the airway.

NECK STRAIN AND WHIPLASH

NECK STRAIN AND WHIPLASH

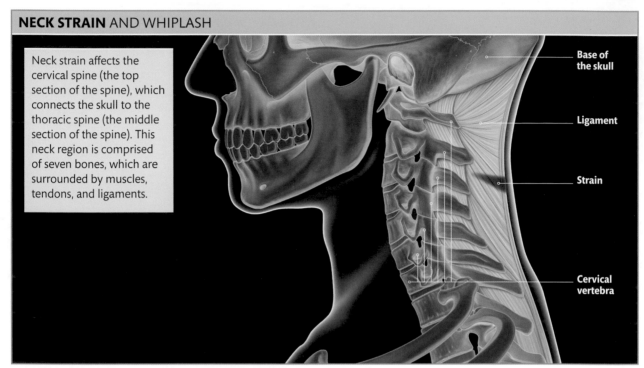

Neck strain affects the cervical spine (the top section of the spine), which connects the skull to the thoracic spine (the middle section of the spine). This neck region is comprised of seven bones, which are surrounded by muscles, tendons, and ligaments.

Base of the skull

Ligament

Strain

Cervical vertebra

Neck strain is a general term for strains of the muscles, tendons, and ligaments around the cervical spine. Whiplash is a form of neck strain caused by violent jolting of the head back and forth, usually as the result of a sudden impact.

CAUSES

Neck strain is common in sports that involve some form of impact or collision, from rugby to martial arts to diving. A fall or a sudden blow to, or twisting of, the neck can put stress on the muscles, tendons, or ligaments connecting the cervical vertebrae. Whiplash, a form of neck strain, is most common in car accidents, but can also occur in contact sports if a player's head is suddenly forced backward, forward, or sideways, or they receive a blow to the head.

SYMPTOMS AND DIAGNOSIS

With neck strain, you may feel pain in your neck at the time of injury, but this pain is likely to be minimal at first, with the pain worsening over the following 12–72 hours. You may feel a "crackling" sensation and weakness in your neck, and pain in your head. The symptoms of whiplash can include

neck and shoulder pain, stiffness, fatigue, blurring of your eyesight, and "ringing" in your ears, but a pain or tingling in your shoulders that runs down your arm may be symptomatic of damage to one of your vertebrae. Your physician will diagnose the condition via an assessment of your symptoms and they may use an X-ray, CT scan, MRI scan, or myelography to confirm the severity of the strain and to check for other conditions, such as spinal cord injury.

RISKS AND COMPLICATIONS

Untreated, neck strain and whiplash can cause long-term pain, restricted movement of your neck, and sleep loss. Undiagnosed "neck injuries" may actually be a neck fracture or a symptom of a back injury, both of which are potentially serious and could cause paralysis. As a consequence, you should always seek immediate medical attention if you have injured your neck.

WHEN WILL I BE FULLY FIT?

You should make a full recovery in 4–6 weeks, though severe neck strain or whiplash—where a tendon has ruptured, for example—can take up to 6 months to heal, and may need surgery. Only return to sports when you are fully pain-free.

TREATMENT

➕ SEEK IMMEDIATE MEDICAL ATTENTION

MEDICAL

IMMEDIATE ▶	SHORT TERM ▶	MEDIUM TERM ▶	LONG TERM
■ If you think you may have strained your neck, you should: ▶ immobilize your neck to protect your spine (**»p.171**). ▶ seek medical attention.	■ If you are diagnosed with neck strain or whiplash, your physician may: ▶ advise you to rest for a day or two, until the pain eases. ▶ prescribe analgesic medication. ▶ fit a neck brace for support. ▶ recommend ice treatment or heat packs. ▶ advise you to exercise your neck gently to prevent stiffness, moving your head through the whole range of neck movements. ■ If the strain is very severe, you may have damaged your tendons, in which case your physician may: ▶ recommend immediate surgery to repair the tendon.	■ Once your injury has healed, usually within 4–6 weeks, your physician may: ▶ refer you to a physical therapist to help you improve the strength, flexibility, and mobility of your muscles (see table below).	■ If short- and medium-term treatments fail, this may be a sign of more serious damage to your neck muscles, tendons, or ligaments. In this case your physician may: ▶ recommend surgery to repair the damage. ■ After surgery, your physician may: ▶ refer you to a physical therapist for a program of rehabilitation (see table below).

PHYSICAL THERAPY

EARLY STAGE ▶	INTERMEDIATE STAGE ▶	ADVANCED STAGE ▶	RETURN TO SPORT
■ Once your physician has referred you, your physical therapist may: ▶ suggest various treatments, such as electrotherapy, to reduce local inflammation. ▶ use soft tissue release therapy and manual therapy to relieve symptoms. ■ You should now be able to: ▶ return to daily activities with only minimal discomfort. ■ You may begin: ▶ exercises to test the range of motion in your neck, thoracic spine, and shoulders, such as neck rotations (**»p.174**), shoulder rotations (**»p.175**), and torso rotations (**»p176**), as pain allows.	■ You should now be able to: ▶ demonstrate a full range of motion in your cervical and thoracic spine. ▶ perform daily activities without pain. ■ Your physical therapist may: ▶ suggest exercises to target the deep, stabilizing muscles of your neck, once your range of motion is restored. ■ You may begin: ▶ exercises for balance and control, such as scapular circles (**»p.251**).	■ You should now be able to: ▶ demonstrate relatively pain-free movement of your neck. ■ Your physical therapist may: ▶ test your grip strength. ■ You may begin: ▶ contact drills that are relevant to your sport, as pain allows. ▶ manual isometric exercises (**»p.220**) ▶ upper-limb weights, such as dumbbell bench presses (**»p.210**), as pain and swelling allows; start at 50% of your one-rep max; aim for 4 sets x 8–12 reps. ▶ participating in noncontact sports training.	■ You should now be able to: ▶ perform any weights exercises or training, without pain. ▶ demonstrate neck and upper-limb strength; your injured side should have only 10% less ability than your uninjured side. ▶ complete full neck bridging exercises, such as isometric bridging (**»p.220**), pain-free. ▶ engage in progressively challenging contact activities specific to your sport. ▶ participate in full training.

NECK NERVE INJURIES

Nerves in the neck emerge from the cervical vertebrae (the top section of the spine) and may become compressed or inflamed, a condition known as neck nerve entrapment. The brachial plexus is a network of nerves that originate from the spine at the base of the neck and supply the arms, hands, and shoulders. When these nerves become stretched or compressed, the condition is known as neck stretch syndrome.

CAUSES

Neck nerve entrapment is often caused by sports involving repetitive stress in the neck area, such as weight lifting. This can cause injury or degeneration of the neck bones (cervical vertebrae), which may then irritate—or trap—the nerves. Neck stretch syndrome occurs in sports such as rugby or football, in which a direct blow to the side of the head or neck, overstretching of the neck, or ear-to-shoulder head rotation can cause the brachial plexus to become stretched or compressed, leading to inflammation.

SYMPTOMS AND DIAGNOSIS

If you have an irritated nerve you may have pain, weakness, and loss of movement in your neck. Numbness in your fingers and weakness in the muscles of your arm and chest are also common symptoms. If you are suffering from cervical nerve stretch syndrome you may feel a sharp pain in your neck, which extends to your shoulder and down the arm, as well as pins and needles or abnormal sensations in your arm. You may also have muscle weakness around your shoulder and arm. Your physician will make a diagnosis through a physical examination and by manipulating your neck. You may also have an X-ray, a CT scan, or an MRI scan.

RISKS AND COMPLICATIONS

If either condition is left untreated, the pain will get worse. There is a risk that your nerves may become permanently damaged, which could lead to more serious conditions affecting the spine. Undiagnosed neck injuries are potentially dangerous. As a consequence, you should always seek immediate medical attention.

WHEN WILL I BE FULLY FIT?

If you do not need surgery, you should be fit within 1 month. If you have had surgery, rehabilitation may take 3 months.

NECK NERVE ENTRAPMENT

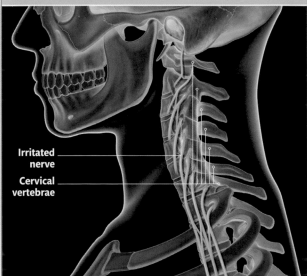

Irritated nerve

Cervical vertebrae

Any of the large number of nerve fibers that extend from the cervical vertebrae and control the shoulder, arm, and hand, may become trapped if the bones are injured.

NECK STRETCH SYNDROME

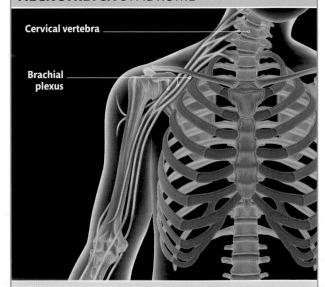

Cervical vertebra

Brachial plexus

Neck stretch syndrome affects the brachial plexus, a network of nerves that originates in the cervical vertebrae and stimulates the muscles of the arm.

TREATMENT

➕ SEEK IMMEDIATE MEDICAL ATTENTION

	IMMEDIATE ▶	SHORT TERM ▶	MEDIUM TERM ▶	LONG TERM
MEDICAL	■ If you think you may have a trapped nerve or neck stretch syndrome, you should: ▶ stop activity. ▶ immobilize your neck to prevent further damage (**》p.171**). ▶ apply ice (**》p.165**). ▶ seek medical attention.	■ If you are diagnosed with a mild-to-moderate case of trapped nerve or neck stretch syndrome, your physician may: ▶ recommend rest. ▶ prescribe analgesic medication. ▶ refer you to a physical therapist for treatment to restore range of movement and strength in your neck (see table below). ■ If you are diagnosed with a severe case of trapped nerve or neck stretch syndrome, your physician may: ▶ recommend surgery to relieve nerve compression.	■ If your trapped nerve fails to respond to physical therapy treatment your physician may: ▶ give you an injection of corticosteroids to reduce inflammation. ■ If you have had surgery, your physician may: ▶ refer you to a physical therapist for treatment to improve movement in your neck (see table below).	■ In rare cases, if your mild-to-moderate trapped nerve or neck stretch syndrome fails to improve with nonsurgical treatment, your physician may: ▶ recommend surgery to relieve nerve compression. ■ After surgery, your physician may: ▶ refer you to a physical therapist for a program of rehabilitation (see table below).

	EARLY STAGE ▶	INTERMEDIATE STAGE ▶	ADVANCED STAGE ▶	RETURN TO SPORT
PHYSICAL THERAPY	■ Once your physician has referred you, your physical therapist may: ▶ suggest various treatments, such as electrotherapy, to reduce local inflammation. ▶ use soft tissue therapy and manual therapy to help relieve your symptoms. ■ You may begin: ▶ neck extensions and flexions (**》p.175**), as pain allows.	■ You should now be able to: ▶ demonstrate a full range of motion in your cervical and thoracic spine (the top and middle sections of your spine), and shoulder. ■ Your physical therapist may: ▶ suggest exercises to target the deep, stabilizing muscles of the neck, once your range of motion is restored. ■ You may begin: ▶ exercises for balance and control, such as scapular circles (**》p.251**); aim for 5 sets x 10 reps—and four-point kneels (**》p.247**). ▶ exercises to strengthen the muscles of your neck, such as manual isometrics (**》p.220**), neck extensions and flexions (**》p.175**), and neck side flexions (**》p.174**).	■ You should now be able to: ▶ complete resistance holds with a pulley (this should not involve any movement of the joint) (**》p.220**); aim for 3 reps x 6–10 secs, without pain. ■ Your physical therapist may: ▶ test the power in your neck and upper limbs to check you are at full strength. ■ You may begin: ▶ upper-limb weights exercises, such as assisted chin-ups (**》p.207**); start at 50% of your one-rep max; aim for 4 sets x 8–12 reps, as pain allows. ▶ noncontact training.	■ You should now be able to: ▶ perform any weights exercises or training, without pain. ▶ demonstrate neck and upper-limb strength; your injured side should have only 10% less ability than your uninjured side. ▶ lift upper-body weights that are at least 80% of your one-rep max. ▶ complete full isometric bridging exercises (**》p.220**), without pain. ▶ engage in progressively challenging contact activities specific to your sport. ▶ participate in full training.

LOW BACK PAIN AND SCIATICA

Between each vertebra of the spine is a disk of cartilage that acts as a shock-absorbing pad—these disks have a soft, jellylike center and a tough, fibrous outer layer. If the disks herniate or burst (known medically as a herniated disk), the gel puts pressure on the spinal nerve roots. Sciatica is a general term for lower back pain that extends into the buttock, thigh, or calf.

CAUSES

Bending forward (flexing) to pick up a heavy object, particularly in activities such as weight lifting, puts increased pressure on the disks of the spine. This kind of stress can cause the outer layer of a disk to rupture, allowing the jellylike contents to protrude, putting pressure onto the nearby nerve roots, which are close to the spine. Herniated disks usually occur in the lower back, although they can happen in any area of the spine. The resulting pressure that is put on the nerve is one of the causes of pain in the lower back, known as sciatica; other causes of sciatica include piriformis syndrome (»p.64).

SYMPTOMS AND DIAGNOSIS

Back pain is extremely common, but most low back pain is not due to herniated disks—if you also have a shooting pain down the back of one leg, usually on flexing or bending sideways, and "pins and needles," numbness, or weakness in your legs, you may also have sciatica.This is typically experienced on one side only. The affected disk may protrude from your spine but should, in most cases, eventually shrink back. Your physician will make a diagnosis from your symptoms and a physical examination, but an MRI is required to confirm sciatica resulting from a herniated disk.

RISKS AND COMPLICATIONS

Secondary pressure on other joints of your spine may lead to arthritis. If your spinal cord is compressed, you may have weakness in both legs, and bowel or bladder dysfunction, or loss of feeling around your perineum or anus—this rare medical emergency is called cauda equina syndrome.

WHEN WILL I BE FULLY FIT?

Recovery may range from a few weeks to months depending on how your injury responds to treatment. If you have sciatica and it is not due to a herniated disk, recovery will occur within 8 weeks. Most cases of sciatica will disappear within 12 weeks.

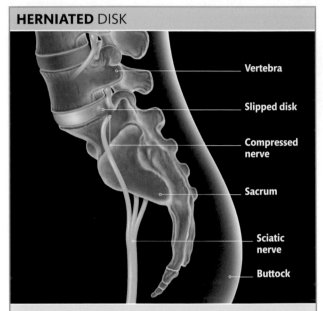

HERNIATED DISK

Vertebra

Slipped disk

Compressed nerve

Sacrum

Sciatic nerve

Buttock

The joints of the spine are formed by a disk sitting between two vertebra. When a disk slips, the nearby nerves can become compressed.

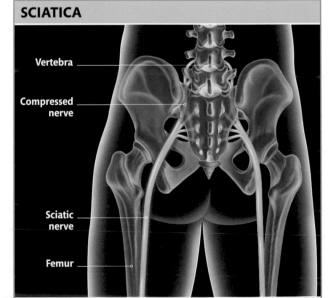

SCIATICA

Vertebra

Compressed nerve

Sciatic nerve

Femur

The sciatic nerves, the two largest nerves in the body, run from the base of the spine to the foot. Pain from sciatica may occur anywhere along the sciatic nerve.

TREATMENT

	IMMEDIATE ▶	SHORT TERM ▶	MEDIUM TERM ▶	LONG TERM
MEDICAL	■ If you think you may have a slipped disk or sciatica, you should: ▶ stop sports, but continue with normal activities, if pain allows. If the pain is severe, you may need to rest in bed for 1–2 days. ▶ apply heat to alleviate spasm in the surrounding muscles of your back. ■ If your symptoms fail to respond to self-treatment, you should: ▶ seek medical attention.	■ If your symptoms are mild, your physician may: ▶ refer you to a physical therapist to treat the spine and restore movement (see table below). ■ If your symptoms are severe your physician may: ▶ prescribe muscle relaxants or strong analgesic medication. ▶ give you an epidural injection to alleviate the pain. ■ Once your pain has subsided, your physician may: ▶ refer you to a physical therapist to treat your spine and restore movement (see table below).	■ If you are among the 10% of patients with true sciatica due to a herniated disk, whose symptoms fail to respond to nonsurgical treatment , your physician may: ▶ recommend surgery to remove the piece of disk that is bulging out. This surgery is highly (90%) successful.	■ After surgery, your physician may: ▶ refer you to a physical therapist for a program of rehabilitation (see table below).

	EARLY STAGE ▶	INTERMEDIATE STAGE ▶	ADVANCED STAGE ▶	RETURN TO SPORT
PHYSICAL THERAPY	■ Once your physician has referred you, your physical therapist may: ▶ suggest various treatments, such as electrotherapy, to reduce local inflammation. ▶ perform a full spinal and pelvic assessment. ▶ use soft tissue therapy and manual therapy to help alleviate your symptoms. ▶ put strapping on the affected area to reduce the load on it. ▶ suggest spinal extension exercises, such as McKenzie extensions (>>p.234), and neural mobility exercises, such as neural glides (>>p.188).	■ You should now be able to: ▶ perform daily activities with reduced levels of pain and discomfort. ■ Your physical therapist may: ▶ assess the length of your quadriceps, hamstrings, gluteals, hip flexors, and latissimus dorsi muscles, to correct any asymmetries. ■ You may begin: ▶ low-level core exercises, such as kneeling supermen, level 1 (>>p.228). ▶ lower-limb bodyweight exercises, such as hip-hitchers (>>p.186). ▶ non-impact conditioning exercise, such as bicycling, walking (either outdoors or on a treadmill), and working on a cross-trainer. ▶ upper-limb weights exercises, such as dumbbell bench presses (>>p.210), as pain allows; start at 50% of your one-rep max; aim for 4 sets x 8–12 reps.	■ You should now be able to: ▶ perform daily activities with no pain or discomfort. ▶ complete moderate- to high-level core exercises, such as extension holds, levels 2–3 (>>p.235), without pain. ■ You may begin: ▶ functional warm-up drills, such as walking lunges (>>p.180), and low-level foot plyometrics, such as A-walks (>>p.254). ▶ low-level skills, such as ball handling, as pain allows. ▶ low-level running, as pain allows. ▶ lower-limb weights, such as Bulgarian dumbbell split squats (>>p.194). ■ Your physical therapist may: ▶ continue to monitor your spinal recovery.	■ You should now be able to: ▶ demonstrate a full active range of motion in your pelvis and lumbar spine. ▶ demonstrate a normal degree of strength and flexibility in your spine. ▶ complete high-level core exercises, such as curl-ups, levels 3–4 (>>p.221) and side planks, levels 2–3 (>>pp.226–27), without pain. ▶ lift upper- and lower-body weights that are at least 80% of your one-rep max, without pain. ▶ complete lower-limb plyometrics, such as hops and jumps (>>pp.256–58), without pain. ▶ complete high-level running at distances relevant to your sport, without pain. ▶ complete sport-specific drills without difficulty. ▶ participate in full training.

SACROILIAC JOINT INFLAMMATION

SACROILIAC JOINT INFLAMMATION

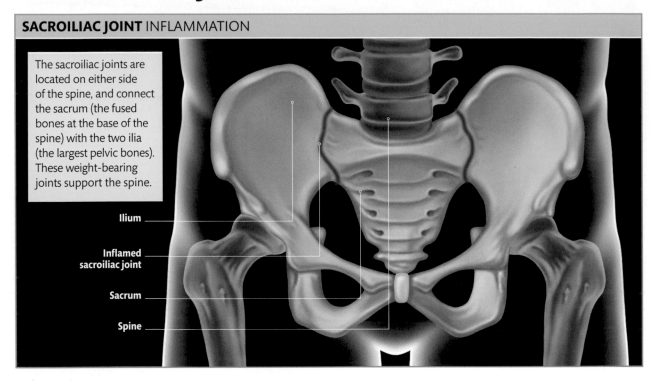

The sacroiliac joints are located on either side of the spine, and connect the sacrum (the fused bones at the base of the spine) with the two ilia (the largest pelvic bones). These weight-bearing joints support the spine.

Ilium

Inflamed sacroiliac joint

Sacrum

Spine

The sacroiliac joints function as a shock absorber for the body. They move very little but are key in transferring weight from the upper body to the legs, and enabling the body to twist when the legs are moving. Inflammation can occur due to injury or from wear and tear, and is a common cause of low back pain.

CAUSES
Injuries to the sacroiliac joints can occur in many sports, and are usually caused by a fall, or a direct blow to the buttocks that jolts the pelvis. Such falls are common in skating, skiing, and horseback riding, and injuries can occur in most collision sports, too. The ligaments supporting the joints are often damaged in the process. Biomechanical abnormalities, such as unequal leg length, are another common cause.

SYMPTOMS AND DIAGNOSIS
You will usually feel pain on either side of your lower back, depending on where the injury has occurred. This pain may spread to your buttocks, the back of your thigh, your groin, and, in rare cases, down to your knee. The pain may

feel worse when you exercise, and also after sitting in the same position for a while. You may suffer stiffness after sitting or walking for long periods, and rolling over in bed may be painful. Your physician will consider your medical history, then carry out a physical examination. He or she may also recommend tests such as blood tests, X-rays, or an MRI scan, to determine if either of your sacroiliac joints are inflamed.

RISKS AND COMPLICATIONS
If you wake every morning with a stiff lower back that lasts for more than 30 minutes, seek medical attention. This may signify inflammatory arthritis, an infrequent but important cause of sacroiliac joint pain.

WHEN WILL I BE FULLY FIT?
With careful exercise you are likely to improve within a period of 2–3 weeks, but you may need to continue the exercises that have been suggested by your physical therapist on a long-term basis in order to prevent the inflammation from coming back. Seek the advice of your physician and physical therapist on when you can safely return to your sport.

TREATMENT

IMMEDIATE ▶	SHORT TERM ▶	MEDIUM TERM ▶	LONG TERM
■ If you think you may have injured your sacroiliac joint, you should: ▶ stop activity. ▶ rest. ▶ seek medical attention.	■ If you are diagnosed with sacroiliac joint inflammation, your physician may: ▶ prescribe analgesic medication. ▶ provide you with a sacroiliac belt, to support the joint. ▶ refer you to a physical therapist for treatment to help strengthen your muscles and improve flexibility around the joint (see table below). Your physical therapist will also be able to correct any abnormalities of posture or sporting technique that are contributing to your pain.	■ If your symptoms fail to respond to physical therapy, your physician may: ▶ prescribe a course of corticosteroid injections to reduce inflammation and prevent scarring.	■ As a last resort, if all other treatments fail, your physician may: ▶ recommend surgery to fuse the joint. ■ After surgery, your physician may: ▶ refer you to a physical therapist for a program of rehabilitation (see table below).

(Left margin label: MEDICAL)

EARLY STAGE ▶	INTERMEDIATE STAGE ▶	ADVANCED STAGE ▶	RETURN TO SPORT
■ Once your physician has referred you, your physical therapist may: ▶ suggest various treatments, such as electrotherapy, to reduce local inflammation. ▶ use soft tissue release therapy and manual therapy to help alleviate your symptoms. ▶ put strapping on the affected area to reduce the load on it. ▶ recommend a pelvic belt. ▶ assess the length of your quadriceps, hamstrings, gluteals, hip flexors, and latissimus dorsi muscles, to correct any asymmetries. ■ You may begin: ▶ low-level core exercises, such as side planks, level 1 (**》p.226**).	■ You should now be able to: ▶ demonstrate a full range of motion in your sacroiliac joint, lumbar spine, and thoracic spine, without pain. ■ You may begin: ▶ lower-limb bodyweight exercises, such as hip hitchers (**》p.186**). ▶ nonimpact conditioning exercise, such as bicycling, walking (either outdoors or on a treadmill), and working on a cross-trainer. ▶ upper-limb weights exercises, such as lat pull-downs (**》p.206**), as pain allows; start at 50% of your one-rep max and aim for 4 sets x 8–12 reps. ▶ moderate level core exercises such as curl-ups, level 2 (**》p.221**).	■ You should now be able to: ▶ complete moderate core exercises, such as those using a Swiss ball (**》pp.222–24**), without pain. ■ You may begin: ▶ functional warm-up drills, such as rotational lunges (**》p.181**), and low-level foot plyometrics, such as A-walks (**》p.254**). ▶ low-level skills, such as ball handling, as pain allows. ▶ low-level running, as pain allows. ▶ lower-limb weights exercises, such as barbell lunges (**》p.194**), as pain allows; start at 50% of your one-rep max and aim for 4 sets x 8–12 reps.	■ You should now be able to: ▶ demonstrate a full active range of motion in your pelvis and lumbar spine. ▶ complete high-level core exercises, such as kneeling supermen, level 3 (**》p.229**), without pain. ▶ complete lower-limb plyometrics, such as hops and jumps (**》pp.256–58**), without pain. ▶ complete high-level running at distances relevant to your sport, without pain. ▶ lift upper- and lower-body weights that are at least 80% of your one-rep max, without pain. ▶ complete sport-specific drills, without difficulty. ▶ participate in full training.

(Left margin label: PHYSICAL THERAPY)

PIRIFORMIS SYNDROME

The piriformis muscle helps the hip joint rotate outward and abduct the thigh (move it away from the body). Piriformis syndrome occurs when the muscle compresses or irritates the sciatic nerve, causing pain in the buttocks and along the back of the thigh, and is a rare cause of the condition sciatica (»p.60).

CAUSES

In most people, the sciatic nerve runs below the piriformis muscle, but in around 15 percent of the population it runs right through the muscle. It is thought that people with this irregularity are predisposed to piriformis syndrome. The condition may also develop through incorrect gait when walking or jogging, or by overexertion in sports that involve sitting, such as rowing or bicycling, which can all result in damage to the piriformis muscle.

SYMPTOMS AND DIAGNOSIS

You will feel pain deep in your buttocks that travels along the sciatic nerve down the back of your leg. The pain will get worse when you sit, climb stairs or steep slopes, or perform squats. Your physician will usually be able to diagnose the condition on the basis of your symptoms and a physical examination, and may also arrange for you to have an X-ray or MRI scan to rule out other causes of pain.

RISKS AND COMPLICATIONS

Prolonged irritation of your piriformis muscle may cause your tendons to become scarred and lead to chronic symptoms such as persistent pain, reduced motion in your hip joint, numbness in your foot, and difficulty walking.

WHEN WILL I BE FULLY FIT?

You can return to sport when normal, pain-free movement of your legs, and muscle strength and power, have returned. With physical therapy and rest, you should be fully fit within 4–8 weeks. If your symptoms are severe and persist even after nonsurgical treatment, you may require surgery. If so, your recovery time is likely to be at least 3 months.

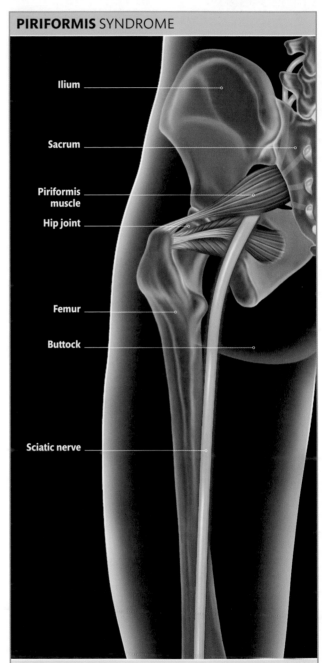

PIRIFORMIS SYNDROME

Ilium

Sacrum

Piriformis muscle

Hip joint

Femur

Buttock

Sciatic nerve

The piriformis muscle is located deep within the buttock tissue, and connects the front of the sacrum (the fused bones at the base of the spine) with the top of the femur (thighbone). It runs in close proximity to the sciatic nerve.

TREATMENT

IMMEDIATE	SHORT TERM	MEDIUM TERM	LONG TERM
■ If you think you may have piriformis syndrome, you should: ▶ stop activity. ▶ minimize movement of the affected area. ▶ massage the affected area. ▶ seek medical attention.	■ If you are diagnosed with piriformis syndrome, your physician may: ▶ prescribe analgesic medication. ▶ refer you to a physical therapist for treatment to relieve your symptoms and restore strength and mobility. (see table below).	■ If your symptoms fail to respond to physical therapy, your physician may: ▶ give you an injection into your piriformis muscle and surrounding tissue, of corticosteroid, local anaesthetic, or botulinum toxin (botox) to help alleviate your symptoms.	■ As a last resort, if all other treatment fails, your physician may: ▶ recommend surgery to loosen your piriformis muscle and help relieve pressure on the sciatic nerve. ■ After surgery, your physician may: ▶ refer you to a physical therapist for a program of rehabilitation (see table below).

MEDICAL (side label)

EARLY STAGE	INTERMEDIATE STAGE	ADVANCED STAGE	RETURN TO SPORT
■ Once your physician has referred you, your physical therapist may: ▶ suggest various treatments, such as electrotherapy, to reduce local inflammation. ▶ perform a full assessment of your spine, pelvis, and hips. ▶ use soft tissue release therapy and manual therapy to help alleviate your symptoms. ▶ assess the length of your quadriceps, hamstrings, gluteals, hip flexors, and latissimus dorsi muscles to correct any asymmetries. ▶ use neural flossing techniques, such as neural glides (»p.188).	■ You should now be able to: ▶ walk and sit with little or no pain. ■ You may begin: ▶ low-level core exercises, such as bridges (»p.236). ▶ lower-limb bodyweight exercises, such as hip hitchers (»p.186) and box step-ups (»p.203). ▶ nonimpact conditioning exercise, such as bicycling, walking (either outdoors or on a treadmill), and work on a cross-trainer.	■ You should now be able to: ▶ complete moderate- to high-level core exercises, such as side planks, level 2 (»p.226), without pain. ■ Your physical therapist may: ▶ continue to monitor your spine to check its mobility. ■ You may begin: ▶ upper-limb weights exercises, such as dumbbell bench presses (»p.210), with no pain or swelling; start at 50% of your one-rep max and aim for 4 sets x 8–12 reps. ▶ functional warm-up drills, such as kneeling supermen (»pp.228–29), and low-level foot plyometrics, such as straight-leg circles-in (»p.255). ▶ low-level skills, such as ball handling, as pain allows. ▶ low-level running, as pain allows.	■ You should now be able to: ▶ demonstrate a full active range of motion in your pelvis and lower spine. ▶ demonstrate a normal degree of strength and flexibility in your spine. ▶ complete high-level core exercises, such as curl-ups, levels 2–4 (»p.221), without pain. ▶ lift upper- and lower-body weights that are at least 80% of your one-rep max, without pain. ▶ complete lower-limb plyometrics, such as hops and jumps (»pp.256–59), without pain. ▶ complete high-level running at distances relevant to your sport, without pain. ▶ complete sport-specific drills without difficulty. ▶ participate in full training.

PHYSICAL THERAPY (side label)

COLLARBONE FRACTURE

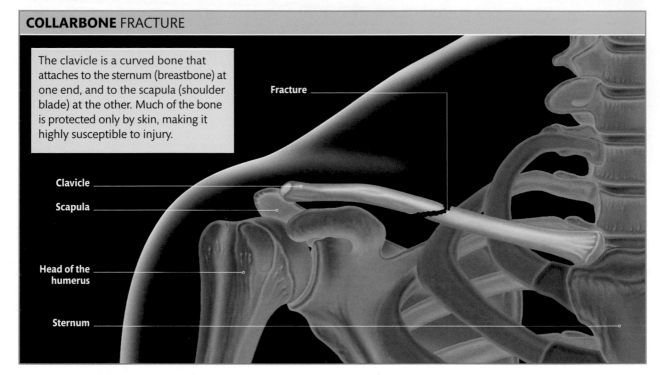

COLLARBONE FRACTURE

The clavicle is a curved bone that attaches to the sternum (breastbone) at one end, and to the scapula (shoulder blade) at the other. Much of the bone is protected only by skin, making it highly susceptible to injury.

Fracture

Clavicle

Scapula

Head of the humerus

Sternum

The clavicle (collarbone) makes up part of the shoulder, and helps keep the shoulder blade in the correct position. Fractures of the collarbone, while serious in themselves, can also result in damage to the nerves and blood vessels in this part of the body.

CAUSES
Fractured collarbones are a feature of sports in which falls onto the shoulder or direct blows to the collarbone are a regular occurrence. They commonly occur when people fall from a bicycle or a horse, either directly onto a shoulder or an outstretched arm, or when players collide during contact sports such as football, rugby, and soccer.

SYMPTOMS AND DIAGNOSIS
You will usually feel immediate pain along the length of your collarbone. You will see and feel swelling, including a firm lump around the fracture, especially if the bone ends are displaced. There may also be redness and bruising around your injury. Lifting your arm may be extremely painful and you may need to support it. Occasionally, you may feel

pins and needles in your arm and hand. Your physician will make a diagnosis through a physical examination, and may confirm the size and location of the break with an X-ray.

RISKS AND COMPLICATIONS
Occasionally, if it is very badly displaced, the bone may fail to fuse properly while healing, leading to a deformity in the shoulder. However, this is very rare. If you do not allow enough time for a fracture to heal before returning to sport, there is a risk of osteoarthritis.

WHEN WILL I BE FULLY FIT?
You may resume contact sports, or sports involving overhead arm movement, after about 12 weeks in most cases, but this will depend on the individual. As a general rule, you should be able to return to sports more quickly after surgery.

TREATMENT

⊕ SEEK IMMEDIATE MEDICAL ATTENTION

MEDICAL

IMMEDIATE ▶	SHORT TERM ▶	MEDIUM TERM ▶	LONG TERM
■ If you think you may have fractured your collarbone, you should: ▶ follow a RICE procedure (**»p.170**). ▶ put your arm in a supportive sling (**»p.170**). ▶ seek medical attention.	■ If you are diagnosed with an undisplaced fracture (in which the bone does not separate), your physician may: ▶ prescribe analgesic medication. ▶ put your arm in a sling for 3–6 weeks. ■ If you are diagnosed with a displaced fracture (in which the bone separates), your physician may: ▶ recommend surgery to realign the ends of the bone. ▶ recommend using low-intensity pulsed ultrasound to help heal the bone.	■ After surgery, your physician may: ▶ put your arm in a sling for around 3–6 weeks.	■ If you have had surgery, your physician may: ▶ monitor your progress for the 3–6 weeks while your arm is in a sling, with occasional X-rays to ensure that your shoulder is healing as expected. ■ Whether you have had surgery or not, once your arm is out of the sling, your physician may: ▶ refer you to a physical therapist for a program of rehabilitation (see table below).

PHYSICAL THERAPY

EARLY STAGE ▶	INTERMEDIATE STAGE ▶	ADVANCED STAGE ▶	RETURN TO SPORT
■ Once your physician has referred you, your physical therapist may: ▶ suggest various treatments, such as electrotherapy, to reduce local inflammation. ▶ take your shoulder through a series of movements (within pain limits) to assess the range of motion in your joint—this will involve no effort from you (passive range of motion); as you recover you will be able to initiate these movements yourself (your active range of motion). ■ You may begin: ▶ exercises to promote control of your shoulder blade, such as scapular clocks (**»p.251**), as pain allows. ▶ strengthening exercises for your shoulder, elbow, and wrist that use resistance without joint movement, such as shoulder isometrics (**»p.212**). ▶ testing the range of motion in your fingers, wrist, and elbow.	■ You should now be able to: ▶ demonstrate no swelling in the affected area. ▶ demonstrate a full range of motion in your fingers, hand, wrist, elbow, and shoulder. ▶ put full weight on your shoulder, with minimal pain. ■ Your physical therapist may: ▶ assess your grip strength; your injured arm should have only 10% less ability than your uninjured one. ▶ test the muscle function of your shoulder in all directions; your injured shoulder should have only 10% less ability than your uninjured one. ■ You may begin: ▶ strengthening exercises, such as side-lying Ls (**»p.214**), initially below your maximum effort, as pain allows; aim for 4 sets x 8 reps.	■ You should now be able to: ▶ complete upper-limb plyometrics, such as medicine ball chest throws (**»p.216**), without pain. ▶ complete balance and control exercises for the shoulder, elbow and wrist, such as four-point kneels (**»p.247**). ▶ put full weight on your shoulder, without pain. ■ You may begin: ▶ upper-limb weights exercises, such as dumbbell bench presses (**»p.210**), as pain allows; start at 50% of your one-rep max and aim for 4 sets x 8–12 reps.	■ You should now be able to: ▶ demonstrate a full active range of motion in your shoulder, and should not feel apprehensive when this is tested by your physical therapist. ▶ lift upper-body weights that are at least 80% of your one-rep max, without pain. ▶ complete high-level running at distances relevant to your sport, without pain. ▶ complete sport-specific drills without difficulty. ▶ participate in full training for at least 2 weeks.

COLLARBONE JOINT INJURIES

A heavy impact, or strain, can cause the ligaments of the acromioclavicular or sternoclavicular joints to tear, leading to a separation of the clavicle (collarbone) from the acromion (the tip of the shoulder), or the sternum (breastbone) respectively.

CAUSES

Separations of the acromioclavicular joint are normally the result of landing on the tip of the shoulder or falling on an outstretched arm, while sternoclavicular joint separations are usually the result of a heavy blow to the chest. Collarbone joint injuries occur frequently in high-impact sports, such as football, ice hockey, rugby, and martial arts; they are also common in sports that carry a high risk of falling, such as horseback riding, bicycling, and skiing.

SYMPTOMS AND DIAGNOSIS

You will feel pain in the joint immediately, along with swelling and a firm lump over the injury. Your arm will be too painful to raise unassisted. Your physician will make a diagnosis from your symptoms and from a physical examination. You may be given an X-ray to assess the severity of the injury and to rule out fractures.

RISKS AND COMPLICATIONS

Acromioclavicular joint injuries may lead to persistent pain and restricted movement if you do not seek prompt medical attention, or if you do not give the injury sufficient time to heal. Sternoclavicular joint injuries may be accompanied by damage to your heart, major blood vessels, and trachea (windpipe), which lie just under the joint. These complications are serious and require emergency treatment.

WHEN WILL I BE FULLY FIT?

In most cases, you should have made a full recovery roughly 12 weeks after injury. With serious complications (see above), your recovery may take substantially longer.

ACROMIOCLAVICULAR INJURY

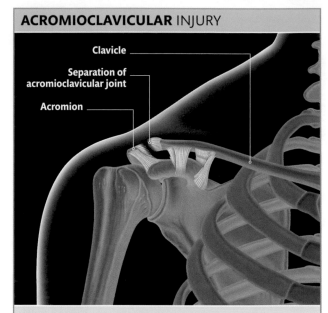

The clavicle and the acromion are joined together by the acromioclavicular joint. Separation occurs when the ligaments that bind the two are torn.

STERNOCLAVICULAR INJURY

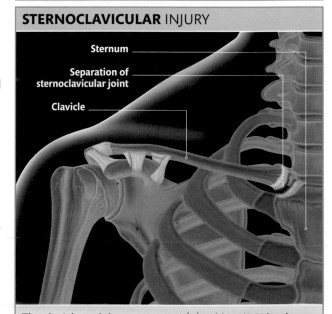

The clavicle and the sternum are joined together by the sternoclavicular joint. Separation occurs when the ligaments that bind the two are torn.

TREATMENT

⊕ SEEK IMMEDIATE MEDICAL ATTENTION

MEDICAL

IMMEDIATE ▶	SHORT TERM ▶	MEDIUM TERM ▶	LONG TERM
■ If you think you may have a collarbone joint injury, you should: ▶ put your arm in a supportive sling (**》p.170**). ▶ apply ice to the affected area (**》p.165**). ▶ seek medical attention.	■ If you are diagnosed with a mild to moderate collarbone injury, your physician may: ▶ prescribe analgesic medication. ▶ recommend rest. ▶ put your arm in a sling for 6–8 weeks. ■ If you are diagnosed with a severe collarbone injury, your physician may: ▶ recommend immediate surgery to repair the joint.	■ If your injury was mild to moderate and has failed to respond to 6–8 weeks of rest, your physician may: ▶ refer you to a physical therapist for treatment to improve range of movement (see table below).	■ If your injury fails to respond to physical therapy, your physician may: ▶ recommend surgery to realign the bones. ■ After surgery, your physician may: ▶ refer you to a physical therapist for a program of rehabilitation (see table below).

PHYSICAL THERAPY

EARLY STAGE ▶	INTERMEDIATE STAGE ▶	ADVANCED STAGE ▶	RETURN TO SPORT
■ Once your physician has referred you, your physical therapist may: ▶ take your arm through a series of movements (within pain limits) to assess the range of motion in your joint—this will involve no effort from you (passive range of motion). ▶ suggest exercises to help you initiate control over your shoulder blade, once pain allows. ■ You may begin: ▶ deep-water pool jogging for 30 minutes at a time, as pain allows. ▶ bicycling 5–7 days after your injury; aim for 20 minutes at 85rpm, level 6, as pain allows. ▶ kinetic chain exercises, such as shoulder dumps (**》p.182**); perform these while wearing your sling.	■ You should now be able to: ▶ lift your arm to 90 degrees flexion and abduction. ■ Your physical therapist may: ▶ continue to assess the range of motion in your shoulder. This time you will be required to actively move the joint. ■ You may begin: ▶ exercises to stretch the back of your shoulder, such as sleeper stretches (**》p.245**). ▶ shoulder isometrics exercises in all directions (**》p.212**); these should involve no joint movement. ▶ using an electrical muscle stimulator on your posterior shoulder muscle. ▶ exercises for the shoulder blade, such as low rows (**》p.209**); aim for 4 sets x 10 reps. ▶ lower-limb exercises, such as leg presses (**》p.195**), with no shoulder involvement. ▶ interval bicycling at a low-moderate intensity. ▶ upper-limb weights exercises with your uninjured arm. ▶ exercises to promote shoulder control, such as lawnmowers (**》p.190**).	■ Your physical therapist may: ▶ perform another assessment of your active range of motion to check for improvements in your movements. ▶ test the muscle function of your injured shoulder; it should only have 30% less ability than your uninjured one. ■ You may begin: ▶ strengthening exercises, such as standing Ys (**》p.215**) below maximum effort; aim for 4 sets x 8 reps. ▶ full-body exercises, such as punch lunges (**》p.182**); aim for 4 sets x 8 reps. ▶ interval bicycling at a moderate intensity. ▶ upper-limb weights exercises such as dumbbell bench presses (**》p.210**), as pain allows; start at 50% of your one-rep max and aim for 4 sets x 8–12 reps.	■ You should now be able to: ▶ demonstrate a full active range of motion in your shoulder, without difficulty or unnatural elevation of the shoulder ("hitching"). ▶ complete upper-limb plyometrics, such as medicine ball chest throws (**》p.216**), without pain. ▶ lift upper-body weights that are at least 80% of your one-rep max, without pain. ▶ complete high-level running at distances relevant to your sport, without pain. ▶ complete sport-specific drills without difficulty. ▶ participate in full training.

ROTATOR CUFF INJURIES

ROTATOR CUFF INJURY

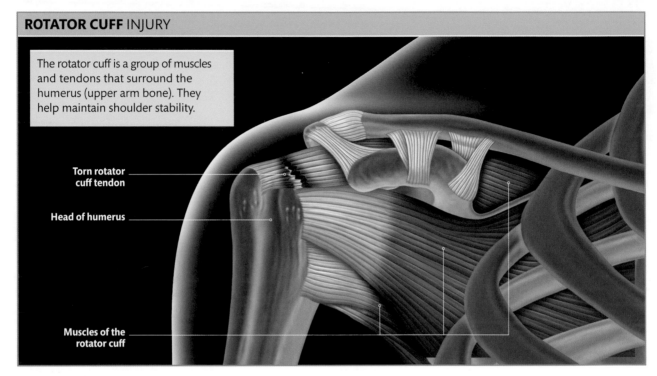

The rotator cuff is a group of muscles and tendons that surround the humerus (upper arm bone). They help maintain shoulder stability.

Torn rotator cuff tendon

Head of humerus

Muscles of the rotator cuff

Tears to the rotator cuff often occur with a sudden, overhead movement of the arm. Chronic tears and rotator cuff tendinopathy, both caused by years of repetitive overhead arm actions, are more common.

CAUSES
Rotator cuff injuries are common in sports involving some form of overhead arm movement, such as volleyball, baseball, swimming, and tennis. Sports such as these can give rise to the quick, violent movements of the shoulder that may lead to a tear in the rotator cuff. The repetition of overhead arm actions is a more common cause of rotator cuff tendinopathy.

SYMPTOMS AND DIAGNOSIS
Symptoms of a rotator cuff tear include a sudden tearing feeling in your shoulder, limited movement, severe pain and weakness in your shoulder, and an inability to move your arm out to the side. Tendinopathy symptoms are similar but also include a "popping" or "cracking" sensation in your shoulder when you move it. Both conditions may also

cause pain when you lie on your shoulder. Your physician will check your range of movement and you may have an X-ray to rule out fractures or bone spurs (malformations of the bone). You may be given an arthrogram (a dye is inserted into your shoulder joint before an X-ray, and if the dye leaks from the area, this indicates a tear in the tendon).

RISKS AND COMPLICATIONS
An untreated rotator cuff injury will become increasingly inflamed and painful, and motion can be reduced, leading to an inability to rotate your shoulder. In the long term, you may develop bone spurs.

WHEN WILL I BE FULLY FIT?
It may take at least 3–6 months' rehabilitation before you can return to sport, although you should make a full recovery. If you have a serious tear to your rotator cuff you may require surgery, followed by an 18-month recovery period. If the surgery is performed early you are likely to be able to return to a relatively high level of activity, but full recovery is unlikely.

TREATMENT

MEDICAL

IMMEDIATE ▶	SHORT TERM ▶	MEDIUM TERM ▶	LONG TERM
■ If you think you may have a rotator cuff injury, you should: ▶ stop activity. ▶ follow a RICE procedure (》p.170). ■ If the pain in your shoulder has not subsided within 2–3 days, you should: ▶ seek medical attention.	■ If you are diagnosed with a rotator cuff injury, your physician may: ▶ prescribe analgesic medication. ▶ advise you to rest your shoulder, allowing time for your injury to heal. ■ When your symptoms have subsided, your physician may: ▶ prescribe a course of corticosteroid injections to promote recovery. ▶ refer you to a physical therapist for treatment to help strengthen your muscles and restore motion (see table below).	■ If your injury fails to respond to nonsurgical treatment, your physician may: ▶ recommend surgery (open surgery or keyhole surgery, depending on the nature of your injury) to reattach the tendon to the bone. ■ After surgery, your physician may: ▶ immobilize your arm in a sling, to give the injury time to heal. You may also be given special apparatus to protect the repaired rotator cuff.	■ After the sling and apparatus used to protect the repaired rotator cuff are removed, your physician may: ▶ refer you to a physical therapist for a program of rehabilitation (see table below).

PHYSICAL THERAPY

EARLY STAGE ▶	INTERMEDIATE STAGE ▶	ADVANCED STAGE ▶	RETURN TO SPORT
■ Once your physician has referred you, your physical therapist may: ▶ suggest exercises such as scapular clocks (》p.251), to help you regain control of your shoulder blade. ▶ take your arm through a series of movements (within pain limits) to assess the range of motion in your joint—this will involve no effort from you (passive range of motion). ■ You may begin: ▶ bicycling 1–2 days after the operation; aim for 20 minutes at 85rpm, level 6, as pain allows. ▶ pool jogging in a sling; aim to jog for up to 30 minutes. ▶ resistance exercises for your shoulder that involve no joint movement 2 weeks after your operation, such as shoulder isometrics (》p.212); test it in all directions, as pain allows. ▶ full-body exercises that you can perform while wearing your sling, such as shoulder dumps (》p.182).	■ You should now be able to: ▶ demonstrate a full range of motion in your elbow, wrist, and hand. ■ Your physical therapist may: ▶ continue to test your passive range of motion; as your shoulder recovers you will be able to initiate these movements yourself (your active range of motion). ■ You may begin: ▶ exercises to stretch the back of your shoulder, such as sleeper stretches (》p.245). ▶ lower-limb weight exercises with no shoulder involvement. ▶ using an electrical muscle stimulator on the back of your shoulder muscles. ▶ exercises where one hand stays in contact with a surface, such as scapular clocks (》p.251) and kneeling supermen (》pp.228–29). ▶ low–moderate interval bicycling (stationary). ▶ upper-limb weights with your uninjured arm.	■ You should now be able to: ▶ demonstrate almost a full active range of motion in your shoulder without any abnormal movement. ■ Your physical therapist may: ▶ perform a muscle function test; your injured arm should demonstrate only 20% less ability than your uninjured one. ▶ continue to test your shoulder's range of motion. ■ You may begin: ▶ strengthening exercises, such as standing Ys (》p.215); aim for 4 sets x 8 reps below maximum effort, and side-lying Ls (》p.214). ▶ full-body exercises, such as push-ups (》pp.228–29); aim for 4 sets x 8 reps. ▶ lower-limb weights; include upper limbs (not overhead). ▶ upper-limb weights training, such as dumbbell bench presses (》p.210); start at 50% of your one-rep max and aim for 4 sets x 8–12 reps. ▶ stationary low-level skills, such as ball handling.	■ You should now be able to: ▶ demonstrate a full active range of motion in your shoulder, and should not feel apprehensive when this is tested by your physical therapist. ▶ complete upper-limb plyometrics, such as medicine ball chest throws (》p.216), without pain. ▶ complete isokinetic testing (》p.263), with internal and external shoulder rotation for both shoulders within 10%. ▶ lift upper-limb weights that are at least 80% of your one-rep max, without pain. ▶ complete high-level running at distances relevant to your sport, without pain. ▶ complete sport-specific drills without difficulty. ▶ participate in full training.

SHOULDER JOINT INFLAMMATION

The shoulder joint consists of a ball and socket—the head of the humerus (upper arm bone) and the glenoid cavity—surrounded by muscles, ligaments, tendons, and soft tissue.

CAUSES

Shoulder bursitis is an inflammation of the bursae (fluid-filled sacs) that act as "cushions" between bones and muscles in the shoulder joint. Frozen shoulder, or adhesive capsulitis, is a mild inflammation of the soft tissue in the joint. Both conditions are linked to sports that put repetitive strain on the shoulder, such as tennis and baseball. An associated condition, impingement syndrome, is common in swimmers and tennis players, and in sports involving overarm throwing. These strain the tendons of the rotator cuff (»p.70), causing them to swell and to be "impinged" by the joint.

SYMPTOMS AND DIAGNOSIS

Shoulder bursitis will be painful when you perform overhead movements or put weight on your shoulder. You may have limited movement in your shoulder, loss of arm strength, and swelling on the outside of your arm. With a frozen shoulder you may have pain that worsens at night or when you try to lift your arm, and reduced movement. Symptoms of impingement syndrome include shoulder pain, difficulty raising your arm, pain when reaching behind you, and a "grinding" sensation on moving your shoulder. Your physician will diagnose these conditions with an assessment of your symptoms, and by using X-rays, and MRI scans.

RISKS AND COMPLICATIONS

Untreated bursitis may lead to further inflammation and possible infection of the fluid inside your bursae, which may require surgery, while untreated impingement syndrome may cause your shoulder to become stiff and immobile, and your tendons to tear, if you engage in sports. Frozen shoulder may initially worsen, leading to further lack of mobility, although it can eventually improve on its own. A buildup of scar tissue on your muscles, however, may result in your needing surgery.

WHEN WILL I BE FULLY FIT?

Recovery from frozen shoulder can take up to 18 months. Following surgery, recovery can take 6 months. Impingement syndrome may need 3–6 months of physical therapy. Bursitis can take 6 months of rehabilitation; if you have had surgery you will require a 6-month recovery period.

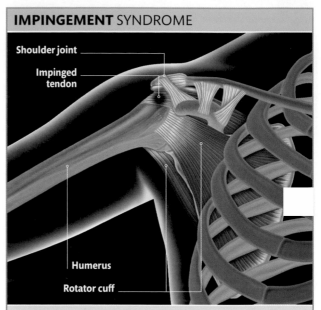

IMPINGEMENT SYNDROME

Shoulder joint
Impinged tendon
Humerus
Rotator cuff

Damage to the muscles of the rotator cuff may cause the head of the humerus to move up, leading to reduced space in the shoulder joint, causing impingement.

SHOULDER BURSITIS

Muscle
Inflamed shoulder bursa
Humerus

Repetitive strain on the shoulder or overhead arm movements can cause the bursa at the head of the humerus to become compressed and inflamed.

TREATMENT

➕ SEEK IMMEDIATE MEDICAL ATTENTION

MEDICAL

IMMEDIATE ▶	SHORT TERM ▶	MEDIUM TERM ▶	LONG TERM
■ If you think you may have a frozen shoulder, you should: ▶ apply heat and muscle relaxant to loosen the joint. ■ If you think you may have shoulder bursitis, you should: ▶ stop activity. ▶ follow a RICE procedure (**»p.170**). ▶ apply heat. ■ If you think you may have impingement syndrome, you should: ▶ apply ice to the affected area (**»p.165**). ▶ seek medical attention.	■ If you are diagnosed with a frozen shoulder, your physician may: ▶ prescribe corticosteroids to reduce the inflammation. ■ If you are diagnosed with bursitis, your physician may: ▶ prescribe corticosteroids to reduce the inflammation. ▶ refer you to a physical therapist (see table below). ■ If you are diagnosed with impingement syndrome, your physician may: ▶ advise you to abstain from repetitive shoulder movements. ▶ refer you to a physical therapist (see table below).	■ If your frozen shoulder fails to respond to nonsurgical treatment, your physician may: ▶ recommend surgery to remove adhesions. ■ If your bursa becomes infected, your physician may: ▶ drain it. ▶ recommend surgery to remove it. ■ If your impingement syndrome fails to respond to nonsurgical treatment, your physician may: ▶ recommend surgery to release the impinged ligament.	■ After surgery for any of these injuries, your physician may: ▶ refer you to a physical therapist for a program of rehabilitation (see table below).

PHYSICAL THERAPY

EARLY STAGE ▶	INTERMEDIATE STAGE ▶	ADVANCED STAGE ▶	RETURN TO SPORT
■ Once your physician has referred you, your physical therapist may: ▶ suggest various treatments, such as electrotherapy, to reduce inflammation. ▶ use soft tissue therapy to release tight muscles, such as your latissimus dorsi, posterior shoulder capsule, and your pectorals. ■ You may begin: ▶ pec stretches (**»p.240**). ▶ posterior capsule stretches, such as sleeper stretches (**»p.245**). ▶ lower-limb weights with no shoulder involvement. ▶ interval cycling at a low–moderate intensity. ▶ upper-limb weights with your uninjured arm.	■ You should now be able to: ▶ demonstrate full cervical and thoracic spine movement. ■ Your physical therapist may: ▶ suggest exercises to improve movement in your shoulder. ■ You may begin: ▶ resistance exercises for your shoulder that involve no joint movement, such as shoulder isometrics (**»p.212**); test all directions; aim for 10 reps x 10 secs. ▶ exercises for your shoulder blade in which one hand stays in contact with a surface, such as scapular clocks (**»p.251**); aim for 10 sets x 10 reps. ▶ full-body exercises (below maximum effort), such as lawnmowers (**»p.190**) and box step-ups (**»p.203**); aim for 4 sets x 8 reps.	■ Your physical therapist may: ▶ perform a muscle function test: your injured shoulder should have only 20% less ability than your uninjured one. ■ You may begin: ▶ strengthening exercises, such as standing Ys (**»p.215**), below maximum effort; aim for 4 sets x 8 reps. ▶ interval bicycling at a moderate intensity. ▶ lower-limb weights exercises that include your upper limbs; do not lift weights over your head. ▶ upper-limb weights exercises, such as dumbbell bench presses (**»p.210**), at 50% of your one rep max; aim for 4 sets x 8-12 reps. ▶ stationary low-level skills, such as ball handling. ▶ low-level running, as pain allows.	■ You should now be able to: ▶ demonstrate a full range of motion in your shoulder, and should not feel apprehensive when this is tested by your physical therapist. ▶ lift upper-body weights that are at least 80% of your one-rep max. ▶ complete high-level running at distances relevant to your sport, without pain. ▶ complete sport-specific drills without difficulty. ▶ participate in full training for at least 1 week.

SHOULDER JOINT INJURIES

The shoulder joint has the greatest mobility of any joint in the body and is more susceptible to dislocation than to any other type of injury. However, it takes considerable force for dislocation or subluxation (partial dislocation) to take place. Dislocations and subluxations occur in a forward (anterior) or backward (posterior) direction; anterior ones are more common.

CAUSES

Shoulder joint injuries are usually associated with collision sports, such as rugby and American football. Direct force to the shoulder in a violent collision between players, for example, may cause the head of the humerus (upper arm bone) to pull free of the shoulder socket, in the case of dislocation, or to pull partially free, in the case of subluxation. Indirect force, such as falling onto an outstretched arm, may cause dislocation or subluxation, while subluxation can result from swinging the arm strenuously into an awkward position.

SYMPTOMS AND DIAGNOSIS

With dislocation you may feel severe pain in your shoulder and a loss of mobility and sensitivity in your arm. Your shoulder may look deformed. With subluxation your shoulder may feel "loose," as if it is slipping in and out of the joint. You may also feel pain and experience a loss of sensitivity in your shoulder or arm. The physician will make a diagnosis through physical examination and an X-ray to identify the injury. You may also need an MRI scan to rule out other injuries, such as rotator cuff tears (»p.70) or ligament ruptures.

RISKS AND COMPLICATIONS

During dislocation your ligaments can tear, and this can leave your shoulder susceptible to further dislocation. Untreated subluxation can cause your shoulder joint to "wear out" over time, and you may require surgery as a result.

WHEN WILL I BE FULLY FIT?

Recovery time is very much dependent on the severity of your injury. Typically, it will be several weeks before you can return to normal activities, and several months before you can return to contact sports. Rehabilitation after surgery may take 3–6 months.

SHOULDER DISLOCATION

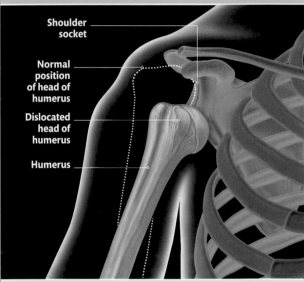

Shoulder socket

Normal position of head of humerus

Dislocated head of humerus

Humerus

The shoulder is a ball-and-socket joint, in which the ball-shaped head of the humerus fits into the shoulder socket. In a dislocation, the humerus pulls free of the socket.

SHOULDER SUBLUXATION

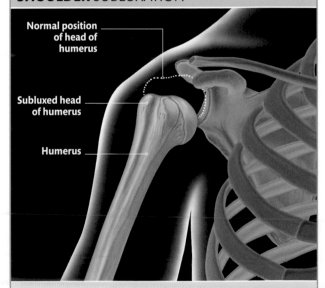

Normal position of head of humerus

Subluxed head of humerus

Humerus

In a subluxation of the shoulder, the ligaments of the joint are torn, and the head of the humerus pulls partially free of the socket.

TREATMENT

➕ SEEK IMMEDIATE MEDICAL ATTENTION

MEDICAL

IMMEDIATE ▶	SHORT TERM ▶	MEDIUM TERM ▶	LONG TERM
■ If you think you may have injured your shoulder joint, you should: ▶ immobilize your shoulder (**»p.170**). ▶ seek medical attention.	■ If you are diagnosed with a shoulder joint injury, your physician may: ▶ assess the sensitivity around your shoulder to check for nerve damage. ▶ put your shoulder back in place. This is usually carried out under anesthetic. ▶ prescribe pain-relief medication. ■ If you have additional injuries such as fractures or torn ligaments, your physician may: ▶ recommend surgery to repair any damaged ligaments or bones in your shoulder joint.	■ If you have not had surgery, after repositioning your shoulder your physician may: ▶ immobilize your arm in a sling for 2–3 weeks. ▶ refer you to a physical therapist for treatment to reduce inflammation and strengthen your shoulder muscles (see table below). ■ After you recover from surgery, your physician may: ▶ immobilize your arm in a sling for 2–3 weeks. ▶ refer you to a physical therapist for a program of rehabilitation (see table below).	■ If your shoulder repeatedly dislocates or subluxates, your physician may: ▶ recommend surgery to correct the problem. ■ After surgery, your physician may: ▶ refer you to a physical therapist for a program of rehabilitation (see table below). ■ Torn ligaments may heal very slowly, in this case your physician may: ▶ refer you to a physical therapist for a program of rehabilitation (see table below).

PHYSICAL THERAPY

EARLY STAGE ▶	INTERMEDIATE STAGE ▶	ADVANCED STAGE ▶	RETURN TO SPORT
■ Once your physician has referred you, your physical therapist may: ▶ suggest various treatments, such as electrotherapy, to reduce local inflammation. ▶ perform soft-tissue massage to surrounding areas to help with pain relief. ▶ suggest exercises you can do in your sling that will help build control in your shoulder blade, such as lawnmowers (**»p.190**) and shoulder dumps (**»p.182**). ■ You may begin: ▶ using an electrical muscle stimulator on your shoulder muscles to help maintain bulk. ▶ low–moderate interval bicycling. First do this with a sling, then continue without.	■ You should now be able to: ▶ demonstrate full cervical and thoracic spine movement. ■ Your physical therapist may: ▶ perform various exercises to help restore range of motion in your shoulder. ■ You may begin: ▶ resistance exercises for your shoulder in all directions, such as shoulder isometrics (**»p.212**), as pain allows; aim for 10 reps, lasting for 10 seconds each. ▶ exercises for the shoulder blade in which one hand stays in contact with a surface, such as scapular clocks (**»p.251**); aim for 10 sets x 10 reps. ▶ full-body exercises, such as lawnmowers (**»p.190**), as pain allows; aim for 4 x 8 reps, first with a sling, then without. ▶ lower-limb weights with no shoulder involvement.	■ You should now be able to: ▶ demonstrate almost a full range of shoulder motion. ■ Your physical therapist may: ▶ perform a muscle function test; your injured arm should demonstrate only 30% less ability than your uninjured one. ▶ continue to test the range of motion in your shoulder. ■ You may begin: ▶ strengthening exercises, such as standing Ys (**»p.215**); aim for 4 sets x 8 reps, below maximum effort. ▶ interval bicycling at a moderate–high intensity. ▶ lower-limb with upper-limb weights; do not lift any weights over your head. ▶ upper-limb weight training, such as dumbbell bench presses (**»p.210**), at 50% of your one-rep max; aim for 4 sets x 8–12 reps. ▶ stationary low-level skills, such as ball handling. ▶ low-level running.	■ You should now be able to: ▶ demonstrate a full range of motion in your shoulder, initiating all movements without pain (active range of motion). You should not feel apprehensive when this is tested by your physical therapist. ▶ complete upper-limb plyometrics, such as medicine ball chest throws (**»p.216**), without pain. ▶ lift upper-limb weights that are at least 80% of your one-rep max, without pain. ▶ complete high-level running at distances relevant to your sport, without pain. ▶ complete sport-specific drills without difficulty. ▶ participate in full training.

SIMPLE RIB FRACTURE

The ribs protect the heart, lungs, and other underlying organs from injury. Heavy impact to the torso can lead to the ribs being fractured.

CAUSES
Rib fractures are usually the result of a blow and occur mainly in collision sports such as rugby. Stress fractures are less common and occur mostly in sports that involve repetitive upper-body activity, such as rowing and golf.

SYMPTOMS AND DIAGNOSIS
You will feel pain in your ribs, which may increase when you inhale or cough. Your physician will usually make a diagnosis through a physical examination, and may also suggest an X-ray to confirm it.

RISKS AND COMPLICATIONS
Pain from a rib fracture may cause you to take shallow breaths and suppress coughing, which can ultimately lead to a chest infection. In more serious fractures, there may be damage to underlying organs such as your lungs.

WHEN WILL I BE FULLY FIT?
With rest, your rib should heal within 3–6 weeks. You may return to your sport when training causes no pain. Further injury to a fractured rib can prolong the healing time.

SIMPLE RIB FRACTURE

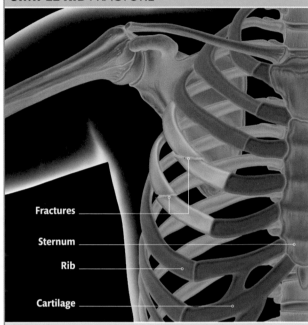

Fractures

Sternum

Rib

Cartilage

A rib fracture is a crack or split in any of the 12 pairs of ribs, or in the cartilage that connects each of them to the sternum (breastbone).

TREATMENT   SEEK IMMEDIATE MEDICAL ATTENTION

MEDICAL

IMMEDIATE
- If you think you may have a rib fracture, you should:
  ▶ apply ice to the affected area (**》p.165**).
  ▶ seek medical attention.

SHORT TERM
- If you are diagnosed with a rib fracture, your physician may: ▶ prescribe analgesic medication. ▶ encourage you to breathe normally and cough frequently, despite the increased pain, to prevent mucus from accumulating in your chest.

MEDIUM TERM
- Your physician may advise you to: ▶ rest until the pain has eased.

LONG TERM
- Your rib should heal within 3–6 weeks, after which your physician may: ▶ refer you to a physical therapist for a rehabilitation program (see table right).

PHYSICAL THERAPY

EARLY STAGE
- Your physical therapist may: ▶ use electrotherapy to reduce inflammation. ▶ assess the range of motion in your spine.

INTERMEDIATE STAGE
- You should have: ▶ no swelling and a near-full range of spinal motion with minimal pain. ■ You may begin: ▶ running, as pain allows. ▶ low-level core-stability exercises, such as pulley chops, level 1 (**》p.230**).

ADVANCED STAGE
- You should now be able to: ▶ perform low-level running, without pain. ▶ perform medium-level core exercises, such as curl-ups, levels 2–3 (**》p.221**), without pain. ■ You may begin: ▶ using upper- and lower-body weights. ▶ advanced-level core-stability exercises, such as pulley chops, level 4 (**》p.231**).

RETURN TO SPORT
- You should now be able to: ▶ demonstrate full active range of motion. ▶ complete upper-limb plyometrics. ▶ train normally.

ELBOW BURSITIS

The elbow bursa is a fluid-filled sac that reduces friction at the point where tendons and muscles move over bone. An injured bursa may produce excess fluid, causing painful swelling.

CAUSES
A blow to your elbow, from a hard object such as a hockey stick, or from a fall, may cause a bursa to become inflamed. Repetitive use of the elbow, such as in swimming or tennis, or bowling in cricket, may also cause inflammation.

SYMPTOMS AND DIAGNOSIS
Your elbow may be painful and tender and swell over the tip. Movement may be difficult. Your physician will usually make a diagnosis through physical examination, and may also suggest an X-ray or MRI scan to confirm it.

RISKS AND COMPLICATIONS
Sometimes an untreated elbow bursa can become infected. If your bursa is infected, the elbow may be red. Infection can cause the elbow joint to deteriorate over time.

WHEN WILL I BE FULLY FIT?
If your bursa has been drained, you may need a few days' rest before feeling fit. After surgical removal of a bursa, you will need at least 6 weeks to regain full fitness.

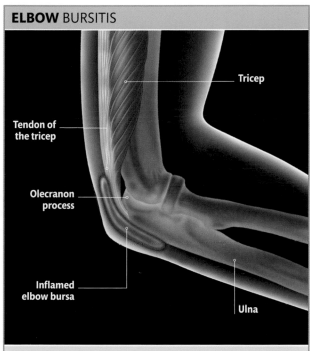

ELBOW BURSITIS

Tricep

Tendon of the tricep

Olecranon process

Inflamed elbow bursa

Ulna

As the elbow joint moves, the elbow bursa reduces friction between the tip of the ulna (known as the olecranon process) and adjacent tendons, such as that of the tricep.

TREATMENT   SEEK IMMEDIATE MEDICAL ATTENTION

MEDICAL

IMMEDIATE
■ If you think you may have elbow bursitis you should: ▶ stop activity. ▶ follow a RICE procedure (**》p.170**). ▶ seek medical attention.

SHORT TERM
■ If there is no improvement after 6 weeks, you should: ▶ seek medical attention. ■ Your physician may: ▶ prescribe antibiotics and analgesic medication. ▶ give you a corticosteroid injection. ▶ drain fluid from bursa. ▶ refer you to a physical therapist for treatment to ease pain and restore movement (see table right).

MEDIUM TERM
■ If the bursitis persists, as a last resort your physician may: ▶ recommend surgery to remove the bursa.

LONG TERM
■ After surgery, your physician may: ▶ immobilize your arm in a cast for 2–3 weeks. ▶ once the cast is off, refer you to a physical therapist for rehabilitation (see table right).

PHYSICAL THERAPY

EARLY STAGE
■ You should now be able to: ▶ move your elbow as much as pain allows, without increasing the swelling or pain.

INTERMEDIATE STAGE
■ You should now be able to: ▶ demonstrate a full range of motion in your fingers, hand, wrist, elbow, and shoulder, without causing swelling. ■ You may begin: ▶ exercises such as Swiss ball donkeys (**》p.222**), and standing Ys (**》p.215**).

ADVANCED STAGE
■ You should now be able to: ▶ complete balance and control exercises for the shoulder, elbow, and wrist, such as four-point kneels (**》p.247**). ■ Your physical therapist may assess your grip strength.

RETURN TO SPORT
■ You should now be able to: ▶ demonstrate a full range of motion in your elbow. ▶ complete upper-limb plyometrics, such as medicine ball chest throws (**》p.216**), without pain.

ELBOW TENDON INJURIES

Lateral epicondylitis (tennis elbow) is inflammation where the tendons join the outer "point" of the humerus (upper arm bone), while medial epicondylitis (golfer's elbow) is inflammation where the tendons join the inner point of the humerus. Thrower's elbow causes pain on both sides of the joint. All these injuries are the result of overuse of the elbow joint.

CAUSES
The extensor muscles, which run down the forearm to the wrist, are used for gripping. Overusing these muscles—especially when the wrist is bent back against resistance (for example, to return a serve)—can cause lateral epicondylitis, as can a direct blow to the elbow. Medial epicondylitis is thought to occur because the action of repeatedly striking a ball with a golf club can jar the elbow but can also be triggered by working out in the gym or repeatedly using topspin for a forehand shot in tennis. A golfer can also develop lateral epicondylitis in the elbow of the lead arm. Thrower's elbow can be triggered by repeated overhead throwing motions.

SYMPTOMS AND DIAGNOSIS
If you have lateral epicondylitis, you will feel pain or a burning sensation on the outside of your upper forearm, sometimes extending along your arm to your wrist, while golfer's elbow will cause you pain on the inside of your elbow, or around the bony point of the joint. If you have thrower's elbow, you will feel pain on both sides of the joint. Weakness in your wrist is common in all three conditions. Your physician may give you an X-ray to check for conditions such as arthritis, and an MRI scan to check for neck or disk problems (injuries such as these may cause symptoms similar to those of elbow tendon injuries). In rare cases, your physician may recommend an electromyogram, in which electrodes are used to check for nerve compression.

RISKS AND COMPLICATIONS
If these conditions are not treated correctly you may experience long-term loss of strength and flexibility, as well as pain when performing everyday tasks.

WHEN WILL I BE FULLY FIT?
You will be fully fit once you no longer have symptoms, which may take weeks or even months. If you need surgery, it will take 4–6 months before you can return to sports.

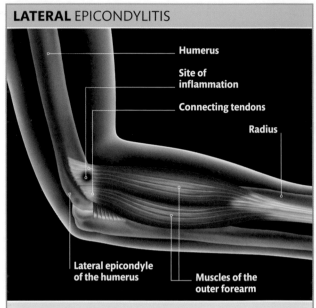

LATERAL EPICONDYLITIS

Humerus

Site of inflammation

Connecting tendons

Radius

Lateral epicondyle of the humerus

Muscles of the outer forearm

Inflammation can occur to the tendons which connect the muscles of the outer forearm to a "bump" (the lateral epicondyle) on the outside of the humerus.

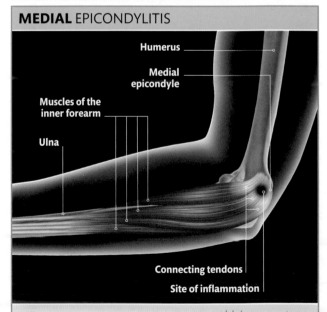

MEDIAL EPICONDYLITIS

Humerus

Medial epicondyle

Muscles of the inner forearm

Ulna

Connecting tendons

Site of inflammation

Inflammation can occur to the tendons which connect the muscles of the inner forearm to a "bump" (the medial epicondyle) on the inside of the humerus.

TREATMENT

⊕ SEEK IMMEDIATE MEDICAL ATTENTION

MEDICAL

IMMEDIATE	SHORT TERM	MEDIUM TERM	LONG TERM
■ If you suspect you have an elbow tendon injury, you should: ▶ stop any activity that causes you pain. ▶ immobilize your forearm (»p.170). ▶ apply ice to the affected area (»p.165) up to six times a day for two days, 15 minutes at a time. ■ If your symptoms do not respond to self-treatment, you should: ▶ seek medical attention.	■ If you are diagnosed with an elbow tendon injury, your physician may: ▶ prescribe pain-relief medication. ▶ prescribe a course of corticosteroid injections to relieve your symptoms and reduce the inflammation. ▶ refer you to a physical therapist for treatment to reduce inflammation and improve strength and motion (see below).	■ If your symptoms fail to respond to nonsurgical treatment, your physician may: ▶ recommend surgery to repair the damaged tissue. ■ After surgery, your physician may: ▶ advise you to rest for around 6 weeks.	■ When you have recovered from surgery, your physician may: ▶ refer you to a physical therapist for a program of rehabilitation (see below).

PHYSICAL THERAPY

EARLY STAGE	INTERMEDIATE STAGE	ADVANCED STAGE	RETURN TO SPORT
■ Your physical therapist may: ▶ suggest treatments to reduce local inflammation, such as electrotherapy. ▶ use soft-tissue massage to help relieve your symptoms. ▶ put strapping on your forearm to ease the load on it. ▶ assess your grip strength. ▶ assess the range of motion in your neck, shoulder, elbow and wrist. ■ You may begin: ▶ eccentric wrist extensions (»p.219); aim for 3 sets x 15 reps twice daily and use a light dumbbell. These should be painful. ▶ core-stability and gluteal exercises, such as dead bugs (»p.225). ▶ lower-limb weights that do not involve the upper limbs. ▶ bicycling, running, and work on a cross-trainer to maintain overall fitness.	■ You should now be able to: ▶ carry out daily activities with no pain. ▶ demonstrate full range of motion in your neck, shoulder, elbow, and wrist. ▶ fully weight-bear on your arm. ■ You may begin: ▶ lower-limb bodyweight exercises, such as single-leg squats (»p.193). ▶ eccentric wrist extensions (»p.219) with heavy dumbbell (men: 15kg; women: 8kg); aim for 3 sets x 15 reps. ▶ strengthening exercises, such as side-lying Ls (»p.214), below maximum effort; aim for 4 sets x 8 reps without pain.	■ You should now be able to: ▶ perform upper-limb plyometrics, such as medicine ball chest throws (»p.216), pain-free. ▶ perform balance and control exercises for the shoulder, elbow, and wrist, such as four-point kneels (»p.247). ■ Your physical therapist may: ▶ retest your grip strength; your injured arm should have only 10% less ability than the uninjured arm. ■ You may begin: ▶ upper-limb weights exercises, such as dumbbell bench presses (»p.210), at 50% of your one-rep max; aim for 4 sets x 8–12 reps, if pain-free. ▶ lower-limb weights that include the upper limbs, such as push presses (»p.238), as pain allows.	■ You should now be able to: ▶ demonstrate a full active range of motion in your elbow, generating all movements without pain. You should not feel apprehensive when this is tested by your physical therapist. ▶ lift upper-limb and lower-limb weights that are at least 80% of your one-rep max. ▶ complete sport-specific drills without difficulty.

HUMERUS FRACTURE

Most fractures of the humerus (the upper arm bone) occur when an older person breaks a fall with an arm extended. However, in a sporting context, humerus fractures also occur through heavy impact.

CAUSES

Humerus fractures are often associated with contact sports such as football, and can be caused by two athletes colliding, resulting in a direct blow to the humerus. Humerus fractures may also result from a fall onto an outstretched arm. In sports such as rugby and football, in which multiple collisions occur, fractures can be caused by one player falling onto the outstretched arm of another, for example when a scrum collapses.

SYMPTOMS AND DIAGNOSIS

Your arm will be painful and swollen, with restricted movement. There may also be bruising around the fracture. Your physician will make a diagnosis by assessing your symptoms and carrying out a physical examination. Your physician will then recommend an X-ray to ascertain the severity and extent of your fracture.

RISKS AND COMPLICATIONS

If you have a very severe fracture, particularly if you are elderly, there is a risk of some permanent loss of mobility of your arm. If your injury is not given sufficient time to heal, there is a risk that you may develop osteoarthritis.

WHEN WILL I BE FULLY FIT?

You will be able to return to sports once full, pain-free movement and flexibility of the upper arm has returned. This usually takes around 3 months. If you have had surgery, you will require 2–3 months after the operation, or possibly up to 6 months, before you can return to sports.

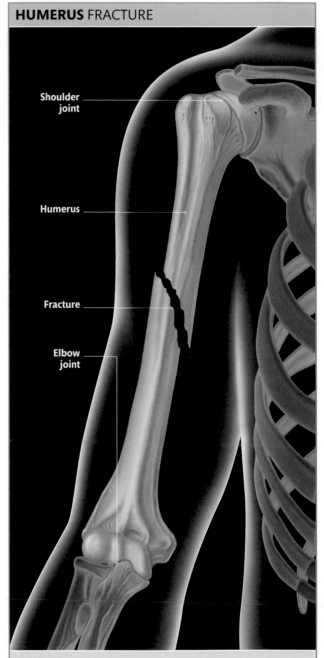

HUMERUS FRACTURE

Shoulder joint

Humerus

Fracture

Elbow joint

The humerus runs between the shoulder and the elbow and is the largest and longest bone in the arm. Because of its size and strength, fractures of this bone usually involve considerable force.

TREATMENT

(+) SEEK IMMEDIATE MEDICAL ATTENTION

MEDICAL

IMMEDIATE	SHORT TERM	MEDIUM TERM	LONG TERM
■ If you think you may have fractured your humerus, you should: ▶ immobilize your upper arm in a sling (**》p.170**). ▶ seek immediate medical attention.	■ If you are diagnosed with a simple fracture of the humerus, your physician may: ▶ nonsurgically realign the affected bones and immobilize your arm with a sling, splint, or cast for around 6 weeks. ▶ prescribe analgesic medication. ■ If your fracture is severe, your physician may: ▶ recommend immediate surgery to repair the fracture.	■ If your bones have been realigned without surgery and have healed as expected, your physician may: ▶ refer you to a physical therapist for treatment to help improve your muscle strength and range of motion (see table below). ■ If your bones have been realigned without surgery, but have failed to heal as expected, your physician may: ▶ recommend surgery to fully repair the fracture.	■ After surgery, your physician may: ▶ immobilize your arm in a cast or sling for 6 weeks. ▶ refer you to a physical therapist for a program of rehabilitation (see table below).

PHYSICAL THERAPY

EARLY STAGE	INTERMEDIATE STAGE	ADVANCED STAGE	RETURN TO SPORT
■ Once your physician has referred you, your physical therapist may: ▶ suggest various treatments, such as electrotherapy, to reduce local inflammation. ▶ recommend ultrasound to promote bone healing. ▶ perform various exercises to help restore range of movement in your shoulder. ■ You may begin: ▶ resistance exercises for your shoulder that involve no joint movement, such as pushing both hands against a wall, or holding a small dumbbell, with your elbow at a right angle for a few seconds, repeating after a pause, as pain allows; aim for 10 reps x 10 secs; test in all directions. ▶ full-body exercises, such as shoulder dumps (**》p.182**), as pain allows; aim for 4 sets x 12 reps, first with a sling, then continue without.	■ You should now be able to: ▶ demonstrate 90 degrees' flexion and abduction in your shoulder, with good shoulder blade control. ■ You may begin: ▶ exercises for the shoulder blade where one hand stays in contact with a surface, such as scapular clocks (**》p.251**); aim for 10 sets x 10 reps. ▶ lower-limb weights exercises with no upper limb involvement, such as 45-degree leg presses (**》p.195**). ▶ low–moderate interval cycling, with a sling.	■ You should now be able to: ▶ demonstrate a near full range of motion in your shoulder. ■ Your physical therapist may: ▶ perform a muscle function test; your injured arm should demonstrate only 20% less ability than the uninjured one. ■ You may begin: ▶ strengthening exercises such as standing Ys (**》p.215**); aim for 4 sets x 8 reps, below maximum effort. ▶ interval cycling at a moderate intensity. ▶ lower- and upper-limb weights exercises, such as straight-leg and single-leg deadlifts (**》p.197**). Do not lift any weights over your head. ▶ upper-limb weight training, such as dumbbell bench presses (**》p.210**), at 50% of your one-rep max; aim for 4 sets x 8–12 reps. ▶ stationary low-level skills. ▶ low-level running. You should not feel any pain.	■ You should now be able to: ▶ demonstrate a full range of motion in your shoulder, generating all movements without assistance. You should not feel apprehensive when tested by your physical therapist. ▶ complete upper-limb plyometrics, such as medicine ball chest throws (**》p.216**), without pain. ▶ lift upper-limb weights that are at least 80% of your one-rep max, without pain. ▶ complete high-level running at distances relevant to your sport, without pain. ▶ complete sport-specific drills without difficulty. ▶ participate in full training for at least 2–3 weeks. ▶ do full contact training drills, without pain.

FOREARM FRACTURES

In many sports, there is huge potential for falling onto the forearm or for the forearm to receive a powerful blow. Consequently, the bones of the forearm—the radius and the ulna—are vulnerable to fracture.

CAUSES
Fractures often occur in contact sports, where falls or direct force on the forearm are common, or in sports such as skateboarding or bicycling, where falls on hard surfaces, impacting the forearm, may occur. Fractures can also be the result of overuse, particularly for tennis players or golfers. A fracture of a forearm bone can be accompanied by dislocation of the elbow or wrist (»p.86).

SYMPTOMS AND DIAGNOSIS
If you have broken either one or both of the bones in your forearm, you may have severe pain and swelling in the limb and be unable to move it. Your forearm may also be visibly deformed, for example if the fracture is displaced or the skin is broken by the fragmented bone. Your physician will carry out a physical examination and arrange for an X-ray to confirm the diagnosis. The X-ray will also establish whether you have sustained any other injuries, such as a wrist or elbow dislocation.

RISKS AND COMPLICATIONS
Various complications may arise: delayed union (slow joining of your bones), malunion (your bones join but are not perfectly aligned), and cross union (your ulna and radius join at the site of the fracture) are possible, but rare. If you suffer loss of bone from a complex break, then you may need a bone graft, an operation in which the missing bone is replaced with an artificial substitute or with bone taken from elsewhere in the body.

WHEN WILL I BE FULLY FIT?
Your cast will be removed after 4–6 weeks. After this, you will need supervised rehabilitation to regain strength and movement in your forearm. This can take 3–6 months.

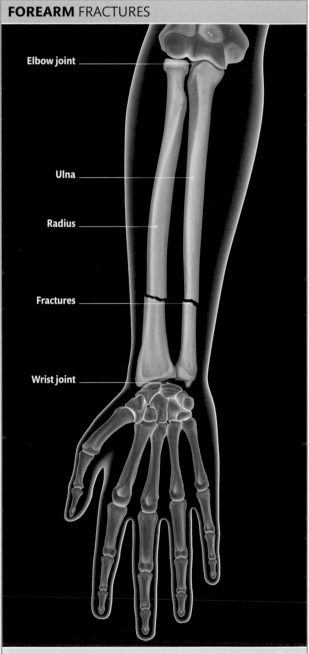

FOREARM FRACTURES

Elbow joint

Ulna

Radius

Fractures

Wrist joint

The two bones of the forearm, the radius and the ulna, run together between the elbow and the wrist. Forearm fractures may involve one or both of these bones, although isolated radial fractures are rare.

TREATMENT

⊕ SEEK IMMEDIATE MEDICAL ATTENTION

MEDICAL

IMMEDIATE ▶	SHORT TERM ▶	MEDIUM TERM ▶	LONG TERM
■ If you think you may have fractured your forearm, you should: ▶ elevate your arm. ▶ immobilize your arm in a sling (**》p.170**). ▶ seek medical attention.	■ If you are diagnosed with a simple forearm fracture, in which the skin is not broken, your physician may: ▶ realign your broken bone and put your arm in a cast; after a week, the position of the fracture will be checked on X-ray. ▶ prescribe analgesic medication. ■ If an open complex forearm fracture, in which your skin is broken by your bone and the fracture is displaced, is diagnosed, your physician may: ▶ recommend surgery to repair the bone.	■ If you have had nonsurgical treatment, your physician may: ▶ X-ray your arm to check how your fracture is healing. ■ If the position of your bones is not correct, your physician may: ▶ recommend surgery to repair the fracture. ■ If you have had surgery, your physician may: ▶ X-ray your arm to check how your fracture is healing. ■ After surgery, your physician may: ▶ put your arm in a cast for up to 6 weeks.	■ After your cast has been removed—whether you have had surgery or not—your physician may: ▶ refer you to a physical therapist for a program of rehabilitation (see table below).

PHYSICAL THERAPY

EARLY STAGE ▶	INTERMEDIATE STAGE ▶	ADVANCED STAGE ▶	RETURN TO SPORT
■ Once your physician has referred you, your physical therapist may: ▶ suggest various treatments, such as electrotherapy, to reduce local inflammation. ▶ perform various exercises to help restore range of movement in your elbow. ▶ assess your grip strength. ▶ advise you to keep moving your hand and fingers. ■ You may begin: ▶ low to moderate stationary bicycling, with your sling.	■ You should now be able to: ▶ demonstrate an increased grip strength; aim for 30% difference between your injured arm and your uninjured one. ■ You may begin: ▶ squeezing a ball in the hand of your injured arm. ▶ isometric shoulder exercises (**》p.212**). ▶ shoulder blade exercises in which one hand maintains contact with a surface, such as scapular clocks (**》p.251**); aim for 10 sets x 10 reps. ▶ lower-limb weights with no shoulder involvement. ▶ upper-limb weights with your uninjured arm. ▶ moderate stationary bicycling.	■ You should now be able to: ▶ demonstrate an increased grip strength; aim for 20% difference between your injured arm and your uninjured one. ■ You may begin: ▶ strengthening exercises such as standing Ys (**》p.215**); aim for 4 sets x 8 reps, below maximum effort. ▶ full-body exercises, such as lawnmowers (**》p.190**); aim for 4 sets x 8 reps, below maximum effort. ▶ moderate-high intensity stationary bicycling, cross-training, and stepping. ▶ upper-limb weights training, such as dumbbell bench presses (**》p.210**), tricep push-downs (**》p.217**), and hammer dumbbell curls (**》p.218**); perform them at 50% of your one-rep max, and aim for 4 sets x 8–12 reps. ▶ stationary low-level skills, such as ball handling.	■ You should now be able to: ▶ demonstrate a full active range of motion in your elbow, generating all movements without assistance. You should not feel apprehensive when this is tested by your physical therapist. ▶ demonstrate grip strength within 10% of that of the uninjured arm. ▶ complete upper-limb plyometrics, such as medicine ball chest throws (**》p.216**), without pain. ▶ lift upper-limb weights that are at least 80% of your one-rep max, without pain. ▶ complete high-level running at distances relevant to your sport, without pain. ▶ complete sport-specific drills without difficulty. ▶ participate in full training.

WRIST FRACTURES

The wrist joint is composed of eight connecting bones, together with the lower ends of the radius and ulna (the bones of the forearm). Wrist fractures—especially to the radius or ulna—are a frequent injury among athletes because the arm is instinctively used to break a fall. They can be difficult to diagnose, however, since symptoms are not always obvious.

CAUSES
Fractured wrists are linked with sports such as bicycling, running, roller blading, or skateboarding, and are usually caused by a fall onto an outstretched hand. A direct blow to, or twisting of the wrist, perhaps incurred during contact sports such as rugby or football, are also common causes of these injuries.

SYMPTOMS AND DIAGNOSIS
You may experience pain, swelling, and tenderness in your wrist, as well as difficulty bending it. You may also have a visible deformity of your wrist, although some fractures are not obvious; for example, a scaphoid bone fracture may have no visible external signs, without even a bruise present. In some cases you will only be aware of the fracture when the pain becomes severe. A wrist fracture may also be accompanied by a dislocation (»p.86). Your physician will examine your wrist and you will have an X-ray or a CT scan to determine the extent of your break and to ensure that you have not suffered additional injuries, such as a fractured forearm (»p.80).

RISKS AND COMPLICATIONS
If the fracture remains untreated, there is a high risk that you will experience complications such as the nonunion of bone fragments, and avascular necrosis (the death of the bone caused by absence of blood supply). Untreated fractures can also lead to loss of mobility in your wrist, and osteoarthritis. Surgery leads to physical therapy being started earlier and muscle atrophy is less, allowing for more rapid rehabilitation.

WHEN WILL I BE FULLY FIT?
If your wrist is placed in a cast you may need 8–12 weeks for healing. After the cast is removed, you can start to use your hand again, avoiding all activities that may cause you pain. With proper rehabilitation, you should be fully fit after about 3 months. After surgery you will need 3 months to recover before resuming your sport.

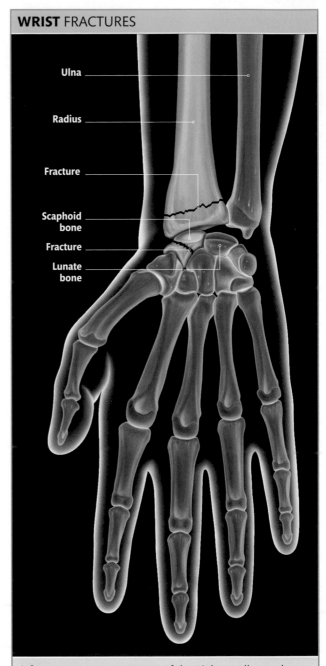

WRIST FRACTURES

Ulna

Radius

Fracture

Scaphoid bone

Fracture

Lunate bone

A fracture may occur to any of the eight small carpal bones that interconnect in the wrist via a series of ligaments, or to the lower ends of the ulna or radius, which sit next to the upper two carpal bones, the scaphoid and lunate.

TREATMENT

⊕ SEEK IMMEDIATE MEDICAL ATTENTION

MEDICAL

IMMEDIATE ▶	SHORT TERM ▶	MEDIUM TERM ▶	LONG TERM
■ If you think you may have fractured your wrist, you should: ▶ follow a RICE procedure (»p.170). ▶ immobilize your arm in a sling (»p.170). ▶ seek immediate medical attention.	■ If you are diagnosed with an undisplaced fracture (your bones are still in the correct position), your physician may: ▶ immobilize your wrist in a short arm cast for 4–6 weeks. ▶ prescribe analgesic medication for 1–2 weeks. ■ If you are diagnosed with a displaced or multiple fracture, your physician may: ▶ recommend surgery to repair your bones.	■ If you have not had surgery and your injury has healed well, your physician may: ▶ refer you to a physical therapist for treatment to improve strength and movement in your wrist (see table below). ■ If you have not had surgery and your injury has failed to heal as expected, your physician may: ▶ recommend surgery to reposition and repair your bones.	■ After surgery: ▶ your arm will be put in a cast for about 4 weeks. ■ After the cast is removed, your physician may: ▶ refer you to a physical therapist for a program of rehabilitation (see table below).

PHYSICAL THERAPY

EARLY STAGE ▶	INTERMEDIATE STAGE ▶	ADVANCED STAGE ▶	RETURN TO SPORT
■ Once your physician has referred you, your physical therapist may: ▶ suggest various treatments, such as electrotherapy, to reduce local inflammation. ▶ advise you to wear a wrist splint and compression bandage after your cast has been removed, to help alleviate symptoms. ▶ take your wrist through a series of movements (within pain limits) to assess the range of motion in your joint—this will involve no effort from you (passive range of motion); as you recover you will be able to initiate these movements yourself (active range of motion). ▶ test that you have full range of motion in your elbow and shoulder. ■ You may begin: ▶ isometric exercises that will strengthen the elbow and wrist, but involve no movement; stop if you feel pain.	■ You should now be able to: ▶ demonstrate no swelling in the affected area. ▶ experience a full range of motion in your fingers, hand, wrist, elbow, and shoulder. ▶ fully weight-bear, without pain. ■ Your physical therapist may: ▶ assess your grip strength to establish a baseline marker for recovery. ■ You may begin: ▶ weight-bearing exercises, such as four-point kneels (»p.247), level 1.	■ You should now be able to: ▶ complete upper-limb plyometrics, such as mini trampoline throws (»p.216), without pain. ▶ complete balance and control exercises for your shoulder, elbow, and wrist, such as scapular circles (»p.251). ■ Your physical therapist may: ▶ retest your grip strength; your injured arm should have only 10% less ability than your uninjured one. ■ You may begin: ▶ upper-limb weights exercises such as dumbbell bench presses (»p.210), as pain allows; start at 50% of your one-rep max and aim for 4 sets x 8–12 reps. You may need to wear wrist straps to strengthen your grip. ▶ lower-limb weight exercises that include the upper limbs, as pain allows. You may need to wear wrist straps to strengthen your grip.	■ You should now be able to: ▶ demonstrate a full active range of motion in your whole arm, and should not feel apprehensive when this is tested by your physical therapist. ▶ complete ball skills, without pain. ▶ lift upper-body weights that are at least 80% of your one-rep max, without pain. ▶ complete sport-specific drills without difficulty. ▶ participate in full training for at least 2–3 weeks.

WRIST DISLOCATION AND SPRAIN

The numerous bones and ligaments that make up the wrist allow the hand to perform a variety of movements. The wrist is highly susceptible to injury because of its exposed position and its key role in many sports. Dislocations normally involve the lunate bone in the wrist, while sprains can affect any of the ligaments.

CAUSES

Injuries to the wrist can occur in any sport in which falling is a hazard, but are most common in skiing, snowboarding, skating, soccer, bicycling, and gymnastics. Falling onto an outstretched hand is the most common cause of dislocations and sprains. When a bone is dislocated it becomes displaced or misaligned, making the joint unstable and affecting the surrounding soft tissue. Sprains involve damage to the ligaments of the wrist, and are classed as mild, moderate, or severe, depending on how badly the ligaments are torn.

SYMPTOMS AND DIAGNOSIS

If you dislocate a bone in your wrist, you will feel pain and there may be swelling, tenderness, and loss of movement. When nerves and blood vessels are damaged, you may experience numbness or paralysis in your wrist and hand. If you have injured your ligaments, you will have bruising and are likely to feel pain during weight-bearing or twisting actions. Your physician will give you a physical examination and may organize an X-ray to determine the severity of the injury and to see whether you also have a wrist fracture (»p.84).

RISKS AND COMPLICATIONS

If you leave a dislocation or sprain untreated, you may suffer a loss of strength and movement in your wrist, as well as impaired sensation in the case of a dislocation. There is also a possibility that your injury may lead to carpal tunnel syndrome (»p.90). Even after treatment your wrist may be susceptible to osteoarthritis, and there is a good chance of developing permanent or residual stiffness, swelling, and weakness.

WHEN WILL I BE FULLY FIT?

Recovery time for a sprain depends on the extent of the damage, but may take 6–10 weeks. Following surgery for a dislocation or a severe sprain you will be in a cast or splint for 1–2 months. After this, it may take 6 weeks for you to recover full strength and range of motion.

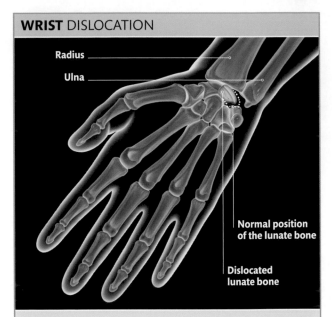

WRIST DISLOCATION

Radius
Ulna

Normal position of the lunate bone

Dislocated lunate bone

Most wrist dislocations involve the lunate bone, one of the carpal bones closest to the arm, which partially spans the base of the ulna and the radius (the bones of the forearm).

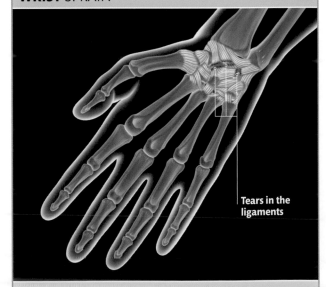

WRIST SPRAIN

Tears in the ligaments

Wrist sprains occur when any of the complex network of ligaments that connect the carpal bones are stretched beyond their normal limits.

TREATMENT

⊕ SEEK IMMEDIATE MEDICAL ATTENTION

MEDICAL

IMMEDIATE ▶	SHORT TERM ▶	MEDIUM TERM ▶	LONG TERM
■ If you think you may have dislocated or sprained your wrist, you should: ▶ follow a RICE procedure (»p.170). ▶ immobilize the injured area with a splint or cast (»p.170). ▶ seek medical attention.	■ If you are diagnosed with a mild wrist sprain, your physician may: ▶ bandage your wrist and recommend that you rest it. ▶ prescribe analgesic medication. ■ If you are diagnosed with a dislocated wrist or a severe sprain, in which the ligaments are badly damaged, your physician may: ▶ recommend surgery to realign your bone or repair the damaged ligament in your wrist.	■ If you have not had surgery, and your wrist has healed as expected, your physician may: ▶ refer you to a physical therapist for treatment to build strength and help regain mobility in your wrist (see table below). ■ If you have had surgery, your surgeon may: ▶ immobilize your wrist in a cast for 4–8 weeks until it is fully healed.	■ After your cast is removed following surgery and your wrist is completely healed, your physician may: ▶ refer you to a physical therapist for a program of rehabilitation (see table below).

PHYSICAL THERAPY

EARLY STAGE ▶	INTERMEDIATE STAGE ▶	ADVANCED STAGE ▶	RETURN TO SPORT
■ Once your physician has referred you, your physical therapist may: ▶ suggest various treatments, such as electrotherapy, to reduce local inflammation. ▶ take your wrist through a series of movements (within pain limits) to assess the range of motion in your joint—this will involve no effort from you (passive range of motion); as your wrist recovers you will be able to initiate these movements yourself (active range of motion). ▶ ensure that you have a full range of motion in your elbow and shoulder. ■ You may begin: ▶ resistance strengthening exercises for your shoulder, elbow, wrist, and hand that do not involve joint movement, such as shoulder isometrics (»p.212) and wrist extension exercises (»p.219).	■ You should now be able to: ▶ demonstrate no swelling in the affected area. ▶ demonstrate a full active range of motion in your wrist, elbow, and shoulder, without pain. ▶ bear your full weight, without pain. ■ Your physical therapist may: ▶ assess your grip strength; your injured hand should have only 10% less ability than your uninjured one.	■ You should now be able to: ▶ complete low-level ball handling, without pain. ■ You may begin: ▶ upper-limb and lower-limb weights, as pain allows; start at 80% of your one-rep max and aim for 4 sets x 8–12 reps. ▶ upper-limb plyometrics that are relevant to your sport, such as medicine ball chest throws (»p.216).	■ You should now be able to: ▶ complete high-level skills that are relevant to your sport, without pain. ▶ complete sport-specific drills without difficulty. ▶ participate in full training. ▶ complete contact drills that are relevant to your sport, pain-free and without feeling apprehensive.

WRIST AND HAND TENDON DISORDERS

Injuries to the tendons in the hand and wrist are common in many sports. Any of the tendons may be affected, but there are two disorders that are particularly prevalent: de Quervain's syndrome and intersection syndrome. These are both caused by an inflammation of the tunnel-like sheath that surrounds the two tendons that control the thumb.

CAUSES

Both of these syndromes are repetitive strain injuries, caused by prolonged or repeated gripping, squeezing, and pulling movements. They are most common in sports such as tennis, rowing, skiing, and weight lifting. In de Quervain's syndrome, the tendon sheath becomes strained, while in intersection syndrome, the sheath is irritated as it rubs against the two thumb muscles. In both cases this leads to inflammation and swelling of the sheath, which in turn leads to restricted movement of the tendons.

SYMPTOMS AND DIAGNOSIS

Your wrist will feel sore and the area may be red. The pain may extend into your thumb or along the inside of your forearm. Although the symptoms are very similar, the two conditions can be distinguished from one another because the pain occurs in different places. De Quervain's syndrome will cause pain and tenderness at the side of your wrist beneath the base of your thumb. Intersection syndrome will cause pain just above the back of your wrist joint, on top of your forearm.

RISKS AND COMPLICATIONS

These disorders usually respond well to self-treatment, but they can take a long time to heal. If you return to your sport without resolving the problem, you risk reinjuring yourself and suffering long-term pain. If you rely on analgesics you may not realize the strain you are putting on your wrist, and this may lead to a rupture of your tendons. If nonsurgical treatments do not improve your condition, you may need surgery to free the tendons.

WHEN WILL I BE FULLY FIT?

These conditions will usually heal within 4–6 weeks, but if you have had surgery your rehabilitation period will be longer. However, you should spend at least 6 months rehabilitating and strengthening your wrist before returning to full activity.

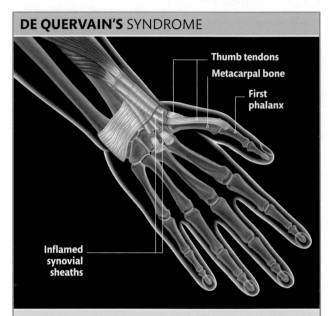

DE QUERVAIN'S SYNDROME

Thumb tendons
Metacarpal bone
First phalanx
Inflamed synovial sheaths

The two tendons that control the thumb are encased in fibrous sheaths (known as synovial sheaths). They attach to the metacarpal bone and the first phalanx (finger bone).

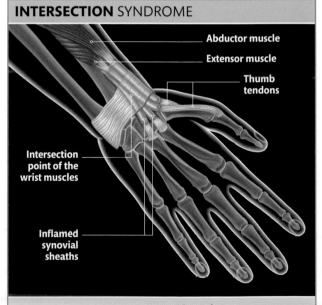

INTERSECTION SYNDROME

Abductor muscle
Extensor muscle
Thumb tendons
Intersection point of the wrist muscles
Inflamed synovial sheaths

The tendons of the thumb extend from the extensor and abductor muscles in the forearm and intersect with two key muscles in the wrist.

TREATMENT

MEDICAL

IMMEDIATE ▶	SHORT TERM ▶	MEDIUM TERM ▶	LONG TERM
■ If you think you may have a tendon disorder in your wrist or hand, you should: ▶ stop any activity that causes pain. ▶ follow a RICE procedure (**》p.170**). ■ If your symptoms fail to improve with self-treatment, you should: ▶ seek medical attention.	■ If a tendon disorder in your wrist or hand is diagnosed, your physician may: ▶ put your wrist and thumb in a splint to immobilize them. ▶ prescribe analgesic medication. ▶ advise you to avoid repetitive thumb and hand movements and to take frequent breaks when performing any activity in which you have to use your hands and wrists.	■ If your injury is healing as expected, your physician may: ▶ refer you to a physical therapist for treatment to relieve symptoms and improve strength and movement in your hand (see table below). ■ If your injury fails to heal as expected, your physician may: ▶ give you an injection of corticosteroids to temporarily bring down the inflammation.	■ If your injury fails to respond to nonsurgical treatment, your physician may: ▶ recommend surgery to widen the tendon tunnel. ■ After surgery, your physician may: ▶ recommend you wear a cast or splint for 3–4 weeks. ▶ refer you to a physical therapist for a program of rehabilitation (see table below).

PHYSICAL THERAPY

EARLY STAGE ▶	INTERMEDIATE STAGE ▶	ADVANCED STAGE ▶	RETURN TO SPORT
■ Once your physician has referred you, your physical therapist may: ▶ suggest various treatments, such as electrotherapy, to reduce local inflammation. ▶ recommend a wrist splint and compression bandage to help alleviate symptoms. ▶ take your wrist through a series of movements (within pain limits) to assess the range of motion in your joint—this will involve no effort from you (passive range of motion); as you recover you will be able to initiate the actions yourself (active range of motion). ▶ use manual therapy and soft tissue therapy to help relieve your symptoms. ▶ test that you have a full range of motion in your elbow and shoulder. ■ You may begin: ▶ resistance strengthening exercises for your shoulder, elbow, and wrist that do not involve joint movement, such as shoulder isometrics (**》p.212**), as pain allows.	■ You should now be able to: ▶ demonstrate no swelling in the affected area, even when performing daily activities. ▶ demonstrate a full range of motion in your neck, shoulder, elbow, and wrist, without pain. ▶ bear your full weight, without pain. ■ Your physical therapist may: ▶ test your grip strength.	■ You should now be able to: ▶ complete upper-limb plyometrics, such as mini trampoline throws (**》p.216**), without pain. ▶ complete shoulder, elbow, and wrist proprioceptive exercises, such as scapular circles (**》p.251**). ■ Your physical therapist may: ▶ retest your grip strength; your injured arm should have only 10% less ability than your uninjured one. ■ You may begin: ▶ upper-limb weights exercises, such as dumbbell bench presses (**》p.210**), as pain allows; start at 50% of your one-rep max and aim for 4 sets x 8–12 reps. (You may need to modify the lifts or use wrist straps.) ▶ lower-limb weight exercises that include the upper limbs, such as push presses (**》p.238**), as pain allows.	■ You should now be able to: ▶ demonstrate a full active range of motion when tested by your physical therapist. ▶ lift upper-body weights that are at least 80% of your one-rep max, without pain. ▶ complete sport-specific drills without difficulty. ▶ participate in full training.

CARPAL TUNNEL SYNDROME

Carpal tunnel syndrome (CTS) is caused by compression of the median nerve that supplies part of the hand. The nerve runs through the carpal tunnel, a narrow space at the wrist.

CAUSES
Compression of the median nerve is commonly caused by sports that involve repetitive movements of the wrist, such as rowing or racket sports. It may also be the result of a blow to the wrist, from a hockey or lacrosse stick, for example, but many cases have no known cause.

SYMPTOMS AND DIAGNOSIS
There may be pain, numbness, or tingling in your thumb and fingers, and you may find manual tasks difficult. Your physician may use a nerve conduction velocity test to make a diagnosis.

RISKS AND COMPLICATIONS
Over time, the muscles at the base of your hand may weaken, causing reduced function. Even after surgery, carpal tunnel syndrome may return if you use your hand as before.

WHEN WILL I BE FULLY FIT?
Carpal tunnel syndrome may clear up without treatment. If you have surgery, you may need to rest your arm and hand for 4–6 weeks before you can take up your sport again.

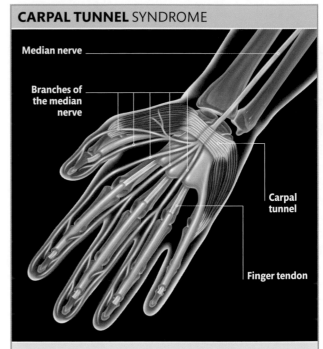

CARPAL TUNNEL SYNDROME

Median nerve

Branches of the median nerve

Carpal tunnel

Finger tendon

The carpal tunnel is a narrow passage in the wrist. It houses the median nerve, which runs down the arm, through the carpal tunnel, to the hand and fingers.

TREATMENT

MEDICAL

IMMEDIATE
■ If you think you may have carpal tunnel syndrome, you should: ▶ stop activity. ▶ immobilize your wrist (**≫p.170**).

SHORT TERM
■ If you are diagnosed with carpal tunnel syndrome, your physician may: ▶ give you a corticosteroid injection to reduce the pain and swelling. ▶ put your wrist in a splint.

MEDIUM TERM
■ If your symptoms fail to respond to nonsurgical treatment, your physician may: ▶ recommend surgery to relieve the pressure on your median nerve. ■ After surgery your physician may: ▶ advise you to rest for 4–6 weeks, and refrain from any sporting activities.

LONG TERM
■ Once you have recovered from surgery, your physician may: ▶ refer you to a physical therapist for a program of rehabilitation (see table right).

PHYSICAL THERAPY

EARLY STAGE
■ Your physical therapist may: ▶ assess your neck, shoulder, elbow, and wrist. ▶ use manual and soft tissue therapy to relieve your symptoms. ▶ suggest wrist flexor stretches. ▶ give advice on posture.

INTERMEDIATE STAGE
■ You should have: ▶ no unusual sensations in your wrist. ■ Your physical therapist will: ▶ assess your grip strength.

ADVANCED STAGE
■ You should now be able to: ▶ demonstrate a full range of motion in your wrist, without pain. ■ You may begin: ▶ upper-limb weights exercises, such as dumbbell bench presses (**≫p.210**)—starting at 50% of your one-rep max—and balance and control exercises, such as scapular circles (**≫p.251**).

RETURN TO SPORT
■ You should now be able to: ▶ demonstrate a full active range of movement; complete sport-specific drills without difficulty.

METACARPAL FRACTURE

Fracture of the metacarpals (the long bones in the hand) is a common sports injury. A heavy impact may break one or more bones.

CAUSES
A direct blow to the back of the hand during combat sports, such as martial arts, or contact sports, such as rugby, may cause metacarpal fractures. Falling on the hand during noncontact sport may also lead to this injury.

SYMPTOMS AND DIAGNOSIS
Your hand may be painful and you may not be able to move your fingers or make a fist. If you can make a fist, your fingers may not align. Bruising may appear a few days after injury and your finger may seem twisted, or shorter. Your physician will make a diagnosis through physical examination and an X-ray.

RISKS AND COMPLICATIONS
If a broken bone heals irregularly, you may be at risk of osteoarthritis. You may also have fragments of broken bone in your hand, which could require surgery to remove them.

WHEN WILL I BE FULLY FIT?
With nonsurgical treatment, a fracture should heal in about 6 weeks. Recovery after surgery may take 6–8 weeks. You can return to your sport once you regain full use of your hand.

METACARPAL FRACTURE

Metacarpal bones

Fracture

Carpal bones

Phalanges

The five metacarpals are the long bones of the hand. They lie between the carpal bones of the wrist and the phalanges (finger bones). All are vulnerable to injury.

TREATMENT ⊕ SEEK IMMEDIATE MEDICAL ATTENTION

MEDICAL

IMMEDIATE
■ If you think you may have a metacarpal fracture, you should: ▶ seek medical attention.

SHORT TERM
■ If you are diagnosed with a simple fracture, your physician may: ▶ nonsurgically realign your bones. ▶ immobilize your hand in a cast, splint, or brace for 6 weeks. ■ For a severe fracture or dislocation, your physician may: ▶ recommend surgery to stabilize and align the bones. ■ After surgery, your physician may: ▶ immobilize your hand in a cast for 4–6 weeks.

MEDIUM TERM
■ your physician may: ▶ arrange for you to have periodic X-rays to check that your bones are healing.

LONG TERM
■ After your cast is removed, whether you have had surgery or not, your physician may: ▶ refer you to a physical therapist for a program of rehabilitation (see table right).

PHYSICAL THERAPY

EARLY STAGE
■ Your physical therapist may: ▶ take you through a series of hand movements to test your passive range of motion.

INTERMEDIATE STAGE
■ You should be able to: ▶ demonstrate no swelling and a full range of motion in the upper limb. ▶ fully bear your weight.

ADVANCED STAGE
■ You should be able to: ▶ demonstrate a grip strength of less than 10% difference between hands. ■ Your physical therapist will: ▶ assess your grip strength. ■ You may begin: ▶ upper-limb weights exercises, such as dumbbell bench presses (》p.210), starting at 50% of your one-rep max. ▶ balance and control exercises, such as scapular circles (》p.251).

RETURN TO SPORT
■ You should be able to: ▶ demonstrate a full range of motion. ▶ complete sport-specific drills without difficulty. ▶ train fully with no pain for 1–2 weeks.

HAND AND FINGER TENDON INJURIES

The tendons of the hands are susceptible to injury in almost every sport, and can be strained, lacerated, or torn away from the phalanx (finger bone). The extensor tendons are particularly at risk of injury from cuts, due to their prominent position, and the flexor tendons can rupture when the fingers are overstretched.

CAUSES

Injury to the extensor tendons – known as mallet finger – is common, especially in sports such as basketball, baseball, and cricket. If a ball moving at speed strikes the tip of the finger it can tear the extensor tendon (which straightens the end joint of the finger) away from the bone. A tiny fragment of bone may be pulled away too—this is known as a mallet fracture. In both cases, the tip of the finger droops down and cannot be straightened. Injuries to the flexor tendons, which enable the fingers to bend, are most common among climbers and gymnasts, and are usually the result of using too forceful a grip. This is known as a bowstring injury.

SYMPTOMS AND DIAGNOSIS

When a tendon in your hand or finger has been injured you will feel pain, swelling, and tenderness at the site of the injury. Your finger or hand may be deformed into a bent position, or you may be unable to hold your finger or hand straight without using your other hand to help. In a bowstring injury you may be unable to bend the fingers of your injured hand, or it may hurt when you attempt to do so. To diagnose your injury, your physician will carry out a physical examination and may suggest an MRI scan.

RISKS AND COMPLICATIONS

Mallet fractures can leave a small bump on top of the end joint of your finger and you may never regain full flexibility in the joint. You may experience redness, tenderness, and swelling at the site of the injury for several months. Left untreated, there is a high risk of your losing finger or hand function.

WHEN WILL I BE FULLY FIT?

Without surgery, it usually takes about 6 weeks for these injuries to heal. If you have had surgery, it will be another few weeks after the splint or wire has been removed before you regain full strength and mobility in the affected finger.

EXTENSOR TENDON INJURY (MALLET FINGER)

Proximal phalanx

Extensor tendon

Middle phalanx

Tear

Distal phalanx

The extensor tendons run along the back of each finger and thumb, attached to the middle and distal phalanges, allowing the fingers and thumbs to straighten.

FLEXOR TENDON INJURY (BOWSTRING INJURY)

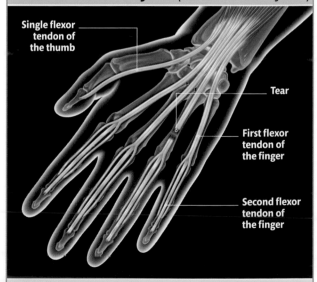

Single flexor tendon of the thumb

Tear

First flexor tendon of the finger

Second flexor tendon of the finger

Each finger has two flexor tendons and the thumb has one. They run along the palm side of the hand (close to the skin) and enable the fingers and thumbs to bend.

TREATMENT

➕ SEEK IMMEDIATE MEDICAL ATTENTION

	IMMEDIATE	SHORT TERM	MEDIUM TERM	LONG TERM
MEDICAL	■ If you think you have injured a tendon in your hand, you should: ▶ seek medical attention.	■ If you are diagnosed with mild to moderate mallet finger, your physician may: ▶ put your finger in a splint for 6-8 weeks, while the tendon heals. ■ If you have a severe mallet fracture or an injury to a flexor tendon, your physician may: ▶ recommend surgery to reattach the tendon.	■ If you have not had surgery and your injury is healing as expected, your physician may: ▶ advise you to wear a splint at night for another 6 weeks, or whenever there is a possibility of reinjury. ▶ refer you to a physical therapist for treatment to help you regain mobility and strength in the joint (see table below). ■ If your finger fails to respond to nonsurgical treatment, your physician may: ▶ recommend surgery to pin or wire the joint.	■ After surgery, your physician may: ▶ refer you to a physical therapist for a program of rehabilitation (see table below).

	EARLY STAGE	INTERMEDIATE STAGE	ADVANCED STAGE	RETURN TO SPORT
PHYSICAL THERAPY	■ Once your physician has referred you, your physical therapist may: ▶ take your hand through a series of movements (within pain limits) to assess the range of motion in your joints—this will involve no effort from you (passive range of motion); as your hand recovers you will be able to initiate these movements yourself (active range of motion). ▶ advise you to try resistance strengthening exercises for your elbow and wrist that do not involve joint movement.	■ You should now be able to: ▶ demonstrate no swelling in the affected area. ■ Your physical therapist may: ▶ test your grip strength. ■ You may begin: ▶ weight-bearing exercises, such as press-ups (**》p.184**), modified at first to decrease weight on the hand.	■ You should now be able to: ▶ complete upper-limb plyometrics, such as mini trampoline throws (**》p.216**), without pain. ▶ complete balance and control exercises for the shoulder, elbow, and wrist, such as four-point kneels (**》p.247**). ■ Your physical therapist may: ▶ retest your grip strength; your injured hand should have only 10% less ability than your uninjured one. ■ You may begin: ▶ upper-limb weights exercises such as dumbbell bench presses (**》p.210**), as pain allows; start at 50% of your one-rep max and aim for 4 sets x 8–12 reps. (You may need to modify the lifts or use wrist straps.) ▶ lower-limb weight exercises that include the upper limbs, such as push presses (**》p.238**), as pain allows.	■ You should now be able to: ▶ demonstrate a full active range of motion when tested by your physical therapist. ▶ lift upper-body weights that are at least 80% of your one-rep max, without pain. ▶ complete sport-specific drills without difficulty. ▶ participate in full training for at least 1–2 weeks.

FINGER FRACTURE AND DISLOCATION

Fractures and dislocations of the finger and thumb bones (phalanges) are very common injuries, particularly among players of basketball, soccer, rugby, and tennis. These injuries can seriously affect the functioning of the hand if not diagnosed and treated appropriately.

CAUSES

Finger injuries are common in collision and contact sports such as rugby and football, and in sports in which the hands are exposed to injury, such as basketball, tennis, and cricket. The finger bones are particularly vulnerable to injury because they do not have a thick, protective covering of soft tissue. Falls onto hard surfaces, sudden contact with a ball—a cricket ball coming off a bat at speed directly striking the end of the finger, for example—direct blows (punches), and indirect force applied to a finger by accidental collision with another athlete may all cause a fracture or dislocation.

SYMPTOMS AND DIAGNOSIS

Fingers can be fractured or dislocated in many different ways, but the symptoms are similar: you will experience pain when touching your finger and have difficulty moving it, as well as swelling, stiffness, and tenderness. Your finger may suddenly appear crooked. If your fracture is close to the nail bed, a bruise may be visible under your nail. Knuckle joints are also often dislocated. Your physician will carry out a physical examination and you will have an X-ray to confirm the severity of your fracture or dislocation.

RISKS AND COMPLICATIONS

It is difficult to assess the severity of a finger injury; often symptoms for mild and serious injuries are the same. If you simply tape your finger without proper diagnosis and delay seeking medical help, or leave the injury untreated, you may end up with long-term pain, swelling, stiffness, deformity, and reduced mobility.

WHEN WILL I BE FULLY FIT?

Your finger may be taped or in a splint for 4–6 weeks. After the tape or splint is removed, it is normal for you to experience some stiffness in your injured finger for several weeks, and you are advised to spend 2–3 weeks on a physical therapy program. Once this is completed, you may consider returning to sports.

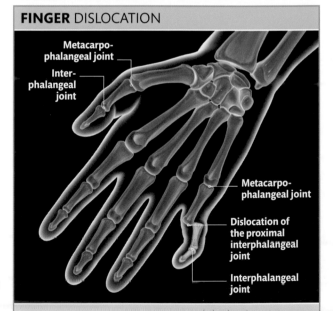

FINGER FRACTURE

Proximal phalanx

Distal phalanx

Proximal phalanx

Middle phalanx

Fracture

Distal phalanx

The fingers each have three phalanges—the proximal, middle, and distal—while the thumb has two. A forceful impact can cause a fracture in any of these bones.

FINGER DISLOCATION

Metacarpophalangeal joint

Interphalangeal joint

Metacarpophalangeal joint

Dislocation of the proximal interphalangeal joint

Interphalangeal joint

Each of the fingers has three joints, while the thumb has two (labeled above). The most commonly dislocated are the proximal interphalangeal joints of the fingers.

TREATMENT

⊕ SEEK IMMEDIATE MEDICAL ATTENTION

	IMMEDIATE ▶	SHORT TERM ▶	MEDIUM TERM ▶	LONG TERM
MEDICAL	■ If you think you may have dislocated or fractured your finger, you should: ▶ apply ice (**》p.165**). ▶ immobilize your finger with a splint, or by taping it to the adjacent finger (**》p.170**). ▶ elevate your arm to prevent swelling. ▶ seek medical attention.	■ If you are diagnosed with a mild-to-moderate dislocation or fracture, your physician may: ▶ manipulate your finger back into its correct position, then tape it to the adjacent finger or place it in a splint for support. ▶ prescribe pain-relief medication. ■ If you are diagnosed with a severe fracture, your physician may: ▶ recommend surgery to realign and support the broken fragments with pins, plates, and screws.	■ Regardless of whether you have had surgical or nonsurgical treatment, your physician may: ▶ leave your finger in a splint, or taped, for 4–6 weeks while it heals. ■ If you have had surgery, your physician may: ▶ X-ray your finger while it is splinted or taped to ensure that it is healing as expected.	■ After your splint or taping has been removed, your physician may: ▶ refer you to a physical therapist for a program of rehabilitation (see table below).
	EARLY STAGE ▶	INTERMEDIATE STAGE ▶	ADVANCED STAGE ▶	RETURN TO SPORT
PHYSIOTHERAPY	■ Once your physician has referred you, your physical therapist may: ▶ suggest various treatments, such as electrotherapy, to reduce local inflammation. ▶ advise you to wear a finger splint and compression bandage to help alleviate symptoms. ▶ take your hand through a series of movements (within pain limits) to assess the range of motion in your finger—this will involve no effort from you (passive range of motion); as your hand recovers you will be able to initiate these movements yourself (active range of motion). ▶ test that you have a full range of motion in your elbow, wrist, and shoulder. ■ You may begin: ▶ shoulder isometrics (**》p.212**) to build up strength, as pain allows.	■ You should now be able to: ▶ demonstrate no swelling in the affected area. ▶ put full weight on your hand, without pain. ■ Your physical therapist may: ▶ test your grip strength.	■ You should now be able to: ▶ complete upper-limb plyometrics, such as mini-trampoline throws (**》p.216**), without pain. ▶ complete balance and control exercises for your shoulder, elbow, and wrist, such as four-point kneels (**》p.247**). ■ Your physical therapist may: ▶ retest your grip strength; your injured hand should have only 10% less ability than your uninjured one. ■ You may begin: ▶ upper-limb weights exercises, such as dumbbell bench presses (**》p.210**), as pain allows; start at 50% of your one-rep max and aim for 4 sets x 8–12 reps. You may need to modify the lifts or use wrist straps. ▶ lower-limb weights exercises that include the upper limbs, as pain allows. You may need to modify the lifts or use wrist straps.	■ You should now be able to: ▶ demonstrate a full active range of motion when tested by your physical therapist. ▶ lift upper-body weights that are at least 80% of your one-rep max, without pain. ▶ complete sport-specific drills without difficulty. ▶ participate in full training.

HIP FRACTURES

The hip is a ball-and-socket joint connecting the femur (thighbone) to the pelvis. Fractures to the neck of the femur are the most common type of hip fracture. The area of the pelvis around the hip joint is also susceptible to avulsion fractures, in which a tendon or ligament pulls away from the pelvis, taking a fragment of bone with it.

CAUSES

Fractures of the neck of the femur may be caused by a forceful blow, such as those experienced in collision sports, including rugby or football, or by a heavy fall in sports such as horseback riding. Avulsion fractures are usually caused by a rapid and powerful contraction of one of the quadriceps or hamstring muscles in the thigh, and is most commonly seen in sports that involve rapid acceleration and deceleration, such as soccer or basketball.

SYMPTOMS AND DIAGNOSIS

If your fracture is the result of a blow, you will feel pain in your hip immediately after the impact, and moving your leg will cause you pain. If you have an avulsion fracture you may feel a sudden pain in your hip when you accelerate, with the pain moving down the muscle that has pulled away from the bone. Your physician will make a diagnosis through a combination of physical examination and X-ray, to determine the location of the fracture and its severity.

RISKS AND COMPLICATIONS

If you have a hip fracture that is not properly treated, long-term damage to the muscles and hip joint can occur. There is also a risk of internal bleeding with hip fractures, so seeking specialist medical attention is essential.

WHEN WILL I BE FULLY FIT?

If you have a hip fracture in which your bone was broken you will need surgery to repair the bone—this may take up to 12 months to heal fully. If you have an avulsion fracture and it is treated properly, you can expect it to heal within 3 months.

FEMORAL NECK FRACTURE

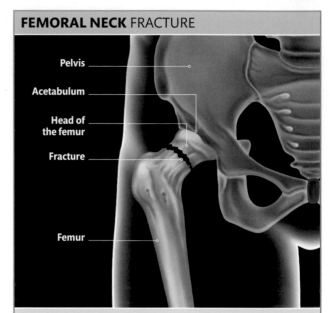

Pelvis

Acetabulum

Head of the femur

Fracture

Femur

In a femoral neck fracture, the head of the femur, which is held within the acetabulum (the socket of the pelvis), becomes disconnected from the rest of the femur.

AVULSION FRACTURE

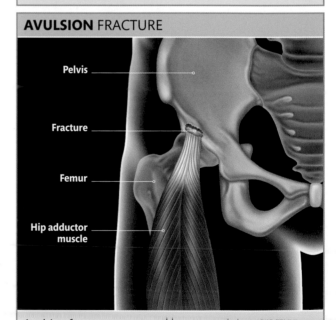

Pelvis

Fracture

Femur

Hip adductor muscle

Avulsion fractures are caused by a powerful contraction of one of the muscles of the upper leg, which causes some of the bone to be pulled away from the pelvis.

TREATMENT

⊕ SEEK IMMEDIATE MEDICAL ATTENTION

MEDICAL

IMMEDIATE ▶	SHORT TERM ▶	MEDIUM TERM ▶	LONG TERM
■ If you think you may have fractured your hip, you should: ▶ stop activity. ▶ immobilize the joint (**》pp.170–71**). ▶ seek medical attention.	■ If you are diagnosed with an avulsion fracture of the hip, your physician may: ▶ advise you to rest until the fracture has healed. This can take up to 3 months. ■ If you have a fracture in which bone is broken, your physician may: ▶ recommend surgery to fix the bone.	■ Once your avulsion fracture has healed, your physician may: ▶ refer you to a physical therapist for treatment to regain strength and mobility in the joint (see table below). ■ If you have had surgery, your physician may: ▶ advise you to use crutches for up to 6 weeks.	■ It may take up to a year to recover fully from a fracture in which bone has broken. After surgery, when your fracture has healed, your physician may: ▶ refer you to a physical therapist for a program of rehabilitation (see table below).

PHYSICAL THERAPY

EARLY STAGE ▶	INTERMEDIATE STAGE ▶	ADVANCED STAGE ▶	RETURN TO SPORT
■ Once your physician has referred you, your physical therapist may: ▶ use manual therapy and soft tissue therapy to help relieve your symptoms. ▶ gently test the range of motion in your hip; this will be guided by your pain limits. ■ You may begin: ▶ resistance exercises, such as squeezes, for the buttocks, quadriceps, adductors, and hamstrings, as pain allows; aim for 10 reps x 10 secs every 2–3 hours. ▶ gentle stretches of your hip flexors, quadriceps, adductors, hamstrings, internal and external hip rotators, and calf muscles, on both legs; aim for 2 reps x 30 secs on each muscle group, 3–4 times daily. ▶ gentle walking in the pool to help regain your normal walking pattern. ▶ walking with crutches, aiming to increase bodyweight loading, as pain allows.	■ You should now be able to: ▶ demonstrate a near full range of motion in both hips. ■ You may begin: ▶ deep-water running and swimming; aim for 20–30 minutes at high intensity intervals. Avoid breaststroke for 4–6 weeks after surgery. ▶ trying to walk normally without a limp. ▶ walking on a treadmill until you can jog without pain. ▶ bicycling and working on a cross-trainer and stepper, as pain allows; aim for 20 minutes at 85rpm, level 6. ▶ core-stability and gluteal exercises, such as single-leg bridges (**》p.236**) and pilates reformer exercises (**》p.237**). Start with modified versions and light resistance, and build toward a normal technique.	■ You should now be able to: ▶ perform low-level jogging, without pain or limping and with a full range of motion in your hips. ■ You may begin: ▶ lower-limb bodyweight exercises, such as step-up and holds (**》p.250**). ▶ functional warm-up drills, such as pike walks (**》p.177**), full-body exercises, such as punch lunges (**》p.182**), and low-level foot plyometrics, such as walking pop-ups (**》p.254**). ▶ lower-limb strength training, such as squats (**》p.180**), calf raises (**》p.204**), and Nordic hamstring lowers (**》p.202**); start at 50% of your one-rep max and aim for 4 sets x 8–12 reps. ▶ walk-jog drills (**》p.252**), as pain allows, building to 10 lengths of a soccer field, working up toward low-level running.	■ You should now be able to: ▶ lift leg weights that are at least 80% of your one-rep max, without pain. ▶ complete foot plyometrics, such as jumps and hops (**》pp.256–58**), and speed drills (**》pp.252–53**), without pain. ▶ perform single vertical and horizontal hops (**》p.261**) and adapted cross-over hops (**》p.262**); your injured leg should have only 10% less ability than your uninjured one. ▶ complete a T-test (**》p.263**); aim for 11 seconds if you are male, and 15 seconds if you are female. ▶ complete high-level running at distances relevant to your sport, without pain. ▶ complete sport-specific drills without difficulty. ▶ participate in full training.

TROCHANTERIC BURSITIS

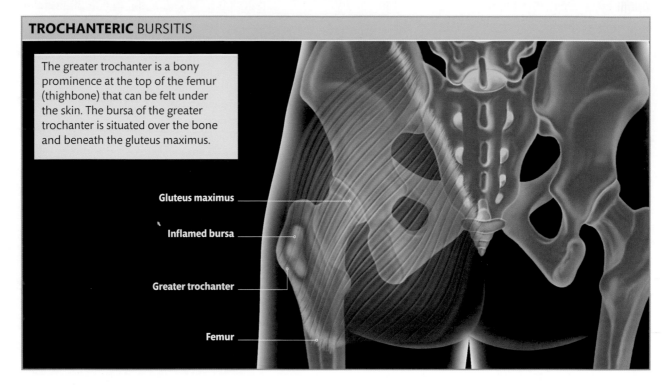

TROCHANTERIC BURSITIS

The greater trochanter is a bony prominence at the top of the femur (thighbone) that can be felt under the skin. The bursa of the greater trochanter is situated over the bone and beneath the gluteus maximus.

Gluteus maximus

Inflamed bursa

Greater trochanter

Femur

Trochanteric bursitis is an inflammatory disorder that affects the greater trochanter, a bony point at the side of the hip. The condition occurs when the bursa of the greater trochanter—a fluid-filled sac that eases movement between the trochanter and the gluteus maximus—becomes aggravated by overuse.

CAUSES
This condition is associated with sports that involve a lot of running, quick changes of direction, or weight-bearing activity, such as soccer, hockey, and track and field. All of these cause repetitive friction between the greater trochanter of the femur and the gluteus maximus, which can lead to inflammation of the bursa. Biomechanical abnormalities, such as unequal leg lengths, may also increase the likelihood of trochanteric bursitis.

SYMPTOMS AND DIAGNOSIS
You may feel some tenderness over the bony upper part of your thigh, and pain running across your hip or down your outer thigh. You may also feel some swelling in the area around the bursa. Bending or extending your hip during walking or sports activities, for example, will cause burning, or aches and pains at the top of your thigh. Your physician will diagnose your condition through physical examination and may recommend an ultrasound or MRI scan to confirm the diagnosis.

RISKS AND COMPLICATIONS
If you leave trochanteric bursitis untreated, and continue to play sports, you will experience ongoing hip pain. The pain may stay at the same level of intensity, but in some cases it could increase in severity.

WHEN WILL I BE FULLY FIT?
In all but the most extreme cases of trochanteric bursitis, you should recover quickly and be able to return to sports 1–2 weeks after treatment. If you have had surgery to remove the bursa, you should be fully fit within 6–8 weeks.

TREATMENT

MEDICAL	IMMEDIATE	SHORT TERM	MEDIUM TERM	LONG TERM
	■ If you think you may have trochanteric bursitis, you should: ▶ stop any activity that causes pain. ▶ apply ice (**》p.165**). ▶ seek medical attention.	■ If you are diagnosed with trochanteric bursitis, your physician may: ▶ recommend that you continue to rest, avoiding any activities that could inflame your bursa. ▶ prescribe analgesic medication. ▶ refer you to a physical therapist for treatment to help release the affected area and strengthen the hip muscles (see table below).	■ If your injury fails to respond to rest and/or physical therapy, your physician may: ▶ give you a local anesthetic and inject corticosteroids into the affected area. ▶ recommend extracorporeal shockwave treatment (EST), in which soundwaves are directed at the area of pain, to speed up the healing process.	■ If all other treatments have failed, as a last resort your physician may: ▶ recommend surgery to remove the bursa. ■ After surgery, your physician may: ▶ advise you to use crutches for up to 2 weeks. ▶ refer you to a physical therapist for a program of rehabilitation (see table below).

PHYSICAL THERAPY	EARLY STAGE	INTERMEDIATE STAGE	ADVANCED STAGE	RETURN TO SPORT
	■ Once your physician has referred you, your physical therapist may: ▶ suggest various treatments, such as electrotherapy, to reduce local inflammation. ▶ use manual therapy and soft tissue therapy to help relieve your symptoms. ▶ assess the intensity and duration of your training, and correct these accordingly. ▶ perform a full biomechanical foot and ankle assessment to judge if you need insoles or orthotics to support your medial arch, or a correct footwear prescription. ■ You may begin: ▶ self-massage of your iliotibial band with a hard foam roller (**》p.191**); spend 6 x 30 seconds on each leg daily, even if it is painful. ▶ exercises to activate and strengthen your gluteal muscles, such as single-leg bridges (**》p.236**), clams (**》p.187**), and hip hitchers (**》p.186**), as pain allows.	■ You should now be able to: ▶ walk without pain. ■ Your physical therapist may: ▶ assess your single vertical and horizontal hops (**》p.261**) and adapted cross-over hops (**》p.262**) to establish baseline scores. ■ You may begin: ▶ core-stability exercises, such as dead bugs (**》p.225**). ▶ functional warm-up drills, such as walking kick-outs (**》p.185**), full-body exercises, such as multidirectional lunges (**》p.249**), and low-level foot plyometrics, such as A-walks (**》p.254**). ▶ low-level running and sporting activities, as pain allows. ▶ interval bicycling and work on a cross-trainer and stepper; build to 20 minutes at 80rpm, level 6, as pain allows. ▶ stretches of your quadriceps, adductors, hamstrings, soleus, gastrocnemius, and gluteal muscles (**》pp.176–81; 186–89; 241–45**). Aim for equal stretches both sides.	■ You should now be able to: ▶ perform interval bicycling at a moderate–high intensity, with little or no pain. ▶ complete low-level running, without pain. ■ You may begin: ▶ lower-limb strength training at 50% of your one-rep max; aim for 4 sets x 8–12 reps of barbell squats (**》p.192**), straight-leg deadlifts (**》p.197**), and Nordic hamstring lowers (**》p.202**).	■ You should now be able to: ▶ lift leg weights that are at least 80% of your one-rep max, without pain. ▶ perform single vertical and horizontal hops (**》p.261**) and adapted cross-over hops (**》p.262**); your injured leg should have only 10% less ability than your uninjured one. ▶ complete foot plyometrics, such as jumps and hops (**》pp.256–58**), and speed drills (**》pp.252–53**), without pain. ▶ complete high-level running at distances relevant to your sport, without pain. ▶ complete sport-specific drills without difficulty. ▶ participate in full training.

HIP LABRAL TEARS AND FAI

The hip joint is comprised of a ball (the head of the femur) and socket (the acetabulum). The hard cartilage (labrum) that stabilizes the hip joint is vulnerable to tearing during sport. Femoroacetabular impingement (FAI) is a hip condition in which the head of the femur (thigh bone) rubs abnormally against the rim of the acetabulum, causing friction. This may "impinge" or "pinch," and eventually damage, the labrum.

CAUSES

Labral tears occur in sports which involve sudden stops and turns combined with jumping and landing, such as soccer, rugby, tennis, or baseball, or sports that involve extreme movement, such as rowing or martial arts. A structural defect of the acetabulum, often where it is too shallow, may lead to tearing where there is trauma or overuse. Gymnasts are particularly affected by this. Femoroacetabular impingement (FAI) occurs as a result of the particular shape of the head of the femur and/or the acetabulum.

SYMPTOMS AND DIAGNOSIS

If you have labral tears, there may be swelling around the joint, causing pain in your hip and groin. There may also be a clicking, catching, locking, or pinching sensation in the affected areas. However, sometimes labral tears produce no immediate symptoms. With FAI, you may feel pain in your hip or lower back, and pain in your groin that radiates to your buttock. There may also be a clicking or pinching sensation in the affected areas, and you may experience stiffness or loss of motion in your hip. Your physician will make a diagnosis with an X-ray, an MRI, or a CT scan.

RISKS AND COMPLICATIONS

Without treatment, both hip labral tears and FAI may lead to hip osteoarthritis.

WHEN WILL I BE FULLY FIT?

If you do not need surgery, you will usually see an improvement in both labral tears and FAI within 2–3 weeks. If you have surgery, a partial labrum excision will need 6–8 weeks recovery, the repair of a torn labrum 3–4 months; surgery for FAI usually needs 3–6 months or longer.

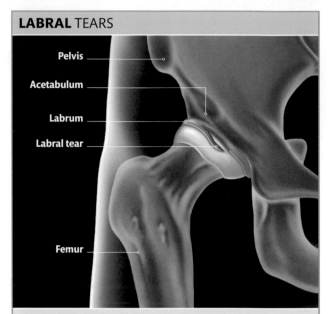

LABRAL TEARS

Pelvis

Acetabulum

Labrum

Labral tear

Femur

Labral tears affect the labrum, a ring of cartilage that surrounds the acetabulum. The labrum holds the head of the femur in place while allowing flexibility in the joint.

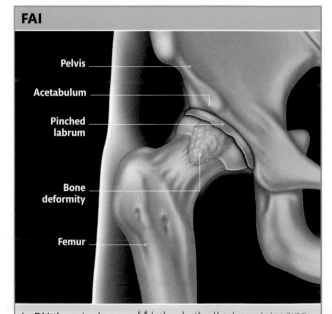

FAI

Pelvis

Acetabulum

Pinched labrum

Bone deformity

Femur

In FAI there is abnormal friction in the thigh joint, leading to pinching of the labrum. The condition is caused by a deformity in the femur or the acetabulum, or, usually, both.

TREATMENT

➕ SEEK IMMEDIATE MEDICAL ATTENTION

MEDICAL

IMMEDIATE ▶	SHORT TERM ▶	MEDIUM TERM ▶	LONG TERM
■ If you think you may have a labral tear or FAI, you should: ▶ seek medical attention.	■ If you are diagnosed with a hip labral tear or FAI, your physician may: ▶ advise you to rest. ▶ give you corticosteroid injections to reduce the inflammation. ▶ prescribe analgesic medication. ▶ advise you to use crutches until you can walk without pain. ▶ refer you to a physical therapist for treatment to help strengthen your hip (see table below).	■ If your symptoms have failed to respond to 2–3 weeks of nonsurgical treatment for either condition, your physician may: ▶ recommend surgery to repair the tear and stimulate new cartilage growth, or to perform FAI decompression.	■ After surgery, your physician may: ▶ refer you to a physical therapist for a program of rehabilitation (see table below).

PHYSICAL THERAPY

EARLY STAGE ▶	INTERMEDIATE STAGE ▶	ADVANCED STAGE ▶	RETURN TO SPORT
■ Once your physician has referred you, your physical therapist may: ▶ use manual therapy and soft tissue therapy to help relieve your symptoms. ▶ test the range of motion in your hip and spine, within pain limits. ■ You may begin: ▶ resistance exercises for the buttocks, quadriceps, adductors, and hamstrings, such as isometric adductor squeezes (**》p.203**), as pain allows; aim for 10 sets x 10 secs every 2–3 hours. ▶ stretches for your hip flexors, quadriceps, hamstrings, adductors, internal and external hip rotators, and calf muscles (**》pp.176–81; 186–89; 241–45**), on both left and right sides; aim for 2 reps x 30 secs on each muscle group, 3–4 times daily. ▶ walking in the pool and gentle swimming (freestyle).	■ You should now be able to: ▶ demonstrate almost a full range of motion in your hip. ▶ walk without pain. ■ You may begin: ▶ deep-water running and swimming; aim for 20–30 minutes at high intensity intervals. Avoid breaststroke for 4–6 weeks after surgery. ▶ trying to walk normally without a limp. ▶ walking on a treadmill until you can jog without pain. ▶ bicycling and working on a cross-trainer and stepper, as pain allows; aim for 20 minutes at 85rpm, level 6. ▶ box step-ups (**》p.203**); aim for 3 sets x 15 reps. ▶ core-stability and gluteal activation exercises, such as single-leg bridges (**》p.236**); start with modified versions and light resistance, and build toward a normal technique.	■ You should now be able to: ▶ demonstrate a full range of motion in your hip. ■ You may begin: ▶ lower-limb bodyweight exercises, such as hip hitchers (**》p.186**), step-up and holds (**》p.250**), and walking lunges (**》p.180**). ▶ functional warm-up drills, such as walking kick-outs (**》p.185**), full-body exercises, such as pike walks (**》p.177**), and low-level foot plyometrics, such as A-walks (**》p.254**). ▶ lower-limb strength training; start at 50% of your one-rep max and aim for 4 sets x 8–12 reps of barbell squats (**》p.192**), Nordic hamstring lowers (**》p.202**), and calf raises (**》p.204**). ▶ working on a rower; start at levels 3–4 for 10 minutes, at a comfortable pace. Increase your time by 10–15% weekly. ▶ walk-jog drills (**》p.252**), building to 10 lengths of a field, without pain, progressing to low-level running.	■ You should now be able to: ▶ lift leg weights that are at least 80% of your one-rep max. ▶ complete foot plyometrics, such as jumps and hops (**》pp.256–58**), and speed drills (**》pp.252–53**), without pain. ▶ perform single vertical and horizontal hops (**》p.261**) and adapted cross-over hops (**》p.262**); your injured leg should have only 10% less ability than your uninjured one. ▶ complete a T-test (**》p.263**); aim for 11 seconds if you are male, and 15 seconds if you are female. ▶ complete high-level running at distances relevant to your sport, without pain. ▶ complete sport-specific drills without difficulty.

OSTEITIS PUBIS

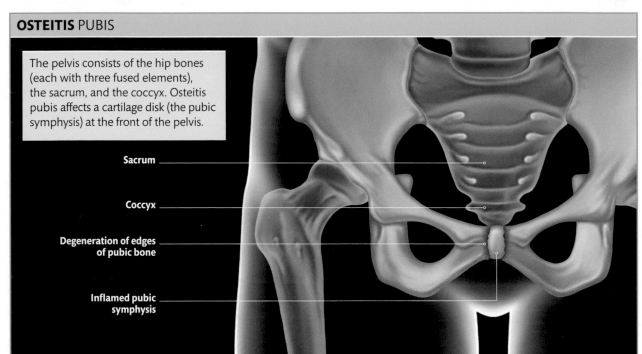

OSTEITIS PUBIS

The pelvis consists of the hip bones (each with three fused elements), the sacrum, and the coccyx. Osteitis pubis affects a cartilage disk (the pubic symphysis) at the front of the pelvis.

Sacrum

Coccyx

Degeneration of edges of pubic bone

Inflamed pubic symphysis

Osteitis pubis is an inflammation of the pubic symphysis (the cartilage joint between the pubic bones that form the front of the pelvis). The disorder, which can occur when the pelvis is subjected to excessive or repetitive stress, causes pain and may also lead to bone degeneration.

CAUSES

The condition is commonly associated with sports that involve a lot of running, sudden changes of direction, or weight-bearing activity, such as soccer, hockey, tennis, and track and field (marathon runners are particularly susceptible to osteitis pubis). Anatomical problems such as stiff hip joints or unequal leg length can also be a factor.

SYMPTOMS AND DIAGNOSIS

The onset of symptoms may be sudden or gradual. You will feel pain low down in your abdomen, in one or both sides of your groin, and along the inside of your thigh. Exercise will aggravate your symptoms. Your physician should be able to diagnose osteitis pubis through physical examination, and will search for hip problems, unequal leg length, or other

underlying conditions that might be the cause of the inflammation. You may also have an X-ray or MRI scan to assess the severity of the disorder.

RISKS AND COMPLICATIONS

If you spend insufficient time on rehabilitation, you may suffer from long-term pain as a result. Once the condition becomes chronic, recovery time increases significantly and there is a greater risk of recurrence. Untreated, osteitis pubis may also cause erosion at the edges of your pubic bones.

WHEN WILL I BE FULLY FIT?

In most cases, you should have made a full recovery within 6–12 weeks, but recovery can take as long as 6 months, depending on how long you have had the injury before you receive treatment. The earlier you start treatment and rehabilitation, the sooner you will return to fitness.

TREATMENT

⊕ SEEK IMMEDIATE MEDICAL ATTENTION

MEDICAL

IMMEDIATE ▶	SHORT TERM ▶	MEDIUM TERM ▶	LONG TERM
■ If you think you may have osteitis pubis, you should: ▶ stop any activity that increases the pain. ▶ follow a RICE procedure (》p.170). ▶ seek medical attention.	■ If osteitis pubis is diagnosed, your physician may: ▶ give you a corticosteroid injection into, or around, the pubic symphysis. If you have bone bruising on either side of the joint, you may be given another injection of a specialized drug. ▶ prescribe analgesic medication. ▶ refer you to a physical therapist for treatment to improve your core stability and strengthen your thigh muscles (see table below).	■ If, once other causes are ruled out, your condition is attributed to overuse, your physician may: ▶ advise you to avoid any activities that place stress on your pelvis.	■ If the injury fails to respond to nonsurgical treatment (this is rare), your physician may: ▶ recommend surgery to stabilize your pubis symphysis with a plate and screws. ■ After surgery your physician may: ▶ advise you to refrain from sport for up to 6 months. ▶ refer you to a physical therapist for a program of rehabilitation (see table below).

PHYSICAL THERAPY

EARLY STAGE ▶	INTERMEDIATE STAGE ▶	ADVANCED STAGE ▶	RETURN TO SPORT
■ Once your physician has referred you, your physical therapist may: ▶ use manual therapy and soft tissue therapy to help relieve your symptoms. ▶ assess the intensity and duration of your training, and correct these accordingly. ▶ perform various physical tests of your adductor muscles and your pubic symphysis in order to monitor your recovery. ■ You may begin: ▶ gentle stretches of your quadriceps, adductors, soleus, hamstrings, gastrocnemius, and gluteal muscles (》pp.176–81; 183–89; 240–45). Aim for equal stretches on both sides. ▶ isometric adductor squeezes (》p.199) at a moderate effort; aim for 10 reps x 10 secs at 0, 60, and 90 degrees of knee flexion daily. ▶ deep-water pool running; aim for 30 minutes at high-intensity intervals.	■ Your physical therapist may: ▶ continue to assess your adductor muscles and your pubic symphysis at each session; you should feel only minimal discomfort. ■ You may begin: ▶ double- and single-leg squats (》p.180): aim for 4 sets x 20 reps of each. ▶ functional warm-up drills such as walking kick-outs (》p.185), full-body exercises, such as push-ups (》pp.228–29), and low-level foot plyometrics such as A-walks (》p.254). ▶ upper-limb weight exercises, such as dumbbell bench presses (》p.210); start at 50% of your one-rep max. ▶ adductor pulley exercises (》p.201); aim for 4 sets x 15–20 reps. ▶ core-stability exercises, such as dead bugs (》p.225), side planks, level 1 (》p.226), kneeling supermen, levels 1–2 (》pp.228–29), and curl-ups (》p.221).	■ You should now be able to: ▶ complete high-level sideways drills, such as carioca sidesteps (》p.188). ▶ perform upper-limb weights with no restrictions or pain. ■ Your physical therapist may: ▶ continue to assess your adductors and your pubic symphysis; you should feel no discomfort when tested. ▶ suggest slide-board exercises (》p.200). ■ You may begin: ▶ lower-limb strength training at 50% of your one-rep max; aim for 4 sets x 8–12 reps of barbell squats (》p.192), straight-leg deadlifts (》p.197), and Nordic hamstring lowers (》p.202). ▶ short-lever adductor manuals (》p.198); aim for 3 sets x 15 reps. ▶ interval walking, jogging, and bicycling, as pain allows. ▶ core-stability exercises, such as side planks, levels 2–3 (》pp.226–27) and kneeling supermen, levels 2–3 (》p.229).	■ You should now be able to: ▶ lift leg weights that are at least 80% of your one-rep max, without pain. ▶ complete long-lever adductor drops (》p.199) starting with a 1kg (2 ¼lb) load, aiming for 3 sets x 12 reps with an 11 lb (5 kg) load. ▶ complete foot plyometrics, such as jumps and hops, (》pp.256–59) and speed drills (》pp.252–53), without pain. ▶ complete a T-test (》p.263): aim for 11 seconds if you are male, and 15 seconds if you are female. ▶ complete high-level running at distances relevant to your sport, without pain. ▶ participate in full training, without pain. ■ You may begin: ▶ high-level core-stability exercises, such as side planks, levels 3–4 (》p.227), kneeling supermen, level 3 (》p.229), and extension holds, level 3 (》p.235).

GROIN STRAIN

The term "groin strain," or "adductor strain," refers to the overstretching, tearing, or rupturing of any of the five adductor muscles of the inner thigh. In most cases, groin strains are minor tears of a few muscle fibers, with the bulk of the muscle remaining intact.

CAUSES

Groin strain is frequently caused by strenuous stretching movements of the legs—when sprinting or kicking a ball, for example—or by sudden changes in direction, which can occur in a range of sports, such as soccer, hockey, or tennis. Overuse of the adductor muscles can lead to inflammation in the groin (adductor tendinitis).

SYMPTOMS AND DIAGNOSIS

Depending on the severity of the strain, you may feel mild discomfort to severe pain toward the top of your inner thigh. You may also find it painful to pull your leg against resistance, and there may be swelling and bruising on your inner thigh. Your physician will diagnose the condition from your medical history and a physical examination. You may be given an ultrasound or MRI scan to confirm the diagnosis.

RISKS AND COMPLICATIONS

Groin strain usually heals without any problems. Although stretching exercises are an important part of rehabilitation and treatment, overdoing them may result in your injury taking a longer time to heal.

WHEN WILL I BE FULLY FIT?

Most groin strains take approximately 4–6 weeks to heal, depending on the severity of your injury. However, you may not regain full fitness for another 2 weeks. If you have had surgery, your rehabilitation period is likely to be 3–6 months or longer.

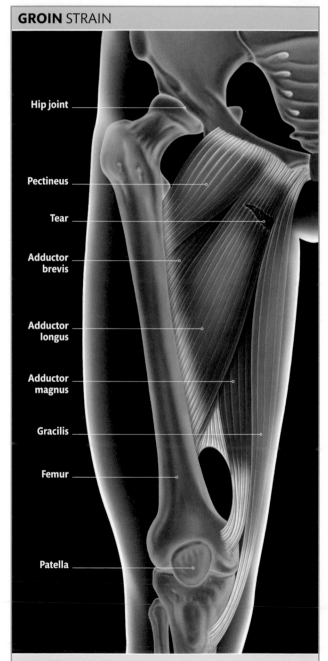

GROIN STRAIN

Hip joint
Pectineus
Tear
Adductor brevis
Adductor longus
Adductor magnus
Gracilis
Femur
Patella

Groin strain can affect any of the five hip adductor muscles (labeled above), whose main function is to pull the leg upward and toward the center of the body while walking and running.

TREATMENT

⊕ SEEK IMMEDIATE MEDICAL ATTENTION

MEDICAL

IMMEDIATE ▶	SHORT TERM ▶	MEDIUM TERM ▶	LONG TERM
■ If you think you may have injured your groin, you should: ▶ follow a RICE procedure (**»p.170**). ▶ seek medical attention.	■ If you are diagnosed with a mild-to-moderate groin strain, your physician may: ▶ prescribe pain-relief medication. ▶ refer you to a physical therapist for treatment to improve muscle strength (see table below). ■ If you are diagnosed with a complete tear of the muscle, your physician may: ▶ recommend surgery to repair the tear.	■ If you have not had surgery, and your injury is not healing as expected, your physician may: ▶ give you a corticosteroid injection to reduce inflammation.	■ After surgery or corticosteroid treatment, your physician may: ▶ refer you to a physical therapist for a program of rehabilitation (see table below).

PHYSICAL THERAPY

EARLY STAGE ▶	INTERMEDIATE STAGE ▶	ADVANCED STAGE ▶	RETURN TO SPORT
■ Once your physician has referred you, your physical therapist may: ▶ use manual therapy and soft tissue therapy to help relieve your symptoms. ▶ suggest you use crutches to take the weight off your groin. ▶ assess the strength of your adductor muscles. ■ You may begin: ▶ gentle stretches of your quadriceps, adductors, soleus, hamstrings, gastrocnemius, and gluteal muscles (**»pp.176–81; 185–89; 241–44**). Aim for equal stretches on both sides. ▶ low-intensity isometric adductor squeezes (**»p.199**); aim for 10 sets x 10 reps, flexing your knee to 0, 60, and 90 degrees. ▶ deep-water pool running, as pain allows; aim for 20–30 minutes of high intensity intervals. ▶ low-level core-stability exercises, such as single arm and leg raises (**»p.224**).	■ You should now be able to: ▶ perform isometric adductor squeezes (**»p.199**) with minimal pain. ■ Your physical therapist may: ▶ assess the function of your adductors. You should feel minimal discomfort. ■ You may begin: ▶ squats (**»p.180**) and single-leg squats (**»p.193**); aim for 4 sets x 20 reps of each. Stop if you feel pain. ▶ functional warm-up drills, such as walking lunges (**»p.180**), full-body exercises, such as lawnmowers (**»p.190**), and low-level foot plyometrics, such as A-walks (**»p.254**). You should not feel any pain. ▶ upper-limb strength training. Do not exert your injured adductor. ▶ box step-ups; aim for 4 sets x 6 reps. ▶ adductor pulley exercises (**»p.201**); aim for 4 sets x 15–20 reps. You should not feel pain. ▶ moderate-level core-stability exercises, such as side planks (**»pp.226–27**).	■ You should now be able to: ▶ perform isometric adductor squeezes (**»p.199**) with no pain and even greater power. ▶ complete high-level sideways drills such as carioca sidesteps (**»p.188**). ▶ lift upper-limb weights as you did before injury. ■ You may begin: ▶ lower-limb strength training, starting at 50% of your one-rep max. Include barbell squats (**»p.192**) and Romanian deadlifts (**»p.196**); aim for 4 sets x 8–12 reps. ▶ interval bicycling. ▶ short-lever adductor manuals (**»p.198**), aiming for 3 sets x 15 reps; stop if you feel pain. ▶ walk-jog drills (**»p.252**), building to 10 lengths of a soccer field; when you have succeeded, move on to low-intensity running. ▶ high-level core-stability exercises, such as Swiss ball jack-knives (**»p.223**).	■ You should now be able to: ▶ lift leg weights that are at least 80% of your one-rep max. ▶ complete long-lever adductor drops (**»p.199**); start with a 1 kg load and aim for 3 sets x 12 reps with 5 kg. ▶ complete foot plyometrics, such as jumps and hops (**»pp.256–57**), and speed drills (**»pp.252–53**), without pain. ▶ perform single vertical and horizontal hops (**»p.261**) and adapted cross-over hops (**»p.262**); your injured leg should have only 10% less ability than your uninjured one. ▶ complete a T-test (**»p.263**): aim for 11 seconds if you are male, and 15 seconds if you are female. ▶ complete high-level running at distances relevant to your sport, without pain. ▶ complete sport-specific drills without difficulty. ▶ complete full training for 2 weeks, without pain.

HERNIAS

A hernia occurs when weakened or torn tissues allow part of an organ to protrude from its normal site. Hernias most often occur in the abdominal or groin area, appearing either as an inguinal hernia (detected as a bulge in the groin or scrotum) or a femoral hernia (detected as a bulge at the top of the thigh).

CAUSES
Hernias are most commonly associated with sports that involve twisting and turning or bending actions—such as hockey, soccer, and tennis. When excessive pressure is placed on the muscles of the abdomen or groin area, they can weaken or tear, allowing part of the intestine to push through at the weak point.

SYMPTOMS AND DIAGNOSIS
You may experience pain at the site of the hernia that increases with exercise, straining, coughing, and sneezing. You may feel a bulge at the site, which you can usually push back through the weakened area. Your physician will diagnose your condition through physical examination and may use an ultrasound or a CT scan to confirm the diagnosis.

RISKS AND COMPLICATIONS
Occasionally, the bulge cannot be pushed back into place, causing a blockage that cuts off the blood supply—a condition known as strangulation that causes severe pain and can lead to the intestine becoming gangrenous. A strangulated hernia is a medical emergency that requires immediate surgery. If you have had treatment for any type of hernia, there is a risk that it will recur.

WHEN WILL I BE FULLY FIT?
Your recovery time will depend on the severity of your hernia and whether you need an operation to repair the weakened area. Following surgery, the time taken to return to fitness also depends on whether laparoscopic ("keyhole") or open surgery was performed, but generally is about 2–6 weeks.

INGUINAL HERNIA

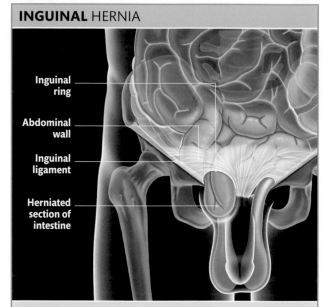

Inguinal ring

Abdominal wall

Inguinal ligament

Herniated section of intestine

An inguinal hernia occurs when part of the small intestine pushes through a weak area of muscle at the opening of the inguinal canal, between the abdomen and the thigh.

FEMORAL HERNIA

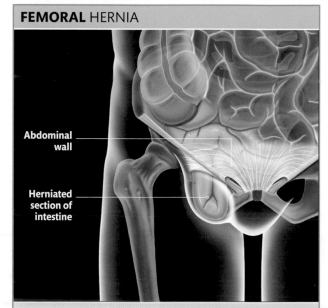

Abdominal wall

Herniated section of intestine

Femoral hernias (more common in women than in men) occur in the area of the groin where the femoral artery and vein pass from the abdomen into the thigh.

TREATMENT

⊕ SEEK IMMEDIATE MEDICAL ATTENTION

MEDICAL

IMMEDIATE ▶	SHORT TERM ▶	MEDIUM TERM ▶	LONG TERM
■ If you think you may have a hernia, you should: ▶ stop activity. ▶ apply ice to the site of the pain (**》p.165**). ▶ seek medical attention.	■ If you are diagnosed with an inguinal hernia, your physician may: ▶ prescribe analgesic medication. ▶ try to avoid the need for surgery by referring you to a physical therapist for treatment to strengthen your abdominal muscles (see table below). ■ If you are diagnosed with an abdominal hernia, your physician may: ▶ recommend surgery to repair the hernia. This may be "keyhole" or open surgery.	■ If your inguinal hernia fails to respond to nonsurgical treatment, your physician may: ▶ recommend surgery to repair the hernia. This may be laparoscopic ("keyhole") or open surgery.	■ If you have had "keyhole" surgery for a hernia, your physician may: ▶ advise you to rest for 2–3 weeks. ■ If you have had open surgery for a hernia, your physician may: ▶ advise you to rest for 2–3 weeks, and then refer you to a physical therapist for a program of rehabilitation (see table below).

PHYSICAL THERAPY

EARLY STAGE ▶	INTERMEDIATE STAGE ▶	ADVANCED STAGE ▶	RETURN TO SPORT
■ Once your physician has referred you, your physical therapist may: ▶ assess your range of motion in your hips and spine. ▶ test the strength of your adductor muscles. ▶ use manual therapy and soft tissue therapy to help relieve your symptoms. ■ You may begin: ▶ gentle lower-limb stretches of your quadriceps, adductors, hamstrings, gastrocnemius, soleus, and gluteal muscles; aim for equal stretches on both sides. ▶ deep-water running, once your wounds have healed; aim for 20–30 minutes of high-intensity intervals. ▶ low-level core-stability exercises, such as bridges (**》p.236**). ▶ adductor lifts (**》p.201**).	■ You should now be able to: ▶ perform double- and single-leg squats, without pain; aim for 3 sets x 20 reps. ■ Your physical therapist may: ▶ retest your adductor muscle strength weekly; you should feel only minimal discomfort. ■ You may begin: ▶ functional warm-up drills such as walking kick-outs (**》p.185**), full-body exercises such as lawnmowers (**》p.190**), and low-level foot plyometrics such as A-walks (**》p.254**). ▶ upper-limb weights exercises that do not strain your abdomen. ▶ bicycling; aim for 20 minutes at 85rpm level 6. ▶ box step-ups (**》p.203**); aim for 4 sets x 6 reps. ▶ adductor pulley exercises (**》p.201**); aim for 4 sets x 15–20 reps. ▶ Moderate-level core-stability exercises, such as pulley lifts, level 3 (**》p.233**).	■ You should now be able to: ▶ complete high-level sideways drills, such as carioca sidesteps (**》p.188**). ▶ do normal upper-limb weights, without pain. ■ Your physical therapist may: ▶ check your adductor muscle strength tests are pain-free. ▶ suggest you exercise with a slide board (**》p.200**). ■ You may begin: ▶ lower-limb strength training; start at 50% of your one-rep max and aim for 4 sets x 8–12 repetitions of good mornings (**》p.208**), calf raises (**》p.204**), and Nordic hamstring lowers (**》p.202**). ▶ walk-jog drills (**》p.252**), as pain allows; build to 10 lengths of a football field; when you have succeeded, move to low-intensity running. ▶ low-level skills training. ▶ high-level core training exercises, such as Swiss ball donkeys (**》p.222**).	■ You should now be able to: ▶ complete dynamic, high-level ball skills, without pain. ▶ perform long-lever adductor drops (**》p.199**); start with an 11 lb (5 kg) load and aim for 3 sets x 12 reps with 11 lb (5 kg). ▶ complete foot plyometrics—such as skips and jumps—and speed drills, without pain. ▶ perform single vertical and horizontal hops (**》p.261**) and adapted cross-over hops (**》p.262**), your injured side should have only 10% less ability than your uninjured side. ▶ complete a T-test (**》p.263**); aim for 11 seconds if you are a male, and 15 seconds if you are a female. ▶ complete high-level running at distances relevant to your sport, without pain. ▶ complete sport-specific drills without difficulty. ▶ participate in full training for at least 2 weeks, without pain.

HAMSTRING INJURIES

Each of the muscles of the hamstrings is susceptible to strains and ruptures. Hamstring injuries can vary in severity from fairly minor contusions (bruises) and moderately serious stretches and strains up to full-scale ruptures.

CAUSES

Contusions (bruises) are caused by heavy impact to the muscle from a collision or a fall. Hamstring strains occur in sports in which an athlete has to accelerate suddenly, or when the muscles are subject to sudden, forceful stretching or contraction: for example, in soccer, basketball, or running and jumping activities. Poor technique, muscle fatigue, and an inadequate warm-up may also make the injury more likely. In severe cases, excessive stretching of the muscle against a force, for example during weight lifting or in a rugby scrum, may cause complete rupture of the muscle.

SYMPTOMS AND DIAGNOSIS

Contusions may be accompanied by pain, swelling, and skin discoloration. A hamstring strain could cause swelling in the back of your thigh and in severe cases you may hear a "pop" at the moment of injury. You may feel twinges of pain in this area during exercise, and when you apply pressure or bend or straighten your knee. The back of your thigh may feel tight and cause difficulty walking: this can range from a slight limp to your needing crutches, depending on the severity of the strain. If you have a complete rupture, you will have intense pain at the back of your leg and be unable to bear weight on it. Your physician will make a diagnosis through physical examination and perhaps an ultrasound or MRI scan.

RISKS AND COMPLICATIONS

Returning to sport before your hamstrings heal properly can lead to the injury recurring. Left untreated, it may cause the tightness in your hamstrings to become worse. "Hamstring syndrome" may develop, in which scar tissue from injured muscles traps your sciatic nerve (**»p.60**), causing more pain.

WHEN WILL I BE FULLY FIT?

If you have a contusion, you should be able to return to your sport once you have no pain. In the case of a mild strain, recovery may take 2–3 weeks. Moderate strains will need 6–8 weeks but can take longer. Rupture of the muscle may require surgery, after which your recovery time may be 4–6 months.

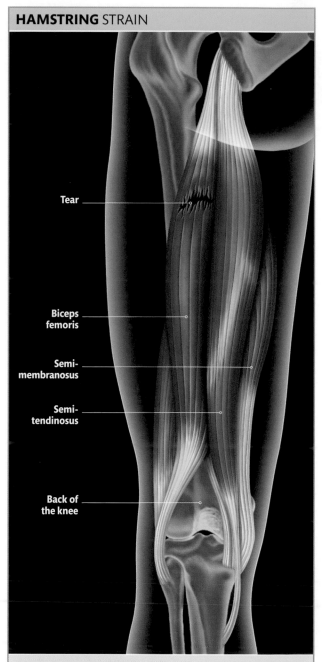

HAMSTRING STRAIN

Tear

Biceps femoris

Semi-membranosus

Semi-tendinosus

Back of the knee

The hamstrings are a group of three muscles at the back of the thigh (labeled above). They are integral to extending the leg and flexing the knee, so any injury to the hamstrings will have an adverse impact on walking and running.

TREATMENT

⊕ SEEK IMMEDIATE MEDICAL ATTENTION

MEDICAL

IMMEDIATE ▶	SHORT TERM ▶	MEDIUM TERM ▶	LONG TERM
■ If you think you may have a mild hamstring strain, you should: ▶ follow a RICE procedure (**»p.170**), keeping your hamstring stretched. ▶ seek medical attention. ■ If you think you may have a ruptured hamstring (you cannot walk unaided), you should: ▶ seek medical attention.	■ If you are diagnosed with a mild hamstring strain, your physician may: ▶ prescribe analgesic medication. ▶ refer you to a physical therapist for treatment to improve your muscle strength (see table below). ■ If you are diagnosed with a ruptured hamstring, your physician may: ▶ recommend surgery to stitch the damaged tissue.	■ If you have had surgery, your physician may: ▶ put your leg in a brace and advise you to rest for 4–6 weeks, or until the muscle has healed.	■ If your injury has healed as expected, your physician may: ▶ refer you to a physical therapist for a program of rehabilitation (see table below).

PHYSICAL THERAPY

EARLY STAGE ▶	INTERMEDIATE STAGE ▶	ADVANCED STAGE ▶	RETURN TO SPORT
■ Once your physician has referred you, your physical therapist may: ▶ use soft tissue massage to help relieve your symptoms. ▶ put strapping on your hamstring to prevent you from overexerting it. ▶ suggest you continue to use crutches until you can walk normally, without limping. ▶ assess the range of motion in your injured hamstring. ■ You may begin: ▶ bridges (**»p.236**) with your knee flexed at 60 degrees; aim for 3 sets x 10 reps, without pain. ▶ deep-water pool jogging, aiming for 20 minutes. You should not feel any pain. ▶ bicycling for 20 minutes at 85rpm, level 6. Stop if you feel pain. ▶ active knee extension within your pain-free range while sitting on a chair; aim for 6 reps x 30 secs every 2 hours. ▶ core-stability and gluteal exercises, such as dead bugs (**»p.225**).	■ You should now be able to: ▶ go up and down stairs, without pain. ▶ perform single-leg bridges (**»p.236**) with your knee flexed at 60 degrees, without pain; aim for 4 sets x 15 reps. ▶ perform straight-leg raises (**»p.193**) with the same ability in each leg. ■ You may begin: ▶ gentle stretches of your quadriceps, adductors, hamstrings, gastrocnemius, soleus, and gluteal muscles (**»pp.176–81; 185–88; 240–45**). Aim for symmetry. ▶ low-intensity sideways drills, such as carioca sidesteps (**»p.188**). ▶ interval bicycling at medium–high intensity. ▶ box step-ups (**»p.203**); aim for 4 sets x 6 reps. ▶ low-level running.	■ You should now be able to: ▶ complete high-intensity sideways drills, such as carioca sidesteps (**»p.188**). ▶ perform single-leg bridges (**»p.236**) with your knee flexed at 30 degrees. Aim for 3 sets x 15 reps, stopping if you feel pain. ■ Your physical therapist may: ▶ assess your single vertical and horizontal hops (**»p.261**) and adapted cross-over hops (**»p.262**) to establish baseline scores. ■ You may begin: ▶ lower-limb strength training at 50% of your one-rep max; aim for 4 sets x 8–12 reps of barbell squats (**»p.192**), straight-leg deadlifts (**»p.197**), and Nordic hamstring lowers (**»p.202**). ▶ foot plyometrics, such as A-skips (**»p.254**), walking pop-ups (**»p.254**), and straight-leg scratches (**»p.256**). ▶ medium-intensity running at distances relevant to your sport. You should not feel pain. ▶ low-level skills training.	■ You should now be able to: ▶ lift leg weights that are at least 80% of your one-rep max, without pain. ▶ complete foot plyometrics, such as jumps and hops (**»pp.256–59**), and speed drills (**»pp.252–53**), without pain. ▶ perform single vertical and horizontal hops (**»p.261**) and adapted cross-over hops (**»p.262**); your injured leg should have only 10% less ability than your uninjured one. ▶ complete a T-test (**»p.263**): aim for 11 seconds if you are male, and 15 seconds if you are female. ▶ complete high-level running at distances relevant to your sport, without pain. ▶ complete sport-specific drills without difficulty. ■ You may begin: ▶ exercises that focus on strengthening the hamstring, such as Nordic hamstring lowers (**»p.202**) and straight-leg deadlifts (**»p.197**); continue these after you return to sport.

QUADRICEPS INJURIES

The four quadriceps muscles are involved in walking, running, and straightening and bending the leg. They are all susceptible to injury, as are the tendons in the thigh. The severity of injuries to these muscles ranges from contusions (bruises), strains (small tears) of the tendon or muscle, to ruptures (complete tears).

CAUSES
Quadriceps strains usually affect the rectus femoris muscle and occur during sports that involve sprinting, jumping, or kicking, such as soccer. In extreme cases, the force that these activities place on the muscle cause it to rupture completely. Sustaining a contusion, or bruise, is a common occurrence in contact sports, where a direct blow to the muscle can lead to localized bleeding in the muscle and under the skin.

SYMPTOMS AND DIAGNOSIS
Symptoms of strains and contusions vary depending on the severity of your injury. You will usually feel pain and tenderness, and perhaps some weakness in your leg. There may also be bruising on your leg and some swelling. If you have ruptured your quadriceps tendon, there may be an audible "pop" at the moment of injury. You will experience pain and swelling, and you may feel a "gap" in your muscle at the site of the rupture. You may also be unable to straighten your knee and find walking difficult. If you have a severe contusion, an X-ray may be done to rule out bone damage. If you have a suspected strain or rupture, diagnosis will be made through physical examination; an ultrasound or MRI scan may also be needed. Ruptures of the quadriceps and patellar tendons (**»pp.122-23**) are, together, called ruptures of the extensor mechanism of the knee.

RISKS AND COMPLICATIONS
An untreated tear can lead to severe loss of mobility and flexibility in the affected area. Rarely, a contusion can lead to myositis ossificans, a painful condition involving muscle calcification (when bone starts to grow within the muscle).

WHEN WILL I BE FULLY FIT?
Most people recover from a strained muscle within 4 weeks, while rehabilitation for a contusion can take 4–8 weeks, depending on the severity of the injury. If you have completely ruptured your quadriceps tendon, you will need surgery and may take 4–6 months to recover fully.

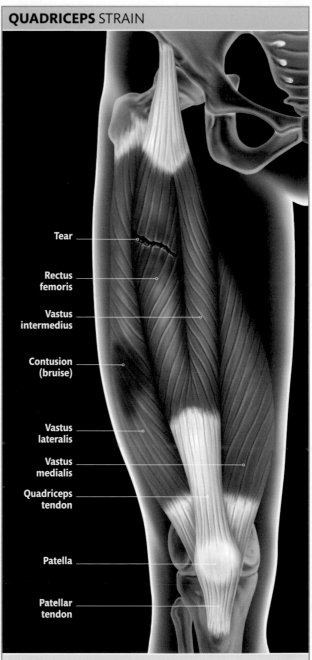

QUADRICEPS STRAIN

Tear

Rectus femoris

Vastus intermedius

Contusion (bruise)

Vastus lateralis

Vastus medialis

Quadriceps tendon

Patella

Patellar tendon

Quadriceps strain can affect any of the four muscles at the front of the thigh (labeled above) that connect to the patella via the quadriceps tendon. They allow the knee to bend and, in the case of the rectus femoris, the hip to flex.

TREATMENT

⊕ SEEK IMMEDIATE MEDICAL ATTENTION

MEDICAL

IMMEDIATE ▶	SHORT TERM ▶	MEDIUM TERM ▶	LONG TERM
■ If you think you may have injured your quadriceps, you should: ▶ follow a RICE procedure (**》p.170**) for 24 hours with your knee at maximum flexion; see icing of quadriceps (**》p.245**). ▶ immobilize your leg (**》pp.170–71**). ▶ seek medical attention.	■ If you are diagnosed with a serious contusion or strain, your physician may: ▶ advise you to continue with RICE for up to 72 hours. ▶ prescribe analgesic medication. ▶ refer you to a physical therapist for treatment (see table below). ■ If a severely strained (partially ruptured) tendon, is diagnosed, your physician may: ▶ put your leg in a cast or brace for 4–6 weeks. ■ If a complete tendon rupture is diagnosed, your physician may: ▶ recommend early surgery to stitch the damaged tissue.	■ Most quadriceps strains heal within 4 weeks, and contusions within 4–8 weeks. If your injury is healing as expected, your physician may: ▶ refer you to a physical therapist for treatment to improve muscle strength and elasticity (see table below). ■ If your severely strained (partially ruptured) tendon has failed to respond to nonsurgical treatment, your physician may: ▶ recommend surgery to repair the tendon.	■ After surgery, your physician may: ▶ put your leg in a cast or brace for 4–6 weeks. You will need crutches for 6–8 weeks. ■ When you are able to walk without crutches, your physician may: ▶ refer you to a physical therapist for a program of rehabilitation (see table below).

PHYSICAL THERAPY

EARLY STAGE ▶	INTERMEDIATE STAGE ▶	ADVANCED STAGE ▶	RETURN TO SPORT
■ Once your physician has referred you, your physical therapist may: ▶ use soft tissue massage to help relieve your symptoms. ▶ suggest you continue to use crutches until you can walk normally without limping. ■ You may begin: ▶ practicing squats (**》p.180**); aim for 3 sets x 20 reps. This should cause minimal pain. ▶ deep-water running; aim for 20–30 minutes, at high-intensity intervals. ▶ upper-limb weights (non-weight-bearing) 1 day after the injury. ▶ bicycling 1–2 days after the injury, as pain allows. Aim for 20 minutes at 85rpm, level 6.	■ You should now be able to: ▶ go up and down stairs, pain-free. ▶ complete single-leg squats (**》p.193**); aim for 3 sets x 10 reps at 90 degrees. ■ You may begin: ▶ gentle stretches of your quadriceps (**》p.243**). Aim for symmetry in both legs. ▶ functional warm-up drills, such as walking lunges (**》p.180**), full-body exercises, such as Swiss ball donkeys (**》p.190**), low-level foot plyometrics, such as A-walks (**》p.254**), and low-level sideways drills, such as carioca sidesteps (**》p.188**), pain-free. ▶ box step-ups (**》p.203**), aiming for 4 sets x 6 reps. ▶ interval bicycling at a medium–high intensity. ▶ low-level running.	■ You should now be able to: ▶ run at low intensity without pain or swelling. ▶ perform high-level sideways drills, such as carioca sidesteps (**》p.188**), without pain. ■ Your physical therapist may: ▶ assess your single vertical and horizontal hops (**》p.261**) and adapted cross-over hops (**》p.262**) to establish baseline scores. ■ You may begin: ▶ moderate-to-high level running at sport-specific distances. You should not feel any pain. ▶ lower-limb strength training; aim for 4 sets x 8–12 reps of barbell squats (**》p.192**) and Romanian deadlifts (**》p.196**); start at 50% of your one-rep max. ▶ low-level skills training.	■ You should now be able to: ▶ lift leg weights that are at least 80% of your one-rep max, without pain. ▶ complete foot plyometrics, such as jumps and hops (**》pp.257–58**), and speed drills (**》pp.252–53**), without pain. ▶ perform single vertical and horizontal hops (**》p.261**) and adapted cross-over hops (**》p.262**); your injured leg should have only 10% less ability than your uninjured one. ▶ complete a T-test (**》p.263**): aim for 11 seconds if you are male, and 15 seconds if you are female. ▶ complete high-level running at distances specific to your sport, without pain. ▶ complete sport-specific drills without difficulty. ▶ participate in full training.

PATELLA FRACTURE

The patella (kneecap) covers the front of the knee joint. Together with the femur (thighbone) and quadriceps (front thigh muscles), it is involved in bending and straightening the knee. Fractures of the patella can vary in severity, from a single crack to cracks in several places.

CAUSES

Fractures of the patella often occur in contact sports such as soccer or rugby, in which it can be common for knees to receive a direct blow, perhaps from a kick. The knees also come under constant stress during these types of sports as the result of explosive movement. This can cause the quadriceps muscle (»p.110) to contract too heavily, putting strain on the kneecap, and potentially causing a fracture.

SYMPTOMS AND DIAGNOSIS

If you have fractured your kneecap, there may be immediate severe pain and rapid swelling of your knee. You may not be able to lift your leg with a straight knee or to put any weight on your leg. In some very severe cases, where your kneecap has been fractured all the way across, you may feel a "gap" in the top of your knee. Your physician will make a diagnosis from a physical examination and usually advise an X-ray to confirm the diagnosis.

RISKS AND COMPLICATIONS

Generally most fractures respond well to treatment, although you may still experience some long-term stiffness and lack of mobility. You may experience similar but more severe problems in cases where surgery was required but was not carried out early enough. Fractures of the patella can also occur in athletes who have had anterior cruciale ligament repair (»p.124) using a patellar tendon bone graft (which uses a piece of patella), and return to sports too soon. There is also a risk of osteoarthritis.

WHEN WILL I BE FULLY FIT?

Regardless of whether or not you have had surgery, your knee will need to be in plaster for around 6 weeks. In all cases, you should expect some residual stiffness in your knee joint. This may continue to affect sporting performance for 3–12 months, after which you should be fully fit.

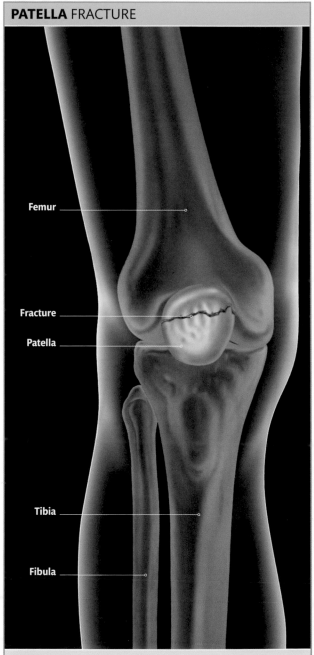

PATELLA FRACTURE

Femur

Fracture

Patella

Tibia

Fibula

The patella is a thick bone located at the point at which the femur and the tibia (shinbone) meet. It serves to protect the knee joint and aid leg movement. Because of its exposed position, it is susceptible to injury.

TREATMENT

⊕ SEEK IMMEDIATE MEDICAL ATTENTION

MEDICAL

IMMEDIATE ▶	SHORT TERM ▶	MEDIUM TERM ▶	LONG TERM
■ If you think you may have fractured your patella, you should: ▶ stop activity. ▶ apply ice to the affected area (»p.165). ▶ seek medical attention.	■ If you are diagnosed with a minor fracture, your physician may: ▶ immobilize your knee in a cast for around 6 weeks. ▶ prescribe analgesic medication. ■ If you are diagnosed with a severe fracture, your physician may: ▶ recommend surgery to repair your kneecap with pins and surgical wire. ▶ recommend surgery to remove your kneecap, if it is impossible to repair, to prevent the onset of arthritis.	■ After surgery to repair or remove your kneecap, your physician may: ▶ immobilize your knee in a cast for around 6 weeks. ■ If your knee is healing as expected after 2–3 weeks, your physician may: ▶ replace the plaster with a knee brace.	■ After your cast or brace has been removed, your physician may: ▶ advise you to use crutches for 2–3 weeks. ▶ refer you to a physical therapist for a program of rehabilitation (see table below). ■ Pain may continue, even after the injury is fully healed, in which case your physician may: ▶ recommend using a brace to support your knee.

PHYSICAL THERAPY

EARLY STAGE ▶	INTERMEDIATE STAGE ▶	ADVANCED STAGE ▶	RETURN TO SPORT
■ Once your physician has referred you, your physical therapist may: ▶ suggest various treatments, such as electrotherapy, to help alleviate your symptoms. ■ You may begin: ▶ bending your knee, as pain allows; aim to achieve 90-degree flexion and full extension. ▶ non-weight-bearing hip exercises, such as clams (»p.187). ▶ using an electrical muscle stimulator on your quadriceps, hamstrings, and calf muscles, to maintain bulk. ▶ trying to walk normally without a limp. ▶ core-stability exercises, such as single arm and leg raises (»p.224).	■ You should now be able to: ▶ demonstrate a full range of motion in your hip, ankle, and foot. ▶ perform straight-leg raises (»p.193) with your leg fully extended, without pain. ▶ bear your full weight, without pain. ■ You may begin: ▶ lower-limb bodyweight exercises, such as single-leg squats (»p.193). ▶ weight-bearing; aim to add 15–20% of bodyweight every 1–2 weeks as pain, swelling, and range of movement allow. ▶ walking on a treadmill (once your limp has gone) until you can jog without pain. ▶ stationary bicycling; aim for 20 minutes at 80rpm, level 6. ▶ deep-water running; aim for up to 30 minutes at high intensity intervals.	■ You should now be able to: ▶ perform single-leg squats (»p.193) with 90-degree flexion, without pain or apprehension. ▶ perform step-up and holds (»p.250), without pain. ■ Your physical therapist may: ▶ assess your single vertical and horizontal hops (»p.261) and adapted cross-over hops (»p.262) for baseline scores. ■ You may begin: ▶ interval bicycling at a low-medium intensity. ▶ functional warm-up drills, such as skating slide-boards (»p.200), full-body exercises, such as Swiss ball donkeys (»p.222), and low-level foot plyometrics, such as A-skips (»p.254). ▶ lower-limb strength training; start at 50% of your one-rep max and aim for 4 sets x 8–12 reps of barbell squats (»p.192). ▶ stationary low-level training and low-level running.	■ You should now be able to: ▶ lift leg weights that are at least 80% of your one-rep max, without pain. ▶ do foot plyometrics, such as jumps and hops (»pp.256–59), and speed drills (»pp.252–53), without pain. ▶ perform single vertical and horizontal hops (»p.261) and adapted cross-over hops (»p.262); your injured side should have only 10% less ability than your uninjured side. ▶ complete a T-test (»p.263): aim for 11 seconds if you are male, and 15 seconds if you are female. ▶ complete high-level running at distances relevant to your sport. ▶ complete sport-specific drills without difficulty. ▶ participate in full training.

PATELLAR DISLOCATION

The patella (kneecap) glides up and down a groove (the femoral trochlear groove) in the femur (thighbone) as the knee bends and straightens. Sometimes the surrounding tendons and ligaments are unable to hold the patella in the groove, enabling it to dislocate ("pop out") or subluxate (partially dislocate), usually outward or laterally.

CAUSES

Dislocation of the patella is associated with sports that involve repetitive running, jumping, or kicking, such as soccer. Such activities can lead to stress on the kneecap and cause it to either fully or partially dislocate from the femoral trochlear groove. Not running properly or wearing the wrong type of shoes can increase the likelihood of this happening. A sharp blow to the kneecap can also dislodge the kneecap.

SYMPTOMS AND DIAGNOSIS

You may feel pain in your knee, and there may be swelling and stiffness in the area. You may hear creaking and crackling sounds when you move your knee, and you may feel it "catch." In more extreme cases, your knee may buckle under your weight and your kneecap may slip off to one side. In an acute dislocation, you may hear a "pop" and feel your knee collapse suddenly. Your physician will usually make a diagnosis through physical examination, but you may need an X-ray or MRI scan to pinpoint the position of the patella and assess any damage to the surrounding tissue.

RISKS AND COMPLICATIONS

If left untreated, a dislocation of your kneecap may lead to the production of loose fragments of cartilage and bone in your knee, causing further degeneration of the joint and the risk of osteoarthritis in the future. One or more dislocations can lead to patellar instability, in which the damaged ligaments and tendons are unable to hold your kneecap securely, and it will continue to feel unstable even after it has been reduced (put back in place).

WHEN WILL I BE FULLY FIT?

For dislocations that do not require surgical treatment, you should be able to return to sports within 4–6 weeks of the start of treatment. After surgery, you will need 4–6 months to recover fully.

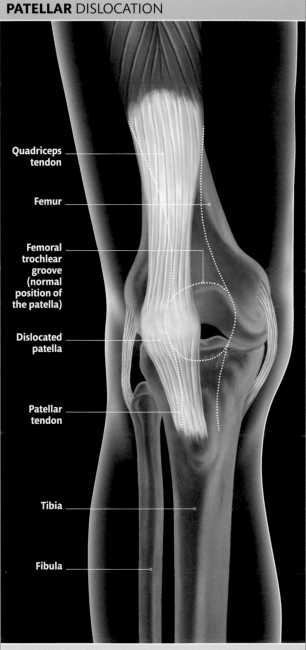

PATELLAR DISLOCATION

Quadriceps tendon

Femur

Femoral trochlear groove (normal position of the patella)

Dislocated patella

Patellar tendon

Tibia

Fibula

The patellar tendon connects the patella to the tibia (shinbone), and the quadriceps tendon, to the femur. In a dislocation, the tendons are unable to hold the patella in place, allowing it to slip out of the femoral trochlear groove.

TREATMENT

⊕ SEEK IMMEDIATE MEDICAL ATTENTION

MEDICAL	IMMEDIATE ▶	SHORT TERM ▶	MEDIUM TERM ▶	LONG TERM
	■ If you think you may have dislocated your kneecap, you should: ▶ stop activity. ▶ follow a RICE procedure (**》p.170**). ▶ seek medical attention.	■ If you are diagnosed with a dislocated kneecap, your physician may: ▶ reduce your patella (relocate it), although in some cases reduction may occur by itself. ▶ prescribe analgesic medication. ▶ immobilize your knee with an extension splint for 2–3 weeks. ▶ advise you to use crutches for 2–3 weeks.	■ When your symptoms have subsided, your physician may: ▶ put a splint on your knee to reduce the lateral movement of your kneecap, while still allowing some movement of the knee. ▶ refer you to a physical therapist for treatment to improve muscle strength and movement in your knee (see table below).	■ If your kneecap continues to be unstable, your physician may: ▶ recommend surgery to repair a damaged ligament or tendon in the knee. ■ After surgery, your physician may: ▶ refer you to a physical therapist for a program of rehabilitation (see table below).

PHYSICAL THERAPY	EARLY STAGE ▶	INTERMEDIATE STAGE ▶	ADVANCED STAGE ▶	RETURN TO SPORT
	■ Once your physician has referred you, your physical therapist may: ▶ use an electrical muscle stimulator on your quadriceps, hamstrings, and calf muscles to maintain muscle bulk. ■ You may begin: ▶ gluteal strengthening and activation exercises, such as clams (**》p.187**). You should not feel any pain. ▶ bending your knee, as pain allows; aim to achieve 90-degree flexion, with full extension. ▶ weight-bearing; aim to add 15–20% of bodyweight every 1–2 weeks as pain, swelling, and range of movement allow. ▶ trying to walk normally, without a limp. ▶ static quadriceps exercises, such as straight-leg raises (**》p.193**). ▶ walking in a pool and swimming, as pain allows.	■ You should now be able to: ▶ demonstrate a full range of motion in your hip, ankle, and foot. ▶ bear your full weight. ▶ perform straight-leg raises (**》p.193**) with your leg fully extended, without pain. ■ You may begin: ▶ lower-limb bodyweight exercises, such as single-leg squats (**》p.193**). ▶ walking on a treadmill (once your gait is normal), until you can jog without pain. ▶ stationary bicycling for 20 minutes at 80rpm, level 6. ▶ deep-water running; aim for up to 30 minutes, at high intensity intervals. ▶ core-stability exercises, such as dead bugs (**》p.225**). ▶ weight-bearing gluteal exercises, such as hip hitchers (**》p.186**).	■ You should now be able to: ▶ perform single-leg squats (**》p.193**) with 90-degree flexion, without pain or apprehension. ▶ perform box step-downs (**》p.203**) without pain or apprehension. ■ You may begin: ▶ interval bicycling at a low–medium intensity. ▶ work on a cross-trainer and stepper; build toward 20 minutes at 80rpm, level 6. ▶ functional warm-up drills, such as walking kick outs (**》p.185**), exercises, such as box step-ups (**》p.203**), and low-level foot plyometrics, such as straight-leg scratches (**》p.256**). ▶ lower-limb strength training; start at 50% of your one-rep max and aim for 4 sets x 8–12 reps of Romanian deadlifts (**》p.196**). ▶ stationary low-level skills, such as ball handling. ▶ low-level running. You should not feel any pain.	■ You should now be able to: ▶ lift leg weights that are at least 80% of your one-rep max, without pain. ▶ complete foot plyometrics, such as jumps and hops (**》p.256–59**), and speed drills (**》p.252–53**), without pain. ▶ complete a T test (**》p.263**): aim for 11 seconds if you are male, and 15 seconds if you are female. ▶ complete high-level running at distances relevant to your sport, without pain. ▶ complete sport-specific drills without difficulty. ▶ participate in full training.

PATELLOFEMORAL PAIN SYNDROME

This common knee condition occurs when the movement of the patella (kneecap) over the femur (thighbone) causes pain at the front of the knee. It is not associated with specific signs of damage to the joint.

CAUSES

This condition can be caused by muscle weakness or imbalance, tight tendons, or abnormal movement of the kneecap over the thighbone. Patellofemoral pain syndrome can also be caused and aggravated by repetitive movements of the knee.

SYMPTOMS AND DIAGNOSIS

You will feel a general ache or pain at the front of your knee, behind or around your kneecap. The pain may be triggered when you place pressure on your knee, when walking up or down stairs, or running (especially downhill), for example. Strenuous exercise, squats, and weight-bearing movements that involve bending your knee may also cause you pain. You may have swelling around your kneecap and a grating sensation (known as crepitus) within the knee joint. Symptoms can be difficult to pinpoint, so your physician may need to perform a variety of tests to make a diagnosis and exclude any other possible causes.

RISKS AND COMPLICATIONS

If this condition is left untreated, your patellar tendon and the cartilage underneath your kneecap may become inflamed. This inflammation can get progressively worse, leading to permanent damage in the joint. It is important to rest your knee and follow any physical therapy program that is recommended, or it may take longer for the condition to improve. This syndrome can also lead to patellofemoral cartilage damage.

WHEN WILL I BE FULLY FIT?

In most cases, if you follow a rehabilitation program, you should see a substantial improvement in a few weeks to a month, and will have made a full recovery within 4–6 months. If you have had surgery, your recovery period is likely to be 3 months.

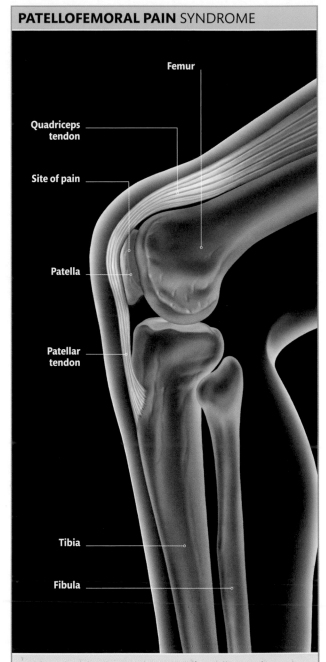

PATELLOFEMORAL PAIN SYNDROME

Femur

Quadriceps tendon

Site of pain

Patella

Patellar tendon

Tibia

Fibula

Held in place by the quadriceps and patellar tendons, the patella glides up and down in a groove in the femur, allowing smooth movement of the knee. Pain occurs when this smooth movement is disturbed for any reason.

TREATMENT

	IMMEDIATE	SHORT TERM	MEDIUM TERM	LONG TERM
MEDICAL	■ If you think you may have patellofemoral pain syndrome, you should: ▶ stop activity. ▶ rest your knee. ▶ follow a RICE procedure (»p.170). ■ If your symptoms have not responded after 2 weeks of self-treatment, you should: ▶ seek medical attention.	■ If you are diagnosed with patellofemoral pain syndrome, your physician may: ▶ advise you to continue with RICE (»p.170) for 4 weeks. ▶ prescribe analgesic medication. ▶ advise you to avoid strenuous or painful activities until the pain subsides. ▶ advise you to use a knee support.	■ If your condition is improving as expected, your physician may: ▶ refer you to a physical therapist for treatment to restore painless movement (see table below). ■ If your condition has not improved after 6 weeks, your physician may: ▶ look for other possible causes of knee pain. ▶ give you a corticosteroid injection in your knee joint to relieve pain.	■ If your injury fails to respond to nonsurgical treatment (this is rare), and a physical cause can be identified, your physician may: ▶ recommend surgery to smooth out the inside of the patella or reduce lateral pull. ■ Once you have fully recovered from surgery, your physician may: ▶ refer you to a physical therapist for a long-term program of rehabilitation (see table below).

	EARLY STAGE	INTERMEDIATE STAGE	ADVANCED STAGE	RETURN TO SPORT
PHYSICAL THERAPY	■ Once your physician has referred you, your physical therapist may: ▶ suggest various treatments, such as electrotherapy, to reduce local inflammation. ▶ assess your lower spine, hip, knee, and ankle. ▶ perform an assessment of your foot and ankle to see if you need insoles or orthotics to support your medial arch, or different footwear. ▶ use soft tissue massage to help relieve your symptoms. ▶ put strapping on your patella to reduce the strain on it. ■ You may begin: ▶ stretching the quadriceps, hamstrings, gastrocnemius, iliotibial band, soleus, and gluteal muscles (»pp.176–81; 185–88; 240–45). Aim for an equal range of movement on both sides. ▶ self-massage with a hard foam roller; spend 6 x 30 seconds on each leg daily. ▶ using an electrical muscle stimulator to help develop your quadriceps.	■ You should now be able to: ▶ walk normally without a limp. ■ You may begin: ▶ practicing squats (»p.180) with the electrical muscle stimulator strapped to your leg; aim to squat to 90 degrees. ▶ box step-ups (»p.203); aim for 3 sets x 15 reps. ▶ exercise on a cross-trainer and stepper; build to 20 minutes at 80rpm, level 6. ▶ lower-limb strength training; aim for 4 sets x 8–12 reps of barbell squats (»p.192) and Romanian deadlifts (»p.196); start at 50% of your one-rep max. There should be no pain and no increase in swelling. ▶ deep-water pool running; aim for 30 minutes. ▶ walk-jog drills (»p.252) at intervals; gradually build to more jogging than walking. ▶ core-stability exercises, such as dead bugs (»p.225).	■ You should now be able to: ▶ complete high box step-ups (»p.203); aim for 4 sets x 6 reps. ▶ complete box step-downs (»p.203); aim for 3 sets x 15 reps. ■ You may begin: ▶ low-level foot plyometrics, such as A-walks (»p.254). ▶ jumping, hopping, and landing drills (»pp.256–59); stop if you feel pain. ▶ interval bicycling at a medium–high intensity. ▶ increasing your running volume and intensity.	■ You should now be able to: ▶ lift leg weights that are at least 80% of your one-rep max, without pain. ▶ do foot plyometrics, such as jumps and hops (»pp.256–59), and speed drills (»pp.252–53), without pain. ▶ complete high-level running at distances relevant to your sport, without pain. ▶ complete sport-specific drills without difficulty. ▶ participate in full training.

PATELLAR BURSITIS

Bursae are fluid-filled sacs that act as cushions to aid smooth joint movement. Each of the three main knee bursae are susceptible to injury and inflammation. When a knee bursa is inflamed, movement of the knee joint becomes painful—a condition known as patellar bursitis.

CAUSES

Trauma – such as a direct blow or a fall onto the front of the knee – can rupture blood vessels, which then bleed into the prepatellar bursa at the front of the kneecap, causing swelling and inflammation. Prepatellar bursitis is also linked with friction and overuse. The infrapatellar bursa is located just below the kneecap, and swelling here is usually connected to inflammation of the adjacent patellar tendon, often caused by a jumping injury. Bursitis of the suprapatellar, which is located above the kneecap, can be caused by a heavy blow to the knee.

SYMPTOMS AND DIAGNOSIS

You will normally have pain and tenderness in your kneecap and in the immediate surrounding area. You may have swelling in your knee, as well as a feeling of warmth. You may also experience difficulty walking, and kneeling will almost certainly aggravate the pain. Your physician will make a diagnosis through physical examination and may drain some fluid from the bursa to send for analysis if infection is suspected. Your physician may also suggest that you have an X-ray to rule out other potential injuries such as a fracture (**»p.112**) or a dislocation (**»p.114**).

RISKS AND COMPLICATIONS

Occasionally, the skin over your kneecap may be broken, allowing bacteria to spread into the fluid of the bursa, causing an infection. If an inflamed bursa is left untreated, you may develop chronic bursitis.

WHEN WILL I BE FULLY FIT?

Unless you experience complications, patellar bursitis should respond well to a period of rest, ice treatment, and pain-relief medication. You should be able to return to your sport within 1–2 weeks. The recovery period for an infected bursa is unpredictable, and it can take up to 2 months to return to sport. If you have had surgery, you should expect to be fully fit within 4–6 weeks, depending on your sport.

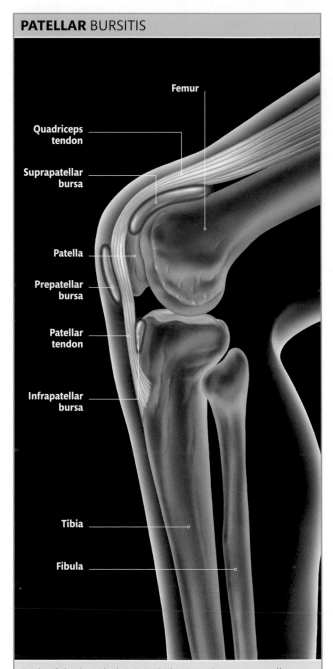

PATELLAR BURSITIS

Femur

Quadriceps tendon

Suprapatellar bursa

Patella

Prepatellar bursa

Patellar tendon

Infrapatellar bursa

Tibia

Fibula

Each of the knee's three main bursae, the suprapatellar, the prepatellar, and the infrapatellar, are located in an area in which tendons and bones move across each other. Any of them may become inflamed through injury or overuse.

TREATMENT

IMMEDIATE ▶	SHORT TERM ▶	MEDIUM TERM ▶	LONG TERM
MEDICAL ■ If you think you may have patellar bursitis, you should: ▶ stop activity. ▶ follow a RICE procedure (»p.170). ▶ seek medical attention.	■ If you are diagnosed with patellar bursitis, your physician may: ▶ prescribe analgesic medication. ▶ advise you to continue with ice treatment and rest. ▶ refer you to a physical therapist for treatment to build strength in your knee (see table below). ■ If an infection is present, your physician may: ▶ prescribe a course of antibiotics.	■ If the symptoms persist, your physician may: ▶ give you an injection of corticosteroids directly into the inflamed bursa. ▶ drain fluid from the inflamed bursa.	■ In very rare cases, if the injury is severe and fails to respond to nonsurgical treatment, your physician may: ▶ recommend surgery to completely remove the bursa. ■ After surgery, your physician may: ▶ refer you to a physical therapist for a program of rehabilitation (see table below).

EARLY STAGE ▶	INTERMEDIATE STAGE ▶	ADVANCED STAGE ▶	RETURN TO SPORT
PHYSICAL THERAPY ■ Once your physician has referred you, your physical therapist may: ▶ suggest various treatments, such as electrotherapy, to help reduce local inflammation. ▶ perform a full biomechanical foot and ankle assessment to determine whether you need insoles or orthotics to support your medial arch, or a correct footwear prescription. ■ You may begin: ▶ straight-leg raises (»p.193).	■ You should now be able to: ▶ demonstrate a full range of motion in your hip, knee, and ankle, without pain. ■ You may begin: ▶ bodyweight lower-limb exercises such as box step-ups (»p.203), squats (»p.180), and single-leg squats (»p.193). ▶ interval bicycling, and work on a cross-trainer and stepper, as pain allows; build toward 20 minutes at 80rpm, level 6. ▶ full-body exercises, such as lawnmowers (»p.190) ▶ low-level foot plyometrics, such as A-walks (»p.254).	■ You should now be able to: ▶ complete interval bicycling at a moderate–high intensity, without pain. ■ Your physical therapist may: ▶ assess your single vertical and horizontal hops (»p.261) and adapted cross-over hops (»p.262) for baseline scores. ■ You may begin: ▶ lower-limb strength training; start at 50% of your one-rep max and aim for 4 sets x 8–12 reps of barbell squats (»p.180), straight-leg deadlifts (»p.197), and Nordic hamstring lowers (»p.202). ▶ high-level, lower-limb exercises, such as box step-downs (»p.203).	■ You should now be able to: ▶ complete foot plyometrics, such as jumps and hops (»pp.256–59), and speed drills (»pp.252–53), without pain. ▶ perform single vertical and horizontal hops (»p.261) and adapted cross-over hops (»p.262); your injured side should have only 10% less ability than your uninjured side. ▶ complete a T-test (»p.263); aim for 11 seconds if you are male, and 15 seconds if you are female. ▶ complete high-level running at distances relevant to your sport, without pain. ▶ complete sport-specific drills without difficulty. ▶ participate in full training, for at least 1 week, without pain.

OSTEOCHONDRITIS DISSECANS

Osteochondritis dissecans of the knee occurs when cartilage in the knee joint—sometimes with a section of bone attached—breaks away. Such a fragment may become lodged in the joint, which can limit the range of motion in the knee.

CAUSES
Osteochondritis dissecans can be caused by an injury or a series of injuries to your knee, which are most likely to occur in collision and contact sports such as rugby and soccer. Impact or repetitive stress from running on a hard surface, for example, can lead to cartilage tearing or fragmenting. When the bone under your cartilage is injured, blood supply may be restricted; this can lead to bone tissue dying, causing the cartilage to fragment and become dislodged. The condition occurs most frequently in teenagers.

SYMPTOMS AND DIAGNOSIS
The onset of symptoms is gradual. You may feel stiffness, weakness, and occasional swelling in your knee. Pain may be located in the center of your knee, or it may be a general ache, and the movement of your knee will be restricted. When bending or straightening your knee, you may experience a clicking or grating sensation within it and it may "lock." There may also be some tenderness at the lower end of your thighbone. Your physician will assess your symptoms and recommend an X-ray to confirm the diagnosis.

RISKS AND COMPLICATIONS
If you leave osteochondritis dissecans untreated, loose fragments of cartilage or bone could cause further damage inside your knee joint, leading to chronic pain, impaired function and, ultimately, early osteoarthritis.

WHEN WILL I BE FULLY FIT?
If you have not had surgery, you can return gradually to activity as part of your rehabilitation, which may take up to a year. In younger people, osteochondritis dissecans is more likely to heal without surgery. After surgery, you will not be able to put weight on your knee for 6–8 weeks. This rest period should be followed by 6–8 months of physical therapy. Older people may not heal without surgery and, even with surgery, there is a greater risk that they will not heal fully and may develop conditions such as osteoarthritis.

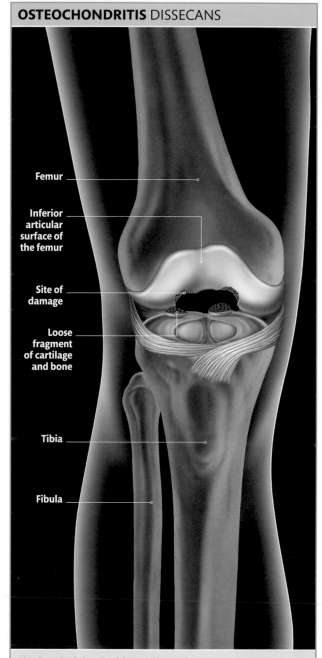

OSTEOCHONDRITIS DISSECANS

Femur

Inferior articular surface of the femur

Site of damage

Loose fragment of cartilage and bone

Tibia

Fibula

The head of the thighbone (femur) is covered with articular cartilage, which helps the knee joint move smoothly. Osteochondritis dissecans occurs when this cartilage is pulled away from the bone.

TREATMENT

⊕ SEEK IMMEDIATE MEDICAL ATTENTION

MEDICAL

IMMEDIATE ▶	SHORT TERM ▶	MEDIUM TERM ▶	LONG TERM
■ If you think you may have osteochondritis dissecans, you should: ▶ stop any activity that causes pain. ▶ follow a RICE procedure (**》p.170**) ▶ immobilize your knee in a straight position (**》p.170–71**) and rest. ▶ seek medical attention.	■ If you are diagnosed with osteochondritis dissecans, your physician may: ▶ immobilize your knee in a cast or brace for 4–6 weeks. ▶ prescribe analgesic medication. ▶ refer you to a physical therapist for treatment to strengthen the muscles around your knee (see table below). ■ If bone in your knee has fragmented and broken away, your physician may: ▶ recommend surgery to remove any loose fragments and repair the damaged bone.	■ If no bone fragments have broken away, your knee should heal naturally over time. However, if your injury fails to respond to non-surgical treatment, your physician may: ▶ recommend surgery to repair the damaged bone.	■ After surgery, your physician may: ▶ advise you to restrict the amount of weight you place on your knee until it is fully healed. ■ After 1–2 weeks, if your injury has healed as expected, your physician may: ▶ refer you to a physical therapist for a program of rehabilitation (see table below).

PHYSICAL THERAPY

EARLY STAGE ▶	INTERMEDIATE STAGE ▶	ADVANCED STAGE ▶	RETURN TO SPORT
■ Once your physician has referred you, your physical therapist may: ▶ suggest various treatments, such as electrotherapy, to reduce local inflammation. ▶ assess the length of your quadriceps, hamstrings, hip flexor, and calf muscles to check that they are symmetrical. ■ You may begin: ▶ core-stability and gluteal exercises, such as dead bugs (**》p.225**). ▶ non-weight bearing exercises, such as clams (**》p.187**), and straight-leg raises (**》p.193**). ▶ using an electrical muscle stimulator on the affected area to help build up the muscle.	■ You should now be able to: ▶ perform weight-bearing gluteal exercises, such as hip hitchers (**》p.186**). ■ You may begin: ▶ functional warm-up drills such as kneeling supermen (**》pp.228–229**), full-body exercises such as lawnmowers (**》p.190**), and low-level foot plyometrics such as A-walks (**》p.254**). ▶ low-level running and sporting activities, as pain allows. ▶ bicycling and working on a cross-trainer and stepper; build to 20 minutes at 80rpm, level 6.	■ You should now be able to: ▶ perform lower-limb strength training, without pain and with no increase in swelling. Aim for 4 sets x 8–12 reps of barbell squats (**》p.192**) and Romanian deadlifts (**》p.196**); start at 50% of your one-rep max. ▶ perform high-level foot plyometrics, such as A-skips (**》p.254**) and bounding (**》p.259**).	■ You should now be able to: ▶ lift leg weights that are at least 80% of your one-rep max, without pain. ▶ complete foot plyometrics, such as jumps and hops (**》pp.256–259**), and speed drills (**》pp.252–253**), without pain. ▶ complete high-level running at distances relevant to your sport, without pain. ▶ complete sport-specific drills without difficulty. ▶ participate in full training.

KNEE TENDON INJURIES

The patellar tendon connects the patella (kneecap) to the tibia (shinbone) at the tibial tuberosity (the bony bump at the top of the shin). Patellar tendinopathy is a common injury in athletes; rupture of the patellar tendon is less common but more serious. Osgood-Schlatter syndrome (OSS), an inflammation of the area around the tibial tuberosity, is most common in teenagers.

CAUSES

Patellar tendinopathy usually occurs in sports that involve repeated jumping, such as volleyball, and it is often called "jumper's knee." A rupture of the patellar tendon can be caused by a sudden contraction of the quadriceps (the large muscle at the front of the thigh), when landing hard from a jump. Osgood-Schlatter syndrome affects teenagers, whose bones grow rapidly: it causes the quadriceps to tighten and may lead to inflammation and pain around the tibial tuberosity.

SYMPTOMS

Patellar tendinopathy will cause pain and swelling at the top of your shin. As with a rupture of your quadriceps tendon (**»p.110**), if you have ruptured your patellar tendon, there may be an audible "pop" at the time of injury and you may be unable to straighten or bear weight on your leg. Osgood-Schlatter symptoms are similar to tendinopathy but less severe, and will worsen if you extend your leg fully or squat. Your physician will carry out a physical examination. If Osgood-Schlatter syndrome is suspected, an X-ray may be used to confirm the diagnosis.

RISKS AND COMPLICATIONS

Without treatment, patellar tendinopathy can lead to a weakening of your leg muscles and long-term knee pain. Complications of a tendon rupture are similar, but also include infection and possible displacement of your kneecap. Left untreated, Osgood-Schlatter syndrome could lead to further knee pain and swelling, and muscle loss in your patellar tendon.

WHEN WILL I BE FULLY FIT?

If patellar tendinopathy is correctly managed, you should be able to return to sports within 6 months. Rehabilitation after surgery for a patellar tendon rupture may take 9–12 months; Osgood-Schlatter syndrome should heal within 3 months.

PATELLAR TENDINOPATHY

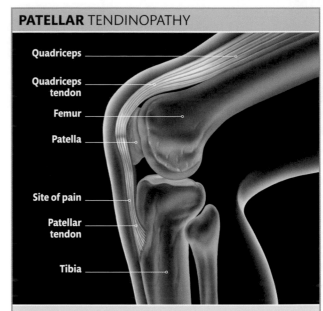

Quadriceps
Quadriceps tendon
Femur
Patella
Site of pain
Patellar tendon
Tibia

The patellar tendon anchors the patella to the tibia. Repeated stress on this tendon can cause small tears, resulting in pain and swelling (tendinopathy).

PATELLAR TENDON RUPTURE

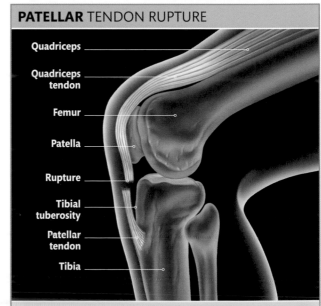

Quadriceps
Quadriceps tendon
Femur
Patella
Rupture
Tibial tuberosity
Patellar tendon
Tibia

If the patellar tendon ruptures completely, the patella breaks free and may be pulled upward by the large quadriceps muscles in the front of the thigh.

TREATMENT

⊕ SEEK IMMEDIATE MEDICAL ATTENTION

MEDICAL

IMMEDIATE ▶	SHORT TERM ▶	MEDIUM TERM ▶	LONG TERM
■ If you think you may have a knee tendon injury, you should: ▶ stop activity. ▶ follow a RICE procedure (**》p.170**). ▶ seek medical attention.	■ If you are diagnosed with patellar tendinopathy or OSS, your physician may: ▶ prescribe analgesic medication. ▶ advise you to rest until your symptoms subside. ▶ refer you to a physical therapist for treatment to help strengthen the muscles (see table below). ■ If you are diagnosed with a ruptured patellar tendon, your physician may: ▶ recommend surgery to repair the tendon.	■ If you have had surgery for a rupture of your patellar tendon, your physician may: ▶ immobilize your leg in a brace for 6 weeks.	■ If patellar tendinopathy fails to respond to nonsurgical treatment after 6–12 months, your physician may: ▶ recommend surgery to remove damaged tissue and repair the tendon. ■ After surgery, or the removal of your leg brace, your physician may: ▶ refer you to a physical therapist for a program of rehabilitation (see table below).

PHYSICAL THERAPY

EARLY STAGE ▶	INTERMEDIATE STAGE ▶	ADVANCED STAGE ▶	RETURN TO SPORT
■ Once your physician has referred you, your physical therapist may: ▶ assess your VISA-P score to determine the severity of your condition. ▶ use manual therapy and soft tissue therapy to help relieve your symptoms. ■ You may begin: ▶ single-leg decline squats (**》p.198**); initially aim for 3 sets x 15 reps twice daily, performed at bodyweight; these will be painful initially. ▶ upper-limb weights, performed in a seated or lying position to off-load weight, such as prone rows (**》p.209**) ▶ core-stability exercises, such as dead bugs (**》p.225**), pulley chops (**》pp.230–31**), and pulley lifts (**》pp.232–33**).	■ You should now be able to: ▶ record an improved VISA-P score. ▶ perform low-level bicycling drills, without pain. ■ You may begin: ▶ single-leg decline squats (**》p.198**) with an 11 lb (5 kg) load (once pain-free using your bodyweight). As these heavier drop downs become pain-free, increase weight by 11 lb (5 kg) at a time. Use a Smith machine or dumbbells. Aim for 3 sets x 15 reps, twice daily. ▶ functional warm-up drills such as walking kick-outs (**》p.185**), exercises such as kneeling supermen (**》pp.228–29**), and low-level foot plyometrics such as A-skips (**》p.254**). ▶ lower-limb weights exercises, as long as they have no knee-pushing movements. For example, try straight-leg deadlifts (**》p.197**), Nordic hamstring lowers (**》p.202**), or single-leg bridges (**》p.236**).	■ You should now be able to: ▶ record a VISA-P score of 80 or above. ▶ feel only minimal morning stiffness or pain in your patella tendon. ▶ participate in normal sport warm-ups with no discomfort (strapping as required). ■ You may begin: ▶ adding heavier loads to your single-leg decline squats, continuing with 3 sets x 15 reps twice daily. Your goal is to add 50% of your bodyweight as your extra load. ▶ low-level jogging, as pain allows; start with straight-line running and gentle figure-eights (**》p.253**).	■ You should now be able to: ▶ record a VISA-P score of 90 or above. ▶ feel no morning stiffness or pain in your patella tendon. ▶ lift leg weights that are at least 80% of your one-rep max, without pain. ▶ perform single vertical and horizontal hops (**》p.261**) and adapted cross-over hops (**》p.262**); your injured side should have only 10% less ability than your uninjured side. ▶ complete foot plyometrics, such as jumps and hops (**》pp.256–59**), and speed drills (**》pp.252–53**), without pain. ▶ complete high-level running at distances relevant to your sport, without pain. ▶ complete sport-specific drills without difficulty. ▶ participate in full training ■ You should continue: ▶ a program of eccentric single-leg decline squats (**》p.193**)—practise these at least once a week for a year.

ANTERIOR CRUCIATE LIGAMENT INJURY

The anterior cruciate ligament (ACL) is one of four main ligaments in the knee that work together to strengthen and stabilize the knee joint. Most sprains and ruptures to this ligament are the result of a sudden twisting movement, but may also be cause by an impact.

CAUSES
In general, knee ligament injuries commonly occur in collision and contact sports, such as football and rugby: when players tackle one another, causing impact on, or twisting of the knee; or if athletes put abnormal strain on the knee when running or jumping. The anterior cruciate ligament may tear if the knee is twisted abnormally or if the leg receives a direct blow, often to the tibia (shinbone), when the foot is firmly planted in the ground, perhaps during a rugby tackle. An awkward fall in a sport such as skiing can also cause injury to this ligament.

SYMPTOMS AND DIAGNOSIS
If you have strained or ruptured your anterior cruciate ligament, you will have severe pain and swelling in your knee. You may also hear an audible "pop" at the time of the injury. Your knee may feel unstable and painful when you put weight on it, and you may not be able to straighten it. Your physician will usually make a diagnosis from a physical examination but may recommend an MRI scan or X-ray to confirm.

RISKS AND COMPLICATIONS
An untreated injury to your anterior cruciate ligament can lead to further damage to your other knee structures, and to permanent instability and pain in your knee. If your case is particularly extreme, you will suffer severe degeneration of the knee, and osteoarthritis may set in.

WHEN WILL I BE FULLY FIT?
If you have not had surgery, you should be able to return to sports within 2–12 weeks. If you have had surgery, then 8–12 months of recovery may be required. However, if your injury is severe, including damage to other knee ligaments, you may not be able to return to any sport in which stress is placed on your knee.

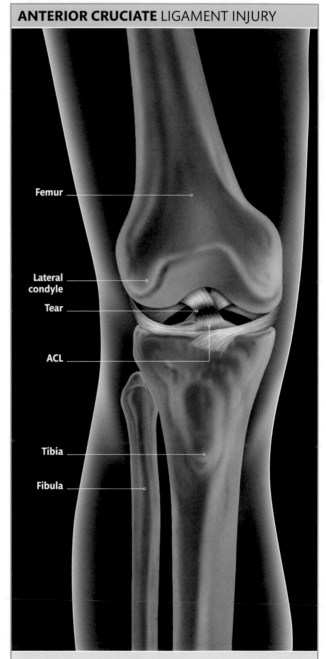

ANTERIOR CRUCIATE LIGAMENT INJURY

Femur

Lateral condyle

Tear

ACL

Tibia

Fibula

The ACL attaches to the "bulge" (the lateral condyle) at the base of the femur (thigh bone) at the back of the knee joint, and connects to the top of the tibia at the front. It is vital for stability in the knee, so injuries can be debilitating.

TREATMENT

⊕ SEEK IMMEDIATE MEDICAL ATTENTION

MEDICAL

IMMEDIATE ▶	SHORT TERM ▶	MEDIUM TERM ▶	LONG TERM
■ If you think you may have sprained or ruptured your ACL, you should: ▶ follow a RICE procedure (**》p.170**). ▶ immobilize your knee (**》pp.170–71**). ▶ seek medical attention.	■ If you are diagnosed with a mild ACL sprain, your physician may: ▶ prescribe analgesic medication. ▶ advise you to use crutches until the swelling and pain have gone. ■ If you are diagnosed with a ruptured ACL, your physician may: ▶ recommend physical therapy to help strengthen your muscles prior to surgery. ▶ advise surgery to repair the ACL using tendon tissue from another part of your body.	■ If you have not had surgery, and your injury is healing as expected, your physician may: ▶ refer you to a physical therapist for treatment to help restore painless movement and regain muscle strength and balance (see table below). ■ If your symptoms have failed to respond to non-surgical treatment, your physician may: ▶ recommend surgery to reconstruct the ACL using tendon tissue from another part of your body.	■ After surgery, your physician may: ▶ place your knee in a brace for up to 4 weeks, and possibly advise the use of crutches. ■ Once your brace has been removed, your physician may: ▶ refer you to a physical therapist for a program of rehabilitation (see table below).

PHYSICAL THERAPY

EARLY STAGE ▶	INTERMEDIATE STAGE ▶	ADVANCED STAGE ▶	RETURN TO SPORT
■ Once your physician has referred you, your physical therapist may: ▶ suggest exercises to help you achieve full knee extension (within 7–10 days) and knee flexion of 90 degrees (within 2 weeks). ■ You may begin: ▶ static quadriceps exercises, such as straight-leg raises (**》p.193**); aim for 4 sets x 10 reps—make sure your knee is completely straight. ▶ single-leg stands (**》p.246**), holding left and right for 30 seconds each. ▶ using an electrical muscle stimulator on your quadriceps and calf muscles to maintain muscle bulk. ▶ upper-limb weights (non-weight-bearing) 10 days after your operation. ▶ core-stability exercises, such as dead bugs (**》p.225**).	■ You should now be able to: ▶ carry out daily activities without pain. ■ Your physical therapist may: ▶ check you have 120 degrees' flexion and full hyperextension of your knee (within 3–4 weeks). ■ You may begin: ▶ trying to walk normally without a limp. ▶ walking on a treadmill (once gait is normal) until you can jog without pain. ▶ functional warmup drills, such as Frankenstein walks (**》pp.177**), and exercises such as hip hitchers (**》p.186**). ▶ box step-ups (**》p.203**); aim for 3 sets x 15 reps. ▶ bicycling and work on a cross-trainer and stepper; build to 20 minutes at 80rpm, level 6. ▶ lower-limb strength training; aim for 4 sets x 8–12 reps of barbell squats (**》p.192**) start at 50% of your one-rep max. ▶ balance exercises, such as hand clock drills (**》p.248**).	■ You should now be able to: ▶ demonstrate full range of motion in your knee. ▶ complete high box step-ups (**》p.203**), as pain allows; aim for 4 sets x 6 reps (with a viper band). ■ Your physical therapist may: ▶ assess your single vertical and horizontal hops (**》p.261**) and adapted cross-over hops (**》p.262**) to establish baseline scores. ■ You may begin: ▶ low-level foot plyometrics such as A-walks (**》p.254**). Also try jumps, hops, and landing drills (**》pp.256–59**), pain-free. ▶ low-level running; start by walking and jogging at intervals (**》p.252**), and then begin running at lower than normal effort. Build to running in different directions by performing T-drills (**》p.263**). ▶ isokinetic machine exercises (**》p.263**) at variable speeds; there should only be 10% difference on each side.	■ You should now be able to: ▶ lift leg weights that are at least 80% of your one-rep max without pain. ▶ complete foot plyometrics, such as jumps and hops (**》pp.256–58**), and speed drills (**》pp.252–53**). You should not feel any pain, nor be apprehensive about performing the exercises. ▶ perform single vertical and horizontal hops (**》p.261**), adapted cross-over hops (**》p.262**) and triple hops (**》p.262**); your injured leg should have only 10% less ability than your uninjured leg. ▶ complete a T-test (**》p.263**): aim for 11 seconds if you are male, and 15 seconds if you are female. ▶ complete high-level running at distances relevant to your sport, without pain. ▶ complete sport-specific drills without difficulty. ▶ participate in full training.

COLLATERAL LIGAMENT INJURIES

The medial collateral ligament (MCL) and the lateral collateral ligament (LCL) are two of the main ligaments that strengthen and stabilize the knee joint. The medial ligament prevents the knee from collapsing inward, while the lateral ligament prevents it from collapsing outward. Rupture of these ligaments is most often seen in collision sports, such as football.

CAUSES

A direct blow to the outside of the knee can lead to a rupture of the medial collateral ligament, while ruptures to the lateral collateral ligament are often the result of a direct blow to the back of the knee. These injuries frequently occur in sports such as rugby and soccer, or if athletes put abnormal stress on the knee when running or jumping. Sprains or tears to the knee ligaments are also common.

SYMPTOMS AND DIAGNOSIS

If you have sprained or ruptured either of your collateral ligaments you will have severe pain around the ligament and swelling in your knee. Your knee may feel unstable and painful when you put weight on it, and you may not be able to straighten it. Your physician will make a diagnosis through physical examination and may recommend an MRI scan or X-ray to confirm the diagnosis.

RISKS AND COMPLICATIONS

If untreated, an injury to one of your ligaments could lead to damage to other parts of your knee and result in permanent instability and pain in the joint. If your case is particularly extreme, recurrent instability can cause severe degeneration of the knee cartilage, and osteoarthritis may develop.

WHEN WILL I BE FULLY FIT?

With most injuries to these ligaments, you should be able to return to sports within 2–12 weeks. If you have had surgery, 8–12 months of recovery may be required. If your case is severe – for example, you have a complex injury that affects other parts of your knee – there is a possibility that you may be unable to return to sports that put your knee under stress.

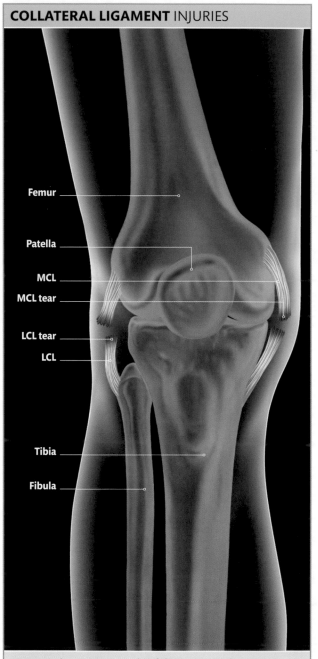

COLLATERAL LIGAMENT INJURIES

Femur
Patella
MCL
MCL tear
LCL tear
LCL
Tibia
Fibula

The MCL (on the inner side of the knee joint) connects the femur (thighbone) to the tibia (shinbone), while the LCL (on the outside of the knee joint) connects the femur to the fibula (calf bone).

TREATMENT

➕ SEEK IMMEDIATE MEDICAL ATTENTION

MEDICAL

IMMEDIATE ▶	SHORT TERM ▶	MEDIUM TERM ▶	LONG TERM
■ If you think you may have injured your MCL or LCL, you should: ▶ stop activity. ▶ follow a RICE procedure (**»p.170**). ▶ immobilize your knee (**»pp.170–71**). ▶ seek medical attention.	■ If you are diagnosed with a mild-to-moderate sprain of the MCL or LCL, your physician may: ▶ put your knee in a brace to stabilize it while it heals. ▶ prescribe analgesic medication. ▶ advise you to use crutches for 2–3 weeks. ■ If you are diagnosed with a severe ligament rupture, your physician may: ▶ recommend surgery to repair the ligament.	■ If you have not had surgery and your injury is healing as expected, your physician may: ▶ refer you to a physical therapist for treatment to improve strength and movement in your knee (see table below). ■ If you have had surgery, your physician may. ▶ monitor your progress to ensure that your injury is healing as expected. ▶ recommend that you wear a brace for up to 6 weeks.	■ After surgery, your physician may: ▶ refer you to a physical therapist for a program of rehabilitation (see table below).

PHYSICAL THERAPY

EARLY STAGE ▶	INTERMEDIATE STAGE ▶	ADVANCED STAGE ▶	RETURN TO SPORT
■ Once your physician has referred you, your physical therapist may: ▶ suggest exercises, such as heel slides (**»p.179**), to help you bend (flex) your knee to 90 degrees and straighten (extend) it fully. ■ You may begin: ▶ static quadriceps exercises, such as straight-leg raises (**»p.193**); aim for 4 sets x 10 reps—make sure your knee is completely straight. ▶ using an electronic muscle stimulator 4–6 hours daily on your quadriceps, hamstrings, and calf muscles to maintain muscle bulk. ▶ core stability exercises, such as dead bugs (**»p.225**). ▶ upper-limb weights (non-weight-bearing) 10 days after your injury. ▶ basic proprioception exercises, such as single-leg stands (**»p.246**), aiming for 30 seconds.	■ You should now be able to: ▶ walk normally without a limp and with no further swelling. ■ Your physical therapist may: ▶ assess your injured knee to check your flexion is within 10% of your uninjured leg, and that extension for both legs is identical. ■ You may begin: ▶ low box step-ups (**»p.203**); aim for 3 sets x 15 reps. ▶ interval bicycling at a low–medium intensity. ▶ work on a cross-trainer and stepper; build to 20 minutes at 80rpm, level 6. ▶ functional warm-up drills, such as kneeling supermen (**»pp.228–29**) and full-body exercises, such as lawnmowers (**»p.190**). ▶ lower-limb strength training; aim for 4 sets x 8–12 reps barbell squats (**»p.180**), starting at 50% of your one-rep max. ▶ a walk-jog programme (**»p.252**).	■ You should now be able to: ▶ demonstrate a full range of motion in your knee. ▶ complete box step-ups and step-downs (**»p.203**) as pain allows; aim for 4 sets x 6 reps. ■ Your physical therapist may: ▶ test the ability of your ligament—you should not feel any pain, nor be apprehensive about being tested. ▶ assess your single vertical and horizontal hops (**»p.261**) and adapted cross-over hops (**»p.262**) to establish baseline scores. ■ You may begin: ▶ low-level foot plyometrics such as A-walks (**»p.254**). Also try jumping, hopping, and landing drills (**»pp.256–59**). You should not feel any pain. ▶ a low-level running program; start by walking and jogging at intervals (**»p.252**), and then begin running at lower than normal effort. Build up to figure-eights and shuttle-run drills (**»p.253**).	■ You should now be able to: ▶ lift leg weights that are at least 80% of your one-rep max, without pain. ▶ complete foot plyometrics, such as jumps and hops (**»pp.256–58**), and speed drills (**»pp.252–53**), without pain. ▶ perform single vertical and horizontal hops (**»p.261**), adapted cross-over hops (**»p.262**), and triple hops (**»p.262**); your injured leg should have only 10% less ability than your uninjured one. ▶ complete a T-test (**»p.263**); aim for 11 seconds if you are male, and 15 seconds if you are female. ▶ complete high-level running at distances relevant to your sport, without pain. ▶ complete sport-specific drills without difficulty. ▶ participate in full training for at least 1–2 weeks.

POSTERIOR CRUCIATE LIGAMENT INJURY

The posterior cruciate ligament (PCL) is one of four main ligaments that work together to strengthen and stabilize the knee joint. Its role is to prevent the femur (thighbone) from sliding over the tibia (shinbone), as well as to prevent the knee from overextending. Direct blows to the tibia can cause a strain or rupture of this ligament.

CAUSES

Knee ligament injuries commonly occur in contact sports, such as football and rugby, as a result of impact or sudden twisting movements. Damage or tears to the posterior cruciate ligament are often caused by a direct blow to the tibia that is sustained when the knee is in a flexed position with the foot firmly planted on the ground, perhaps during a football tackle.

SYMPTOMS AND DIAGNOSIS

You will feel severe pain in the knee, sometimes with swelling in the joint. Putting weight on the injured knee will be painful, and it may also feel unstable, or even "give way" when you are going downstairs, or down a hill. You may be unable to straighten your leg at the knee. After a time you may experience ongoing grating, cracking, or popping sounds (known as crepitus), as well as pain, in the joint. Your physician will usually make his initial diagnosis through a physical examination—this diagnosis is likely to be confirmed with an MRI scan. He may use an X-ray to check whether you have damaged your bones.

RISKS AND COMPLICATIONS

If left untreated, an injury to your posterior cruciate ligament can lead to further damage to other structures in your knee, and to permanent instability and pain in the joint.

WHEN WILL I BE FULLY FIT?

For less severe injuries, you should be able to return to sports within 2–12 weeks. If you have had surgery, 8–12 months may be required. If your injury is severe and includes damage to other knee structures, you may not be able to return to sports that involve excessive stress being put on your knee joint.

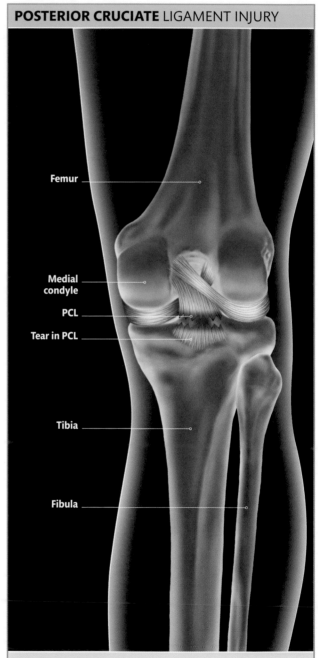

POSTERIOR CRUCIATE LIGAMENT INJURY

Femur

Medial condyle

PCL

Tear in PCL

Tibia

Fibula

The PCL is one of the four major ligaments of the knee. It runs from the back of the tibia, travels through the knee joint, and attaches to the inner protrusion (the medial condyle) on the base of the femur.

TREATMENT

➕ SEEK IMMEDIATE MEDICAL ATTENTION

MEDICAL

IMMEDIATE
- If you think you may have a PCL injury, you should:
  ▶ immobilize your knee (**pp.170–71**).
  ▶ follow a RICE procedure (**p.170**).
  ▶ seek medical attention.

SHORT TERM
- If you are diagnosed with a PCL injury, your physician may:
  ▶ advise you to use crutches until the pain and swelling have gone.
  ▶ place your knee in a brace to stabilize it while it heals, and until the pain and swelling have gone.
- If you are diagnosed with a ruptured ligament, your physician may:
  ▶ recommend surgery to repair the ligament.

MEDIUM TERM
- If you have not had surgery, and your injury is healing as expected, your physician may:
  ▶ refer you to a physical therapist for treatment to restore knee movement and regain muscle strength, particularly for the quadriceps, and balance (see table below).
- If, after a period of time, your PCL does not respond to treatment and the knee remains unstable, your physician may:
  ▶ recommend surgery to repair the ligament.

LONG TERM
- After surgery, your physician may:
  ▶ place your leg in a brace for 2–3 weeks.
- Once the brace has been removed, your physician may:
  ▶ refer you to a physical therapist for a program of rehabilitation (see table below).

PHYSICAL THERAPY

EARLY STAGE
- Once your physician has referred you, your physical therapist may:
  ▶ advise exercises to help you bend your knee to 90 degrees and straighten it fully.
- You may begin:
  ▶ static quadriceps exercises, such as straight-leg raises (**p.193**); aim for 4 sets x 10 reps—ensure that your knee is completely straight.
  ▶ single leg stands (**p.246**), holding left and right for 30 seconds each.
  ▶ using an electrical muscle stimulator on your quadriceps and calf muscles to maintain muscle bulk.
  ▶ upper-limb weights (non-weight-bearing) 10 days after your injury.
  ▶ core-stability exercises, such as pulley chops (**p.230–31**) and pulley lifts (**pp.232–33**).

INTERMEDIATE STAGE
- You should now be able to:
  ▶ walk normally with no limp and no increased swelling.
- Your physical therapist may:
  ▶ assess your knee's range of motion; your injured knee should have only 10% less ability than your uninjured knee.
- You may begin:
  ▶ deep-water running; aim for up to 30 minutes, at high intensity intervals.
  ▶ warmup drills, such as kneeling supermen (**pp.228–29**) and full-body exercises, such as pike walks (**p.177**).
  ▶ box step-ups (**p.203**); aim for 3 x 15 reps.
  ▶ cycling and work on a cross-trainer and stepper; build to 20 minutes at 80rpm, level 6.
  ▶ lower-limb strength training, such as barbell squats (**p.180**); start at 50% of your one-rep max and aim for 4 x 8–12 reps.
  ▶ balance exercises, such as foot clock drills (**p.248**).

ADVANCED STAGE
- You should now be able to:
  ▶ demonstrate a full range of motion in your knee.
  ▶ complete high box step-ups (**p.203**), as pain allows; aim for 4 sets x 6 reps.
- Your physical therapist may:
  ▶ assess your single vertical and horizontal hops (**p.261**) and adapted cross-over hops (**p.262**) to establish baseline scores.
  ▶ test the ability of your PCL ligament—you should not feel any pain, nor feel apprehensive at being tested.
- You may begin:
  ▶ low-level foot plyometrics such as straight-leg scratches (**p.256**). Also try jumps, hops, and landing drills (**pp.256–59**), if pain-free.
  ▶ a low-level running programme: start by walking and jogging at intervals (**p.252**), and then begin running at lower than normal effort. Build to running in a figure-8.

RETURN TO SPORT
- You should now be able to:
  ▶ lift leg weights that are at least 80% of your one-rep max, without pain.
  ▶ complete foot plyometrics, such as jumps and hops (**pp.256–59**), and speed drills (**pp.252–53**), without pain.
  ▶ perform single vertical and horizontal hops (**p.261**), adapted cross-over hops (**p.262**), and triple hops (**p.262**); your injured leg should have only 10% less ability than your uninjured one.
  ▶ complete a T-test (**p.263**): aim for 11 seconds if you are male and 15 if you are female.
  ▶ complete high-level running at distances relevant to your sport, without pain.
  ▶ complete sport-specific drills without difficulty.
  ▶ participate in full training.

MENISCUS TEAR

Meniscus tears are among the most common knee injuries. Their severity can range from minor tears that cause only slight discomfort and grind away until they become smooth, to more severe cases that inhibit the joint's function and may require surgery.

CAUSES

Meniscus tears are commonly associated with sports such as basketball and soccer, and are usually the result of forceful twisting of the leg when the foot is planted on the ground and the knee is flexed. Sometimes a direct blow to the knee can cause damage. Menisci become less resilient with age, so simple rotation of the knee may be enough to cause damage in older people.

SYMPTOMS AND DIAGNOSIS

You will feel pain in one side of your knee and there may be swelling. You may hear a clicking noise when you bend your knee and you may not be able to put weight on your affected leg. Your knee may feel as if it is locking or giving way, and could lock completely if a torn meniscus part-displaces into your knee. Your physician will diagnose your condition through a physical examination of your knee, and may recommend an MRI scan to confirm the diagnosis.

RISKS AND COMPLICATIONS

A torn meniscus may leave your knee joint with jagged edges and loose pieces of cartilage. If left untreated these can cause the cartilage at the ends of your tibia (shinbone), femur (thighbone), and patella (kneecap) to become worn, possibly leading to arthritis. In the case of surgery (meniscectomy), the aim is to preserve as much of your meniscus as possible because total removal may lead to further degeneration and future osteoarthritis.

WHEN WILL I BE FULLY FIT?

In most cases, you will recover after nonsurgical treatment within 2–4 weeks. If you have had part of your meniscus removed with surgery, you should recover in around 5–8 weeks. A full surgical repair of your meniscus may mean a delay in your return to sport of approximately 3–4 months.

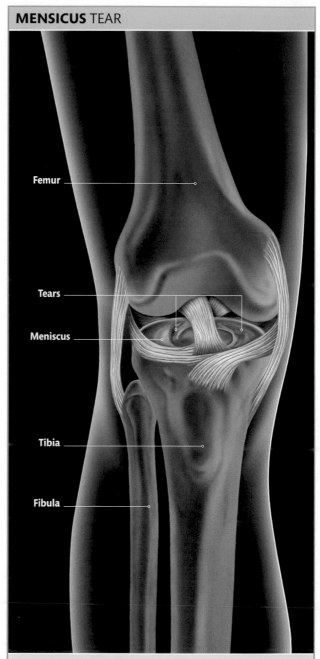

MENSICUS TEAR

Femur

Tears

Meniscus

Tibia

Fibula

The two menisci in the knee are made up of tough cartilage, and act as cushions between the tibia and the femur. They reduce friction, provide shock absorption, and distribute weight evenly across the knee.

TREATMENT

✚ SEEK IMMEDIATE MEDICAL ATTENTION

MEDICAL	IMMEDIATE ▶	SHORT TERM ▶	MEDIUM TERM ▶	LONG TERM
	■ If you think you may have a meniscus tear, you should: ▶ stop activity. ▶ follow a RICE procedure (»p.170). ▶ seek medical attention.	■ If you have been diagnosed with a meniscus tear, your physician may: ▶ advise you to rest your knee completely for 3–4 weeks. ▶ advise you to use crutches. ■ If your knee is locked as a result of your injury, your physician may: ▶ recommend surgery to repair the damaged tissue, or, if the injury is severe, to remove it.	■ If, after 3–4 weeks of nonsurgical treatment, your injury is healing as expected, your physician may: ▶ refer you to a physical therapist for treatment to improve muscle strength (see table below). ■ If your symptoms have failed to respond after 3–4 weeks of nonsurgical treatment, your physician may: ▶ recommend surgery to repair the damaged tissue, or, if the injury is severe, to remove it.	■ After surgery, your physician may: ▶ refer you to a physical therapist for a program of rehabilitation (see table below).

PHYSICAL THERAPY	EARLY STAGE ▶	INTERMEDIATE STAGE ▶	ADVANCED STAGE ▶	RETURN TO SPORT
	■ Once your physician has referred you, your physical therapist may: ▶ use an electrical muscle stimulator on your quadriceps, hamstrings, and calf muscles to maintain muscle bulk. ■ You may begin: ▶ straight-leg raises (»p.193); aim for 4 sets x 10 reps, ensuring that your leg is completely straight. ▶ single-leg stands (»p.246), standing on your left and right legs for 30 seconds each. ▶ deep-water pool running, once your wounds have healed; aim for 20–30 minutes, at high-intensity intervals. ▶ stationary bicycling for 20 minutes at 85rpm, level 6. ▶ core-stability exercises, such as dead bugs (»p.225). ▶ upper-limb weights (non-weight-bearing) 10 days after the operation.	■ You should now be able to: ▶ fully flex and extend your knee with minimal swelling. ■ You may begin: ▶ trying to walk with no limp. ▶ a walk-jog programme (»p.252). ▶ practicing squats (»p.180) with an electrical muscle stimulator strapped to your leg; aim to squat to 90 degrees. ▶ box step-ups (»p.203); aim for 3 sets x 15 reps. ▶ lower-limb strength training, as long as you have no pain or increase in swelling. Start at 50% of your one-rep max and aim for 4 sets x 8–12 reps of barbell squats (»p.192) and Romanian deadlifts (»p.196). ▶ interval bicycling at a low–medium intensity. ▶ work on a cross-trainer and stepper, as pain allows; build to 20 minutes at 80rpm, level 6.	■ You should now be able to: ▶ demonstrate a full range of motion in your knee with no swelling. ▶ complete low-level foot plyometrics, such as jumping and hopping (»pp.256–259), without pain. ■ Your physical therapist may: ▶ assess your single vertical and horizontal hops (»p.261) and your adapted cross-over hops (»p.262) for baseline scores. ■ You may begin: ▶ high box step-ups (»p.203), as pain allows; aim for 4 sets x 6 reps. You may use a viper band. ▶ low-level running; start at 50-60% effort, building to 60-70% effort. Try figure-eight running drills (»p.253) at 60-70% effort.	■ You should now be able to: ▶ lift leg weights that are at least 80% of your one-rep max, without pain. ▶ complete speed drills (»pp.252–253), without pain. ▶ perform single vertical and horizontal hops (»p.261), adapted cross-over hops (»p.262), and triple hops (»p.262); your injured side should have only 10% less ability than your uninjured side. ▶ complete a T-test (»p.263); aim for 11 seconds if you are male, and 15 seconds if you are female. ▶ complete high-level running at distances relevant to your sport, without pain. ▶ complete sport-specific drills without difficulty. ▶ participate in full training.

ILIOTIBIAL BAND SYNDROME

The iliotibial band (ITB) is involved in extending (straightening) the knee, moving the hip sideways, and stabilizing the leg during running. Overuse of this tendon can cause iliotibial band syndrome, in which the ilitiobial band becomes painful.

CAUSES
This condition is common in sports such as running, bicycling, or rowing, which can overuse the iliotibial band. It is caused by repetitive rubbing of this tendon over the outside of the femur (thighbone) close to the knee, and repeated bending of the knee. This causes friction, followed by inflammation and pain in the tendon; inflammation of the bursa (a fluid-filled sac) beneath the tendon can also occur. Iliotibial band syndrome may also result from athletes overtraining, from muscle imbalance, for example when running repeatedly on an uneven surface, incorrect running technique, and changes to a training routine.

SYMPTOMS AND DIAGNOSIS
The first sign of iliotibial band syndrome may be pain on the outside of your knee, particularly when walking down stairs. Running may make the pain worse, especially when going downhill. You may also notice a swelling or thickening of the tissue, or tightness, around the outside of your upper leg. Your knee may also be painful when you bend or straighten it and you may experience weakness when you move your hips sideways. Your physician will usually make a diagnosis by assessing your symptoms, although an ultrasound or an MRI scan may be recommended to confirm the diagnosis.

RISKS AND COMPLICATIONS
If iliotibial band syndrome is left untreated, you may experience persistent long-term pain in your knee and hip.

WHEN WILL I BE FULLY FIT?
ITB syndrome should clear up with rest and analgesic medication, and you should recover fully within 8 weeks. On the rare occasions that surgery is necessary, most people recover fully within 8 weeks of the operation.

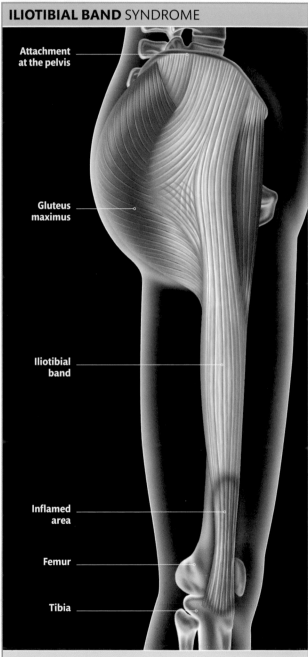

ILIOTIBIAL BAND SYNDROME

Attachment at the pelvis

Gluteus maximus

Iliotibial band

Inflamed area

Femur

Tibia

ITB syndrome affects the iliotibial band—a long, thick, tendonlike structure that runs from the pelvis down the outside of the femur to just below the knee, where it connects to the tibia (shin bone).

TREATMENT

	IMMEDIATE	SHORT TERM	MEDIUM TERM	LONG TERM
MEDICAL	■ If you think you may have ITB syndrome, you should: ▶ stop any activity that causes or increases the pain. ▶ follow a RICE procedure (»p.170). ▶ seek medical attention.	■ If you are diagnosed with ITB syndrome, your physician may: ▶ advise you to rest. ▶ prescribe analgesic medication. ▶ recommend you continue to follow a RICE procedure until the pain improves. ▶ refer you to a physical therapist for treatment to stretch your ITB, correct muscle imbalance, and improve muscle strength (see table below).	■ If your symptoms have not improved within a month, despite rest and short-term treatment, your physician may: ▶ give you an injection of corticosteroids into the area to relieve pain. ▶ recommend some manual therapy techniques, such as massage by a trained therapist, or self-massage.	■ In very rare circumstances, if all nonsurgical treatment fails, your physician may: ▶ recommend surgery to lengthen your ITB in order to reduce friction. ■ After surgery, your physician may: ▶ refer you to a physical therapist for a program of rehabilitation (see table below).

	EARLY STAGE	INTERMEDIATE STAGE	ADVANCED STAGE	RETURN TO SPORT
PHYSICAL THERAPY	■ Once your physician has referred you, your physical therapist may: ▶ suggest various treatments, such as electrotherapy, to reduce inflammation. ▶ assess the intensity and duration of your normal training program and correct accordingly. ▶ perform a foot and ankle assessment to see if you need insoles or orthotics to support your medial arch, or if you need different footwear. ▶ use soft-tissue massage on your ITB, quadriceps, hamstrings, and gluteals, to help relieve your symptoms. ■ You may begin: ▶ self-massage of your iliotibial band with a hard foam roller (»p.191). Aim for 6 reps x 30 secs on each leg daily, even if it is painful. ▶ core-stability and gluteal exercises, such as side planks (»p.226), to maintain your overall fitness; stop if you feel any pain.	■ You should now be able to: ▶ perform weight-bearing gluteal exercises, such as step-up and holds (»p.250), without pain. ■ Your physical therapist may: ▶ assess the length of your quadriceps, hamstrings, hip flexors, and calf muscles to check that they are symmetrical. ■ You may begin: ▶ functional warm-up drills, such as overhead lunges (»p.181), full-body exercises, such as Swiss ball jack-knives (»p.190), and low-level foot plyometrics, such as straight-leg circles-out (»p.255). ▶ low-level running and sporting activities, as pain allows. ▶ bicycling, and working on the cross-trainer and stepper, as pain allows; build toward 20 minutes at 80rpm, level 6.	■ You should now be able to: ▶ complete low-level running, without pain. ▶ perform lower-limb strength training, with no pain and no increase in swelling; aim for 4 sets x 8–12 reps of Bulgarian dumbbell split squats (»p.194) and Romanian deadlifts (»p.196); start at 50% of your one-rep max. ▶ perform running drills, such as T-drills (»p.263) and sprints.	■ You should now be able to: ▶ lift leg weights that are at least 80% of your one-rep max, without pain. ▶ do foot plyometrics, such as jumps and hops (»pp.256–58), and speed drills (»pp.252–53), without pain. ▶ complete high-level running at distances relevant to your sport, without pain. ▶ complete sport-specific drills without difficulty. ▶ participate in full training.

LOWER LEG FRACTURE

The two bones of the leg, the tibia (shinbone) and fibula (calfbone), often sustain fractures. The tibia, which is the second-longest bone in the body, gets broken more often than any other long bone.

CAUSES

Any strong force, direct or indirect, applied to the tibia and fibula can cause a fracture. In contact sports, this may be the impact of a direct blow to the leg by another player; it can also occur if a player's foot is firmly planted on the ground and the leg is twisted. In skiing, when the binding attached to the ski does not release in a fall and enough force is applied, both bones will snap just above the top of the boot.

SYMPTOMS AND DIAGNOSIS

You will feel severe pain and be unable to put any weight on your leg. If the fracture has displaced the bones or soft tissue and torn open the skin, you will be able to see a visible deformity. Your knee may be tense and stiff, while your foot may be pale and cool, indicating a disruption to the blood supply, or numb, indicating nerve injury. Your physician will make a diagnosis by assessing your symptoms and examining your leg. You will be given an X-ray to ascertain the severity and location of the fracture.

RISKS AND COMPLICATIONS

If you break both bones, your leg will be highly unstable. A severe fracture of the tibia with torn skin, soft tissue loss, and damage to the blood vessels, nerves, and ligaments, carries a high risk of complication and infection, and you will need emergency surgery. The blood supply in some areas of the tibia is sparse, so it tends to heal slowly and poorly. If the bone has not been properly set, your leg may be disfigured and may not return to full function, with limited mobility in your knee, ankle, and foot joints. You may experience further complications including long-term pain in your leg or compartment syndrome (»p.139).

WHEN WILL I BE FULLY FIT?

Depending on the nature of your fracture, after removal of the cast or after surgery, you may need a further 6–12 months' intensive supervised rehabilitation before you will be able to return to your sport.

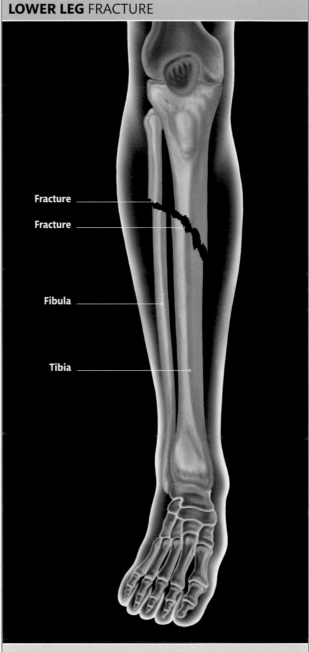

LOWER LEG FRACTURE

Fracture

Fracture

Fibula

Tibia

The tibia and fibula run together between the knee and the ankle. Because there is only a thin layer of skin protecting the front of the tibia, fractures are often open, with bony fragments breaking through the skin.

TREATMENT

⊕ SEEK IMMEDIATE MEDICAL ATTENTION

MEDICAL

IMMEDIATE ▶	SHORT TERM ▶	MEDIUM TERM ▶	LONG TERM
■ If you think you may have fractured your leg, you should: ▶ immobilize your leg (»p.171). ▶ avoid putting any weight on your leg. ▶ seek medical attention.	■ If you are diagnosed with a simple fracture, with no soft tissue affected, your physician may: ▶ put your leg in a cast and advise you to use crutches for at least 2 months. ▶ prescribe analgesic medication. ■ If you are diagnosed with a more complicated fracture, with some damage to the soft tissue, your physician may: ▶ recommend emergency surgery to realign the bone fragments.	■ If you need surgery, but your leg is too swollen to operate, your physician may: ▶ immobilize your leg, either in a splint or a cast, and delay surgery until your soft tissue has recovered. ■ If you have had surgery, your physician may: ▶ advise you to keep your leg elevated while it is healing, to avoid swelling. It may be placed in either a splint or a cast for several weeks.	■ After you have recovered from surgery, your physician may: ▶ refer you to a physical therapist for a program of rehabilitation (see table below).

PHYSICAL THERAPY

EARLY STAGE ▶	INTERMEDIATE STAGE ▶	ADVANCED STAGE ▶	RETURN TO SPORT
■ Once your physician has referred you, your physical therapist may: ▶ suggest various treatments to help alleviate your symptoms. ■ You may begin: ▶ putting weight on your leg and trying to walk normally without limping. ▶ stationary bicycling; aim for 20 minutes at 85rpm, level 6. ▶ deep-water running; aim for up to 30 minutes at high-intensity intervals. ▶ core-stability exercises, such as dead bugs (»p.225).	■ You should now be able to: ▶ demonstrate full range of motion in your hip, knee, foot, and ankle, without pain. ▶ put full weight on your leg, without pain. ■ You may begin: ▶ walking on a treadmill until you are able to jog without pain. ■ You may begin: ▶ lower-limb bodyweight exercises, such as single-leg squats (»p.193). You should not feel any pain. ▶ functional warm-up drills, such as kneeling supermen (»pp.228–29), full-body exercises such as lawnmowers (»p.190), and low-level foot plyometrics, such as walking pop-ups (»p.254). ▶ interval bicycling at a low–medium intensity. ▶ a walk-jog drill (»p.252).	■ You should now be able to: ▶ complete low-level running, without pain. ■ You may begin: ▶ moderate- to high-level foot plyometrics, such as straight-leg circles-in and -out (»p.255); ▶ interval bicycling at a high intensity. ▶ lower-limb strength training; start at 50% of your one-rep max; aim for 4 sets x 8–12 reps of barbell squats (»p.180). ▶ stationary low-level skills, such as ball handling. ▶ low-level running.	■ You should now be able to: ▶ lift leg weights that are at least 80% of your one-rep max, without pain. ▶ complete foot plyometrics, such as jumps and hops (»pp.256–58), and speed drills (»pp.252–53), without pain. ▶ perform single vertical and horizontal hops (»p.261), adapted cross-over hops (»p.262), and triple hops (»p.262); your injured side should have only 10% less ability than your uninjured side. ▶ complete high-level running at distances relevant to your sport, without pain. ▶ complete sport-specific drills without difficulty. ▶ participate in full training.

CALF INJURIES

The group of muscles that make up the calf provide the power for extending the foot and raising the heel. Explosive contractions of these muscles can cause strains and, less commonly, a rupture of the muscle fibers.

CAUSES

Calf muscle strains are common in sports like athletics or soccer, which involve repeated explosive activities such as sprinting or jumping; or in sports in which athletes push against resistance, for example in weight lifting and in rugby. In both cases an abrupt, forceful contraction occurs, causing strain to the tendons or muscles. Ruptures of the calf usually occur to the gastrocnemius muscle, and are the result of a massive contraction of that muscle, usually when jumping, landing, or accelerating.

SYMPTOMS AND DIAGNOSIS

If you strain your calf muscle, you may have tightness, stiffness, pain, and swelling in your leg. If you have ruptured your gastrocnemius muscle, you may hear a sound similar to the cracking of a whip at the time of injury. Your physician will make a diagnosis through physical examination of your leg, and confirm the extent of the injury with an MRI or ultrasound scan.

RISKS AND COMPLICATIONS

If you think you have damaged your calf, you should always consult a physician as there is a risk that blood clots may form in your leg. In the long term, a severe strain or rupture of the calf muscle may lead you to adjust your running or walking technique, causing injuries in other parts of your body.

WHEN WILL I BE FULLY FIT?

After a calf strain, you should be able to resume sport within 3-12 weeks, depending on the severity of the injury. If you have ruptured one of the muscles in your calf, and have had surgery as a result, it may take 6-9 months for you to recover full fitness.

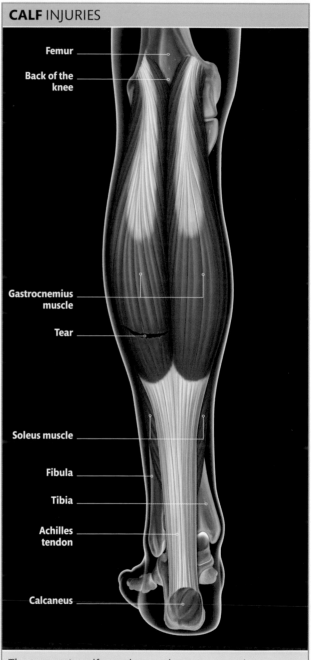

CALF INJURIES

- Femur
- Back of the knee
- Gastrocnemius muscle
- Tear
- Soleus muscle
- Fibula
- Tibia
- Achilles tendon
- Calcaneus

The two main calf muscles are the gastrocnemius, originating at the femur (thighbone), and the soleus, which sits above the tibia and fibula (leg bones). Both connect to the calcaneus (heel bone) via the Achilles tendon.

TREATMENT

➕ SEEK IMMEDIATE MEDICAL ATTENTION

MEDICAL

IMMEDIATE ▶	SHORT TERM ▶	MEDIUM TERM ▶	LONG TERM
■ If you think you may have injured your calf, you should: ▶ follow a RICE procedure (**»p.170**). ▶ seek medical attention.	■ If you are diagnosed with calf strain, your physician may: ▶ prescribe analgesic medication. ▶ advise you to rest until the pain has subsided. ▶ refer you to a physical therapist for treatment to stretch and strengthen the muscle (see table below). ■ If a ruptured calf muscle is diagnosed, your physician may: ▶ recommend surgery to repair the muscle.	■ If you have had surgery for a ruptured calf muscle, your physician may: ▶ put your leg in a cast for 6–8 weeks. ▶ advise you to use crutches, but to put as much weight on your leg as you can bear. ■ After your cast has been removed, your physician may: ▶ refer you to a physical therapist for a program of rehabilitation (see table below).	■ If your injury has not healed after 6 months of nonsurgical treatment, your physician may: ▶ recommend surgery to repair the muscle. ■ After surgery, your physician may: ▶ put your leg in a cast for 6–8 weeks. ▶ advise you to use crutches, but to put as much weight on your leg as you can bear. ■ After your cast has been removed, your physician may: ▶ refer you to a physical therapist for a program of rehabilitation (see table below).

PHYSICAL THERAPY

EARLY STAGE ▶	INTERMEDIATE STAGE ▶	ADVANCED STAGE ▶	RETURN TO SPORT
■ Once your physician has referred you, your physical therapist may: ▶ suggest raising and lowering your foot at the ankle joint to test your range of motion, as pain allows (**»p.179**). ■ You may begin: ▶ resistance exercises that test the foot in a downward direction (but without actually moving the joint), as pain allows. ▶ deep-water pool jogging for up to 30 minutes, as pain allows. ▶ gentle interval bicycling and working on a cross-trainer and stepper, as pain allows; build toward 20 minutes at 80rpm, level 6. ▶ core stability exercises, such as dead bugs (**»p.225**). ▶ calf raises (**»p.204**); start on a flat surface, gradually working toward the edge of a step.	■ You should now be able to: ▶ go up and down stairs with no discomfort. ■ You may begin: ▶ gentle calf stretches (**»p.243**); aim for 2 reps x 30 secs, 4 times daily. ▶ single-leg calf raises (**»p.204**) over the edge of a step; aim for 5 sets x 8–10 reps. ▶ functional warm-up drills such as walking lunges (**»p.180**), full-body exercises such as lawnmowers (**»p.190**), and low-level foot plyometrics such as A-walks (**»p.254**). ▶ box step-ups (**»p.203**); aim for 4 sets x 6 reps. ▶ interval bicycling at a moderate–high intensity. ▶ lower-limb strength training; start at 50% of your one-rep max and aim for 4 sets x 8–12 reps of barbell squats (**»p.192**) and Romanian deadlifts (**»p.196**).	■ You should now be able to: ▶ complete high-level sideways drills, such as carioca sidesteps (**»p.188**). ▶ participate in normal training warm-ups. ■ You may begin: ▶ low-level running; start at 50–60% effort, building to 60–70% effort. Also try figure-eight running (**»p.253**). ▶ single vertical and horizontal hops (**»p.261**) and adapted cross-over hops (**»p.262**); your injured leg should have only 10% less ability than your uninjured one. ▶ bent-knee eccentric calf drops (**»p.205**); aim for 3 sets x 15 reps. ▶ straight-knee eccentric calf drops (**»p.205**); aim for 4 sets x 8 reps.	■ You should now be able to: ▶ demonstrate a full active range of motion in your toe. ▶ lift leg weights that are at least 80% of your one-rep max. ▶ complete normal foot plyometrics, such as jumps and hops (**»pp.256–59**), and speed drills (**»pp.252–53**), without pain. ▶ complete high-level running at distances relevant to your sport, without pain. ▶ complete sport-specific drills without difficulty. ▶ participate in full training for at least 1–2 weeks, without pain.

SHIN SPLINTS

Shin splints is a general term that is often used to describe exercise-induced pain felt in the front of the lower leg.

CAUSES
Shin splints may have various causes but it is usually a result of exercise. Failure to warm up properly before running, or an abrupt increase in training intensity, can lead to shin splints, as can running on hard or inclined surfaces, poor technique, or foot abnormalities that place stress on the leg. It can also be caused by compartment syndrome (see opposite).

SYMPTOMS AND DIAGNOSIS
You may feel a dull ache on the inner side of your shin that intensifies when you begin exercise. There may also be swelling. Your physician will diagnose the condition through physical examination, and rule out other conditions with an MRI.

RISKS AND COMPLICATIONS
Untreated shin splints may stop you from doing any running. In serious cases it may cause stress fractures of the tibia.

WHEN WILL I BE FULLY FIT?
You should be fully fit within 3–6 months. In rare cases, you may require surgery, in which case your recovery time will be 3 months.

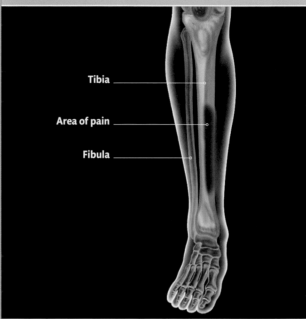

SHIN SPLINTS

Tibia

Area of pain

Fibula

The medical name for this inflammatory condition is medial tibial stress syndrome. Pain is felt at the front of the leg, over the inner part of the tibia (shin bone).

TREATMENT

MEDICAL

IMMEDIATE
■ If you think you may have shin splints, you should: ▶ follow a RICE procedure (**》p.170**). ■ If your symptoms continue for more than 2–3 weeks, you should: ▶ seek medical attention.

SHORT TERM
■ If you are diagnosed with shin splints, your physician may: ▶ prescribe analgesic medication. ▶ refer you to a physical therapist for treatment (see table right).

MEDIUM TERM
■ If your condition fails to respond to physical therapy and your pain is severe, your physician may: ▶ recommend surgery to relieve pressure on your calf muscles.

LONG TERM
■ After surgery, your physician may: ▶ recommend shock wave therapy. ▶ refer you to a physical therapist for a program of rehabilitation (see table right).

PHYSICAL THERAPY

EARLY STAGE
■ Once your physician has referred you, your physical therapist may: ▶ use manual and soft tissue therapy to help relieve your symptoms; do a full biomechanical assessment.

INTERMEDIATE STAGE
■ You should now be able to: ▶ stretch both calf muscles equally. ▶ perform moderate-intensity bibicycling, without pain. ■ You may begin: ▶ warm-ups, such as walking lunges (**》p.180**). ▶ full-body exercises, such as push-ups (**》pp.228–29**). ▶ low-level foot plyometric exercises, such as A-walks (**》p.254**).

ADVANCED STAGE
■ You should now be able to: ▶ perform low-level running, without pain. ■ You may begin: ▶ lower-limb weights training, aim for 4 sets x 8–12 reps at 50% of your one-rep max.

RETURN TO SPORT
■ You should now be able to: ▶ lift lower leg weights at 80% of your one-rep max. ▶ participate in full training, pain-free.

COMPARTMENT SYNDROME

The muscles in the limbs are contained within "compartments," comprised of connective tissue and bone. An increase in pressure within one of these is known as compartment syndrome.

CAUSES
Compartment syndrome can be caused by a one-off injury, such as a bone fracture or tearing of the muscle, which might occur during contact sports, but is more often the result of long-term overuse as a result of running.

SYMPTOMS AND DIAGNOSIS
You will feel intense pain that persists both at rest and during activity. You may have weakness, tingling, or reduced sensation in the limb. Your physician will make a diagnosis through a physical examination, and perhaps with an MRI scan.

RISKS AND COMPLICATIONS
Untreated, this condition may cause lasting nerve and muscle damage (or muscle death), and, in rare cases, loss of the limb. It can also cause the onset of shin splints (see opposite).

WHEN WILL I BE FULLY FIT?
If it is caught early, recovery rates for this condition are good and you should be able to return to your sport in 4–6 weeks. If you have had surgery, recovery may take 1–3 months.

COMPARTMENT SYNDROME

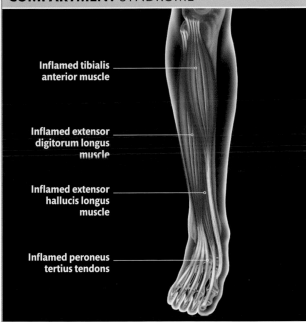

Inflamed tibialis anterior muscle

Inflamed extensor digitorum longus muscle

Inflamed extensor hallucis longus muscle

Inflamed peroneus tertius tendons

This condition most commonly affects the anterior (front) compartment of the lower leg. Swelling within the enclosed area may compress blood vessels and nerves.

TREATMENT SEEK IMMEDIATE MEDICAL ATTENTION

MEDICAL

IMMEDIATE
- If you think you may have compartment syndrome, you should: ▶ rest. ▶ follow a RICE procedure (**》p.170**). ▶ seek medical attention.

SHORT TERM
- If you are diagnosed with compartment syndrome, your physician may: ▶ prescribe analgesic medication. ▶ refer you for compartment pressure testing. ▶ recommend surgery to relieve pressure in the inflamed compartment.

MEDIUM TERM
- After surgery, your physician may: ▶ refer you to a physical therapist for treatment to improve your strength and movement (see table right).

LONG TERM
- After surgery, your physician may: ▶ refer you to a physical therapist for a program of rehabilitation (see table right).

PHYSICAL THERAPY

EARLY STAGE
- You may begin: ▶ nonimpact activities 1 week post-surgery. ▶ upper-limb weights 1 week post-surgery. ▶ core-stability exercises, such as dead bugs (**》p.225**). ▶ low-level bicycling; aim for 20 minutes.

INTERMEDIATE STAGE
- You should now be able to: ▶ exercise a full range of movement in your hip, knee, and ankle. ▶ perform low-moderate level bicycling, without pain.

ADVANCED STAGE
- You should now be able to: ▶ perform your specific sporting activities without pain. ■ You may begin: ▶ lifting lower-limb weights at 50% of your one-rep max. ▶ foot plyometric exercises, such as hurdle jumps (**》pp.257–58**).

RETURN TO SPORT
- You should now be able to: ▶ lift leg weights that are 80% of your one-rep max. ▶ participate in full training without pain.

ACHILLES TENDON RUPTURE

ACHILLES TENDON RUPTURE

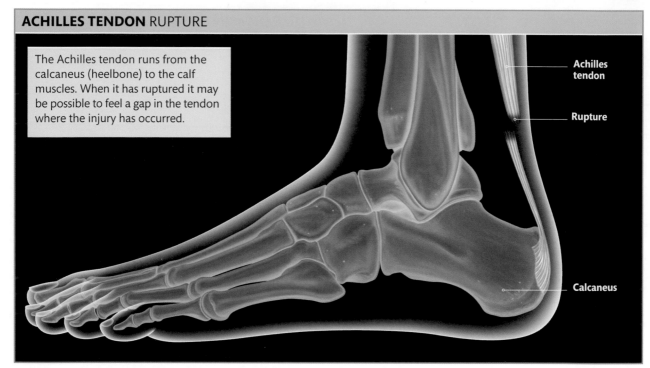

The Achilles tendon runs from the calcaneus (heelbone) to the calf muscles. When it has ruptured it may be possible to feel a gap in the tendon where the injury has occurred.

Achilles tendon

Rupture

Calcaneus

The Achilles tendon is the largest and strongest tendon in the body. It plays an important role in most sports and is particularly vulnerable to overloading. Unsurprisingly, therefore, the Achilles is the most commonly ruptured tendon.

CAUSES

Achilles tendon ruptures mostly occur in sports such as soccer or track and field, which involve repeated sprinting and jumping, or in sports in which athletes push against resistance, such as weight lifting or rugby. In these activities, abrupt, forceful contraction of the calf muscles pulls on the tendon. Ruptures may be partial, although complete ruptures are far more common. The risk of rupture increases if there is an underlying degeneration of the tendon, as in Achilles tendinopathy (»pp.142–43), if you have poor sports technique, or if there is a sudden change in your training pattern.

SYMPTOMS AND DIAGNOSIS

If you sustain an Achilles tendon rupture, you will feel a sudden, usually intense, pain, similar to that of a kick, in your calf. You may have varying degrees of bruising and swelling,

stiffness in your calf and heel, and be unable to stand on tiptoe. In the case of a complete rupture, you may also hear an audible snap, as the tendon tears, and be able to feel a "gap" in your leg at the point of rupture. Your physician will make a diagnosis through an examination of the affected area, and with an X-ray, MRI, or ultrasound scan.

RISKS AND COMPLICATIONS

An untreated partial Achilles rupture can lead to a complete rupture several weeks later. Scar tissue may build up around a partial rupture, resulting in a disabling condition that will cause you chronic pain.

WHEN WILL I BE FULLY FIT?

Ruptures of your Achilles tendon may take up to 10 weeks to heal, depending on the severity of the injury. After a complete rupture, a period of rest and non-weight-bearing will be recommended, and, if you are an athlete, surgery to repair your tendon will be necessary. You may be able to start non-weight-bearing activities, such as swimming, after 8–12 weeks. You can resume your sport 6 months after surgery.

TREATMENT

⊕ SEEK IMMEDIATE MEDICAL ATTENTION

MEDICAL

IMMEDIATE ▶	SHORT TERM ▶	MEDIUM TERM ▶	LONG TERM
■ If you think you may have ruptured your Achilles tendon, you should: ▶ follow a RICE procedure (**»p.170**). ▶ seek medical attention.	■ If you are diagnosed with a ruptured Achilles tendon, your physician may: ▶ recommend surgery to repair the damaged tendon. ▶ advise you to limit the bending of your foot toward your leg (dorsiflexion).	■ After surgery, your physician may: ▶ put your lower leg and foot in a cast or boot for 6–8 weeks, with your foot pointing downward. ▶ give you crutches, but advise you to put as much weight on your foot as you can bear.	■ Your physician may: ▶ refer you to a physical therapist for a program of rehabilitation (see table below).

PHYSICAL THERAPY

EARLY STAGE ▶	INTERMEDIATE STAGE ▶	ADVANCED STAGE ▶	RETURN TO SPORT
■ Once your physician has referred you, your physical therapist may: ▶ massage your calf, 2 weeks after the operation. ▶ advise that you remain with your foot in the boot at all times, apart from when performing your exercises, until at least 8 weeks after the injury. ▶ advise you to increase the range of motion in your ankle gradually over the 8 weeks, but not to stretch the tendon. ■ You may begin: ▶ resistance exercises for your calf that involve no joint movement, as pain allows. ▶ exercising your knees and hips to maintain mobility. ▶ bicycling in your boot, 2–4 weeks after your operation. Build toward 20 minutes at 80rpm, level 6. ▶ core-stability exercises, such as dead bugs (**»p.225**).	■ You should now be able to: ▶ walk in your boot with no limp, fully weight-bearing, at 6–8 weeks. ■ You may begin: ▶ single-leg stands for more than 30 seconds in sneakers on a hard floor (**»p.246**). ▶ trying to walk normally with a ⅓in (1 cm) heel raise in your shoes (8 weeks after operation). ▶ testing your ankle's range of motion, as pain allows. ▶ light resistance exercises, such as pilates reformer exercises (**»p.237**). ▶ calf raises (**»p.204**); start at 50% of your one-rep max and aim for 4 sets x 8–12 reps. ▶ deep-water running, once 90 degrees of ankle flexibility has been achieved. ▶ interval cycling at a low–medium intensity. ▶ work on a cross-trainer and a stepper; build up to 20 minutes at 80rpm, level 6.	■ You should now be able to: ▶ demonstrate a normal walk, but continue to wear a ⅓in (1 cm) heel raise. ■ Your physical therapist may: ▶ assess your single vertical and horizontal hops (**»p.261**) and adapted cross-over hops (**»p.262**) for baseline scores. ■ You may begin: ▶ lower-limb weights, keeping your foot touching the floor. ▶ straight-knee eccentric calf drops (**»p.205**); aim for 3 x 15 reps at 50% bodyweight. ▶ functional warm-up drills, such as Frankenstein walks (**»p.177**), full-body exercises, such as punch lunges (**»p.182**), and low-level foot plyometrics, such as A-walks (**»p.254**). ▶ walking on a treadmill until you can jog without pain; building up to low-level running.	■ You should now be able to: ▶ complete bodyweight bent- and straight-knee eccentric calf drops (**»p.205**); aim for 4 x 8 reps at 100% bodyweight as your extra load. ▶ lift leg weights that are at least 80% of your one-rep max, without pain. ▶ perform single vertical and horizontal hops (**»p.261**) and adapted cross-over hops (**»p.262**); your injured side should have only 10% less ability than your uninjured side. ▶ complete a T-test (**»p.263**); aim for 11 seconds if you are male, and 15 seconds if you are female. ▶ complete foot plyometrics, such as jumps and hops (**»pp.256–59**), and speed drills (**»pp.252–53**), without pain. ▶ complete high-level running without pain. ▶ complete sport-specific drills and full training.

ACHILLES TENDINOPATHY

ACHILLES TENDINOPATHY

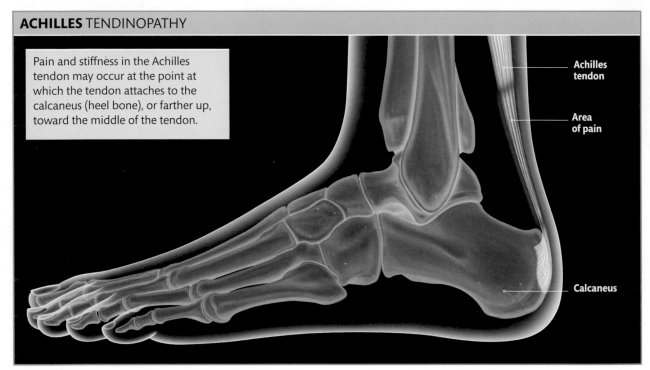

Pain and stiffness in the Achilles tendon may occur at the point at which the tendon attaches to the calcaneus (heel bone), or farther up, toward the middle of the tendon.

Achilles tendon

Area of pain

Calcaneus

Achilles tendinopathy is a degenerative condition characterized by pain and swelling in and around the Achilles tendon at the back of the lower leg.

CAUSES

Achilles tendinopathy is an overuse injury caused by repetitive and excessive stress. It is common in running and jumping sports, such as basketball, soccer, and volleyball. The disorder particularly affects middle-aged people, and is linked to a degeneration of the tendon fibers. Problems with the Achilles tendon can be caused, and worsened, by wearing inappropriate footwear and sudden changes in training patterns. The lack of an effective warm-up may also be a contributing factor.

SYMPTOMS AND DIAGNOSIS

The main symptom of Achilles tendinopathy is pain, which can range from mildly uncomfortable to intense. You may also have swelling and thickening around your tendon. The presentation of the condition, and the type of pain you may experience varies. In some cases, the pain may occur only when you are active, and this could prevent you from participating in your sport. Alternatively, you may experience pain even at rest; you may also have stiffness in your Achilles tendon and lower leg, particularly when getting up in the morning.

RISKS AND COMPLICATIONS

If left untreated, Achilles tendinopathy can produce further degeneration in your tendon and even cause small tears, which may lead to a partial or complete rupture of your Achilles tendon (»pp.140–41).

WHEN WILL I BE FULLY FIT?

A full recovery from Achilles tendinopathy takes several weeks at best. With prompt, appropriate treatment, you are unlikely to require surgery or suffer long-term problems, but even if your symptoms improve, you are at risk of developing another bout of tendinopathy in the future.

TREATMENT

➕ SEEK IMMEDIATE MEDICAL ATTENTION

	IMMEDIATE ▶	SHORT TERM ▶	MEDIUM TERM ▶	LONG TERM
MEDICAL	■ If you think you may have Achilles tendinopathy, you should: ▸ follow a RICE procedure (**》p.170**). ▸ seek medical attention.	■ If you are diagnosed with Achilles tendinopathy, your physician may: ▸ advise you to rest for 5–10 days. ▸ recommend you wear a boot or brace to limit movement of your ankle (dorsiflexion). ▸ prescribe analgesics. ▸ refer you to a physical therapist for exercises to strengthen the tendon (see table below).	■ If your condition has not responded to treatment, your physician may: ▸ recommend an MRI or ultrasound scan to further investigate the injury.	■ If investigations, such as MRI or ultrasound scans, reveal areas of tendinopathy in your Achilles, your physician may: ▸ recommend ultrasound-guided injections. ▸ recommend surgery to repair the damaged tissues.

	EARLY STAGE ▶	INTERMEDIATE STAGE ▶	ADVANCED STAGE ▶	RETURN TO SPORT
PHYSICAL THERAPY	■ Once your physician has referred you, your physical therapist may: ▸ recommend that you refrain from running for at least 2 weeks after the onset of pain. ■ You may begin: ▸ bent- and straight-knee eccentric calf drops (**》p.205**); aim for 3 x 15 reps, 2 times a day; these exercises are only effective if they produce pain in the Achilles tendon. ▸ seated upper-limb weights, such as bench presses (**》p.210**) and shoulder presses (**》p.211**). ▸ core-stability exercises, such as dead bugs (**》p.225**).	■ You should now feel: minimal tendon pain and stiffness when getting out of bed in the morning. ■ You may begin: ▸ bent- and straight-knee eccentric calf drops (**》p.205**); aim for 3 x 15 reps, 2 times a day, loading with 11 lb increments as they become pain-free. ▸ functional warm-up drills such as walking lunges (**》p.205**), kinetic chain exercises, such as lawnmowers (**》p.190**) and low-level foot plyometrics, such as A-walks (**》p.254**). ▸ lower-limb strength training; start at 50% of your one-rep max and aim for 4 sets x 8–12 reps of barbell squats (**》p.180**). ▸ interval cycling at a low–medium intensity. ▸ work on a cross-trainer and a stepper; build up to 20 minutes at 80rpm, level 6.	■ You should now be able to: ▸ participate in team warm-ups without discomfort. ■ You may begin: ▸ bent- and straight-knee eccentric calf drops (**》p.205**); aim for 3 x 15 reps, 2 times a day, aiming for 100% bodyweight as your extra load. ▸ walking on a treadmill until you can jog without pain; then begin low-level running. ▸ regular lower-limb weights.	■ You should now be able to: ▸ lift leg weights that are at least 80% of your one-rep max, without pain. ▸ perform single vertical and horizontal hops (**》p.261**) and adapted cross-over hops (**》p.262**); your injured side should have only 10% less ability than your uninjured side. ▸ complete foot plyometrics, such as jumps and hops (**》p.256–59**), and speed drills (**》p.252–53**), without pain. ▸ complete high-level running without pain. ▸ complete sport-specific drills and full training.

ANKLE FRACTURE

The ankle is one of the most commonly injured parts of the body. Its complexity makes it vulnerable to fractures, which can involve any number of its constituent parts.

CAUSES
Ankle fractures are not always the result of high-speed impacts and they can even occur during walking. However, sports linked with ankle fractures tend to involve running and changing direction—in tennis, for example—or jumping and landing from a height; all of these can lead to fracturing of the ankle. High-impact sports, such as rugby and soccer, can also lead to fractures, either through forceful twisting of the ankle or an impact to the side of the ankle, during a tackle, for example, when the foot is firmly planted on the ground.

SYMPTOMS AND DIAGNOSIS
After the injury, your ankle will be painful to touch. Bruising, swelling, and skin discoloration may also be present, while your ankle may appear deformed. The severity of ankle fractures can range from undisplaced or minimally displaced stable fractures (your fractured bones have stayed mainly in place), which can be treated nonoperatively, to displaced unstable fractures (your bone has moved out of place), which may require surgery. Your physician will make a diagnosis based on your symptoms, and will also manipulate your ankle and may give you an X-ray to confirm the diagnosis.

RISKS AND COMPLICATIONS
If you continue activity after an ankle fracture, you could sustain further injury, not just to your bones, but to ligaments, muscles, blood vessels, and nerves. Left untreated, your bones may not heal in proper alignment. Even with treatment, complications are common. Damage to the joint surfaces,which, after trauma, are no longer smooth, could lead to the onset of osteoarthritis. You may also be at risk of compartment syndrome (**»p.139**), if the bleeding from your fracture increases pressure in your leg.

WHEN WILL I BE FULLY FIT?
Your ankle will be in a cast for up to 6 weeks. After the cast comes off, you will need to learn to walk properly again. Even after your ankle is healed, you will have to wait up to 6 months before resuming sport, depending on the severity of your fracture.

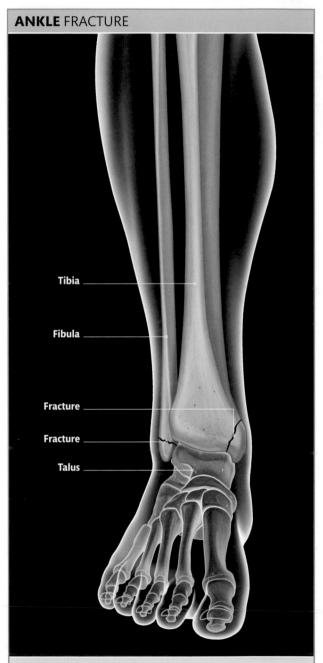

ANKLE FRACTURE

Tibia

Fibula

Fracture

Fracture

Talus

The ankle joint connects the tibia (shinbone) and fibula (calfbone) to the talus—an important bone in the foot. It is a very complex joint in which many bones come together.

TREATMENT

✚ SEEK IMMEDIATE MEDICAL ATTENTION

MEDICAL

IMMEDIATE ▶

- If you think you may have fractured your ankle, you should:
  ▶ stop activity.
  ▶ immobilize the joint (》pp.170–71).
  ▶ follow a RICE procedure (》p.170).
  ▶ seek medical attention.

SHORT TERM ▶

- If you are diagnosed with a mild fracture, your physician may:
  ▶ put your ankle into a splint until the swelling goes down, then replace it with a cast.
  ▶ advise you to use crutches.
  ▶ prescribe analgesic medication.
- If you are diagnosed with a fracture in which the bone has moved, your physician may:
  ▶ reposition your ankle before putting on the cast.
  ▶ suggest surgery.

MEDIUM TERM ▶

- If your ankle is healing as expected after 6 weeks in a cast, your physician may:
  ▶ refer you to a physical therapist for exercises to strengthen the joint (see table below).
- If your fracture has failed to heal after 6 weeks in a cast, your physician may:
  ▶ recommend surgery to fix the broken bones in the correct place.

LONG TERM

- After surgery, your physician may:
  ▶ place your leg in either a cast or a walking boot for at least 6 weeks. You may also be given crutches to use. (Putting weight on the injured leg will depend on the severity of your injury.)
- Once your cast or walking boot has been removed, your physician may:
  ▶ refer you to a physical therapist for a program of rehabilitation (see table below).

PHYSICAL THERAPY

EARLY STAGE ▶

- Once your physician has referred you, your physical therapist may:
  ▶ suggest various treatments, such as electrotherapy, to help alleviate your symptoms.
  ▶ assess your ankle flexibility with knee-to-wall stretches (》p.243).
- You may begin:
  ▶ weight-bearing; aim to add 15–20% of bodyweight every 1–2 weeks as pain, swelling, and range of movement allow.
  ▶ trying to walk normally without limping.
  ▶ stationary bicycling; aim for 20 minutes at 80rpm, level 6.
  ▶ deep-water running; aim for up to 30 minutes at high-intensity intervals.
  ▶ core-stability exercises, such as dead bugs (》p.225).

INTERMEDIATE STAGE ▶

- You should now be able to:
  ▶ demonstrate full range of motion in your hip, knee, and foot, without pain.
  ▶ put full weight on your injured leg, without pain.
- Your physical therapist may:
  ▶ check your ankle flexibility; your injured side should flex only 10% less than your uninjured side.
- You may begin:
  ▶ walking on a treadmill until you can jog without pain (》p.252).
  ▶ lower-limb bodyweight exercises, such as single-leg squats (》p.193).
  ▶ functional warm-up drills, such as kneeling supermen (》pp.228–229), full-body exercises, such as lawnmowers (》p.190), and low-level foot plyometrics, such as A-walks (》p.254).
  ▶ interval bicycling at a low–medium intensity.

ADVANCED STAGE ▶

- Your physical therapist may:
  ▶ assess your single vertical and horizontal hops (》p.261) and adapted cross-over hops (》p.262) for baseline scores.
- You may begin:
  ▶ lower-limb strength training; start at 50% of your one-rep max and aim for 4 sets x 8–12 reps of barbell squats (》p.192).
  ▶ stationary low-level skills, such as ball handling.
  ▶ low-level running, pain-free, with no increase in swelling.
  ▶ low-level foot plyometrics, such as walking pop-ups (》p.254).

RETURN TO SPORT

- You should now be able to:
  ▶ lift leg weights that are 80% of your one-rep max.
  ▶ complete foot plyometrics, such as jumps and hops (》pp.256–259), and speed drills (》pp.252–253), without pain.
  ▶ perform single vertical and horizontal hops (》p.261) and adapted cross-over hops (》p.262); your injured side should have only 10% less ability than your uninjured side.
  ▶ complete high-level running at distances relevant to your sport, without pain.
  ▶ complete sport-specific drills without difficulty.
  ▶ participate in full training.

ANKLE SPRAIN

ANKLE SPRAIN

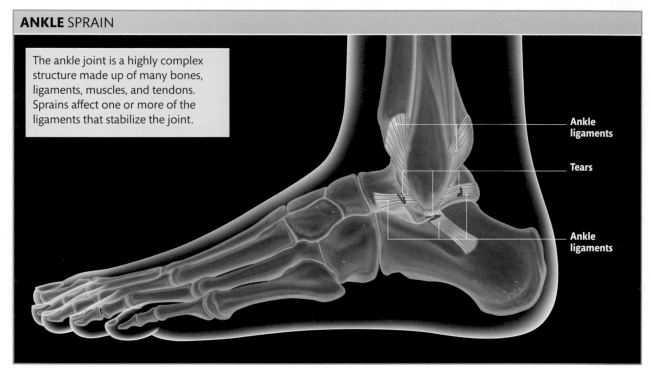

The ankle joint is a highly complex structure made up of many bones, ligaments, muscles, and tendons. Sprains affect one or more of the ligaments that stabilize the joint.

Ankle ligaments

Tears

Ankle ligaments

Ankle sprains are among the most common of all sports-related injuries. The ankle joint is designed to adapt to uneven terrain, but a sudden or forceful twisting motion can result in damage to the ankle ligaments. In severe sprains, the ligaments may be torn and the ankle dislocated. In some cases, the bones around the ankle may also be fractured (**»pp.144–145**).

CAUSES

The most common type of sprain occurs when the ankle turns over so that the sole of the foot faces inward (an inversion sprain), causing the ligaments on the outside of the ankle to stretch beyond their limit. In rare cases the foot is forced outward (an eversion sprain), damaging the ligaments on the inside of the ankle. Ankle sprains are most common in sports that involve side-to-side movement, such as basketball and tennis, or where there is a high risk of your foot being stepped on by another player, such as in soccer. Running on uneven ground can also lead to sprains and inadequate footwear increases the risk of such injuries.

SYMPTOMS AND DIAGNOSIS

You may have pain, stiffness, and swelling around your ankle, and you may not be able to bear weight on it. There may be bruising that moves down your foot toward your toes in the days following the injury. Your physician will do a physical examination to diagnose a sprain and may arrange for an X-ray to check for any other ankle injuries, such as a fracture.

RISKS AND COMPLICATIONS

If the damage to your ligaments is severe, you may be at risk of permanent ankle instability and it is likely that you will sprain your ankle again. If you repeatedly sprain your ankle you may need surgery to tighten the ligaments around the joint. If you do not undergo proper rehabilitation you may suffer from chronic pain and permanent instability, and there is a risk that you will develop osteoarthritis in your ankle.

WHEN WILL I BE FULLY FIT?

With rest and treatment, a mild or moderate sprain should heal in a few weeks. With a severe sprain, you will need a supervised period of rehabilitation of up to 3 months. If you have to undergo surgery, it may take up to 6 months before you can take up your sport again.

TREATMENT

✚ SEEK IMMEDIATE MEDICAL ATTENTION

MEDICAL

IMMEDIATE ▶	SHORT TERM ▶	MEDIUM TERM ▶	LONG TERM
■ If you think you may have sprained your ankle, you should: ▶ follow a RICE procedure (**》p.170**). ▶ seek medical attention.	■ If you are diagnosed with a mild-to-moderate ankle sprain, your physician may: ▶ prescribe analgesic medication. ▶ advise you to use crutches and continue with RICE until the injury has healed. ■ If you are diagnosed with severe ligament damage, your physician may: ▶ recommend surgery to repair the ligament.	■ If you have not had surgery and your injury is healing as expected, your physician may: ▶ refer you to a therapist for treatment to restore range of motion, strength, and flexibility (see table below). ■ If your injury has failed to respond to 2 weeks of nonsurgical treatment you may have torn the ligament, in which case your physician may: ▶ recommend surgery to repair the ligament.	■ After surgery, your physician may: ▶ put your ankle in a brace and give you crutches for 3–4 weeks. ▶ refer you to a physical therapist for a program of rehabilitation (see table below).

PHYSICAL THERAPY

EARLY STAGE ▶	INTERMEDIATE STAGE ▶	ADVANCED STAGE ▶	RETURN TO SPORT
■ Once your physician has referred you, your physical therapist may: ▶ suggest various treatments, such as electrotherapy, to reduce inflammation. ▶ perform manual therapy and soft-tissue release. ▶ advise you to try ankle movements (**》p.179**) within a range that you can tolerate, without increasing pain or swelling. ■ You may begin: ▶ pool walking as a form of resistance therapy; build up to deep-water pool running when you are able. ▶ core-stability exercises, such as dead bugs (**》p.225**). ▶ single-leg stands (**》p.246**); aim for 4 sets x 30 secs.	■ You should now be able to: ▶ demonstrate minimal swelling, with a difference of ½–⅔ in (1–1.5 cm) between each ankle. ■ Your physical therapist may: ▶ test your ankle flexibility with a knee-to-wall measurement (**》p.243**). ■ You may begin: ▶ weight-bearing and trying to walk normally without a limp. ▶ single-leg stands (**》p.246**), as pain allows; aim to hold each leg for 30 seconds. ▶ single-leg calf raises on both legs (**》p.204**); aim for 2 repetitions on each leg. ▶ walking on a treadmill until you can jog without pain (**》p.252**). ▶ functional warm-up drills, such as kneeling supermen (**》pp.228–29**), full-body exercises, such as step-up and holds (**》p.250**), and low-level foot plyometrics, such as A-walks (**》p.254**). ▶ working on a cross-trainer, stepper, or doing interval bicycling; build toward 20 minutes at 80rpm, level 6.	■ You should now be able to: ▶ demonstrate no swelling in your ankle. ▶ participate in warm-ups with no discomfort (strapping your ankle as required). ■ Your physical therapist may: ▶ retest your ankle flexibility to check that your ankles are within 10% of each other's range of motion. ▶ assess your single vertical and horizontal hops (**》p.261**) to establish a baseline score. ■ You may begin: ▶ a low-level running program; start at 50–60% effort, building to 60–70% effort as you feel able. Try figure-eight drills (**》p.253**) at 50–60% effort, and shuttle-run drills (**》p.253**).	■ You should now be able to: ▶ lift leg weights that are at least 80% of your one-rep max. ▶ perform single vertical and horizontal hops (**》p.261**) and adapted cross-over hops (**》p.262**); your injured leg should have only 10% less ability than your uninjured one. ▶ complete foot plyometrics, such as jumping and hopping (**》pp.256–59**), and speed drills (**》pp.252–53**), without pain. ▶ complete high-level running at distances relevant to your sport, without pain. ▶ complete sport-specific drills without difficulty. ▶ participate in full training for at least 1–2 weeks.

HEEL BONE FRACTURE

HEEL BONE FRACTURE

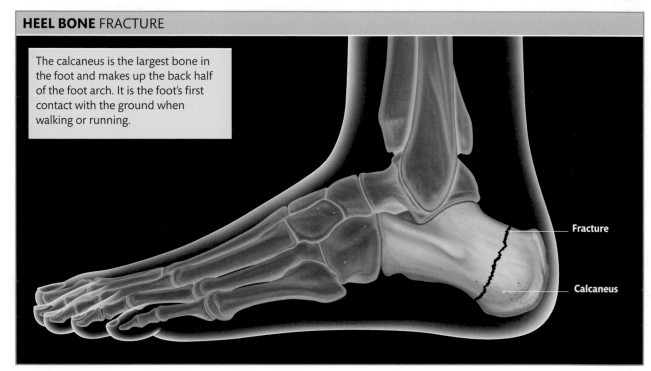

The calcaneus is the largest bone in the foot and makes up the back half of the foot arch. It is the foot's first contact with the ground when walking or running.

Fracture

Calcaneus

During walking, running, and jumping, the calcaneus (heel bone) supports all the weight of the body. Of all the bones in the back of the foot, the heel is the most commonly fractured.

CAUSES
Heel fractures are often connected with sports such as the high jump or the long jump, in which there is a risk of a hard fall—perhaps from a height—directly onto the heels. Fractures of the heel can also be the result of sustained repetitive stress to the back of the foot, of the type found in long-distance running, for example.

SYMPTOMS AND DIAGNOSIS
You may experience severe pain in your heel, as well as swelling and tenderness, and squeezing your heel will be painful. There may also be bruising. You may find that you develop a limp and find it difficult to put your weight on your injured foot. In severe cases, you may be completely unable to walk. In very serious fractures, the broken bone may pierce the skin overlying your heel and be exposed. Your physician will make a diagnosis through physical examination and from looking at your medical history. You may also be given an X-ray to determine the severity, extent, and exact position of the fracture.

RISKS AND COMPLICATIONS
Leaving a fractured calcaneus untreated for too long can lead to severe swelling, which will delay healing. Swelling can also delay healing after surgery. In some severe cases, in which the bone is fragmented, there may be complications such as malunion (when the bony fragments do not heal in the proper position). Very severe fractures can lead to ongoing problems such as chronic foot pain, especially when walking, running, or standing for long periods of time. People who have had a heel fracture are also susceptible to osteoarthritis.

WHEN WILL I BE FULLY FIT?
If the fractured bone has not been knocked out of position by the impact that caused the fracture, it should heal in around 12 weeks, but it may be another 8–12 weeks before you can return to sports. If you have had surgery to repair the fracture, it may take 6–9 months or longer before you are fully fit and, in the worst cases, some patients are never able to return to sports.

TREATMENT

⊕ SEEK IMMEDIATE MEDICAL ATTENTION

MEDICAL

IMMEDIATE ▶	SHORT TERM ▶	MEDIUM TERM ▶	LONG TERM
■ If you think you may have fractured your heel bone, you should: ▶ stop activity. ▶ follow a RICE procedure (»p.170). ▶ seek medical attention.	■ If you are diagnosed with a mild to moderate fracture, your physician may: ▶ prescribe analgesic medication. ▶ immobilize your foot in a cast and give you crutches for 6 weeks. ■ If you are diagnosed with a severe fracture, in which the bone has broken into fragments, your physician may: ▶ recommend surgery to repair the bone.	■ If you have not had surgery, and your injury is healing as expected, your physician may: ▶ refer you to a physical therapist for treatment to help restore full range of motion and strength in your ankle and foot (see table below). ■ If you have not had surgery and your injury has failed to heal as expected, your physician may: ▶ recommend surgery to repair the bone.	■ After surgery, your physician may: ▶ put your foot in a cast for at least six weeks. ▶ advise you to avoid putting full weight on your foot for 2–3 weeks after the operation. ▶ refer you to a physical therapist for a program of rehabilitation (see table below).

PHYSICAL THERAPY

EARLY STAGE ▶	INTERMEDIATE STAGE ▶	ADVANCED STAGE ▶	RETURN TO SPORT
■ Once your physician has referred you, your physical therapist may: ▶ suggest various treatments, such as electrotherapy, to reduce local inflammation. ▶ help you reintroduce weight-bearing, possibly while wearing an aircast boot, depending on your physician's instructions. ▶ assess the intensity and duration of your training, and correct these accordingly. ▶ perform a full biomechanical foot and ankle assessment to see if insoles or orthotics to support your medial arch, or heel pads, would help you. ▶ use manual therapy and soft-tissue therapy to help relieve your symptoms. ▶ advise stretching your soleus, gastrocnemius, and tibialis anterior muscles. ■ You may begin: ▶ deep-water pool running to maintain fitness.	■ You should now be able to: ▶ demonstrate a full range of motion in your hip and knee. ▶ bear your full weight, without pain. ■ You may begin: ▶ lower-limb bodyweight exercises, such as squats (»p.180) and calf raises (»p.204). ▶ functional warm-up drills such as Frankenstein walks (»p.177), full-body exercises such as lawnmowers (»p.190), and low-level foot plyometrics such as A-walks (»p.254). ▶ bicycling and work on a cross-trainer and stepper; build toward 20 minutes at 80rpm, level 6. ▶ core stability exercises, such as dead bugs (»p.225). ▶ pilates reformer exercises (»p.237).	■ You should now be able to: ▶ complete moderate-high intensity interval bicycling. ■ Your physical therapist may: ▶ assess your single vertical and horizontal hops (»p.261) and your adapted cross-over hops (»p.262) for baseline scores. ■ You may begin: ▶ lower-limb strength training, starting at 50% of your one-rep max, without pain and with no increase in swelling; aim for 4 sets x 8-12 reps of barbell squats (»p.180) and Romanian deadlifts (»p.196). ▶ low-level running and sporting activities, as pain allows.	■ You should now be able to: ▶ lift leg weights that are at least 80% of your one-rep max, without pain. ▶ complete foot plyometrics, such as jumps and hops (»pp.256–59), and speed drills (»pp.252–53), without pain. ▶ perform single vertical and horizontal hops (»p.261) and adapted cross-over hops (»p.262); your injured side should have only 10% less ability than your uninjured side. ▶ complete high-level running at distances relevant to your sport, without pain. ▶ complete sport-specific drills without difficulty. ▶ participate in full training for at least 2–3 weeks, without pain.

RETROCALCANEAL BURSITIS

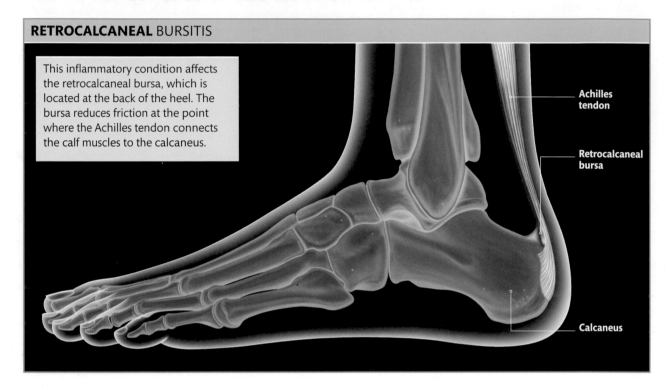

RETROCALCANEAL BURSITIS

This inflammatory condition affects the retrocalcaneal bursa, which is located at the back of the heel. The bursa reduces friction at the point where the Achilles tendon connects the calf muscles to the calcaneus.

Achilles tendon

Retrocalcaneal bursa

Calcaneus

Retrocalcaneal bursitis is inflammation of the retrocalcaneal bursa (a slippery, fluid-filled sac) that cushions the Achilles tendon as it passes over the calcaneus (heel bone). In a related condition, known as Haglund's syndrome, retrocalcaneal bursitis occurs together with inflammation of the Achilles tendon (»pp.142).

CAUSES
Both retrocalcaneal bursitis and Haglund's syndrome are usually linked to sports that involve walking, running, or jumping, where repetitive and excessive stress on the bursa that cushions the Achilles tendon leads to inflammation. Other contributing factors include wearing shoes that are too tight or that do not cushion the foot sufficiently, and an incorrect gait when walking or running.

SYMPTOMS AND DIAGNOSIS
Both conditions will cause pain when running, walking, or jumping. You will feel tenderness in your heel, and there may be redness and swelling in the area. The pain may intensify when you stand on tiptoes. A common symptom of Haglund's syndrome, which is associated with a prominent bony spur at the retrocalcaneal region, is pain at the back of your heel. The pain worsens if you stand or walk for prolonged periods. Your physician will make a diagnosis based on your description of your symptoms and a physical examination.

RISKS AND COMPLICATIONS
If you leave either condition untreated, the bursa may rupture, leaving your Achilles tendon vulnerable to further friction, and possible rupture (»p.140). In Haglund's syndrome, a bony spur often develops on the heel, exacerbating the pain and inflammation.

WHEN WILL I BE FULLY FIT?
If nonsurgical treatment is successful, retrocalcaneal bursitis should improve after around 3 months, but it may take up to 6 months to regain full fitness. If you develop Haglund's syndrome and conservative treatment is not successful, you may need surgery. If this is necessary, it may take you up to a year to recover fully.

TREATMENT

	IMMEDIATE ▶	SHORT TERM ▶	MEDIUM TERM ▶	LONG TERM
MEDICAL	■ If you think you may have retrocalcaneal bursitis or Haglund's syndrome, you should: ▶ stop activity. ▶ follow a RICE procedure (**≫p.170**). ■ If your symptoms do not improve with rest and self-treatment after 6 weeks, you should: ▶ seek medical attention.	■ If you are diagnosed with retrocalcaneal bursitis or Haglund's syndrome, your physician may: ▶ prescribe analgesic medication. ▶ recommend special shoe inserts designed to relieve stress on your heel. ▶ refer you to a physical therapist for treatment to ease your symptoms and improve strength and flexibility in your ankle (see table below).	■ If your retrocalcaneal bursitis fails to respond to nonsurgical treatment, your physician may: ▶ recommend surgery to drain fluid from the inflamed bursa, or to remove the bursa. ■ If your Haglund's syndrome fails to respond to nonsurgical treatment, and you have developed a bony spur, your physician may: ▶ recommend surgery to remove the spur and drain the bursa.	■ After surgery for either condition, your physician may: ▶ refer you to a physical therapist for a program of rehabilitation (see table below).

	EARLY STAGE ▶	INTERMEDIATE STAGE ▶	ADVANCED STAGE ▶	RETURN TO SPORT
PHYSICAL THERAPY	■ Once your physician has referred you, your physical therapist may: ▶ suggest various treatments, such as electrotherapy and possibly a night splint, to reduce local inflammation. ▶ advise you to gently move your ankle within the range that you can tolerate, without increasing swelling or pain. ▶ perform manual therapy and soft tissue release of tight lower-limb muscles as required.	■ You should now be able to: ▶ demonstrate a full range of motion in your hip, knee, and ankle, without pain. ■ You may begin: ▶ single-calf raises over a step on both legs (**≫p.204**); aim for 4 sets x 15 reps; you should not feel any pain. ▶ interval bicycling, and work on a cross-trainer and a stepper; build toward doing 20 minutes at 80rpm, level 6. ▶ full-body exercises, such as overhead lunges (**≫p.181**), and low-level foot plyometrics, such as A-walks (**≫p.254**). ▶ low-level skills specific to your sport, such as ball handling; you should not feel any pain.	■ You should now be able to: ▶ perform low-level running and running drills, without pain. ■ You may begin: ▶ lower-limb strength training; start at 50% of your one-rep max and aim for 4 sets x 8–12 reps of barbell squats (**≫p.192**) and Romanian deadlifts (**≫p.196**). ▶ upper-limb weights training, involving the lower limbs, such as push presses (**≫p.238**), as pain allows.	■ You should now be able to: ▶ demonstrate a full range of motion in your ankle. ▶ lift leg weights that are at least 80% of your one-rep max. ▶ perform single vertical and horizontal hops (**≫p.261**) and adapted cross-over hops (**≫p.262**); your injured leg should have only 10% less ability than your uninjured one. ▶ complete foot plyometrics, such as jumps and hops (**≫pp.256–59**), and speed drills (**≫pp.252–53**), without pain. ▶ complete high-level running at distances relevant to your sport, without pain. ▶ complete sport-specific drills without difficulty. ▶ participate in full training.

TIBIALIS POSTERIOR TENDINOPATHY

Persistent overuse of the tibialis posterior tendon can produce inflammation in the tendon, known as tibialis posterior tendinopathy, which can lead to a rupture of the tendon.

CAUSES
This condition is most commonly seen in runners, but can occur in any sport. Athletes who overpronate (roll the foot inward) are particularly susceptible. Less frequently, this injury may be the result of a direct blow to the foot or ankle.

SYMPTOMS AND DIAGNOSIS
You will feel a gradual onset of pain toward the back of your ankle and there may be swelling. Diagnosis may be made by a physical examination and a nerve conduction velocity test.

RISKS AND COMPLICATIONS
Left untreated, your tendon may rupture, in which case you will need surgery. If the arch of your foot collapses completely, you will be unable to exert pressure on the sole of your foot.

WHEN WILL I BE FULLY FIT?
With nonsurgical treatment, you should be able to return to sports after 12 weeks. If you have had surgery, full recovery could take up to a year.

TIBIALIS POSTERIOR TENDINOPATHY

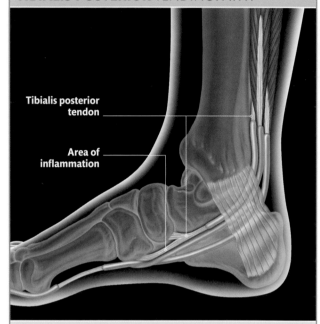

Tibialis posterior tendon

Area of inflammation

The tibialis posterior tendon runs from the back of the lower leg into the instep and attaches to bones in the bottom of the foot. It supports the arch of the foot.

TREATMENT ⊕ SEEK IMMEDIATE MEDICAL ATTENTION

MEDICAL

IMMEDIATE
- If you think you may have tibialis posterior tendinopathy, you should: ▶ follow a RICE procedure (**»p.170**). ▶ seek medical attention.

SHORT TERM
- If you are diagnosed with moderate tendon damage, your physician may: ▶ prescribe analgesic medication. ▶ refer you to a physical therapist for treatment (see table right). ■ If your tendon is ruptured, your physician may: ▶ recommend surgery.

MEDIUM TERM
- If the injury fails to respond to physical therapy, your physician may: ▶ give you an arch support. ▶ recommend surgery to repair the tendon.

LONG TERM
- After surgery, your physician may: ▶ refer you to a physical therapist for a program of rehabilitation (see table right).

PHYSICAL THERAPY

EARLY STAGE
- Once your physician has referred you, your physical therapist may: ▶ assess and correct the intensity and duration of your training. ▶ perform a biomechanical foot and ankle assessment. ▶ perform manual and soft-tissue therapy. ▶ suggest eccentric inversion exercises (**»p.204**).

INTERMEDIATE STAGE
- You should now be able to: ▶ bear your full weight with minimal discomfort. ■ You may begin: ▶ lower-limb bodyweight exercises, such as single-leg squats (**»p.193**).

ADVANCED STAGE
- You should now be able to: ▶ do interval bicycling at a moderate–high intensity. ▶ perform barbell squats (**»p.192**); aim for 4 sets x 8–12 reps at 50% of your one-rep max.

RETURN TO SPORT
- You should now be able to: ▶ lift leg weights that are 80% of your one-rep max. ▶ resume full training, without pain.

SINUS TARSI SYNDROME

Sinus tarsi syndrome is a painful condition in which the fluid and tissue inside the sinus tarsi become inflamed. It is brought on by overuse and is associated with ankle sprains.

CAUSES

Sinus tarsi syndrome occurs commonly in running and stems from overuse of the ankle and overpronation (rolling the foot inward as you land). A past ankle sprain can also be a cause.

SYMPTOMS AND DIAGNOSIS

You may feel pain around the bone on the inside of your ankle and at the entrance to the sinus tarsi on the outside of your foot. Running on curves may be painful. Diagnosis may be by examination, X-ray to rule out fractures, or MRI to detect excessive fluid.

RISKS AND COMPLICATIONS

Sinus tarsi syndrome rarely occurs alone and may indicate that you have another condition. Left unchecked it will become more pronounced, especially when sprinting and jumping.

WHEN WILL I BE FULLY FIT?

If you respond well to nonsurgical treatment you should be fit in around 4–6 weeks. If you need to have surgery, full recovery will take up to 3 months.

SINUS TARSI SYNDROME

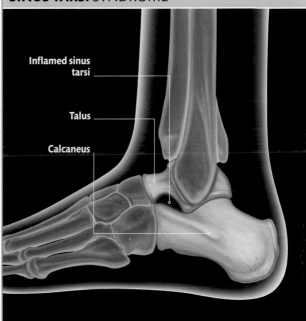

Inflamed sinus tarsi

Talus

Calcaneus

The sinus tarsi is a tunnel bounded by the talus (an ankle bone) and the calcaneus (heel bone). It contains the cervical ligament and the roots of the inferior extensor retinaculum.

TREATMENT   SEEK IMMEDIATE MEDICAL ATTENTION

MEDICAL

IMMEDIATE
■ If you think you may have sinus tarsi syndrome, you should: ▶ stop activity. ▶ follow a RICE procedure (**》p.170**). ▶ seek medical attention.

SHORT TERM
■ If you are diagnosed with sinus tarsi syndrome, your physician may: ▶ advise rest. ▶ prescribe analgesic medication. ▶ put your ankle in a brace for 1 month.

MEDIUM TERM
■ If your symptoms persist, your physician may: ▶ refer you to a physical therapist for treatment to strengthen your ankle (see table right). ▶ prescribe a course of corticosteroids.

LONG TERM
■ If all nonsurgical treatment fails, your physician may: ▶ recommend surgery to remove damaged tissue. ■ After surgery your physician may: ▶ refer you to a physical therapist for a program of rehabilitation (see table right).

PHYSICAL THERAPY

EARLY STAGE
■ Once your physician has referred you, your physical therapist may: ▶ begin to mobilize your joint. ▶ take your foot through movements to test its range of motion (passive).

INTERMEDIATE STAGE
■ You should now be able to: ▶ exercise a full range of motion in your hip, knee, and ankle with assistance (active). ■ You may begin: ▶ calf raises (**》p.204**). ▶ upper-limb weights that involve your legs, such as push presses (**》p.238**).

ADVANCED STAGE
■ You should now be able to: ▶ perform low-level running, without pain or instability. ■ You may begin: ▶ barbell squats (**》p.192**) at 50% of your one-rep max; aim for 4 sets x 8–12 reps.

RETURN TO SPORT
■ You should now be able to: ▶ demonstrate a full active range of motion. ▶ lift leg weights that are 80% of your one-rep max. ▶ complete sport-specific drills without pain.

FOOT TENDON INJURIES

Overuse is the most common cause of sports injury to the extensor tendons, which run along the top of the foot, and the flexor tendons, which run along the bottom of the foot. The extensor tendons may also be damaged by a dropped object or if the foot is stamped on.

CAUSES

Anyone who plays a sport involving jumping or running may damage their foot tendons through overuse (hill running is particularly hard on the extensor tendons). Trainers that fit badly or are too tightly laced can also put excessive pressure on the foot. All of these factors can lead to inflammation of the tendons, a condition called tendinopathy.

SYMPTOMS AND DIAGNOSIS

If you have inflamed extensor tendons, you will have pain and swelling on the top of your foot. The pain will be worse when you are running. If you have inflamed flexor tendons, the underside of your foot will be tender along the course of the tendons, and there will be a stabbing pain in the arch of your foot, especially when you stand on your toes. Swelling and nodules may appear on your foot. Your physician will make a diagnosis through an assessment of your medical history and a physical examination, and may also ask for an X-ray to rule out a metatarsal stress fracture. The sensitivity of your lower limb may be tested, to rule out any nerve damage from an injury.

RISKS AND COMPLICATIONS

Persistent (chronic) tendinopathy is a sign that the tendons are failing to heal properly. The condition is difficult to manage and there is a risk that the tendons will eventually rupture, which may require surgery. In some cases, a foot affected by tendinopathy may never completely return to normal, although it can become quite pain-free.

WHEN WILL I BE FULLY FIT?

Usually, if you follow a treatment program, your foot will heal in 6–12 weeks, depending on the severity of your injury. If you have had surgery to repair a ruptured tendon, it will take you up to 6 months to recover fully.

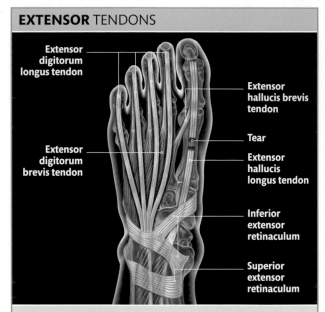

EXTENSOR TENDONS

Extensor digitorum longus tendon

Extensor hallucis brevis tendon

Tear

Extensor digitorum brevis tendon

Extensor hallucis longus tendon

Inferior extensor retinaculum

Superior extensor retinaculum

The extensor tendons (labeled above) straighten, or extend, the toes and bend them upward. They originate in the lower leg muscles and run along the top of the foot.

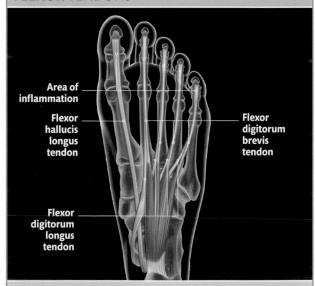

FLEXOR TENDONS

Area of inflammation

Flexor hallucis longus tendon

Flexor digitorum brevis tendon

Flexor digitorum longus tendon

The flexor tendons (labeled above) bend the toes downward. They originate in the calf muscles and run along the inside of the ankle and the sole of the foot.

TREATMENT

⊕ SEEK IMMEDIATE MEDICAL ATTENTION

MEDICAL

IMMEDIATE ▶	SHORT TERM ▶	MEDIUM TERM ▶	LONG TERM
■ If you think you may have injured a tendon in your foot, you should: ▶ stop activity. ▶ follow a RICE procedure (**»p.170**). ▶ seek medical attention.	■ If you are diagnosed with tendinopathy, your physician may: ▶ prescribe analgesic medication. ▶ refer you to a physical therapist for treatment to strengthen and stretch your calf muscles (see table below). ■ If you are diagnosed with a ruptured tendon, your physician may: ▶ recommend surgery to repair the tendon.	■ If your tendinopathy fails to respond to physical therapy, your physician may: ▶ give you an injection of corticosteroids to reduce inflammation. ■ After surgery on a ruptured tendon, your physician may: ▶ put your foot in a splint for around 4 weeks. ▶ advise you to use crutches while your foot is in a splint.	■ After you have had surgery, and when your cast has been removed, your physician may: ▶ refer you to a physical therapist for a program of rehabilitation (see table below).

PHYSICAL THERAPY

EARLY STAGE ▶	INTERMEDIATE STAGE ▶	ADVANCED STAGE ▶	RETURN TO SPORT
■ Once your physician has referred you, your physical therapist may: ▶ suggest various treatments, such as electrotherapy, to reduce local inflammation. ▶ assess the intensity and duration of your normal training, and correct these accordingly. ▶ perform a full biomechanical assessment of your foot and ankle, to see if insoles or orthotics to support the medial arch, or heel pads, would help you. ■ You may begin to: ▶ move your toes within a tolerable range of motion; stop if you have pain or an increase in swelling.	■ You should now be able to: ▶ demonstrate full range of motion in your hip, knee, foot, and ankle, without pain. ▶ experience no morning pain or stiffness in your foot tendons. ■ Your physical therapist may: ▶ assess your ability to perform manual high-load eccentrics. For example, you can use a band as resistance against which to pull and push your foot.	■ You should now be able to: ▶ complete low-level running, without pain and with full range of motion in your foot and ankle. ■ You may now begin: ▶ lower-limb strength training; aim for 4 sets x 8–12 reps of barbell squats (**»p.180**) and Romanian deadlifts (**»p.196**). Start at 50% of your one-rep max. You should not feel any pain and there should be no increase in swelling. ▶ upper-limb weights exercises that involve the lower limbs, such as power cleans (**»pp.238–39**), as pain allows.	■ You should now be able to: ▶ demonstrate full active range of motion. ▶ lift lower-limb weights that are at least 80% of your one-rep max, without pain. ▶ complete foot plyometrics, such as jumps and hops (**»pp.256–58**), and speed drills (**»pp.252–53**), without pain. ▶ complete high-level running at distances relevant to your sport, without pain. ▶ complete sport-specific drills without difficulty. ▶ participate in full training.

FOOT LIGAMENT SPRAINS

Sprains of the ligaments of the feet range from mild injuries to severe ruptures. The ligaments of the toe joints are particularly prone to injury.

CAUSES
Direct impact or an awkward move, for example, in martial arts, may cause foot ligament sprain. A condition called turf toe occurs when a toe is forced upward, spraining a ligament underneath the foot; in sand toe, the reverse injury occurs when a toe is bent downward and a ligament at the top of the foot is damaged.

SYMPTOMS AND DIAGNOSIS
You will feel pain and there may be swelling and bruising in the injured joint. Your physician will make a diagnosis from your medical history, a physical examination, and an X-ray.

RISKS AND COMPLICATIONS
Turf toe can progress into a chronic problem, in which the joint never fully heals, and this may lead to cartilage wear and eventually arthritis.

WHEN WILL I BE FULLY FIT?
Depending on the injury, a return to full fitness may take a few weeks to several months. If you need surgery to repair a rupture, full recovery can take up to 6 months.

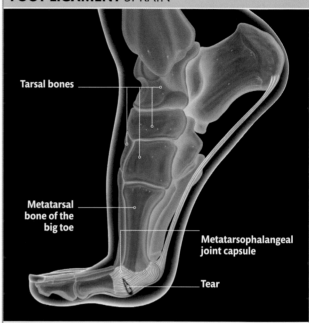

FOOT LIGAMENT SPRAIN

Tarsal bones

Metatarsal bone of the big toe

Metatarsophalangeal joint capsule

Tear

The metatarsophalangeal joint of the big toe is especially vulnerable to injury. Jamming the toe or subjecting it to excessive stress can cause ligament tears.

TREATMENT   SEEK IMMEDIATE MEDICAL ATTENTION

MEDICAL

IMMEDIATE
- If you think you have sprained a foot ligament, you should: ▶ follow a RICE procedure (**》p.170**). ▶ seek medical attention.

SHORT TERM
- If you are diagnosed with a mild sprain, your physician may: ▶ put your lower leg in a splint or cast for 4 weeks. ■ For turf toe, your physician may: ▶ brace your toe. ■ For sand toe, your physician may: ▶ tape your toe. ■ For a rupture your physician may: ▶ recommend surgery to repair the ligament.

MEDIUM TERM
- For mild sprains, once a splint or cast has been removed, and for sand or turf toe, your physician may: ▶ refer you to a physical therapist for treatment (see table right).

LONG TERM
- After surgery, your physician may: ▶ refer you to a physical therapist for a program of rehabilitation (see table right).

PHYSICAL THERAPY

EARLY STAGE
- Once your physician has referred you, your physical therapist may: ▶ perform soft-tissue massage. ▶ tape the joint. ■ You may begin: ▶ moving your toe. ▶ core-stability exercises, such as dead bugs (**》p.225**).

INTERMEDIATE STAGE
- You should now be able to: ▶ walk without pain. ■ You may begin: ▶ calf raises (**》p.204**); aim for 2 reps on each side.

ADVANCED STAGE
- You should now be able to: ▶ perform low-level jogging, without pain. ■ You may begin: ▶ lower-limb strength training, such as Romanian deadlifts (**》p.196**) and 45-degree leg presses (**》p.195**), starting at 50% of your one-rep max.

RETURN TO SPORT
- You should now be able to: ▶ demonstrate full range of motion in your toe. ▶ lift leg weights that are 80% of your one-rep max. ▶ participate in full training.

MORTON'S NEUROMA

Morton's neuroma is a condition affecting one of the plantar nerves that run between the metatarsal bones in the foot.

CAUSES
Sports associated with repetitive stress on the ball of the foot, such as running and jumping, may put pressure on the metatarsals and cause one of the plantar digital nerves to become pinched and to thicken.

SYMPTOMS AND DIAGNOSIS
You may experience pain, burning, or decreased sensation between the toes, and numbness or cramping in the foot. Standing in shoes may cause pain, which is relieved by removing your shoes. Your physician will diagnose the condition through physical examination and an MRI scan.

RISKS AND COMPLICATIONS
Left untreated, Morton's neuroma may cause more severe pain, permanent damage to affected nerves, loss of sensation in your toes and, perhaps, a permanent disability.

WHEN WILL I BE FULLY FIT?
If you respond well to nonsurgical treatment you should be able to return to sport in around 3 weeks. If you need surgery it normally takes around 6 weeks to resume sport.

MORTON'S NEUROMA

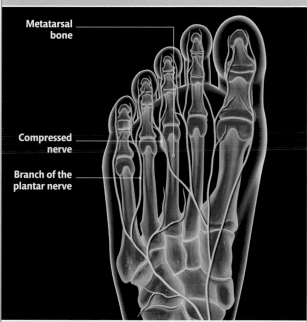

Metatarsal bone

Compressed nerve

Branch of the plantar nerve

Branches of the plantar nerve run between the metatarsal bones of all the toes. Morton's neuroma most commonly affects the nerve between the third and fourth toes.

TREATMENT
 SEEK IMMEDIATE MEDICAL ATTENTION

MEDICAL

IMMEDIATE
- If you think you may have Morton's neuroma, you should: ▶ stop activity. ▶ follow a RICE procedure (**》p.170**). ▶ seek medical attention.

SHORT TERM
- If you are diagnosed with Morton's neuroma, your physician may: ▶ recommend rest, with a gradual return to activity. ▶ advise you on suitable footwear. ▶ give you a corticosteroid injection. ▶ prescribe analgesic medication.

MEDIUM TERM
- If your injury fails to respond to nonsurgical treatment, your physician may: ▶ recommend surgery to relieve pressure on the nerve or to remove it.

LONG TERM
- After surgery, your physician may: ▶ refer you to a physical therapist for a program of rehabilitation (see table right).

PHYSICAL THERAPY

EARLY STAGE
- Once your physician has referred you, your physical therapist may: ▶ mobilize your joint. ▶ massage the thickened tissue. ▶ test your range of motion (passive).
- You may begin to: ▶ weight-bear.

INTERMEDIATE STAGE
- You should now be able to: ▶ demonstrate full range of motion in your hip, knee, foot, and ankle without assistance (active). ■ You may begin: ▶ single-calf raises (**》p.204**) over a step; aim for 4 sets x 12 reps with no pain.

ADVANCED STAGE
- You should now be able to: ▶ perform low-level jogging, without pain. ■ You may begin: ▶ barbell squats (**》p.192**) at 50% of your one-rep max; aim for 4 sets x 8–12 reps.

RETURN TO SPORT
- You should now be able to: ▶ demonstrate full active range of motion. ▶ complete sport-specific drills and train normally.

METATARSAL FRACTURE

Fracture of the metatarsal bones is the most common type of foot injury in sport, and may be caused by sudden trauma or overuse.

CAUSES
Metatarsal fractures often occur during contact sports such as rugby or soccer, usually from a blow to the foot. Stress fractures are associated with running and jumping sports such as athletics, as a result of repetitive trauma.

SYMPTOMS AND DIAGNOSIS
There may be pain, numbness, swelling, discoloration, and deformity of your foot. You may not be able to bear weight on it. Your physician will diagnose a fracture through physical examination, X-ray, and possibly a CT scan.

RISKS AND COMPLICATIONS
An untreated fracture can lead to damage to nerves and blood vessels, and bones may not heal, causing long-term weakness in the foot.

WHEN WILL I BE FULLY FIT?
With an uncomplicated fracture you can return to sport about 4–6 weeks after the cast comes off. After surgery, you may need to wear a protective shoe for about 1 month. A stress fracture requires 1 month of immobilization.

METATARSAL FRACTURE

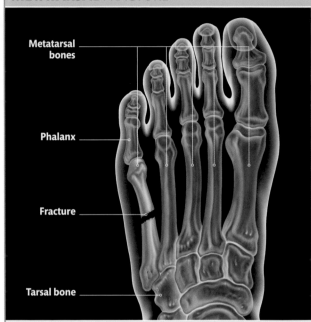

Metatarsal bones

Phalanx

Fracture

Tarsal bone

The five metatarsals—the longest and narrowest of the foot bones—connect the midfoot to the toes. They are especially vulnerable to injury in contact sports.

TREATMENT   SEEK IMMEDIATE MEDICAL ATTENTION

MEDICAL

IMMEDIATE
- If you think you may have a metatarsal fracture you should: ► stop activity. ► follow a RICE procedure (**»p.170**). ► seek medical attention.

SHORT TERM
- If you have an uncomplicated fracture, your physician may: ► put a cast on your foot. ■ For a displaced fracture your physician may: ► recommend surgery to repair the bone.

MEDIUM TERM
- For an uncomplicated fracture, if your injury is healing as expected, your physician may: ► refer you to a physical therapist for treatment to stretch and strengthen the muscles (see table right). ■ If the injury fails to respond to nonsurgical treatment, your physician may: ► recommend surgery to repair the bone.

LONG TERM
- After surgery, your physician may: ► refer you to a physical therapist for a program of rehabilitation (see table right).

PHYSICAL THERAPY

EARLY STAGE
- Once your physician has referred you, your physical therapist may: ► suggest electrotherapy to reduce inflammation and ultrasound to promote healing. ■ You may begin: ► core-stability exercises, such as dead bugs (**»p.225**).

INTERMEDIATE STAGE
- You should now be: ► almost free of pain when your metatarsal joint is touched. ■ You may begin: ► interval cycling—aim for 20 minutes at 80rpm, level 6. ► barbell squats (**»p.192**); aim for 4 sets x 8–12 reps at 50% of your one-rep max.

ADVANCED STAGE
- You should now be able to: ► perform moderate-level interval cycling, pain-free. ■ You may begin: ► foot plyometrics, such as walking pop-ups (**»p.254**). ► low-level running.

RETURN TO SPORT
- You should now be able to: ► complete sport-specific drills, pain-free. ► train fully for at least 2–3 weeks, without pain.

TOE FRACTURE

There are 14 toe bones (phalanges, singular "phalanx") in the foot, which can easily be injured by kicking or stubbing the toe.

CAUSES
Fractures often occur during sports such as rugby or soccer: through direct force from a fall, a blow or kick to the foot, or the force of kicking something too hard; or by indirect force, such as twisting your foot and putting strain on the toes.

SYMPTOMS AND DIAGNOSIS
Common symptoms of a toe fracture are pain, swelling, inability to bear weight on your foot, toe deformity, and discomfort wearing shoes. Your physician will diagnose a fracture through physical examination and an X-ray.

RISKS AND COMPLICATIONS
Untreated fractures of your toes may lead to further damage to nerves and blood vessels, and your bones may not heal properly if they are incorrectly aligned.

WHEN WILL I BE FULLY FIT?
It normally takes 4–6 weeks to regain a good range of motion, and to be able to return to sport. If you require surgery, recovery will take around 4–6 weeks.

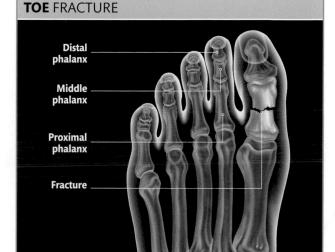

TOE FRACTURE

- Distal phalanx
- Middle phalanx
- Proximal phalanx
- Fracture

Toes have three phalanges: proximal (closest), middle, and distal (furthest). The big toe, however, has only two. When the foot is injured, one or more of them may be fractured.

TREATMENT　　⊕ SEEK IMMEDIATE MEDICAL ATTENTION

MEDICAL

IMMEDIATE
- If you think you may have fractured your toe, you should: ▶ stop activity. ▶ follow a RICE procedure (»p.170). ▶ seek medical attention.

SHORT TERM
- If your toe is not displaced, your physician may: ▶ tape it to the adjacent toe for 1 month. ■ If you have a displaced or joint fracture your physician may: ▶ recommend surgery.

MEDIUM TERM
- If your taped toe is healing as expected, your physician may: ▶ refer you to a physical therapist for treatment to restore range of motion (see table right). ■ If your injury fails to respond to taping, your physician may: ▶ recommend surgery.

LONG TERM
- After surgery, your physician may: ▶ tape your toe. ▶ refer you to a physical therapist for a programme of rehabilitation (see table right).

PHYSICAL THERAPY

EARLY STAGE
- Once your physician has referred you, your physical therapist may: ▶ suggest various treatments, such as electrotherapy, to reduce local inflammation, and low-intensity pulsed ultrasound to promote healing.

INTERMEDIATE STAGE
- You should now be able to: ▶ demonstrate a full range of motion in your hip, knee, foot, and ankle. ■ You may begin: ▶ warm-ups, such as walking lunges (»p.180). ▶ sport-specific skills, such as ball handling.

ADVANCED STAGE
- You should now be able to: ▶ perform low-level jogging, pain-free. ■ You may begin: ▶ barbell squats (»p.192); aim for 4 sets x 8–12 reps at 50% of your one-rep max.

RETURN TO SPORT
- You should now be able to: ▶ lift leg weights that are 80% of your one-rep max. ▶ complete sport-specific drills, pain-free.

PLANTAR FASCIITIS

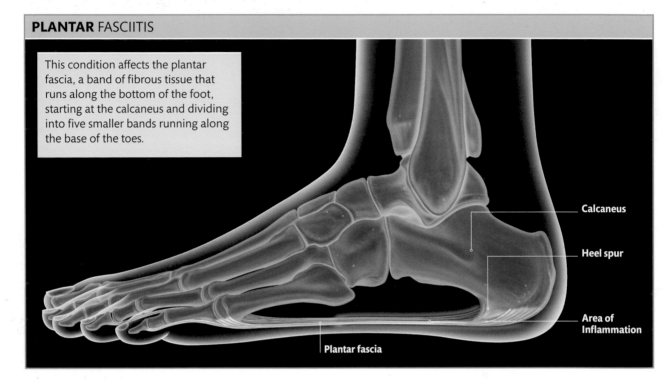

PLANTAR FASCIITIS

This condition affects the plantar fascia, a band of fibrous tissue that runs along the bottom of the foot, starting at the calcaneus and dividing into five smaller bands running along the base of the toes.

Calcaneus

Heel spur

Area of Inflammation

Plantar fascia

The plantar fascia is a thick band of tissue that stretches from the heel to the base of the toes, supporting the arch of the foot. Plantar fasciitis (also known as painful heel syndrome) is a chronic condition in which the plantar fascia becomes inflamed. Often, when an X-ray is taken of the plantar fascia, a calcium deposit—known as a heel spur—is found over the calcaneus (heelbone).

CAUSES

Plantar fasciitis occurs in sports with a lot of running and jumping, and those that are played on hard surfaces, such as basketball. These sports involve repeated stress to the underside of the foot, causing the toe joints to bend and putting pressure on the heel end of the plantar fascia, leading to inflammation. Shoes that do not cushion the foot sufficiently, or support the arch, are also a factor, as is being overweight. Heel spurs occur when the heel bone is irritated by the tendon that attaches the plantar fascia to the heel bone, causing the bone to deposit calcium in the area of the irritation. They sometimes occur with plantar fasciitis, but not always.

SYMPTOMS AND DIAGNOSIS

Plantar fasciitis causes pain on the underside of your heel—this is usually most intense first thing in the morning, although it can worsen through the day. Pain may stop during exercise but will return afterward; you may also feel pain after a prolonged period of rest. Heel spurs also cause pain in your heel, and there may sometimes be a grinding or clicking sensation at the point at which the tendon crosses your heel. Your physician will diagnose both conditions through physical examination, and may use an X-ray to confirm the diagnosis.

RISKS AND COMPLICATIONS

Untreated plantar fasciitis will usually worsen, making walking painful. You may also experience knee, hip, and lower-back problems. An untreated heel spur may make your surrounding tendons inflamed, encouraging calcium deposits and worsening your heel spur.

WHEN WILL I BE FULLY FIT?

Without surgery, plantar fasciitis should heal within a few months; if you have had surgery, you should wait 3–6 months before returning to sport.

TREATMENT

	IMMEDIATE ▶	SHORT TERM ▶	MEDIUM TERM ▶	LONG TERM
MEDICAL	■ If you think you may have plantar fasciitis, you should: ▶ stop activity. ▶ rest until the pain subsides. ▶ apply ice to reduce swelling, then heat to promote blood flow and healing (»p.165). ▶ seek medical attention.	■ If plantar fasciitis is diagnosed, your physician may: ▶ prescribe analgesic medication. ▶ recommend an orthotic insert, such as a heel cup, to reduce stress on your heel, tape to support the plantar fascia, a night splint, and a walking cast. ▶ advise you to rest your foot for 2–4 weeks.	■ If your plantar fasciitis fails to respond to early treatment, your physician may: ▶ give you an injection of corticosteroid to help alleviate your symptoms.	■ If your plantar fasciitis symptoms persist for 6–12 months, your physician may: ▶ recommend surgery to relieve tension and inflammation from the plantar fascia. ■ After surgery, your physician may: ▶ refer you to a physical therapist for a program of rehabilitation (see table below).

	EARLY STAGE ▶	INTERMEDIATE STAGE ▶	ADVANCED STAGE ▶	RETURN TO SPORT
PHYSICAL THERAPY	■ Once your physician has referred you, your physical therapist may: ▶ suggest various treatments, such as electrotherapy, to reduce local inflammation. ▶ use soft-tissue massage to relieve your symptoms. ▶ suggest using a night splint to stretch your plantar fascia. ▶ perform a full biomechanical assessment of your foot and ankle to see if wearing insoles or orthotics to support the medial arch will speed up recovery. ▶ suggest you perform self-massage with a golf ball (»p.245) under the arch of your foot. ■ You may begin: ▶ deep-water pool running to maintain fitness.	■ You should now be able to: ▶ stretch your injured calf to the same extent as your uninjured one. ▶ feel no morning pain or stiffness in your plantar fascia. ■ You may begin: ▶ single-leg calf raises (»p.204) over the edge of a step; aim for 5 sets x 8–10 reps. You should not feel any pain. ▶ functional warm-up drills such as walking kick-outs (»p.185), full-body exercises such as walking lunges (»p.180), and low-level foot plyometrics such as walking pop-ups (»p.254). Stop if you have any pain or swelling.	■ You should now be able to: ▶ perform lower-limb strength training without pain and with no increase in swelling; start at 50% of your one-rep max and aim for 4 sets x 8–12 reps of barbell squats (»p.192) and Romanian deadlifts (»p.196).	■ You should now be able to: ▶ lift leg weights that are at least 80% of your one-rep max. ▶ complete foot plyometrics, such as jumps and hops (»pp.256–59), and speed drills (»pp.252–53), without pain. ▶ perform high-intensity running, at distances relevant to your sport, without pain. ▶ complete sport-specific drills without difficulty. ▶ participate in full training.

TREATMENT & REHABILITATION

From the point of injury to your return to play, appropriate treatment and therapy are key to your recovery. This chapter provides essential information on immediate treatment of various injuries, and guides you step-by-step through a wide range of exercises that may be recommended as part of your rehabilitation program. Make sure you consult your doctor and physical therapist before beginning any exercise program, and follow the general guidelines set out in the introduction of this book.

FIRST AID ESSENTIALS

Proper sports equipment and good technique are key to avoiding sports injuries. If someone is injured, stop play or training and examine him immediately (if it is safe to do so). Some injuries can be dealt with by rest and self-treatment but some require urgent medical help. If you can't contact the emergency services (and if there are enough of you), one person should stay with the victim while two others go for help.

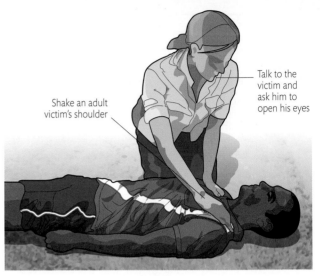

Shake an adult victim's shoulder

Talk to the victim and ask him to open his eyes

PRIORITIES AFTER AN INCIDENT

Assess a situation quickly and methodically. Find out what happened. First, treat victims suffering life-threatening conditions such as unconsciousness (**»p.172**), breathing difficulties (**»p.171**), or severe bleeding (**»p.167**).
Response Is the victim conscious or unconscious? If the victim is responding to you, he is conscious. Shake his shoulders gently if you're not sure.
Airway Is it open and clear? If the victim can talk, it is. If he is unconscious, open and clear it.
Breathing Is it normal? Treat any difficulty such as choking or asthma. If he is unconscious and not breathing, call for emergency help and begin CPR (**»p.93**).
Circulation Are there any signs of severe bleeding?

If so, treat the victim immediately. Once life-threatening conditions are under control, you can make a more detailed assessment. Examine the victim methodically from head to toe. Asking how the injury occurred can help in diagnosis.

WARNING!

Act fast after an accident. Delay can be harmful. Ideally, you should treat the victim while someone else calls 911. If you are on your own, call 911 immediately yourself.

BASIC FIRST AID KIT

Keep your first aid kit dry and accessible. Check seals on sterile dressings—if they're not intact the dressings aren't sterile. Replace anything you use as soon as possible. Sports played in extreme climates of heat or cold require a specialized first aid kit—seek specific advice from a sports retailer or outfitter.

Safety pins for securing bandages

Large scissors are useful for cutting clothing

Combined sterile dressings—these include a dressing pad with bandage attached

Antibiotic eye ointment

Lightweight zip carrier

Waterproof adhesive bandages; gauze pads

Hypoallergenic micropore tape to secure dressings

Gauze roller bandage to secure dressings

Folded triangular bandage

Alcohol-free antiseptic wipes

Antiseptic cream

Disposable gloves (latex free)

MINOR INJURIES

Any injury that breaks the skin carries an infection risk. Infection can come from the air, dirt, or clothing embedded in the wound. Keeping injuries clean is an important part of sports-related first aid.

MINOR CUTS OR ABRASIONS

Any break in the skin must be cleaned and protected from infection. Rinse it with clean cold water and pat it dry. Cover the injury with a dressing pad larger than the wound. For small wounds, use an adhesive bandage; for larger ones, use a sterile pad and a bandage, or a combined sterile dressing.

JOGGER'S NIPPLE

Long-distance runners can suffer from jogger's nipple, a result of clothing rubbing against the nipples over time. Men can prevent this by wearing a well-fitting sports vest. A properly fitting sports bra protects female runners. To treat jogger's nipple, clean the nipple with warm water and air dry. Lubricate with moisturizer or antiseptic ointment. A small adhesive bandage on each nipple acts as a barrier.

NOSE BLEEDS

A severe blow to the nose may cause bleeding, swelling, and bruising around the nose and eyes (a fractured bone will require hospital treatment). A cut to the nose or septum (the partition dividing the nostrils) will also cause nasal bleeding. Before treating a nose bleed, ensure that there are no other head injuries that need urgent medical attention. Severe bleeding may require a hospital visit.

1 Position the victim head-forward, and not leaning back (blood flowing down the throat can block an airway or cause vomiting). Pinch the lower half of his nose to stop the bleeding and create a clot.

2 After 10 minutes release to see if bleeding has stopped. If not, pinch again for 10 minutes. If bleeding lasts more than 30 minutes, go to the hospital.

BLISTERS AND BRUISING

A blister is a fluid-filled "bubble" under the skin caused by repeated rubbing or friction. A bruise is bleeding into the skin and surrounding tissue from a blow that does not break the skin. Both frequently affect athletes.

HOW TO TREAT BLISTERS

The ideal treatment is to rest and wait until it has healed, but this may not be possible if you are in mid-game. Cover with a gel blister adhesive bandage if you have one. Never pierce or burst a blister; this increases the risk of infection.

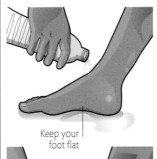

Keep your foot flat

1 Wash the area with clean water and rinse. Pat the area and surrounding skin dry gently and thoroughly with a sterile gauze pad. If it is not possible to wash the area, keep it as clean as possible.

2 Cover the blister with an adhesive dressing; make sure the pad of the adhesive bandage is larger than the blister. A gel blister adhesive bandage has a cushioned pad that provides extra protection and comfort.

HOW TO TREAT BRUISING

To reduce the swelling and pain of a bruise, raise and support the injured area and apply a cold compress. If you have access to cold running water, ice, or snow, soak a cloth and hold it against the bruised area for at least 10 minutes. An ice pack must be wrapped and never make direct contact with the skin. Severe bruising may indicate a more serious injury, such as a broken bone or internal injury, which will require urgent medical attention.

Hold the pack firmly on the affected area. Cool for 10 minutes, adding more ice as required

WOUNDS AND BLEEDING

Some sports injuries can result in severe bleeding, but this can usually be controlled by a combination of direct pressure and elevation of the injury. Reassure the victim while you are treating him. You may also need to treat him for shock (see opposite).

SCALP WOUNDS

A scalp wound can bleed profusely, making it appear worse than it actually is. However, it may mask a more serious head injury. If the victim becomes drowsy, has a headache, or double vision (this can develop hours later), seek emergency medical help. A large scalp wound may require stitches.

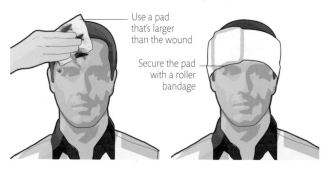

Use a pad that's larger than the wound

Secure the pad with a roller bandage

1 Stop play. Sit the victim down with his head raised. Apply pressure, ideally over a sterile dressing pad.

2 Secure the dressing with a roller bandage. Monitor the victim. If the wound is severe or if his condition deteriorates, get help.

FOREIGN OBJECT IN A WOUND

Any loose foreign objects, such as pieces of dirt or gravel, should be removed from a wound because they may cause infection or delay healing. Either rinse them off with cold running water or carefully remove them with sterile tweezers. If an object is lodged in a wound, don't remove it but bandage as shown below and seek medical advice.

1 Don't try to remove the object, which may be plugging bleeding. Control bleeding by pressing firmly on either side of the wound.
■ Push the edges of the cut together but take care not to press directly on the object.
■ Raise the wound above the level of the victim's heart.

Keep the injured body part raised to slow blood flow to the area

2 Place a piece of gauze lightly over the object to protect it, then build up padding on either side (rolled bandages are ideal). Bandage over the pads and the object in the wound.
■ Check the circulation beyond the bandage every 10 minutes (see Step 3, opposite). Get medical help.

Bandage over the object and padding to prevent further injury

EYE INJURIES

The eye can be seriously injured by a blow from a racquet, hockey stick, or hard ball, risking a ruptured eyeball, facial fractures, or even loss of vision. Always wear the eye protection recommended as appropriate for your sport.

1 Gently lie the victim down with his head on your knee. Cover the injured eye. Ask him to keep both eyes still because moving one eye causes the other to move. If an object is sticking out of the eye, place pads securely around it and seek medical help.

Cover the affected eye with a sterile pad

If you can see an object on the surface of the eye, try lifting it off with the corner of a handkerchief, or washing it out with sterile water, rinsing away from the good eye. Don't remove anything that is sticking to the eye, or embedded in it.

2 Secure the dressing with a bandage. If you're on your own, fix the dressing in place with adhesive bandages or tape and try not to move your eyes. Seek medical help.

Secure the pad with a bandage

SEVERE EXTERNAL BLEEDING

Control the bleeding with direct pressure over a wound and call for emergency help. Never use a tourniquet because this can cause severe tissue damage. Life-threatening shock is likely to develop if blood loss is severe (see below).

1 Apply direct pressure to the wound, over a sterile pad or dressing if you have one. Remove or cut away clothing to expose the wound. Raise the injured limb above the level of the victim's heart to reduce blood flow to the area. Help the victim lie down, and raise his legs.

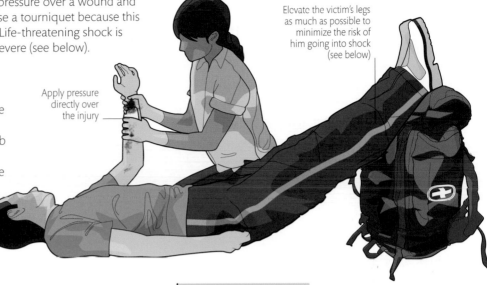

Apply pressure directly over the injury

Elevate the victim's legs as much as possible to minimize the risk of him going into shock (see below)

2 Secure the dressing with a bandage. If blood soaks through, apply a second dressing on top of the first.

3 While waiting for help, every 10 minutes, check that the bandage is not too tight. Gently press a fingernail beyond the dressing. If the skin color does not return quickly, rebandage more loosely.

TREATING SHOCK

Shock is a life-threatening condition that occurs if the circulatory system fails. In sports, the most common cause of shock is severe bleeding. Initially, the victim will have a rapid pulse and pale clammy skin. As the condition progresses, his breathing will become rapid and shallow, his pulse weaker, and his skin a pale gray–blue. Untreated, shock will lead to unconsciousness.

DEALING WITH SHOCK

■ Do not give the victim anything to eat or drink because an anesthetic may be needed; moisten his lips with water if he's thirsty. Call for help; the victim must be transported in the treatment position.

■ Help the victim lie down; insulate him from the ground with blankets. Raise and support his legs as high as you can above heart level.

■ Treat the cause of shock, for example bleeding (see above). Suspect shock, too, if you notice any symptoms, yet can't see any obvious injury—it could be caused by internal bleeding.

■ Loosen tight clothing, for example at the neck, chest, and waist. Keep his head low: this may prevent him from losing consciousness. Keep the victim warm: cover him with a coat, spare clothing, or a blanket.

■ Don't move the victim unnecessarily. Monitor his level of response, breathing, and pulse while waiting for help. Begin cardiopulmonary resuscitation if he loses consciousness (»p.173).

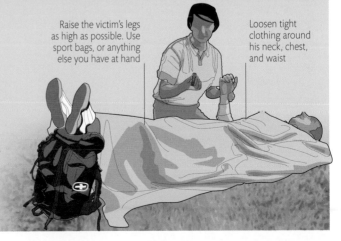

Raise the victim's legs as high as possible. Use sport bags, or anything else you have at hand

Loosen tight clothing around his neck, chest, and waist

ENVIRONMENTAL INJURIES

Some sports expose players to extremes of heat and cold, which can overwhelm the body's ability to regulate temperature. This can be fatal. Wearing the correct sports clothing offers protection, but if there is an emergency, act fast. Don't leave a victim. Call for help or send someone to seek help while you treat the victim.

COLD INJURIES

Exposure to cold, for example during skiing or rock climbing, can cause body parts to freeze (frostnip and frostbite), or the body's core temperature to drop (hypothermia).

FROSTNIP AND FROSTBITE

Frostnip is the freezing of the top layer of skin, usually on the face and extremities. The skin turns numb, white, and hard. Untreated, it can lead to frostbite, which is much more serious—the deeper tissues, and even the bone, freeze. The skin turns white or blue and feels solidly frozen.

Put gloved hands in the armpits

1 If there is no risk of refreezing, warm the area gradually with body heat—place the victim's hands in his own armpits, or his feet in your armpits. He can take acetaminophen if the process is painful. Do not attempt rewarming if there is any risk of refreezing.

2 Remove any rings and raise the injured part to reduce swelling. Ideally, place the affected area in warm water. Then, dress the injury in sterile dressings. Avoid exposing the area to cold and seek medical help.

ALTITUDE SICKNESS

If you are a climber, you might experience symptoms of altitude sickness, which include nausea, appetite loss, shortness of breath, and a headache that's not relieved by medication. You may also have difficulty sleeping and will feel unwell. Start the descent immediately and remain at a lower altitude for a few days. Severe cases will need to be carried.

HYPOTHERMIA

This life-threatening condition develops if the body's core temperature falls below 95°F (35°C). This is a common condition in marathon runners, who rapidly lose heat when they stop running. Treatment aims to prevent further heat loss. It's vital that a victim is warmed up gradually. If he is warmed up too quickly, blood is diverted away from vital organs, such as the heart and brain, to the skin, which can actually speed up cooling of the body. A victim with hypothermia must be moved on a stretcher.

1 If possible, and if there is no risk of further cold, remove any wet clothing and replace with warm, dry clothes.

2 Keep the victim warm by wrapping him in coats, blankets, spare clothes, or a survival foil blanket. Monitor and record the victim's vital signs while waiting for help.

The foil coating of a first aid blanket traps heat and reflects it back toward the body

DROWNING

If you have rescued a person from water, help him lie down with his head low. If he is unconscious and not breathing, call for medical help and begin cardiopulmonary resuscitation, but give five rescue breaths before beginning chest compressions (**»p.173**). Seek medical advice, even if the victim is conscious, because water can also enter the lungs and cause secondary drowning hours after the person appears to have recovered. If a person has been immersed in cold water, there is a high risk of hypothermia (see above).

HEAT INJURIES

Playing sports or training in hot weather without taking the correct precautions will expose you to sunburn, dehydration, and overheating. This will not just hamper your performance; in the worst case scenario, it will threaten your life.

SUNBURN

Protect yourself by avoiding training or playing in the middle of the day. Always wear a hat and suitable ultraviolet-proof clothing recommended for your sport. Before exposure, apply SPF 50 suncream. If you are sunburned, stay out of the sun; use cold compresses, followed by moisturizers on your skin. Take acetaminophen to ease pain. Leave blisters intact.

DEHYDRATION

Vigorous exercise in hot temperatures will require a greater fluid intake than mild exercise in mild climates. Help the victim sit down and give fluids; water or sports drinks are usually sufficient, but rehydration salts mixed with water is best. If the victim complains of cramps, help him stretch the affected muscles, then massage them firmly.

WARNING!

If a victim suffering from heatstroke falls unconscious, be ready to give cardiopulmonary resuscitation (**»p.173**).

HEATSTROKE

This life-threatening condition may follow heat exhaustion or develop swiftly with no warning. Heatstroke causes the body's temperature-control mechanism to fail. If a person complains of headache, feels dizzy, has hot, dry skin, and a raised body temperature, he may have developed heatstroke and will need urgent medical help because he could lose consciousness.

1 Move the victim to a cool place out of the sun. Help him sit or lie down with his head raised and remove as much of his outer clothing as possible. Call for emergency help.

2 Do anything possible to reduce the body temperature quickly. Ideally, wrap him in a cold, wet sheet. Keep the sheet cool by continually pouring water over it.

HEAT EXHAUSTION

If a victim feels dizzy and starts to sweat profusely, but has cold, clammy skin, help him lie down in the shade and offer him fluids to drink. Elevate his legs to help improve blood flow to the brain, and monitor him while he recovers.

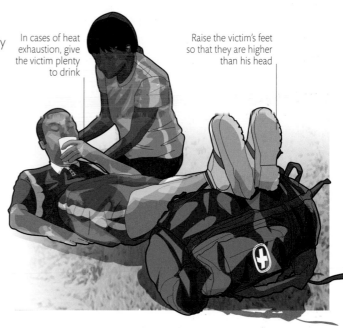

In cases of heat exhaustion, give the victim plenty to drink

Raise the victim's feet so that they are higher than his head

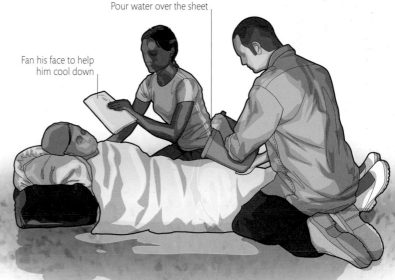

Pour water over the sheet

Fan his face to help him cool down

3 When the victim's temperature drops below 104°F (40°C), replace the wet sheet with a dry one.

4 Monitor his level of response, pulse, and breathing. If his temperature starts to rise again, repeat the treatment.

BONES, JOINTS, AND MUSCLES

It can be difficult to tell whether an injury is a sprain, strain, dislocated joint, or broken bone without an X-ray. If you are in any doubt about an injury it is better to treat it as a fracture because, if it is, the broken bone ends can move, damaging nearby blood vessels or nerves, or can pierce the skin, adding the risk of infection.

SPRAINS AND STRAINS

Injuries to ligaments, tendons, and muscles are a relatively frequent occurrence during sport. A strain is a pulled muscle and is a common sports injury. Sprains occur when ligaments that hold a joint together are damaged. Injuries of this type should be treated with the "RICE" procedure:
R–**Rest** the injured part
I–Cool the injury with an **Ice** pack or a cold pad (aim for 20–30 minutes every 2 hours for at least the first 3 days)
C–Apply **Compression** to the injury
E–**Elevate** the injured part
Once you have given first aid, seek medical advice. Depending on the injury and available transportation, take the victim to the hospital, or wait with him until help arrives.

1 Rest and support the injury. Wrap a cold compress around it for at least 20–30 minutes to reduce swelling and bruising.

Raise the injured area

2 Leave the compress in place, or wrap padding around the injury. Apply a crêpe bandage from the joint below the injury to the joint above it (i.e. toes to knee for a sprained ankle), and seek medical advice.

Bandage a sprained ankle from the victim's toes to his knee

FRACTURES AND DISLOCATIONS

If the victim is in severe pain and you are unsure about the seriousness of the injury, treat it as a break. Strains and sprains may cause swelling and pain, but other signs indicate that an injury is more likely to be a fracture. Compare his injured limb to his uninjured limb. There may be signs of deformity, such as one leg being shorter than the other, or his ankle being turned outward, if both the tibia and the fibula are broken. The victim will not be able to move the limb normally, if at all. If the bone pierces the skin (an open fracture), there is a risk of infection. Internal bleeding and shock (»p.167) are a risk if the victim has broken a large bone.

HAND INJURY

Injuries to the hands are often complicated by bruising or bleeding. Remove jewelry before the area starts to swell. Raise the injured hand and treat bleeding with direct pressure (»p.167). Wrap the hand in padding and support it in a raised position with a sling.

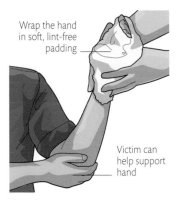

Wrap the hand in soft, lint-free padding

Victim can help support hand

ARM INJURY

Falling onto an outstretched hand can cause a broken wrist, forearm, upper arm, or collarbone, or a dislocated shoulder. Support the affected arm in a sling. If a victim can't bend his arm, he may have injured his elbow, in which case do not use a sling. Wrap padding around the joint instead and secure his arm to his body with folded triangular bandages. To make sure that the bandage isn't too tight, check his wrist pulse.

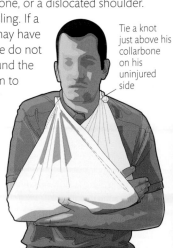

Tie a knot just above his collarbone on his uninjured side

USING A SLING

Slide a triangular bandage between his arm and his chest. Bring the front up over his arm, and tie a square knot on his uninjured side.

CRAMP

This painful muscle spasm can be caused by dehydration and a reduction of body salts through perspiration due to playing sports or training in hot weather. Always make sure you have enough to drink when exercising. Sit down, rest, and stretch the affected muscles.

CALF

Sit the victim down and support his affected leg. Help him straighten his leg, and flex his toes to reverse the spasm. Then massage the painful muscle.

Massage his calf muscles firmly

THIGH

If the cramp is in the back of his thigh, straighten his leg to stretch the muscle; if it's in the front of his thigh, bend the leg. Once the pain eases, massage the affected area.

FOOT

Help the victim stand on his good foot and stretch the muscles to reverse the spasm. Once the cramp has eased, massage the affected area of his foot.

LEG INJURY

Injuries to the leg can be serious—an unstable fracture could pierce a large blood vessel, causing severe bleeding. Don't move the victim unless necessary, making sure his legs have been immobilized first. If you see any signs of shock (»p.167) ensure his head is low, but do not raise his legs.

Support the joints above and below the injury | Keep leg straight

1 Lay the victim down and support the injury to minimize further damage. Call for emergency help. If this is nearby, just maintain this support. You can put rolled-up coats or blankets on either side for extra support.

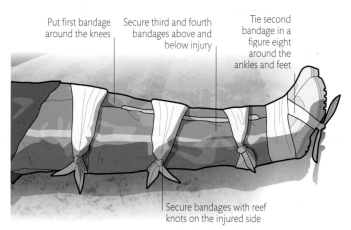

Put first bandage around the knees | Secure third and fourth bandages above and below injury | Tie second bandage in a figure eight around the ankles and feet

Secure bandages with reef knots on the injured side

2 If help is delayed or you need to move the victim, splint his injured leg to the uninjured one. Put bandages around his knees and ankles (and his pelvis, for thigh injuries). Place padding between his legs, and tie the bandages.

SPINAL INJURY

If the victim has fallen on his back, or from a height, it is best to assume that he has a spinal, as well as a head, injury. Don't move him—support his head and neck in line with the rest of his back. Moving him could damage his spinal cord, which may result in permanent paralysis below the injured area. Call for emergency help, or send someone to get help while you stay with him. In the eventuality that you have to leave the victim to get help, and he is unable to maintain an open airway, put him in the recovery position (»p.173).

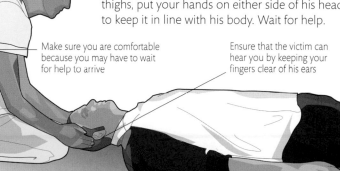

SUPPORT THE HEAD AND NECK

Kneel behind his head. With your elbows on your thighs, put your hands on either side of his head to keep it in line with his body. Wait for help.

Make sure you are comfortable because you may have to wait for help to arrive

Ensure that the victim can hear you by keeping your fingers clear of his ears

UNCONSCIOUSNESS

If someone falls unconscious during a match or in training, your priority is to make sure his airway is open so that he can breathe. Ask someone to call for emergency help while you treat him. Make sure that you don't move the victim, and don't leave him alone unless you have to go and get help yourself.

CHECK FOR RESPONSE
Gently shake the victim's shoulders. Talk to him and watch for a response. If he's alert, he's conscious. If, for example, he reacts weakly, he may not be fully conscious—monitor him for any change, whether this is a deterioration or improvement in his condition (see below). If there's no response, he's unconscious.

OPEN THE AIRWAY
If an unconscious victim is on his back, he's at risk of his tongue falling back and blocking his air passages. Tilting his head and lifting his chin will "lift" his tongue, clearing his airway.

CHECK THE BREATHING
Tilt the victim's head back with one hand and lift his chin with two fingers of your other hand; don't press on the soft tissues under his chin. Keep his airway open, and look, listen, and feel for normal breathing. If the victim's breathing is normal, place him in the recovery position (see opposite). If he's not breathing, begin chest compressions (see opposite).

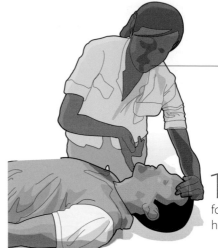

Talk to the victim and ask him to open his eyes

1 Place a hand on the victim's forehead to tilt his head; lift his chin.

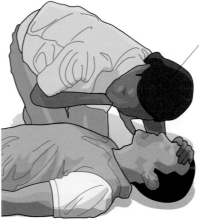

Look, listen, and feel for any breath coming from the victim

2 Look along the victim's chest; listen, and feel, for breath against your cheek for no more than 10 seconds.

MONITORING LEVELS OF CONSCIOUSNESS

If you are checking a person's level of consciousness after an incident you should be aware that this may change. Any injury that has affected the brain in some way (and this may not always be a head injury) can cause unconsciousness. If a victim seems conscious at first, monitor him for any change in his condition, using the AVPU code below. Any sign of deterioration is serious. Call for emergency help.

AVPU SCALE
■ You can assess consciousness levels by checking the victim's level of response to stimuli using the AVPU code.

A—Is the victim **Alert**? Are his eyes open and does he respond to questions?

V—Does the victim respond to **Voice**? Does he answer simple questions and obey commands?

P—Does the victim respond to **Pain**? Does he open his eyes or move if pinched?

U—Is the victim **Unresponsive** to any stimulus?

MONITORING PROGRESS
■ Regularly check and keep a note of any change to the victim's level of response, and the rate and quality of his breathing or pulse (see above).

■ If the victim has had a blow to his head during a match or training, never allow him to continue play without first obtaining medical advice.

■ If the victim appears to have recovered from a head injury, place him in the care of a responsible person. Advise the victim to go to the hospital immediately if he develops symptoms such as a raised temperature, headache, vomiting, confusion, drowsiness, or double vision, because these are symptoms of a serious condition called compression.

CARDIOPULMONARY RESUSCITATION (CPR)

If a victim is not breathing, you must try to keep his body supplied with oxygen using chest compressions and rescue breaths until emergency help arrives. This is known as cardiopulmonary resuscitation (CPR). If an adult collapses, the cause is most likely to be a heart problem, so treat as below. If you have rescued an unconscious victim from water, start with five rescue breaths. If you are unable to give rescue breaths, you can give chest compressions alone.

HOW TO GIVE CPR

Kneel beside the victim, level with his chest so that you don't have to change position. If you have someone else with you, take turns giving CPR so you don't become too exhausted. Change over at the end of each two-minute cycle.

1 Put one hand on the center of the victim's chest—make sure you don't press on his lower abdomen, the tip of his breastbone, or his ribs.

2 Place the heel of your other hand on top of the first and link your fingers together. Keep your fingers off the victim's chest.

3 Start chest compressions. Lean over and, keeping your arms straight, press straight down on the victim's chest, depressing it by 1½–2in (4–5cm). Release the pressure and let his chest come back up, but don't move your hands. Repeat this process 30 times at a rate of 100 compressions per minute.

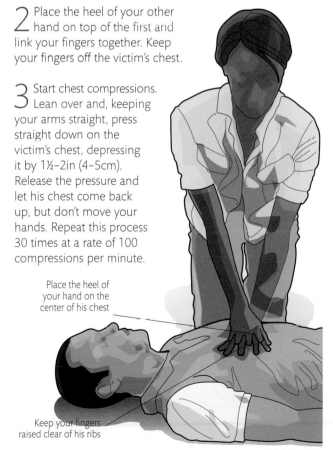

Place the heel of your hand on the center of his chest

Keep your fingers raised clear of his ribs

RECOVERY POSITION

If an unconscious victim is breathing, place him in the recovery position to keep his airway open and clear. Remove anything bulky from his pockets. Kneel beside him. Bend the arm nearest you at a right angle to his body, then bring his other arm across his chest until his hand rests against his near cheek, and hold it there. Bend his far leg at the knee, and, still holding his knee, pull the victim toward you until he is on his side. Adjust his lower arm and thigh as shown here.

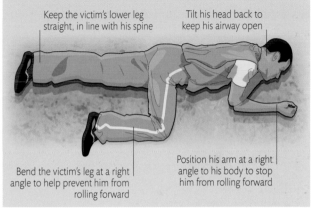

Keep the victim's lower leg straight, in line with his spine

Tilt his head back to keep his airway open

Bend the victim's leg at a right angle to help prevent him from rolling forward

Position his arm at a right angle to his body to stop him from rolling forward

4 Tilt the victim's head to open his airway (see opposite), pinching his nose to close his nostrils. Let his mouth fall open slightly. Lift his chin with the fingers of your other hand.

5 To begin rescue breaths, take a normal breath and seal your lips over those of the victim. Blow into his mouth until you see his chest rise, then lift your mouth away and watch his chest fall. If his chest doesn't rise, adjust his head and try again. Repeat to give a second breath, but don't make more than two attempts at giving rescue breaths before compressing again.

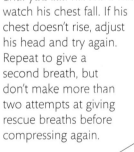

Make a tight seal around his nose

6 Continue the cycle of 30 compressions followed by two rescue breaths until the victim recovers, help arrives, or you are too exhausted to keep going.
■ If at any stage the victim starts breathing normally, place him in the recovery position (see above) and monitor his condition until help arrives.

MOBILITY EXERCISES

Mobility exercises are crucial to the prevention and rehabilitation of injuries. To help prevent injury it is essential that you have sufficient mobility to perform whatever movements are involved in your chosen activity. In rehabilitation you must always regain mobility before you can work on your stability, strength, and power to get you back to full fitness.

1 **NECK** ROTATION

This simple movement helps ease neck ache, maintain neck flexibility, and delay or prevent age-related stiffness. You should be able to rotate your neck through 70–90 degrees on either side without straining.

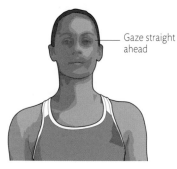
Gaze straight ahead

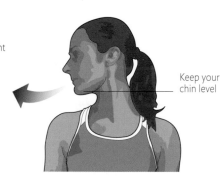
Keep your chin level

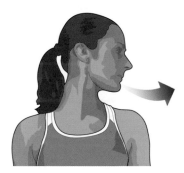

1 Look straight ahead, keeping your spine in a neutral position. Keep your upper body relaxed and your arms loose by your sides.

2 Move your head slowly to the side to look over your right shoulder. Turn it as far as is comfortable, and hold for a few seconds.

3 Move your head back through the starting position, until you are looking over your left shoulder, without straining. Return to the start position.

2 **NECK SIDE** FLEXION

This useful mobility exercise is ideal if you suffer from aching muscles in the upper back and neck. Poor posture or an awkward sleeping position can result in imbalances in the muscles of your neck and shoulders. This may cause pain or even headaches, and can commonly happen to sedentary desk workers.

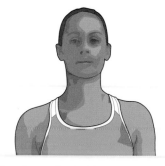

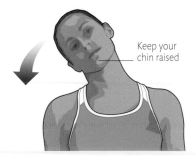
Keep your chin raised

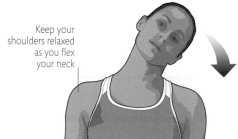
Keep your shoulders relaxed as you flex your neck

1 Stand upright, holding your body in a relaxed posture, with your shoulders loose and your eyes looking straight ahead.

2 Tilt your head so that your right ear moves toward your right shoulder as far as comfortable. Hold for a few seconds.

3 Flex your neck in the opposite direction, passing through the start position to the limit of flexion. Hold and return to the start position.

3 NECK EXTENSION AND FLEXION

This easy movement, which can be carried out either standing or seated, will help prevent general neck stiffness, and will also give you an advantage in sports for which head position and movement are important—for example, when following a fast-moving ball or other moving objects.

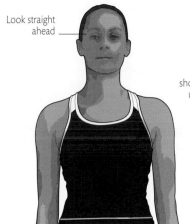
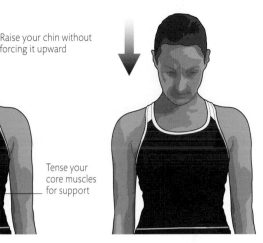

Look straight ahead

Keep your shoulders and upper body relaxed

Raise your chin without forcing it upward

Tense your core muscles for support

1 Stand upright with your arms by your sides in a relaxed posture. Look straight ahead and keep your spine in a neutral position.

2 Extend your neck as far as is comfortable by slowly raising your chin so you are looking directly upward. Hold for a few seconds.

3 Flex your neck by letting your head drop forward without straining. Return your head to the start position.

4 SHOULDER ROTATION

The stability of your shoulder joints stems from the muscles and ligaments around them, rather than from your skeletal system. This exercise frees up your shoulder joints, and also warms up your trapezius muscles (the large muscles on each side of the upper part of your back) before beginning a resistance-training session.

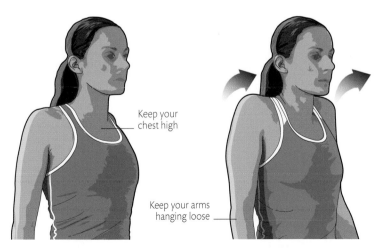
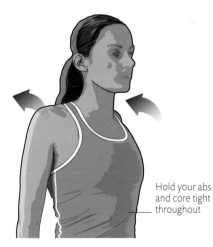

Keep your chest high

Keep your arms hanging loose

Hold your abs and core tight throughout

1 Let your arms hang loose by your sides and relax your shoulders. Keep your head level and your spine in a neutral position.

2 Bring your shoulders forward and inward and raise them slowly up toward your ears.

3 Rotate your shoulders backward and around to the start position, still looking straight ahead.

5 WRIST ROTATION

Good grip is fundamental to many activities. This exercise mobilizes your wrist joints and can help prevent wrist injuries that commonly affect desk workers, such as carpal tunnel syndrome (»p.90).

Keep your shoulders level

Keep your abs and core tight

1 Make small circles with your hands around your wrist joints. Move slowly, rolling your wrists, rather than moving them from side to side. Continue for 20 seconds before reversing the direction of rotation.

6 HIP STRETCH

Good functional hip mobility helps keep your body steady, upright, and well balanced. This simple but effective exercise targets your hips and gluteals, and can be used as part of your training regimen as well as a warm-up exercise.

Feel the stretch in your hip

Extend your arm for balance

Hold your leg parallel to the floor

1 Stand upright with a neutral spine and your head up. Lift your right leg up and across your body, and grip it with your left hand across your shin. Ease your leg up, hold the position, then lower and repeat with your left leg.

7 TORSO ROTATION

This exercise helps you mobilize your core muscles, moving your upper body while keeping your hips stationary.

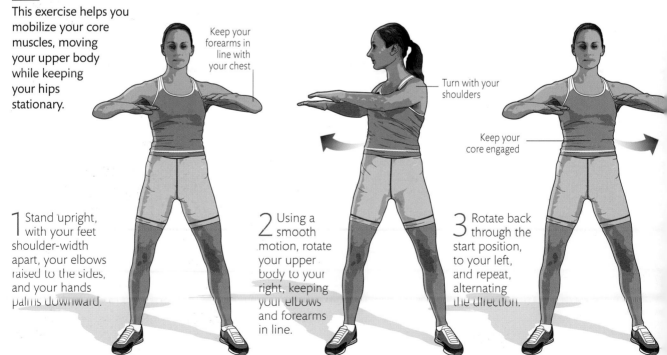

Keep your forearms in line with your chest

Turn with your shoulders

Keep your core engaged

1 Stand upright, with your feet shoulder-width apart, your elbows raised to the sides, and your hands palms downward.

2 Using a smooth motion, rotate your upper body to your right, keeping your elbows and forearms in line.

3 Rotate back through the start position, to your left, and repeat, alternating the direction.

8 FRANKENSTEIN WALK

This exercise mobilizes your hips and hamstrings. You should carry it out walking. Ensure you keep a steady tempo and extend your front leg under tight control rather than letting it swing.

1 Start from a standing position. Keep your body upright, with your right leg slightly behind the line of your body, resting on your toes. Hold your left arm out straight in front of your body.

Extend your hand, palm downward

2 Bring your right leg up to touch your left hand (or as near as your flexibility will allow). Return to an upright stance and repeat with your other leg.

Raise your foot up toward your hand

Keep your right leg as straight as possible

Keep your left leg straight and solid and your foot flat on the floor

9 PIKE WALK

This challenging, functional mobility exercise works your calves, hamstrings, the core muscles of your lower back, and your shoulders. With practice, some people can bend almost in half, but persevere if your movement is limited. Control of your shoulders, pelvis, and spinal position is crucial.

1 Position yourself as if you were about to perform a push-up (>>pp.228–29), with your hands shoulder-width apart and your arms straight.

Keep your spine in a neutral position

Maintain a straight line through your hips

Support your weight on your toes

2 Walk your hands forward as far as possible. Then, keeping your legs straight, slowly walk your feet up toward your hands.

Fold your body at your hips

Keep your core and abs tight

3 When you reach the point at which you cannot continue walking forwards, hold the position for a few moments, then walk your feet back to the start position.

Maintain a straight back throughout

Keep your legs straight

Keep your arms straight and your hands flat on the floor

10 **LEG** ABDUCTION

In this hip mobility exercise you move your leg in a different plane to that in the leg flexion (see below).

This movement works to free up your gluteals and the muscles in your groin area.

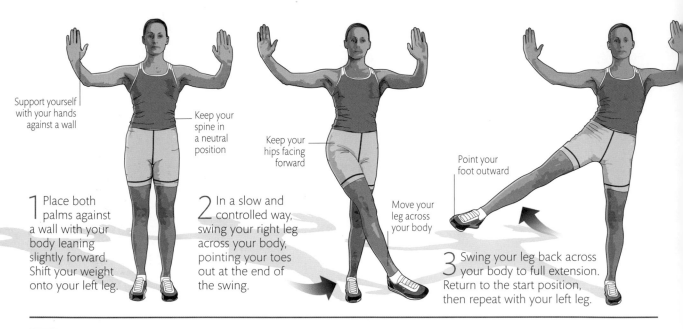

Support yourself with your hands against a wall

Keep your spine in a neutral position

Keep your hips facing forward

Move your leg across your body

Point your foot outward

1 Place both palms against a wall with your body leaning slightly forward. Shift your weight onto your left leg.

2 In a slow and controlled way, swing your right leg across your body, pointing your toes out at the end of the swing.

3 Swing your leg back across your body to full extension. Return to the start position, then repeat with your left leg.

11 **LEG** FLEXION

This movement works your hips and hamstrings. Like the harder Frankenstein walk (»p177), this exercise involves moving one leg at a time, but here both your moving leg and your stabilizing limb are worked at once.

Keep your right leg as straight as possible

1 Stand on your left leg with your right leg slightly behind the line of your body. Rest your right foot on tiptoes. Lightly place your left palm against a wall or piece of apparatus to help maintain your balance.

Bend your knee very slightly for balance

2 Keep your left foot firm and flat on the floor, and bring your right leg forward in front of you. Keep your right knee as straight as possible.

Tense and hold your core muscles for support

Keep your foot flat on the floor

3 Bring your right leg up as high as you can, keeping it straight. Hold for a few seconds, lower it, then repeat with your left leg.

Keep the movement smooth and controlled

12 HEEL SLIDE

This is a simple exercise that can increase the range of motion in your knee and hip. It is an especially useful rehabilitation exercise to help you regain your movement following a knee (»pp.112–31) or hip injury (»pp.96–101), or surgery on either joint.

PROGRESSION

Once you have become familiar with the exercise and increased your range of movement, try sitting upright and hugging your knee into your body to flex your knee a little further.

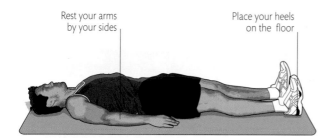

Rest your arms by your sides

Place your heels on the floor

Keep your pelvis neutral

Bend your knee as far as you can

1 Lie on your back with your legs stretched out straight in front of you, your arms by your sides, and your heels pressed against the floor.

2 Slowly bend your right knee up by sliding your right heel along the ground. Bend it as far as you can without hitching your hip. Slide your right leg back to the start position, and repeat with your left leg.

13 ANKLE MOVEMENTS

These movements are essential to the effective functioning of your ankle, and are ideal rehabilitation exercises to help you regain flexibility in your ankle joint, if you have had an ankle injury (»pp.144–47) or ankle surgery.

Maintain a straight back

Keep your heel on the floor

Keep your shoulders up and your back straight

Keep your hips straight and aligned

1 Sit with your right leg straight out in front of you and your left leg bent at a right angle, your left foot flat on the floor. Keeping your right leg straight, pull your right foot up toward you as far as you can, then push your foot back down so your toes are pointing away from you. Do this for at least 20–30 repetitions, then repeat with your left foot.

2 Sit with your right leg straight out in front of you and your left leg bent at a right angle, your left foot flat on the floor. Keeping your legs straight, turn your right foot and ankle inward as far as you can and then outward as far as possible. Do this for at least 20–30 repetitions, then repeat with your left foot.

14 SQUAT

This is one of the key movement patterns for your lower body and core. Good form is key: go as low as possible to improve your range of motion and do not "bounce."

Hold your chest up

Hold your arms out straight with your palms facing down

Keep your spine neutral

Ease your hips back

Ensure that the bend in your knees follows the line of your feet

Hold your torso upright throughout the exercise

Keep your head level

Keep your heels on the ground

Start with your legs straight and your feet turned slightly outward

1 Stand with your spine neutral, your arms out in front of you, and your feet just over shoulder-width apart.

2 Breathe in and, looking straight ahead, bend at your knees and hips, easing your hips backward.

3 Squat down until your thighs are parallel to the floor (or further if you can). Return to the start position.

15 WALKING LUNGE

This is an excellent way to mobilize your hips and thighs. The walking lunge tests both your balance and coordination, making it an excellent mobility exercise for all types of sports. You can also perform it from a fixed position.

1 Stand with your feet hip-width apart and your shoulders, hips, and feet in line.

2 Take a long step forward with your right leg. Drop down and bend at your knees.

3 Push off with your left leg back to an upright position, keeping your core engaged and head up.

4 Step forward with your left leg and drop down again. Return to the start position and repeat.

Maintain a strong posture throughout

Feel the stretch in your hips

Your upper leg should be parallel to the floor

Lift your left leg through in one fluid movement

Rest your back leg on the ball of your foot

Make sure that your knee is over your foot

16 OVERHEAD LUNGE

This demanding lunge mobilizes your hips and thighs along with your thoracic spine and shoulders. Adding a light weight overhead also works the stabilizers in your shoulders and puts emphasis on the mobility of your hips and lower back.

1 Stand with your feet hip-width apart and your shoulders, hips, and feet in line. Hold a light bar at arm's length above your head with your hands widely spaced.

Engage your core muscles

Hold the bar with your arms straight above your shoulders

Keep your chest high and your shoulders back

Keep your back as straight as possible and avoid overarching

Lift your heel off the floor

2 Lunge forward with your right leg, holding the bar above you with straight arms. Push back off your right leg to return to the start position and repeat on your left leg.

17 ROTATIONAL LUNGE

This is another good mobility exercise for your hips and thighs. You should feel it stretching the hip flexor of your back leg and the gluteals of your front leg. In addition, the movement engages your torso, which rotates as you turn your head, first to one side and then to the other.

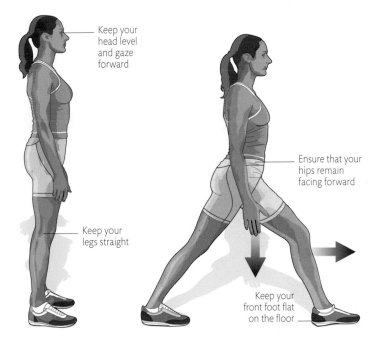

Keep your head level and gaze forward

Keep your legs straight

Ensure that your hips remain facing forward

Keep your front foot flat on the floor

1 Stand with your feet hip-width apart and your shoulders, hips, and feet in line. Make sure that your knees and toes are pointing straight ahead.

2 Step forward with your left leg and lower your body, bending your knees. As you descend, start to turn your torso to the right at your waist.

Extend your right arm out and behind your body, keeping it parallel to the floor

Bring your left arm across your body

Rotate your whole torso, keeping your hips pointing forward

Raise your back heel off the floor

3 Turn your head, extend your left arm across your body, and twist at your waist. Recover to the start position, then repeat with your right leg.

18 PUNCH LUNGE

This exercise is designed to help your hips, torso, upper back, and shoulders to work in unison. It encourages your lower and upper body to work together, which is very important for correct shoulder function following an injury.

1 Stand with your feet shoulder-width apart. Keeping your left arm hanging by your side, bend your right arm and make a fist with your hand.

Slightly rotate your chest and torso

Stand with your feet shoulder-width apart

2 Step forward with your left leg, bending slightly at your knee, and punch fully forward with your right hand, so that your arm is straight out in front of you. Pause, then return to the start position. Repeat for the required number of repetitions and then switch sides.

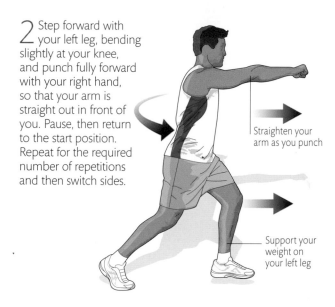

Straighten your arm as you punch

Support your weight on your left leg

19 SHOULDER DUMP

This exercise helps you coordinate the movement of your hips and shoulders to ensure that they work together. Like the punch lunge (see above), the shoulder dump also encourages your lower and upper body to function as a unit, which is very important after any form of shoulder injury.

Keep your back straight

Allow your arms to hang down vertically

1 Stand with your feet shoulder-width apart and your knees bent slightly. Lean forward at your waist, allowing your arms to hang vertically down in front of you, and make loose fists with your hands.

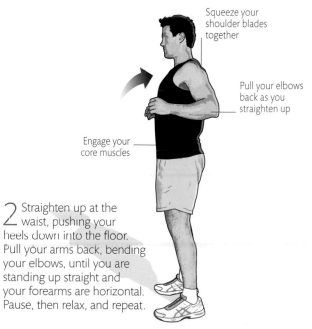

Squeeze your shoulder blades together

Pull your elbows back as you straighten up

Engage your core muscles

2 Straighten up at the waist, pushing your heels down into the floor. Pull your arms back, bending your elbows, until you are standing up straight and your forearms are horizontal. Pause, then relax, and repeat.

20 ROBBERY

Similarly to the shoulder dump (see opposite), this exercise combines upper- and lower-body movements to aid correct shoulder function, but requires a greater range of motion and coordination.

Keep your back straight

Lean forward from your hips

1 Keeping your back straight, lean forward at your hips, bending your knees slightly and allowing your arms to hang straight down in front of you. Clench your hands into loose fists.

Keep your shoulders relaxed but squeeze your shoulder blades together

Push your hips forward

Straighten your knees

2 Push forward at your hips, straightening at your knees and raising your hands upward above you with your elbows bent at right angles. Pause at the top of the movement then return to the start position.

PROGRESSION

Once you are used to the exercise, you can make it harder by holding a dumbbell in each hand. Ensure that you start with light weights and maintain good form.

21 PUSH-UP PLUS

The push-up plus is similar to a normal push-up but requires a little extra push at the very top of the movement. This engages your serratus anterior muscle, helping to improve your shoulder function.

Relax your shoulders

1 Position yourself roughly parallel to the floor, supporting your weight on your palms and your toes.

Keep your pelvis neutral

2 Keeping your back straight, and your core muscles tight, press your palms downward, extending your arms, and raise your torso.

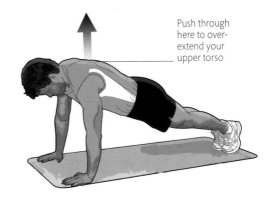

Push through here to over-extend your upper torso

3 As you reach the top of the movement, push up between your shoulder blades as high as you can. Pause, then return to the start position.

22 PRESS-UP

This simple exercise is great for rehabilitation of shoulder injuries (**»pp.70–75**), working the muscles of your upper body and building your core strength. It can be performed on a chair or a bench.

Look straight ahead

Keep your shoulders back and down

Grip the edges of the chair

1 Sit on a chair and grip the outside edges of the seat with your hands. Try to keep your hands in line with your shoulders.

Keep your back straight and squeeze your shoulders together

Engage your core muscles

2 Push down with your hands to raise your body off the chair— you may not be able to lift yourself very high. Pause briefly and lower yourself to the start position.

23 WINDOW-WIPER

This dynamic exercise works your hip joints, upper legs, and shoulders. It helps get your rotator cuff functioning as part of a full-body movement, and makes the lower and upper body work together. It is another useful exercise for the rehabilitation of shoulder injuries (**»pp.70–75**).

Rotate your hand so it points upward

Bend your elbow at about 90 degrees and keep it close to your torso

1 Stand next to a wall with your feet slightly more than shoulder-width apart. Holding a small cloth in your right hand, press it gently against the wall, with your arm bent.

Keep your back straight and your shoulder blades together

Engage your core

Bend your knees

2 Bend your knees and drop down into a squat position, keeping the cloth pressed against the wall. Try to squat as low as possible.

Push up with your arm at a 45-degree angle

Push up through your hips

Straighten your knees

Push down with your heels

3 Straighten up explosively, pushing the cloth upward at an angle of about 45 degrees until you are upright and your arm is fully extended. Pause, then return to the start position. Repeat for the required number of repetitions, then switch arms.

PROGRESSION

Once you have perfected the movement and your strength has improved you can perform the exercise using a dumbbell or hand-weight instead of a cloth. Ensure that you begin with a light weight and maintain good form throughout.

24 WALKING KICK-OUT

This exercise encourages hip mobility in the moving leg and stability in the standing leg, which is great for most sports, because nearly all will require you to have a good range of movement.

Keep your back straight and your upper body balanced

Bend your knee slightly

1 Stand with your body balanced and your feet shoulder-width apart.

2 Transfer your entire weight onto your left leg and lift your right leg up so that your hip and knee are flexed at a right angle.

Balance your body over your standing leg

Try to get your leg horizontal

Feel the stretch in your inner thighs

Transfer your weight forward

3 Kick your right leg out to the side while maintaining your balance on your left leg. Reach your right leg out as far as you can.

4 Step forward with your right leg, then return to the start position, and repeat with your left leg.

25 WALL SIT PRESS

This exercise is great for releasing your thoracic spine and opening up your shoulders and chest region prior to performing upper-body exercises.

Bend your elbows at a right angle

Place the back of your wrists against the wall

1 Sit with your hips, back, shoulders, elbows, wrists, and head flat against a wall, and the soles of your feet placed together. Hold a bar above your head with your elbows bent at 90 degrees.

Raise the bar as high as possible

Maintain your position against the wall

Feel the stretch in your lats

2 Slowly push the bar above your head, maintaining full contact with the wall throughout the entire movement. Once you reach your limit, lower the bar to the start position.

26 STATIONARY SUPERMAN

This exercise is excellent for improving your balance and coordination, as well as your hamstring flexibility. It is an essential exercise for the rehabilitation of lower-body injuries. Practice in front of a mirror to perfect your form.

1 Stand upright with your body balanced and your feet shoulder-width apart.

Keep your pelvis neutral

2 Bend forward at your waist, lifting your right leg back and transferring your weight onto your left leg, bending your knee slightly, and lifting your arms as you do so.

Start to straighten your right leg behind you

3 Continue until your body is as close as you can get to parallel with the floor. Hold, then slowly return to the start position, bringing your right leg down and forward to stand.

Keep your spine straight

Bend your left knee to a maximum of 20–30 degrees

27 HIP HITCHER

This exercise works your abductor muscles. To begin with, you may need to use a swinging bar to support your weight, but as you progress, you will be able to increase the flexion of your hip.

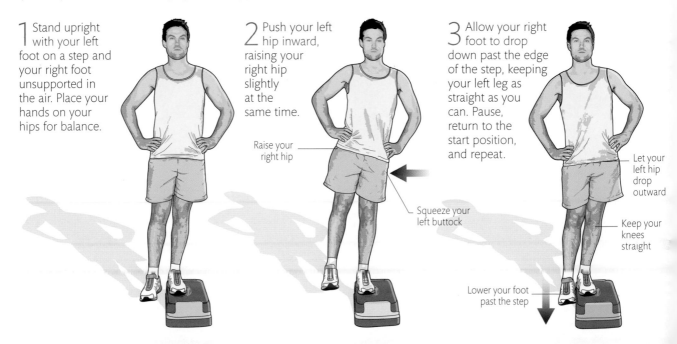

1 Stand upright with your left foot on a step and your right foot unsupported in the air. Place your hands on your hips for balance.

2 Push your left hip inward, raising your right hip slightly at the same time.

Raise your right hip

Squeeze your left buttock

3 Allow your right foot to drop down past the edge of the step, keeping your left leg as straight as you can. Pause, return to the start position, and repeat.

Let your left hip drop outward

Keep your knees straight

Lower your foot past the step

28 CLAM

This straightforward exercise activates your gluteals and hip flexors, while also improving overall stability in your pelvis and abdominals.

1 Lie on your right side bending slightly at your hips and your knees. Extend your right arm so that it is in line with your body, and place your head on it. Bend your left arm at the elbow and rest your left hand on the floor in front of you.

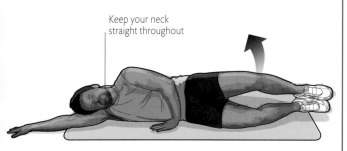

Keep your neck straight throughout

2 Keeping your neck straight, your hips and shoulders in line, and your feet touching, engage your core and begin lifting the knee of your left leg, rotating it at your hip.

Keep your hips forward and aligned

Make sure that your feet stay in contact

3 Lift your left knee as far as it will go, while keeping your hips aligned. Slowly lower your knee back to the start position and repeat for the required number of repetitions before swapping sides.

29 HAMSTRING LOWER

This exercise builds up flexibility and control in your hamstring muscles. It is a progressive exercise that can be made harder as your flexibility improves, and it requires strong core stability.

Rest your left leg against the edge of the doorframe

Position your hips as close as possible to the support

Keep your knees straight

1 Lie on your back with your left leg next to a doorframe. Place a step under your right heel. Lift your legs and prop your left leg against the doorframe. Slide your hips forward until your legs are at right angles to your body.

Keep your back flat against the floor

Keep your right leg straight as you lower it

2 Slowly lower your right leg toward the step, keeping it straight throughout. Touch your heel onto the block, then raise your right leg back to the start position. Complete the desired number of repetitions, then repeat with your left leg.

PROGRESSION—LEVELS 2 AND 3

Once you have full control over the movement, you can progress to Levels 2 and 3. For Level 2, use the doorframe support but remove the step and lower your leg to the floor. For Level 3 (see right), perform the exercise without the doorframe or the block.

30 NEURAL GLIDE

Also known as "flossing," this is a great exercise for helping with neural tension in your spine and legs. When you are starting off, be gentle and don't push it too hard—you will develop the range of movement eventually.

Sit up straight

Flex your neck

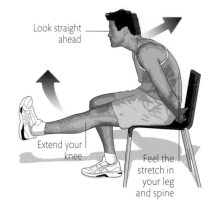

Look straight ahead

Extend your knee

Feel the stretch in your leg and spine

1 Sit on a chair, with your back straight, your spine lengthened, and your arms tucked behind you.

2 Slump down, so that your spine is rounded and your neck is flexed.

3 Straighten your left leg as far as is comfortable and, at the same time, lift your head. Hold the position for 30 seconds. Return to the position in Step 2 and repeat with your right leg.

31 CARIOCA SIDESTEP

This is a simple coordination drill that can be used for any lower-limb injury and also as part of your rehabilitation following a hamstring injury (»pp.108–09). It is also often used as part of a warm-up for numerous sports.

Shift your weight on to your right leg

Shift your weight on to your right leg

1 Stand with your legs roughly shoulder-width apart.

2 Moving to your left, swing your right leg across and in front of your body, and shift your weight onto your right foot.

3 Keeping your weight on your right leg, swing your left leg around from the back, so that your feet are roughly shoulder-width apart again.

4 Continue to move sideways, this time swinging your right leg behind your left, shifting your weight onto your right foot.

5 With your weight on your right leg, swing your left leg in front of your body. Repeat Steps 1–5 over the desired distance, then reverse.

32 SIDEWAYS WALK

This drill helps improve your lateral movement, which is important in most sports, and also helps rehabilitation following a leg injury.

PROGRESSION

Begin the exercise at a walking pace, gradually build to a skip and then try to do the drill as fast as you can. Alternatively, you can try the exercise on your toes or heels.

1 Stand with your legs shoulder-width apart.

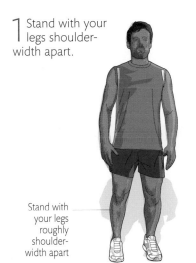

Stand with your legs roughly shoulder-width apart

2 Take a big step to your left, keeping your right foot on the floor. Shift your weight to your left foot as you do so.

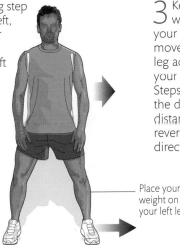

Place your weight on your left leg

3 Keeping your weight on your left leg, move your right leg across toward your left. Repeat Steps 1–3 over the desired distance, then reverse the direction.

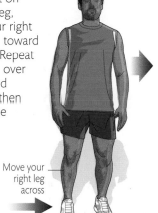

Move your right leg across

33 RESISTED LATERAL WALK

A further progression of the sideways walk (see above), this is a great functional exercise to help engage and build your hip stabilizer muscles.

PROGRESSION

Begin the movement at a walking pace, gradually build to a skip, before performing the drill as fast as you can. Alternatively, you can try doing the drill on your toes or heels.

1 Attach a band or strap to both of your ankles, and stand with your legs shoulder-width apart.

Stand with your legs around shoulder-width apart

2 Step to your left, keeping your right foot on the floor, placing your weight on both legs.

Step sideways with your left leg

3 Bring your right leg toward your left leg. Repeat Steps 1–3 over the desired distance, then reverse the direction.

Move your right leg across toward your left

34 LAWNMOWER

This exercise works the large muscles of your middle and upper back as well as the rotator cuff muscles of your shoulder, helping coordinate your lower and upper body and improve your shoulder control.

Hold your left arm straight out behind you

Keep your back straight

Plant your heels on the floor

1 Stand with your feet slightly more than shoulder-width apart, and hold a dumbbell in your right hand.

2 Bending your knees and leaning forward from your waist, lower the dumbbell across your legs to just above your left foot. Extend your left arm straight out behind you.

Keep your core engaged

Straighten your legs

Follow the movement with your head

Keep your elbow high

Twist at your hips

3 Engaging your core, strongly pull the dumbbell up and across your torso. Straightening your legs, rotate your upper body to the right, and swing your left arm forward.

4 Pull the weight up to shoulder level, so your right elbow is at a right angle, and bring your left arm across your body. Pause, then return to the start position. Switch arms.

35 CAT AND CAMEL

A great muscle-releasing exercise, this stretch helps lubricate your spine and get your spinal disks moving. It is one of the best exercises you can do as part of a general warm-up.

Bend your elbows sligh[t]

1 Kneel on all fours with your hands in line with your shoulders, your fingers pointing forward, and your knees below your hips.

Feel the stretch in your back

Tilt your pelvis upward

Drop you[r] head

2 Round your back upward and pull in your stomach, letting your head drop forward.

Stretch your head upward and backward

3 Reverse the position by curving your spine downward, lifting your head upward, tilting your pelvis downward, and arching your lower back. Return to the start position.

36 GLUTEAL/PIRIFORMIS FOAM ROLLER

This exercise loosens up the gluteals at the outside of your buttocks and the piriformis toward the middle of them.

Feel the stretch here

1 Sit on the roller with your right buttock and cross your right leg over your left leg. Rolling backward and forward, work on the outside of your buttock before shifting your weight to the middle of your buttock. Repeat for at least 30 seconds before switching sides.

37 LATS FOAM ROLLER

This exercise helps loosen up the large muscles of your middle and upper back.

Feel the stretch in your side

1 Lie on your right side over the roller, which should fit under your armpit, and place your hands behind your head for stability. Use your back muscles to roll down from your armpit to the base of your shoulder blade. Roll back up and repeat for at least 30 seconds. Switch sides.

38 ITB FOAM ROLLER

This exercise loosens your iliotibial band (ITB) and your tensor fascia latae. It is great for runners and bicyclists, because they are often prone to ITB syndrome (»p.132).

1 Lie on your right side with the foam roller beneath your outer thigh, just above your knee. Propping yourself up on your right forearm, bend your left arm and place your left hand in front of you for support.

Feel the stretch in your ITB

2 Using your right forearm and left hand, slowly push your body over the roller so that your outer thigh slides across the roller, up toward your hip bone. Slide back the opposite way and repeat for at least 30 seconds, then swap sides.

39 THORACIC FOAM ROLLER

Here the foam roller acts as a hinge to help improve the range of motion in your middle and upper back. It is good for players of contact sports who suffer neck pain.

1 Sit with your heels planted on the floor and the roller beneath the middle of your back. Lie back onto the roller so that it is just below your shoulder blades. Clasp your hands together and lightly cradle your head.

Feel the stretch in your upper back

Roll to here but no farther

2 With your chin tucked in, slide up and down the roller from your neck all the way down to the level of your lowest ribs. Do not go too low into your lumbar spine because this will cause some discomfort. Repeat for at least 30 seconds.

STRENGTH-TRAINING EXERCISES

Strength training is often a crucial part of your rehabilitation program. Your physical therapist will design your exercise regimen under the direction and prescription of your **physician, and must guide your form. Achieving perfect form in these exercises is key to helping you return to your sport with the necessary control, strength, and power.**

40 BARBELL SQUAT

This multi-joint exercise is extremely effective at developing the muscles of your legs, pelvis, and spine. It is a great foundation exercise for building overall power and strength, but must be performed with good form. To improve your form, increase the depth of your squat by placing a small (½–1 in/1–2 cm) block under your heels.

1 Take a balanced grip on the bar on the rack. Duck beneath it and stand up with your feet directly under the bar. Step back and stand upright with the bar resting on the upper part of your back.

Place your feet just wider than shoulder–width apart

Gaze straight ahead

Hold your chest high

2 Breathe deeply and, tensing your abs and gluteals, start the descent. Keep your feet pointing slightly outward, and ensure that your knees follow the angle of your feet as you bend your knees and ease your hips back.

Keep your torso at a constant angle

Drop your buttocks back

3 Maintain a neutral spine and lower your body slowly and under tight control, easing your hips farther back. Bend your knees, making sure you keep them over your toes.

Maintain a neutral back position

Keep the bar centered over your feet

Keep the bar stable and level

4 Continue bending at the knees until your thighs are parallel to the floor. Your torso should be at a 45-degree angle. Return to the start position and repeat as required.

41 SINGLE-LEG SQUAT

This exercise works in a similar way to the squat (»p.180), but is a much more challenging movement to perform correctly because it requires much greater leg strength, balance, and core stability.

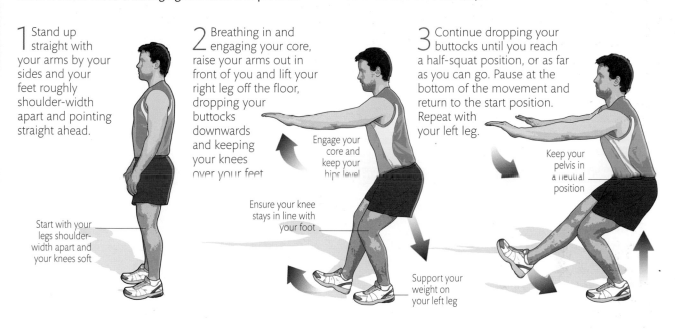

1 Stand up straight with your arms by your sides and your feet roughly shoulder-width apart and pointing straight ahead.

2 Breathing in and engaging your core, raise your arms out in front of you and lift your right leg off the floor, dropping your buttocks downwards and keeping your knees over your feet

3 Continue dropping your buttocks until you reach a half-squat position, or as far as you can go. Pause at the bottom of the movement and return to the start position. Repeat with your left leg.

Start with your legs shoulder-width apart and your knees soft

Ensure your knee stays in line with your foot

Engage your core and keep your hips level

Support your weight on your left leg

Keep your pelvis in a neutral position

42 STRAIGHT-LEG RAISE

The ability to straighten your knee fully is crucial to knee rehabilitation, whatever your injury may be. Learning to tighten your quadriceps and hold them while performing a straight-leg raise is one of the basics you need to master.

Bring your heel off the floor

Fully straighten your left knee

Rotate your left leg outward

Keep your leg straight

1 Sit up straight on the floor with your legs stretched out in front of you. Tighten the quadriceps of your left leg as much as possible to straighten your knee fully.

2 Rotate your left leg out to a 45-degree angle while still keeping your quadriceps tight and your knee as straight as possible.

3 With your quadriceps tight and your leg rotated, lift it 8–12in (20–30cm) off the floor, ensuring that you do not let your knee sag or bend. Pause, then slowly lower your leg to the start position. Repeat with your right leg.

43 BULGARIAN DUMBBELL SPLIT SQUAT

This exercise is similar to the barbell split squat, but holding the dumbbells at your sides gives you a lower center of gravity and improves your stability. It is ideal for improving balance and strength in your hips and thighs.

Let your arms hang vertically

Hold a dumbbell in each hand

Position your right foot just ahead of your torso

Bend your knee toward a right angle

Rest your toes on the bench

Keep your torso upright and your lower back flat

1 With your feet hip-width apart, place your right foot in front of you with your knee slightly bent, and your left foot behind you on top of a bench.

2 Keep your body upright and your head facing forward. Engaging your core and breathing freely, gently lower your left knee almost to the ground.

3 Slowly straighten your right leg to the start position—do not step or hop back with your right foot. Repeat as required, then switch to your left leg.

44 BARBELL LUNGE

This exercise strengthens the large muscles of your legs and your glutes. It is a dynamic movement that is useful in training for racket sports because it improves your ability to reach those difficult shots.

1 Stand with your feet hip-width apart and your knees soft. Rest the barbell across your upper back, holding it with a wide grip, your knuckles facing backward.

Look straight ahead

Keep your knees slightly bent

2 Engage your core muscles and take one long step forwards with your right foot. At the same time, lower your left knee toward the floor, breathing freely.

Bring your left foot up on your toes

3 Let your left knee almost touch the floor, then straighten your right leg and step back to the start position. Complete your set and repeat with your left leg.

Ensure that your left thigh is vertical

45 45-DEGREE LEG PRESS

This simple machine exercise is suitable for those who do not have good core strength and are not familiar with more functional exercises, such as the barbell squat

(»p.192). Performing the movement with only one leg is also a great way to do extra work on an injury as part of your rehabilitation program.

1 Select a weight on the stack and sit on the machine. Place your feet hip-width apart on the platform, take the weight on your legs, release the safety lock, and hold the handle supports.

Bend your knees to at least 90 degrees

Keep your head and back well supported on the pad

2 Push with your legs until they are almost fully extended. Pause at the top of the movement, then return to the start position slowly and under control.

Keep your heels and toes pressed against the platform

Extend your legs almost fully

46 MACHINE LEG CURL

This exercise isolates your hamstrings (which work to bend your knees and extend your hips), making it an excellent

exercise to help protect your knees or assist with rehabilitation after a knee or hamstring injury.

Rest your back against the pad

Align your knee joint with the machine's pivot

1 Select a weight from the stack and sit on the machine. Adjust the moving arm so that it is under your ankles and does not slide up your calves. Position the lap pad above your knees.

Place your ankles on the pad of the moving arm

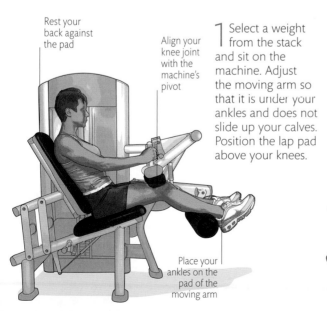

2 Keeping your back stable against the seat, push the moving arm back in a smooth motion by contracting your hamstrings. Return it under control to the start position.

Press your ankles against the pad

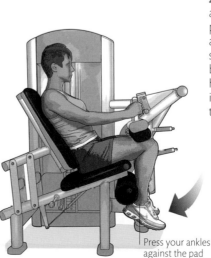

47 ROMANIAN DEADLIFT

This exercise balances work on your quads with development of your hamstrings and gluteals—the muscles that extend your hips. The Romanian deadlift makes an excellent addition to a general training program for most sports, especially for those that require leg strength and power.

1 Squat down so that your feet are under the bar and the bar rests against your shins. Grip the bar using an alternate hook grip to prevent it from rotating. Your hands should be more than shoulder-width apart.

Keep your back flat and tight throughout

Hold the bar with an alternate hook grip—one hand over, and one under

2 Begin lifting the bar with a long, strong leg push, extending your knees and hips. Your knees should be bent as you lift the bar past them.

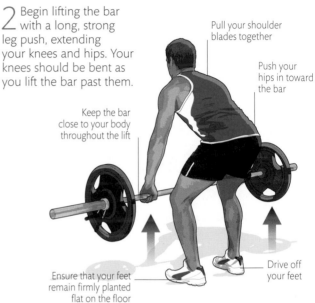

Pull your shoulder blades together

Push your hips in toward the bar

Keep the bar close to your body throughout the lift

Ensure that your feet remain firmly planted flat on the floor

Drive off your feet

3 Continue the lift as if pushing the floor away from you with your feet, until you stand up with your legs straight. Pause, then return to the start position under control.

Brace your shoulders back

Grip tightly so that the bar does not rotate in your hands

VARIATION

Using dumbbells for the deadlift recruits more muscles to control and stabilize movement. It is a good way of developing strength and technique for heavier barbell lifts. Start with light weights to determine your range of motion. As with the barbell lift, keep your back flat and the weights close to your body. Do not pause at the bottom of the movement or allow the weights to "bounce" as you lower them.

WARNING!

Correct lifting technique is essential in this movement. Never lift with your spine flexed forward: not only will the exercise be ineffective, but you also risk spinal injury. Always raise and lower your shoulders and hips together. Keep the bar close to your body and do not drop it at the end of the movement; always lower it under control.

48 STRAIGHT-LEG DEADLIFT

This is a useful exercise for strengthening your lower back and developing your hamstrings and gluteals. It is an excellent movement for anyone who runs or is involved in high-speed and contact sports.

Keep your arms straight

1 Stand upright with your feet hip-width apart and the barbell resting across your upper thighs. Hold the bar with straight arms and an overhand grip.

Keep your back straight throughout

2 With your head facing forward and your knees almost locked, bend from your waist to lower the barbell. Inhale as you do so.

Feel it here

Engage your core muscles

3 Keeping your core muscles tight, slowly pivot at your hips to raise your upper body to the start position, exhaling as you do so.

Bend your knees to a maximum of 30 degrees

49 SINGLE-LEG DEADLIFT

As with the straight-leg deadlift (see above), this exercise strengthens your lower back, gluteals, and hamstrings. Because you have to balance on one leg at a time, this exercise also works your core muscles.

1 Stand with a dumbbell in each hand in an overhand grip, with your feet slightly less than shoulder-width apart. Place your left foot about half a step in front of your right foot.

2 Keeping your abs contracted, your back straight, and your chest lifted, slowly lower the dumbbells toward your left foot. Keep your left leg bent slightly throughout the movement, and lift your right leg for balance.

3 Lower the dumbbells down your shin as far as you can reach. Hold, then flex your left hamstring and push your hips forward to bring your body back to the start position. Repeat with your right leg.

Keep your arms straight

Push your buttocks backward

Bend your knee to a maximum of 20–30 degrees

Keep your back straight throughout

Maintain the angle of your knees

50 ECCENTRIC SINGLE-LEG DECLINE SQUAT

This exercise is used specifically to treat the patella tendon, but can be used in the later stages of any lower-limb injury because it will build eccentric strength in your quadriceps. The important thing is not to push your weight up on the affected leg—use this leg only for lowering your body.

1 Stand with your feet facing forward on a decline board set to an angle of about 25 degrees.

2 Bending your right leg slightly, lift your left foot off the ground until your left knee is almost at a right angle.

3 Standing on your right leg, engage your core and bend your right knee slowly for as deep a squat as possible, and hold briefly.

4 Lower your left foot to the board and lift your right foot off. Push up through your left foot and stand to the start position. Switch feet.

Point your feet forward

Support your weight on your right foot

Engage your core

51 SHORT-LEVER ADDUCTOR MANUAL

This exercise is great for groin and adductor problems and requires no equipment, just a good friend. It can be made as demanding as you want, although it is best to take it easy at first if you are in pain or are very weak. As your strength grows you will be increasingly able to resist your partner's downward force.

Start with your legs at 60 degrees

1 Lie on your back with your legs angled at 60 degrees. Your partner should kneel down, with forearms placed against the inside of your knees.

2 Get your partner to push your knees apart toward the floor. Resist this movement all the way to the bottom of your range of motion. At the bottom of your range, begin to pull your knees back together to the start position, with your partner pushing down much less on the way back up.

52 LONG-LEVER ADDUCTOR DROP

This is an advanced exercise that you should attempt only after doing high-resistance short-lever adductor manuals (see opposite), and once your isometric adductor squeezes (see right) are pain-free. Perform the exercise without weights to begin with, then move up to using ankle weights on your swinging leg as you progress.

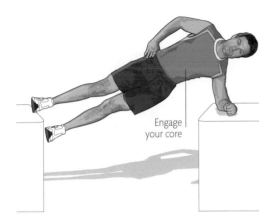

Engage your core

1 Position yourself between two benches with your top leg and bottom forearm supporting your suspended body weight. If using an ankle weight, make sure it is strapped to the bottom leg. Keep your hips and back straight.

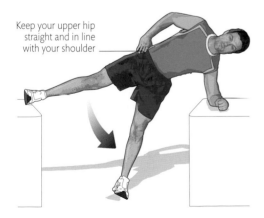

Keep your upper hip straight and in line with your shoulder

2 Slowly lower your bottom leg as far as possible while keeping your hips and back straight. Bring your bottom leg back up to touch your top leg, and then repeat.

53 ISOMETRIC ADDUCTOR SQUEEZE

This is a key exercise for beginning your recovery after a groin or adductor injury. It is also an essential exercise for sacroiliac joint inflamation (»p.62), for which regaining adductor strength is essential.

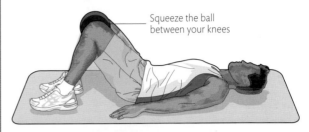

Squeeze the ball between your knees

1 Lie on your back with your pelvis in a neutral position, your knees bent at a right angle, and your feet flat on the ground. Place a medicine ball between your knees. Squeeze as hard as is comfortable, hold for 10 seconds, and relax to the start position. Repeat the movement as required. You should not experience any pain when you squeeze the ball.

2 Place a medicine ball between your ankles. Lie on your back with your pelvis in a neutral position and keep your legs straight. Squeeze the ball between your ankles as hard as you can, holding for 10 seconds, and return to the start position. Repeat the movement as required. This movement should not be causing you any pain.

Maintain a strong back and engage your core

3 Lie on your back with your pelvis in a neutral position and your hips and knees bent at right angles. Place a medicine ball between your knees. Squeeze as hard as is comfortable, hold for 10 seconds, and relax to the start position. Perform the necessary amount of repetitions. You should not experience any pain when you squeeze the ball.

54 SLIDE-BOARD ADDUCTOR AND ABDUCTOR

This movement works your abductor and adductor muscles, which support and stabilize your hips. Begin the movement slowly and carefully; as you progress you can perform the exercise while holding dumbbells.

1 Put on a pair of socks or some shoe covers over your sneakers. Stand on a slide board with your feet as far apart as is comfortable, and your hands held behind your lower back.

Keep your knees straight

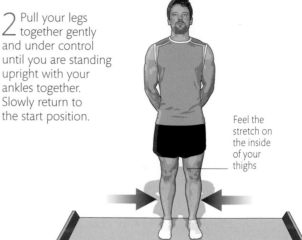

2 Pull your legs together gently and under control until you are standing upright with your ankles together. Slowly return to the start position.

Feel the stretch on the inside of your thighs

55 SKATING SLIDE-BOARD

This exercise works your abductor and adductor muscles, which support your pelvis and groin. Perform the movement slowly at first and build up speed, distance, and the number of repetitions as you progress.

1 Put on a pair of woolen socks or put shoe covers over your sneakers. Stand on the right side of a slide-board with your knees slightly bent.

Slightly bend your knees

2 Push off with your right foot, shifting your weight onto your left side, and skating your left leg across the slide-board.

Drag your right leg across the board

Slide your left foot across the board

3 Keep sliding across the board to your left, dragging your right leg until you reach the left side. Return to the starting stance, then slide back to your right. Build up to a continuous movement.

56 ADDUCTOR LIFT

This exercise is a great for your adductors, and an effective early stage rehabilitation exercise for groin injuries (»p.104) and sacroiliac joint pain (»p.62). As your strength and range of motion increases, use ankle weights to make it harder.

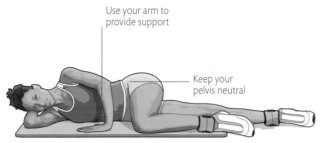

Use your arm to provide support

Keep your pelvis neutral

Feel the stretch on the inside of your right thigh

1 Lie on your right side with your hips stacked and your right arm bent under your head. Shift your weight forward, using your left arm for balance. Bend your left leg to 90 degrees, with your left knee touching the floor. Keep your right leg straight.

2 Raise your right leg off the ground as high as you can, exhaling as you do so. Pause, then return to the start position, inhaling as you do so. Complete your set and switch sides to work your left leg.

57 ADDUCTOR PULLEY

This exercise builds strength and endurance in the adductor muscles of your leg, and is another useful movement in the rehabilitation of groin injuries (»p.104) and pain in your sacroiliac joint (»p.62).

1 Choose a weight on the pulley stack and attach an ankle strap to your left leg. Stand with your right foot on a small step and your left leg next to the pulley station. Make sure your back is straight and your right knee is slightly bent.

2 Keeping your hips aligned and your upper body still, swing your left leg behind your right leg as far as you can. Hold, then return to the start position, and complete your set before switching legs.

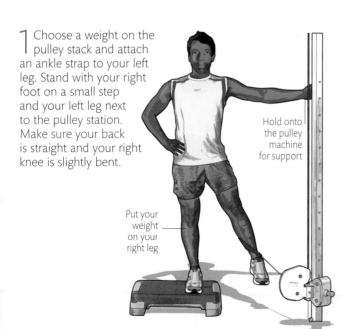

Hold onto the pulley machine for support

Put your weight on your right leg

Keep your core engaged

Keep your hips aligned

58 PULLEY HIP EXTENSION

This simple, pulley-based exercise works your hip extensors, namely your gluteus maximus. It is a useful movement for anyone who is recovering from an injury to the back, hip, or groin.

1 Attach your right leg to a pulley using a strap. Stand with your feet pointing forward and your right foot ahead of your left. Hold onto the pulley rail or a wall for balance.

Put your weight on your left leg

2 Engaging your core muscles to stabilize your movement, pull back with your right leg until it is pointing behind you and you feel the movement in your hip. Return to the starting position and repeat. Swap legs once you have completed your repetitions.

Keep your leg straight

59 NORDIC HAMSTRING LOWER

This exercise is good for strengthening the large muscles of your hamstrings, and is useful for a wide variety of sports. It is an advanced exercise that requires the assistance of a partner, and you should only do it under supervision. It is an excellent exercise if you suffer from recurrent hamstring strains (»p.108).

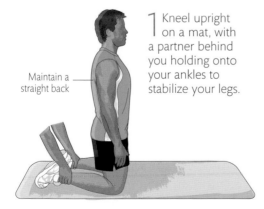

Maintain a straight back

1 Kneel upright on a mat, with a partner behind you holding onto your ankles to stabilize your legs.

Feel the stretch in your hamstrings

Bend your hips slightly

2 Lean forward with your back straight, bending slightly at your hips. Use your hamstrings to control the movement of your body as far as you can, before using your hands to support you toward the floor.

3 As soon as your chest reaches the floor, push back upward with your arms. Extend your arms until your hamstrings can take over and bring you back up to the starting position.

60 BOX STEP-UP

This great exercise targets the main muscles of your leg—your quads, hamstrings, and gluteals. The muscles of your calves assist while your core stops your body from falling forward or twisting. You can begin the movement on a low step or bench, then progress to using bands, and an increasingly high platform, until you can use a high box.

1 Stand facing a step or bench and place your left foot on top, making sure that your heel is not hanging over the edge.

Hold your body upright

2 Push down with your left heel and use your left thigh and gluteal muscles to lift your right foot up onto the bench. Your left knee should be at an angle of about 90 degrees.

Keep your back straight

Put your weight on this knee and contract your quads

3 Drive your body up onto the step, exhaling as you do so. Step down backward, reversing the movement to the start position. Repeat for the required number of repetitions, then swap feet.

Maintain a strong posture throughout

61 BOX STEP-DOWN

This movement also works the main muscles of your leg—your quads, hamstrings, and gluteals. The muscles of your calves also help you, while your core stops your body from falling forward or twisting. This is a more advanced exercise than the step-up (see above), requiring more control from your quadriceps and gluteals.

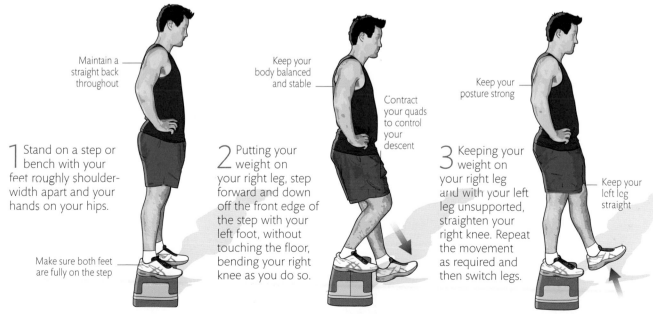

1 Stand on a step or bench with your feet roughly shoulder-width apart and your hands on your hips.

Maintain a straight back throughout

Make sure both feet are fully on the step

2 Putting your weight on your right leg, step forward and down off the front edge of the step with your left foot, without touching the floor, bending your right knee as you do so.

Keep your body balanced and stable

Contract your quads to control your descent

3 Keeping your weight on your right leg and with your left leg unsupported, straighten your right knee. Repeat the movement as required and then switch legs.

Keep your posture strong

Keep your left leg straight

62 ECCENTRIC INVERSION

Eccentric exercises are used to help treat tendon disorders. This exercise works the tendon on the inside of your ankle, which is called your tibialis posterior (»p.152). It may be quite uncomfortable to begin with, but you will gradually be able to increase your range of motion and can use ankle weights as you progress.

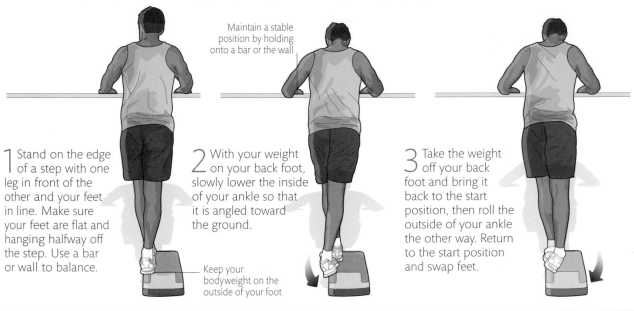

Maintain a stable position by holding onto a bar or the wall

1 Stand on the edge of a step with one leg in front of the other and your feet in line. Make sure your feet are flat and hanging halfway off the step. Use a bar or wall to balance.

2 With your weight on your back foot, slowly lower the inside of your ankle so that it is angled toward the ground.

Keep your bodyweight on the outside of your foot

3 Take the weight off your back foot and bring it back to the start position, then roll the outside of your ankle the other way. Return to the start position and swap feet.

63 CALF RAISE

This exercise develops the muscles of your lower leg. To begin with, work on a Smith machine to help stabilize your body. When you are confident, perform the exercise with heavier free weights, testing your balance further. You can also perform the exercise using one leg at a time, which is useful for the rehabilitation of various lower-limb injuries.

Hang your heels over the edge of the platform

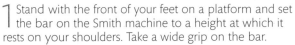

1 Stand with the front of your feet on a platform and set the bar on the Smith machine to a height at which it rests on your shoulders. Take a wide grip on the bar.

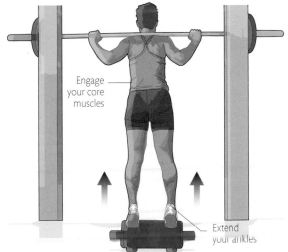

Engage your core muscles

Extend your ankles

2 With your head facing forward, raise both heels up through a full range of movement. Lower your heels to return to the start position.

64 STRAIGHT-KNEE ECCENTRIC CALF DROP

This exercise is used for treating your Achilles tendon (»pp.140–43), and may initially be painful to perform. It is also helpful in the late-stage rehabilitation of calf injuries (»p.136) as it strengthens and lengthens the gastrocnemius muscle. Ensure that you use only your affected leg to lower your weight during the movement.

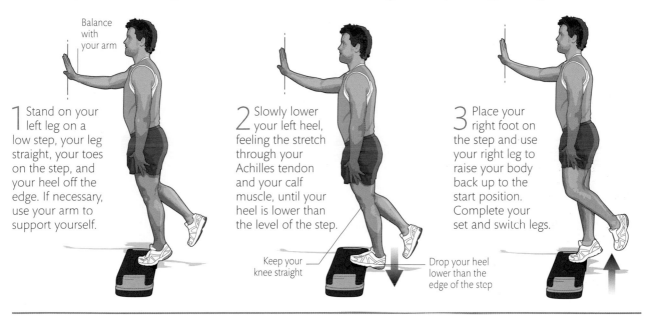

Balance with your arm

1 Stand on your left leg on a low step, your leg straight, your toes on the step, and your heel off the edge. If necessary, use your arm to support yourself.

2 Slowly lower your left heel, feeling the stretch through your Achilles tendon and your calf muscle, until your heel is lower than the level of the step.

Keep your knee straight

3 Place your right foot on the step and use your right leg to raise your body back up to the start position. Complete your set and switch legs.

Drop your heel lower than the edge of the step

65 BENT-KNEE ECCENTRIC CALF DROP

As with the straight-knee eccentric calf drop (see above), this exercise is useful for treating Achilles tendon injuries (»pp.140–43) and in late-stage calf injury rehabilitation (»p.136), but it strengthens and lengthens your soleus muscle as opposed to your gastrocnemius. Use only your affected leg to lower your body during the movement.

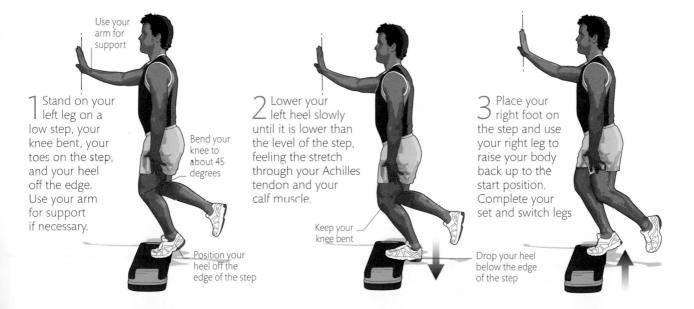

Use your arm for support

1 Stand on your left leg on a low step, your knee bent, your toes on the step, and your heel off the edge. Use your arm for support if necessary.

Bend your knee to about 45 degrees

Position your heel off the edge of the step

2 Lower your left heel slowly until it is lower than the level of the step, feeling the stretch through your Achilles tendon and your calf muscle.

Keep your knee bent

3 Place your right foot on the step and use your right leg to raise your body back up to the start position. Complete your set and switch legs

Drop your heel below the edge of the step

66 ONE-ARM ROW

This is a great exercise for your back and shoulders and one that offers great results in terms of strength and upper-body posture with a low risk of injury. To get the best results, it is important not to rotate your torso or hips.

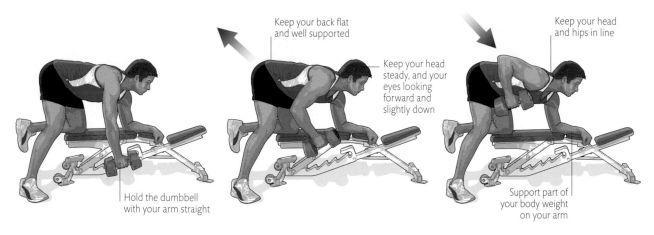

Keep your back flat and well supported

Keep your head steady, and your eyes looking forward and slightly down

Keep your head and hips in line

Hold the dumbbell with your arm straight

Support part of your body weight on your arm

1 Rest your left knee on a bench. Holding your back flat, brace your body with your left arm. Hold the dumbbell with your right hand.

2 Hold your back flat and your shoulders level. Raise the dumbbell toward your body with your elbow pointing up.

3 Pull your elbow as high as possible before returning under control to the start position. Complete your set then repeat with your left arm.

67 LAT PULL-DOWN

This is a good exercise for rehabilitating a bad back or returning from shoulder injuries if you are unable to lift your own body weight in the regular chin-up.

Keep your body upright under the pulley and your arms straight

Keep your thighs anchored under the pad

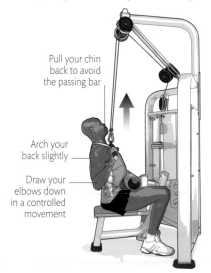

Pull your chin back to avoid the passing bar

Arch your back slightly

Draw your elbows down in a controlled movement

1 Select the weight, grip the bar just wider than shoulder-width apart, and sit down, placing your upper thighs under the pad.

2 Easing your body back slightly, pull the bar down to your upper chest, drawing your elbows in. Pause, and slowly return to the start position.

VARIATION

You can use many varied grips to work your back and arms in different ways. It is useful to train with a variety of grips to ensure all muscle groups are worked. The narrower the grip you use, the more the emphasis is on the smaller muscles of your shoulders; the wider your grip, the more the stress is placed on your lats and your elbows. An underhand grip engages your biceps, making the movement easier than if you use an overhand grip.

68 ASSISTED CHIN-UP

This is a great way to work your big back muscles and practice the movement of the regular chin-up (see below) if you lack the strength to lift your whole body weight. Note that adding weight to the stack makes the exercise easier.

Choose a suitable grip width

Engage your core muscles

Kneel on the pad

Pull until your chin rises above the level of your hands

Hold your feet together

1 Select the weight and stand on the foot rests. Grasp the hand grips and rest your knees on the pad, keeping your arms straight.

2 Bending at your elbows, use your lats to pull your body up until your chin is higher than your hands. Pause, then lower yourself to the start position.

VARIATION

Try varying your grip and hand spacing. As for the lat pull-down (see opposite), an overhand grip uses your biceps less, so is tougher than an underhand grip. A narrow grip works the smaller muscles in your shoulders, while a wide grip is more challenging on your lats.

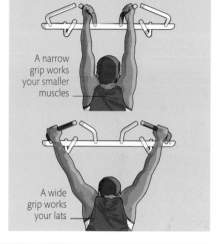

A narrow grip works your smaller muscles

A wide grip works your lats

69 CHIN-UP

This challenging exercise is great for advanced back, shoulder, and arm rehabilitation and ideal for training for sports that involve gripping and grappling. Begin with the assisted version (see above) to build your strength.

Hang on fully extended arms

Take a neutral grip with medium hand spacing to place the least stress on your wrists and elbows

Pull your body upward

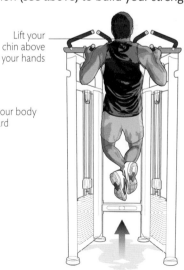

Lift your chin above your hands

1 Select your desired grip (see above) and drop down on fully extended arms. Bend your knees and cross your feet to improve your stability.

2 From a hanging position, flex your elbows and shoulders and pull your body upward. Don't swing your legs or bend at your hips for extra momentum.

3 Keeping your shoulders back, pull your body upward until your chin passes your hands. Pause, then lower yourself slowly to the starting position.

70 GOOD MORNING

This exercise works your glutes and hamstrings, while your large spinal erector muscles hold your back flat.

It is an ideal movement for medium to advanced hamstring rehabilitation after injury or surgery.

Support the bar with your upper arms

Keep your spine neutral

Plant your heels on the floor

1 Hold your body upright, with a barbell resting across your upper back. Keep your knees slightly bent and your spine neutral.

2 Bending at your knees and hips, lean forward under control. Keep your chin up—it will stop you from rounding your back.

3 Continue to lean forward by pivoting at your hips. Keeping your back neutral, lower your chest, letting your knees bend slightly.

4 Flex as far as possible: with practice your back may be parallel to the floor. Return to the start position, breathing out as you go.

71 SEATED PULLEY ROW

This exercise is fantastic for building strength in your back, but good technique is crucial to performing it safely. It can

also be performed with a single arm for the rehabilitation of shoulder injuries or dysfunction.

Begin with your arms straight

Bend at your knees

Maintain your knee angle throughout the exercise

Keep your buttocks fixed in one position

Keep your back at 90 degrees to the bench

1 Select the desired weight from the stack. Push with your legs so that your arms are extended, your back is neutral, and your knees are at an angle of about 90 degrees.

2 Draw your elbows back to pull the handles (or bar), keeping your spine neutral and your body upright. Brace your feet against the footrests as you do so.

3 Pull the handles (or bar) back into your body at the level of your upper abdomen, drawing your elbows back as far as possible. Pause, then slowly return to the start position.

72 PRONE ROW

This exercise is fantastic for developing your upper back and strengthening your core. To make your stabilizers work even harder, you can try performing the movement on a Swiss ball rather than a bench.

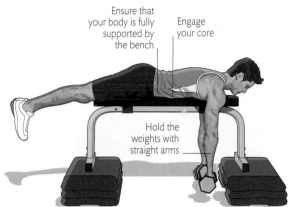

Ensure that your body is fully supported by the bench

Engage your core

Hold the weights with straight arms

Keep your elbows in line with your wrists

Squeeze your shoulder blades together at the top of the movement

1 Lie chest down on a flat bench, holding a pair of dumbbells in an overhand grip, with your arms hanging down below your shoulders. Hold your head level, with your chin resting on the bench.

2 Bending at your elbows, pull your upper arms back as high as comfortable, while keeping them at right angles to your torso. Pause at the top of the movement and return the dumbbells under control to the start position.

73 LOW ROW

This important upper-back exercise works the stabilizers of your core and your posterior shoulder muscles. Practicing this with a single arm is an excellent exercise for people with shoulder injuries or dysfunction.

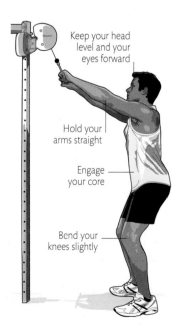

1 Set the pulley high and select the desired weight. Hold the bar straight with both hands in an overhand grip. Brace your legs and glutes.

Keep your head level and your eyes forward

Hold your arms straight

Engage your core

Bend your knees slightly

2 Bring the bar in an arc all the way down to your upper thighs. Pause, then return slowly to the start position following the same trajectory.

Maintain an upright position, ensuring that your weight does not shift forward

Keep your body braced but do not use your hips to "muscle down" the weight

74 DUMBBELL BENCH PRESS

This exercise is great for increasing strength in your chest and shoulder muscles. Dumbbells are especially good for working the smaller muscles around your shoulders, as well as preventing imbalance during the exercise.

Hold your arms at 90 degrees to your body

Lower the weights together, under control

Keep your forearms vertical under the weights

1 Raise the dumbbells over your chest. Stabilize your body, pressing your shoulders, head, and hips against the bench.

2 Lower the weights slowly, keeping them in line with your mid-chest. Pause at the bottom, then push back up to the starting position.

VARIATION

You can perform this exercise using a barbell instead of dumbbells. While the dumbbell bench press offers greater range of motion, some people find it easier to use a barbell. Always use a rack and make sure that someone is on hand to watch or "spot" you while you perform the exercise. Do not overload the barbell because this can lead to poor form.

75 INCLINE DUMBBELL BENCH PRESS

Another great exercise for your chest and shoulders, this variant of the dumbbell bench press (see above) offers you an even greater range of movement.

Allow the weights to touch lightly

Extend your arms straight over your shoulders

Keep your buttocks, head, and shoulders well supported

Keep your feet flat on the floor throughout

1 Stabilize your shoulders and head against the bench. Hold the dumbbells straight above your shoulders so they touch at the top.

2 Lower the weights evenly, until your upper arms are almost vertical and the weights are at shoulder level. Push back up to the starting position.

VARIATION

As with the standard bench press (see above), you can perform the incline bench press with a barbell rather than dumbbells. Always use a rack and have someone watch or "spot" you, and make sure you do not overload the barbell because this can lead to poor movement. Bear in mind that you will be able to lift less weight in an incline position, because the smaller muscles of your shoulders come into play.

76 SHOULDER SHRUG FROM HANG

This is a great end-stage power exercise following any major injury. It works your trapezius muscles, while adding an upward extension of your whole body. This makes it useful if your sport calls for explosive power.

Move your shoulders in front of the bar

Ease your hips back

Keep an overhand grip on the bar

Keep your arms straight

Keep your wrists straight

Maintain a straight back

1 Hold the bar with your arms outside your thighs. Roll your shoulders, bend at your knees and waist, and lower the bar to just above your knees.

2 Drive your body rapidly upward with a powerful vertical shrug, rising up on your toes. Bring your hips up, keeping your arms hanging straight.

3 Once you have reached full body extension, bend your knees, ease your hips back, and lower the bar under full control to the start position.

77 DUMBBELL SHOULDER PRESS

You can perform this exercise seated (as shown here), standing, or with alternate presses. Using dumbbells instead of a barbell helps you avoid muscular imbalance because both of your shoulders are working equally.

Use an overhand grip

Engage your core

Allow the dumbbells to lightly touch behind your head

Keep your elbows soft

Keep your back straight

1 Sit on the end of a bench holding the dumbbells just above shoulder height. Keep your back straight and your feet flat on the ground.

2 Press the weights upward with your shoulders until your arms are fully extended. Hold briefly, without locking your elbows, then lower them to the start position.

78 SHOULDER ISOMETRICS

The muscles of your rotator cuff are vital in stabilizing the movement of your shoulder joints, especially in sports that involve throwing. This series of exercises works your rotator cuff and is used early on after a shoulder injury (»pp.70–75).

Use your right hand to resist the movement of your left shoulder

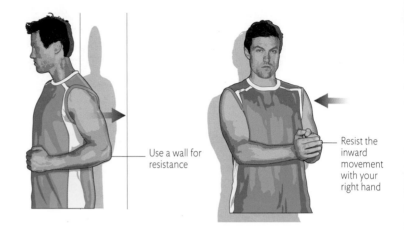

Use a wall for resistance

Resist the inward movement with your right hand

1 Stand with your left arm tight by your side and place your right hand over your left. Push forward with your left shoulder, while resisting with your right hand. Hold for 10 seconds, rest, complete the set, and switch sides.

2 Stand with your left shoulder, upper arm, and elbow against a wall. Push backward with your arm and elbow for 10 seconds then rest. Complete the required number of repetitions and switch arms.

3 Stand with your left arm tight by your side and your right hand positioned over your left. Turn your left shoulder inward and push, resisting with your right hand. Hold for 10 seconds and rest. Repeat as necessary and switch sides.

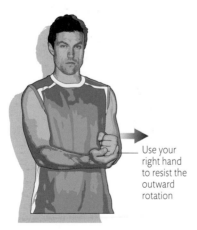

Use your right hand to resist the outward rotation

Lift your left arm away from your body and resist with your right hand

Place a rolled-up towel between your arm and your side

4 Stand with your left arm tight by your side and your right hand underneath your left. Push outward with your shoulder, resisting the movement with your right hand. Hold for 10 seconds, then rest. Repeat the exercise as required and switch sides.

5 Stand with your left arm by your side, holding the elbow of your left arm with your right hand. Lift your elbow away from your side, resisting with your right hand. Hold for 10 seconds, then rest. Complete the set, and switch sides.

6 Stand with your left arm tight by your side, and a rolled-up towel between your elbow and your side. Squeeze your elbow into the side of your body, hold for 10 seconds, rest, and repeat as required. Switch sides once you have completed your set.

79 SCARECROW ROTATION

The muscles of your rotator cuff are vital in stabilizing shoulder movement, especially in sports that involve throwing. This exercise works your rotator cuff and helps you avoid injury.

1 Stand facing a low pulley and grip the handle in your left hand. Raise your elbow to the side in line with your shoulder.

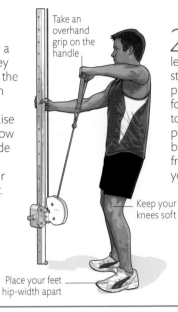

Take an overhand grip on the handle

Keep your knees soft

Place your feet hip-width apart

2 Keeping your left arm still, slowly pivot your forearm up to a vertical position, breathing freely as you do so.

3 Lower your left arm to the start position. Complete your set and repeat with your right arm.

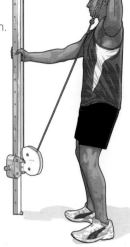

Move your forearm to a vertical position

80 INTERNAL ROTATION

This exercise develops the internal rotator cuff muscles of your shoulder. A simple pulley rehabilitation exercise, it is ideal for a rotator cuff injury (»p.70), especially as you can easily adjust the weight as you progress.

1 Stand sideways to a pulley set at about waist height. Bend your right arm to 90 degrees and then turn it outwards, away from your body.

Grip a folded towel between your arm and chest to help you maintain correct position

Grip the handle securely

Tuck your left arm behind your back

2 Bring your right arm across as far as is comfortable. Return slowly to the start position. Finish the set and repeat with your left arm.

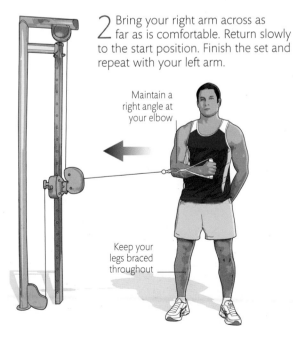

Maintain a right angle at your elbow

Keep your legs braced throughout

81 SIDE-LYING L

This exercise isolates the muscles in the sides of your upper back and shoulders, such as the infraspinatus muscle of your rotator cuff. It is used in the rehabilitation of the shoulder after injury, but is also useful for throwing and racket sports.

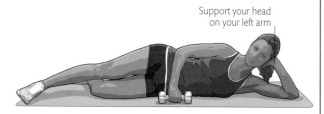

Support your head on your left arm

1 Lie on your left side on an exercise mat. With the elbow of your right arm bent at 90 degrees and your forearm to the front of your body, take an overhand grip on a dumbbell and rest it on the mat.

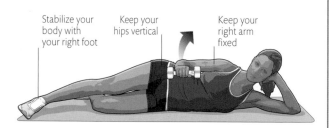

Stabilize your body with your right foot

Keep your hips vertical

Keep your right arm fixed

2 Keeping your right arm still and your elbow fixed against your side, gently raise your forearm through a comfortable range of movement in a smooth, controlled action.

Rotate your forearm to the vertical position but no further

Feel it at the back of your shoulder

3 Maintaining your elbow at a right angle and pressed against your side, lower the dumbbell slowly to the start position and complete the set. Repeat with your left arm.

82 DYNAMIC HUG

This exercise uses the muscles that help your shoulder blades sit properly. It is an essential exercise for treating shoulder impingement problems because the muscle being worked is often very weak.

1 Grab the handles of a pulley system with the cables set to a high position. Raise your arms out sideways and bend your elbows to 90 degrees, with your knuckles pointing forward.

Bend your elbows to 90 degrees

Place one foot out in front

2 Push forward with your hands and shoulders, aiming for a position slightly below and in front of your chest, until you have extended both of your arms fully.

Fully extend your arms

3 Now push a little farther and feel your shoulder blades stretch across your upper back to achieve the extra range. Hold for 2–3 seconds then slowly return to the start position and repeat.

Bring your hands toward each other

83 REAR LATERAL RAISE

This exercise is great for your shoulders and the muscles of your mid-back, such as your rhomboids. You can perform the movement standing, sitting, or lying down, but good body position is key to avoid working the larger muscles of your back.

Keep your spine neutral

Brace your abs and back muscles

Bend your elbows slightly

Keep your torso static during the lift

Raise the weights to the level of your shoulders or just above

Keep your core muscles tight

1 With your knees slightly bent and your back flat, drop forward at your hips with your head looking ahead and slightly down. Flex your elbows a little and rest the plates of the dumbbells on your upper thighs.

2 Lift the dumbbells out to your sides in a smooth motion with the weights moving in symmetry. Keep the weights in line with your shoulders and ensure that your back stays tight.

3 Bring the weights level with your shoulders and depress your shoulder blades. Pause at the top of the movement, and return to the start position slowly and under control.

84 STANDING Y

This exercise strengthens the muscles of your shoulders and upper back, and helps improve the stability of your shoulder joints. In particular, it works your supraspinatus and front deltoid muscles.

VARIATION

Lifting the weights with your knuckles turned in and your thumbs pointing downward puts more emphasis on the front of your shoulders.

Ensure your back is straight

Keep your knees soft

Keep your core engaged

Relax your shoulders

Keep your elbows slightly bent

1 Stand with your feet about hip-width apart and with your knees bent slightly. Hold a dumbbell in each hand in an overhand grip, with your arms straight and the weights resting on the outsides of your thighs.

2 Engaging your core muscles and bending slightly at your elbows, lift the weights vertically upward, with each arm angled at 45 degrees and your thumbs pointing upward and inward.

3 Maintaining the angle of your arms, raise the dumbbells to shoulder-height. Pause, then lower them slowly to the start position.

85 MINI TRAMPOLINE THROW

This exercise works your rotator cuff muscles in a plyometric way, using explosive movements to build muscular power. You should begin with gentle throws, but you can increase the speed of them as you progress.

PROGRESSION

If you find this exercise too hard, start in a kneeling position, then in a split-kneeling position (kneeling on one leg, the other in front of you, foot flat on the floor), before trying the standing position. Raising your hand higher, increases the elevation of your shoulder.

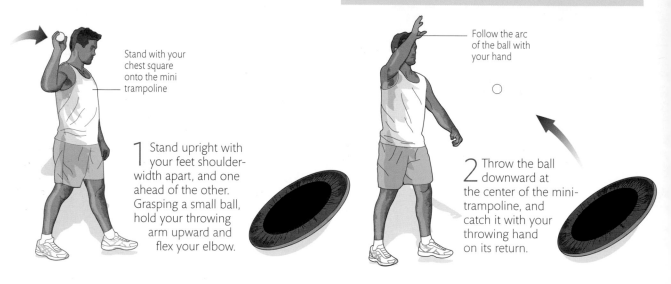

Stand with your chest square onto the mini trampoline

1 Stand upright with your feet shoulder-width apart, and one ahead of the other. Grasping a small ball, hold your throwing arm upward and flex your elbow.

Follow the arc of the ball with your hand

2 Throw the ball downward at the center of the mini-trampoline, and catch it with your throwing hand on its return.

86 MEDICINE BALL CHEST THROW

This is an advanced exercise that requires power in your chest, shoulders, and arms. It is great for anyone recovering from a shoulder injury (»pp.70–75), and for sports involving throwing or hitting. You will need a partner to perform it.

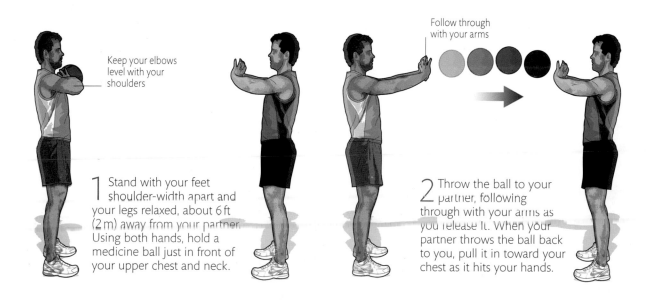

Keep your elbows level with your shoulders

1 Stand with your feet shoulder-width apart and your legs relaxed, about 6 ft (2 m) away from your partner. Using both hands, hold a medicine ball just in front of your upper chest and neck.

Follow through with your arms

2 Throw the ball to your partner, following through with your arms as you release it. When your partner throws the ball back to you, pull it in toward your chest as it hits your hands.

87 ECCENTRIC DROP-CATCH

This exercise is effective in working the muscles of your rotator cuff (in particular your supraspinatus), and is a useful part of rehabilitation for shoulder injuries (»pp.70–75). Increase the weight of the ball as you progress.

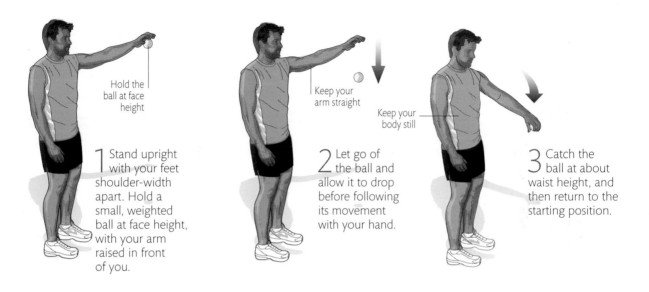

Hold the ball at face height

1 Stand upright with your feet shoulder-width apart. Hold a small, weighted ball at face height, with your arm raised in front of you.

Keep your arm straight

Keep your body still

2 Let go of the ball and allow it to drop before following its movement with your hand.

3 Catch the ball at about waist height, and then return to the starting position.

88 TRICEPS PUSH-DOWN

This is a basic strengthening exercise for your triceps muscles, which form the back of your upper arms.

Reversing the grip on the bar turns this in to a pull-down that also works the muscles of your forearms.

Keep your elbows tight to the sides of your body

1 Set the pulley to a high position, select your desired weight, and take an overhand grip on the bar at chest height.

2 Push the bar down slowly under control, using your elbow joints as pivots. Keep your trunk, legs, and hips stationary.

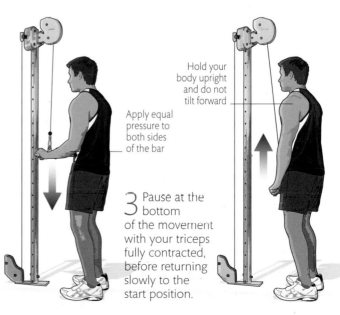

Apply equal pressure to both sides of the bar

Hold your body upright and do not tilt forward

3 Pause at the bottom of the movement with your triceps fully contracted, before returning slowly to the start position.

89 CLOSE-GRIP BENCH PRESS

At first glance this exercise is very similar to the regular barbell bench press (»p.210). However, by bringing your hands closer together on the bar you place far more emphasis on your triceps and anterior deltoids than on your chest, so this one is a useful exercise for strengthening your upper arms.

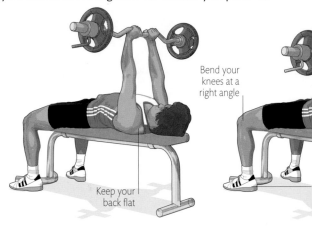

Bend your knees at a right angle

Keep your back flat

Keep the bar level and under control, and hold it vertically over your chest

Push down hard with your feet

Lower the bar until your knuckles touch your chest

1 Lie on a bench with your feet planted on the floor. Hold an EZ bar with an overhand grip at slightly less than shoulder-width. Extend your arms to hold the bar above your upper chest.

2 Ensuring that the bar is stable and under control, unlock your elbows and, keeping them tucked in, lower the bar slowly toward your chest. Inhale as you do so.

3 Lower the bar until your hands make contact with your chest, making sure that your elbows do not flare out. Pause, and, exhaling, drive the bar upward to the start position.

90 HAMMER DUMBBELL CURL

Suitable for those returning from any upper limb injury, this exercise works your forearms in addition to your biceps, but does not put pressure on your wrists. Try sitting on an incline bench to extend the range of possible movement.

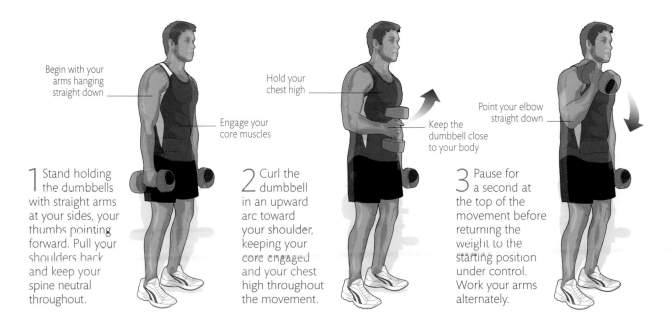

Begin with your arms hanging straight down

Engage your core muscles

Hold your chest high

Keep the dumbbell close to your body

Point your elbow straight down

1 Stand holding the dumbbells with straight arms at your sides, your thumbs pointing forward. Pull your shoulders back and keep your spine neutral throughout.

2 Curl the dumbbell in an upward arc toward your shoulder, keeping your core engaged and your chest high throughout the movement.

3 Pause for a second at the top of the movement before returning the weight to the starting position under control. Work your arms alternately.

91 WRIST EXTENSION

You need a strong grip to work effectively with heavy weights. This exercise strengthens your forearms, allowing you to hold greater loads for longer periods, which will help you work your large muscle groups.

Hold your wrist level with the front of your knee

Slowly move the dumbbell as high as you can

Maintain a neutral spine

Keep your forearm still

Keep your feet flat on the floor

1 Sit on a bench holding one dumbbell in an overhand grip. Rest your forearm along the top of your thigh.

2 Keeping your forearm still, use your wrist to raise the dumbbell slowly and under control beyond the horizontal position.

3 Slowly lower the dumbbell to the start position using only your wrist. Complete the set and repeat with your other arm.

92 ECCENTRIC WRIST EXTENSION

This exercise is specific for tennis elbow (»p.78) and, unlike the wrist extension (see above), it involves lowering rather than raising the weight. It is an important exercise and you will find it painful if you are doing it correctly.

Keep your wrist level with the front of your knee

Keep your spine neutral

Slowly move the dumbbell as low as you can

Keep your forearm still

Keep your feet flat on the floor

1 Sit on a bench holding one dumbbell in an overhand grip. Rest your forearm on your thigh, and use your wrist to raise the weight.

2 Keeping your forearm still, use your wrist to lower the dumbbell slowly and under control below the horizontal position.

3 Pause at the bottom of the movement, then raise the dumbbell to the start position using your wrist. Complete the set and switch arms.

93 ISOMETRIC BRIDGING

Neck strength is crucial in any sport that involves contact, collision, or upper-body strength. These are advanced exercises and should be done under supervision, and only once you have sufficient neck and core strength.

Keep your back straight

Balance your toes on the floor

Press the top of your head into the floor

Rest your knees on the mat

1 Lean forward onto a mat in a bridge position, so that you are supporting your weight on the front of your head, your knees, and your toes, and your back is straight. Controlling your breathing, try to hold the position for 10 seconds to begin with, building toward 30 seconds as you progress.

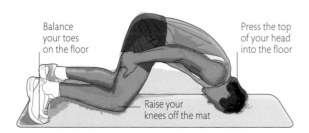

Balance your toes on the floor

Press the top of your head into the floor

Raise your knees off the mat

2 Lie in a bridge position, with the front of your head and your toes resting on a mat, your knees off the ground, and your back straight. Controlling your breathing, begin by trying to hold the position for 10 seconds, building toward 30 seconds as you progress.

Keep your upper legs in line with your torso

Keep your core engaged

Rest the back of your head on the floor

Keep your hips up

3 Lie on a mat with your knees raised and your feet flat on the floor. Raise your body into a bridge position, lifting your shoulders off the floor, so that your weight is resting on your feet and the back of your head. Controlling your breathing, initially try to hold the position for 10 seconds, building toward 30 seconds as you progress.

94 MANUAL ISOMETRICS

These neck-strengthening exercises use your hands for resistance and can be performed either standing or sitting down. These are essential exercises for anyone who has suffered a neck injury (**»pp.56–59**) or who is starting to strengthen their neck. As you progress you can use bands or a pulley machine to provide the required resistance.

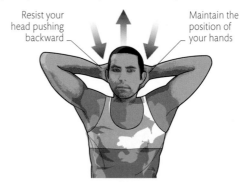

Resist your head pushing backward

Maintain the position of your hands

1 Clasp your hands behind your head. Press your head backward against them, resisting with your hands and ensuring that your head doesn't move. Hold, then relax.

Keep your neck still and do not let your head move

Resist your head pushing sideways

2 Hold the heel of your hand against the side of your head and press your head sideways against it, while resisting with your arm. Pause, then relax, and switch sides.

Keep your head upright and do not allow it to move

Resist your head turning

3 Press your right hand to your temple and your left hand to the back of your head. Turn your head to the right, resisting with both arms, stopping your head from moving. Hold, then relax, then switch hands and direction.

95 CURL-UP

A key part of most exercise programs, this movement strengthens your rectus abdominis muscle, which helps stabilize your pelvis. If it is recommended as part of your rehabilitation, you can increase the difficulty of the exercise through five levels as your strength and endurance gradually improve.

Keep your left foot in line with your right knee

Lift only your chest, shoulders, and head

Keep your right leg straight

1 Lie on your back with one leg straight and the other bent at a 90-degree angle with your foot flat on the floor. Bend your elbows and place your hands palm-down under your lower back. Rest your elbows against the floor.

2 Keeping your elbows on the floor, engage your core to lift your shoulders up, exhaling as you do so, ensuring that you lift only your shoulders off the floor, rather than lifting your upper body and doing a sit-up. Hold for 8 seconds, then return to the start position for 2 seconds. Complete your set then switch leg positions.

PROGRESSION–LEVEL 2

Perform the curl-up as in Level 1, with your hands under the small of your back, this time with your elbows off the floor. As for Level 1, keep one leg straight along the floor and the other bent at a right angle with your foot flat on the floor. Hold for 8 seconds at the top of the movement, then return to the start position for 2 seconds. Complete your set then switch leg positions.

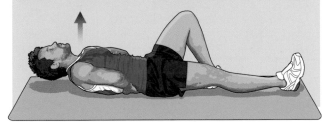

PROGRESSION–LEVEL 3

Place your hands across your chest instead of behind your back, straightening one leg along the floor, bending the other at 90 degrees with your foot flat on the floor, and only lifting your chest, shoulders, and head off the floor. Hold for 8 seconds at the top, then return to the start position for 2 seconds. Complete your set, then switch leg positions.

PROGRESSION–LEVEL 4

Position yourself with a wobble-board under your lower back and your hands across your chest, with one leg straight along the floor and the other bent at a right angle with your foot flat on the floor. Lift your chest, shoulders, and head, hold at the top for 8 seconds, then return to the start position for 2 seconds. Complete your set before switching leg positions.

PROGRESSION–LEVEL 5

Perform the exercise with your lower back positioned on a Swiss ball and your hands across your chest. Plant your feet firmly on the floor and bend your knees at 90 degrees. Hold for 8 seconds, then return to the start position for 2 seconds. Complete your set before switching leg positions.

96 SWISS BALL TWIST

This exercise not only builds strong abs but also strengthens the rotational muscles of your torso. Working on the ball also promotes balance, making this a great exercise for sports such as golf and surfing.

Rest your fingers lightly on the sides of your head, and avoid pulling it forward

1 Lie on the stability ball with your lower back supported, your feet flat on the floor, your knees at right angles, and your hands touching your head.

Use your feet to help stabilize your body

2 Once you feel steady, begin to crunch up. About halfway up, twist your torso to one side—spreading your elbows wide helps you keep your balance.

Contract your abs

3 Pause at the top of the movement, then lower and untwist your upper torso to return to the start position. Repeat for your other side.

97 SWISS BALL DONKEY

This valuable but relatively advanced exercise requires great balance and control along with shoulder stability. It works your abs and the core muscles that flex your hips, and can be used for almost any injury.

Place your feet on top of the ball

Maintain a straight line through your spine and neck to your head

Straighten your elbows without locking them out

1 Start with your body in a push-up position (»p.228). Keep your hands flat on the floor and place the tops of your feet on the ball. Align your head with your spine.

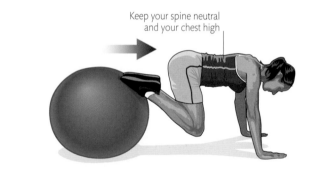

Keep your spine neutral and your chest high

2 Draw your knees toward your chest, maintaining a neutral spine as the ball rolls forward. Your hips will rise a little as the ball moves.

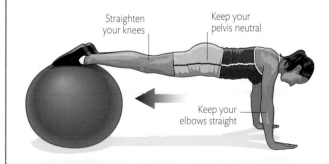

Straighten your knees

Keep your pelvis neutral

Keep your elbows straight

3 Keeping your neck stretched out, roll the ball back by returning your legs to the start position with your knees straight.

98 SWISS BALL JACK-KNIFE

This advanced exercise builds strength and stability in your hip flexors and lower abdominals, and requires a high degree of shoulder stability. This is a high-level exercise and should initially only be attempted under supervision.

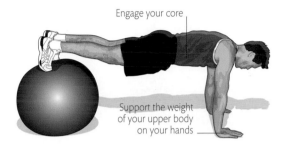

Engage your core

Support the weight of your upper body on your hands

1 Start with your body in a push-up position (»p.228), but with your toes resting on the ball. Engage your core to stop your lower back arching.

Keep your back straight throughout

2 Pull the ball in toward your chest by raising your hips, then roll it forward with your feet so that your knees come in toward your chest.

Keep your movement under control

3 Pause, then roll the ball back out again, straightening your legs to the start position.

99 SWISS BALL ROLL-OUT

This exercise builds stability and strength in your core muscles because it makes your abs and lower back work together, while also strengthening your shoulders.

Ensure that your back is flat

1 Kneel down, resting your hands and lower arms on the top of the ball, and ensure that your back is flat.

Keep your pelvis neutral

Extend your arms forward

2 Roll the ball forward by extending your arms, and follow it with your upper body as far as you can without arching your back. Use your abdominals to pull the ball back to the start position.

VARIATION

Using a barbell instead of a stability ball is a high level variation of this exercise, but should only be attempted once you have no pain and very good abdominal and spinal control. Kneel with your hands on the bar, shoulder-width apart. Keep your back flat as you roll the bar forward and use your abs to pull it back to the starting position.

100 **SWISS BALL** ARM PUSH

This exercise requires you to stabilize your pelvis, lower back, shoulders, and neck while working your abdominals and shoulder-blade stabilizers. It is a full-body exercise that can be used to rehabilitate almost any injury.

Engage
your core

1 Lie on your front over an exercise ball, with your hands on the floor directly below your shoulders. Keep your elbows straight, but not locked, and your shoulders relaxed. Make sure that your back is straight and your pelvis is not tipping forward.

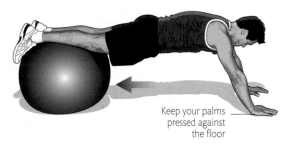

Keep your palms
pressed against
the floor

2 Keeping your body straight and your hands fixed in position, push slowly backward with your arms. Move as far as you can, keeping control of your upper body and abs. Hold for 2–3 seconds.

Maintain a straight
line through your
spine and neck

3 Slowly pull forward through your shoulders and hands and return to your starting position.

101 **SINGLE ARM AND** LEG RAISE

This exercise engages the transversus abdominis muscle of your core, using it to stabilize your pelvis against the motion of your arms and legs. This muscle acts as a natural girdle, flattening your abdomen and supporting your lower back.

Bend your knees to
about 90 degrees

1 Lie on your back with your knees bent, your feet flat on the ground, and your arms extended above you with your palms facing forward.

Keep your right
arm stationary

Relax your
shoulders

Keep your back straight
and your pelvis neutral

2 Lower your left arm to the ground behind you as you lift your right knee directly over your hip, contracting your abdominals as you do so.

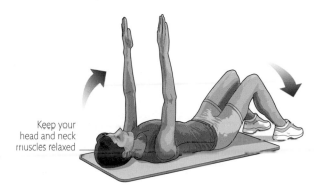

Keep your
head and neck
muscles relaxed

3 Slowly return to the start position and repeat with your right arm and left leg.

102 DEAD BUG

This exercise works your lower back, pelvis, trunk, and shoulders. A moderate- to high-level pilates exercise, it should only be attempted after more basic pilates exercises, such as the single arm and leg raise (see opposite), are mastered. If you are recovering from a back injury, ensure that you keep your lower back pressed against the floor.

Relax your shoulders

Start with your knees bent at a right angle

1 Lie on your back on a mat with your hips and knees bent at 90 degrees, and your feet roughly hip-width apart in the air. Point your arms up directly over your shoulders, palms facing forward, and contract your abs.

Pull your bent leg back toward your chest

Press down slightly into the mat

2 Lower your left arm behind you and extend your right leg, bringing it as close to the floor as possible without arching your back. Draw your left knee in to your chest.

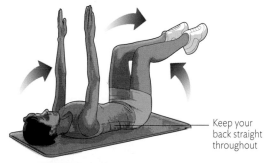

Keep your back straight throughout

3 Briefly hold the position, ensuring that you do not arch your back. Return to the start position and switch sides.

103 PRONE PLANK

This static floor exercise engages your core muscles, plus many of the major muscle groups of your upper and lower body, in order to maintain a fixed position. Use this exercise to help prevent lower-back problems or to rehabilitate after a lower-back injury.

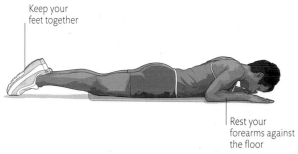

Keep your feet together

Rest your forearms against the floor

1 Lie face down on an exercise mat with your elbows to your sides and your hands alongside your head, palms facing the ground.

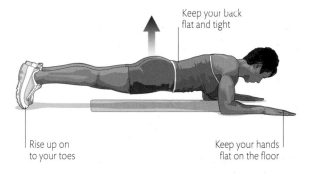

Keep your back flat and tight

Rise up on to your toes

Keep your hands flat on the floor

2 Engaging your core and leg muscles, raise your body from the floor, supporting your weight on your forearms and toes while breathing freely.

Flex your ankles

3 Hold the plank position for a short while—try 20 seconds to start with—then gently lower your body back onto the start position.

104a SIDE PLANK (LEVEL 1)

This exercise works your abdominals as they stabilize your core and your obliques, and support your spine. The most basic form of this exercise is good for initial rehabilitation, and is a starting point for those who have not preformed the movement before or do not have sufficient core stability.

Align your knees with your hips

Keep your elbow directly under your shoulder

Engage your core

Push your hips forward to keep your body in a straight line

1 Lying on your right side, prop yourself up on your right forearm and bend your knees so that your lower legs are behind you. Make sure that your right elbow is directly under your shoulder and in line with your hips. Rest your left arm along the side of your body.

2 Engage your abdominals and push down through your right elbow to raise your hips off the floor, making sure that you keep your ribcage elevated and your shoulder lowered. Hold for 8 seconds, then return to the start position for 2 seconds. Complete your set, then switch sides.

104b SIDE PLANK (LEVEL 2)

This progression of the exercise makes your abdominals and obliques work harder because you are supporting your body weight on your arm and your ankles. You will need to engage your core and stabilize your whole body.

Make sure your hips are aligned and do not drop back

Align your elbow with your hips and feet

Keep your core tight and your ribcage raised

Keep your feet aligned

1 Lying on your right side, prop yourself up on your right forearm. Extend your legs and keep your feet together. Make sure that your right elbow is directly under your shoulder and in line with your hips. Rest your left arm along your side.

2 Engage your abdominals and push downward through your right elbow to raise your hips off the ground, making sure that you keep your ribcage elevated and your shoulder lowered. Hold for 8 seconds, then return to the start position for 2 seconds. Repeat 10 times, then switch sides.

104c SIDE PLANK (LEVEL 3)

This further progression makes it even harder for you to balance. As a result, it works the muscles at the sides of your torso harder and helps improve your posture.

Balance on the side of your foot

1 Lying on your left side, prop yourself up on your forearm. Extend your legs and keep your feet together. Make sure that your left elbow is directly under your shoulder and in line with your hips. Rest your right arm on your side.

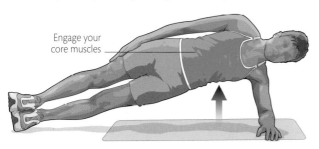

Engage your core muscles

2 Engage your core muscles and push downward through your left elbow to raise your hips off the ground.

Lift your arm to make a right angle with your torso

Keep hips forward and aligned

3 Raise your right arm until it is about 90 degrees to your torso, keeping your ribcage elevated and your shoulder lowered. Hold for 8 seconds, then return to the start position for 2 seconds. Repeat 10 times, then switch sides.

104d SIDE PLANK (LEVEL 4)

This is the most complex version of the exercise. It requires excellent strength and stability in your core stabilizers to keep your body balanced.

Keep your shoulder and elbow aligned

1 Lying on your side, prop yourself up on your forearm. Extend your legs and keep your feet together. Make sure that your supporting elbow is directly under your shoulder and in line with your hips. Rest your upper arm on your side.

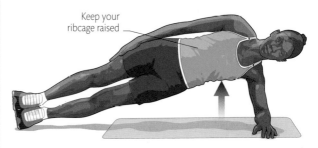

Keep your ribcage raised

2 Engage your core muscles and push downward through your supporting elbow to raise your hips off the ground.

Keep your core tight

Keep your hips straight

3 As you lift your hips, raise your right arm and leg until you make a star shape, keeping your ribcage raised and your shoulder lowered. Hold for 8 seconds, then return to the start position for 2 seconds. Repeat 10 times, then switch sides.

105 PUSH-UP

This is one of the simplest and most effective exercises for your core, chest, shoulders, back, and arms. Its added benefit is that it requires no apparatus—just your own body weight. There are many variations that can be used and this is a great middle- to final-stage exercise for those suffering from lower back pain (»p.60).

WARNING!

Do not let your torso sag as you push yourself up. This will cut down the range of your movement, diminishing the benefit to your chest, shoulders, and arms. Failure to straighten your arms after each rep will also make the exercise less effective.

Tense your spinal erectors

Support your weight on your toes

Tense your abs

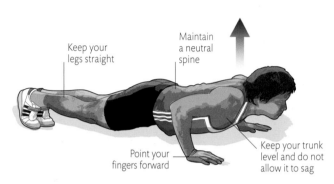

Keep your legs straight

Maintain a neutral spine

Point your fingers forward

Keep your trunk level and do not allow it to sag

1 Support your body on your toes and palms, with your arms straight and your hands in line with, and a little wider than, your shoulders. Inhale and lower your body slowly until your torso just touches the ground.

2 Hold the bottom position for a second, then exhale and push your torso up until your arms are straight and you are back at the start position. Keep the angle of your back constant and your head forward.

106 KNEELING SUPERMAN

This exercise strengthens the spinal extensor muscles, which support the length of the spine, building strength and stability in your core and lower back as well as your abdominals and shoulders. It is a mainstay for a healthy back and crucial to your rehabilitation process after a back injury (»p.60).

Keep your back in a neutral postion

Align your head with your spine

Keep your core muscles tight

Extend your arm straight out in front

1 Kneel on all fours, ensuring that your knees are aligned squarely under your hips. Keep your back straight, and position your hands directly beneath your shoulders, pressing them flat on the ground and pointing forward.

2 Engaging your core, raise one arm in front of you. Hold and return to the start position. Repeat with your other arm.

VARIATION 1

Using a pair of frames will give you a much greater range of movement than in a standard push-up. Position the frames a little wider than shoulder-width apart and, resting on your toes and your straightened arms, engage your core to keep your body straight.

Keep your hips and torso in line

Maintain straight legs

Point each frame inward at 45 degrees

VARIATION 2

Resting the tops of your feet on a stability ball will make your chest, shoulders, and arms work harder than in a standard push-up, and will also require a much greater level of core stability.

Engage your core and keep your pelvis neutral

VARIATION 3

As in the push-up on one leg, having one hand out in front of you makes your core muscles work harder and in a slightly different way, while providing extra benefit to the muscles of your chest, shoulders, and arms. Ensure that you keep your core engaged throughout the movement, and repeat with your other arm.

Keep your pelvis neutral

Position one hand out in front of you

VARIATION 4

Raising one leg during the push-up means that your core stabilizers have to work much harder to keep you balanced. Stretch through your hip to lift your foot off the floor, making sure that you keep your knee extended. Avoid twisting your hips, and hold the lift before returning to the start position. Repeat with your other leg.

Keep your hips and torso in line

Maintain straight legs

PROGRESSION—LEVEL 2

Raising a leg rather than an arm will demand more balance and control. Engage your abdominal muscles and lift your right leg behind you to hip height. Balance and hold, then return to the start position. Being careful to keep your back straight and not to arch your spine, repeat with your other leg.

Stretch your leg straight out behind you

Keep your back in a neutral postion and your chest high

Align your head with your spine

PROGRESSION—LEVEL 3

Combining an arm lift and a leg lift requires good strength and stability. Contracting your abs, lift your right leg behind you to hip height and your left arm forward to shoulder height. Hold, then lower your leg and arm, under control, to the start position. Keeping your body straight, repeat with your other leg and arm.

Make sure you keep your torso stationary and do not leg your shoulders sag

Extend your arm straight out in front

107a PULLEY CHOP (LEVEL 1)

Core stability is about controlling your spine. When you keep your spine still while you are moving your arms and lower body, you are performing true core-stability exercises.

This basic form of the pulley chop puts stress on the muscles of your core as you try to maintain your balance. If you find Level 1 too hard, then begin with a full kneeling position.

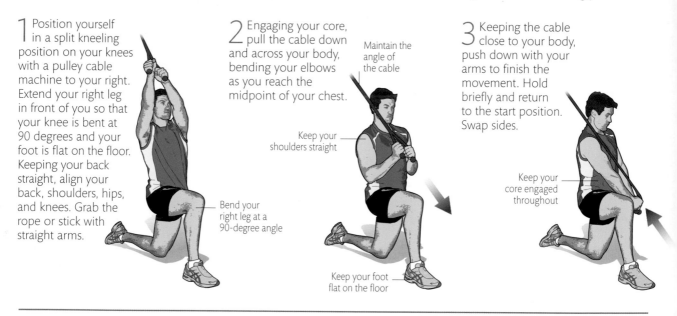

1 Position yourself in a split kneeling position on your knees with a pulley cable machine to your right. Extend your right leg in front of you so that your knee is bent at 90 degrees and your foot is flat on the floor. Keeping your back straight, align your back, shoulders, hips, and knees. Grab the rope or stick with straight arms.

Bend your right leg at a 90-degree angle

2 Engaging your core, pull the cable down and across your body, bending your elbows as you reach the midpoint of your chest.

Maintain the angle of the cable

Keep your shoulders straight

Keep your foot flat on the floor

3 Keeping the cable close to your body, push down with your arms to finish the movement. Hold briefly and return to the start position. Swap sides.

Keep your core engaged throughout

107b PULLEY CHOP (LEVEL 2)

Performing the chop while standing brings your leg muscles into play, in addition to those of your torso and shoulders.

Your core is also being made to work harder, so your strength and stability will improve.

1 Stand with the pulley to your right, keeping your legs straight. Make sure your back is straight and your hips and shoulders are aligned. Keeping your arms extended, grab the cable.

Engage your core

Keep your legs straight

2 Engaging your core, pull the cable down and across your body, bending your elbows as you reach the midpoint of your chest. Keep your shoulders straight and your hips fixed throughout the movement.

Keep your hips facing forward

3 Keeping the cable close to your body, push down with your arms to finish the movement. Hold briefly and return to the start position. Switch sides.

Extend your arms fully

107c PULLEY CHOP (LEVEL 3)

This progression of the movement involves you using a scissors stance (a kind of half-lunge), which is less stable than a standing position. This makes you work your core slightly harder in order to maintain your balance.

1 Stand with the pulley to your right, with your right foot forward, your legs making an angle of about 30 degrees at your hips, and your knees bent slightly. Make sure that your back is straight and that your hips and shoulders are aligned. Hold the cable with your arms extended.

Engage your core

Keep your knees bent slightly

2 While keeping your shoulders straight and your hips still, engage your core to pull the cable down and across your body, bending your elbows as you reach the midpoint of your chest.

Keep your hips still

3 Keeping the cable close to your body, push down with your arms to finish the movement. Hold briefly and return to the start position, before switching sides.

Extend your arms

107d PULLEY CHOP (LEVEL 4)

The most complex variation of this exercise requires very good strength and stability in your core stabilizers. As with the previous levels, the exercise builds strength and stability through your legs, torso, and shoulders, but this version, using a full lunge stance, places additional stress on your core, hip flexors, and gluteals.

1 Stand with the pulley to your right and lunge forward with your right leg. Lift your left heel off the ground. Keep your hips and shoulders aligned and your back straight. Hold the cable with your arms extended above you.

Bend your knee at a right angle

Keep your right foot flat on the floor

2 Keeping your shoulders straight and your hips still, engage your core to pull the cable down and across your body, bending your elbows as you reach the midpoint of your chest.

Keep your back and shoulders straight

3 Keeping the cable close to your body, push down with your arms to finish the movement. Hold briefly, then return to the start position and switch sides.

Maintain the angle of the cable

Fully extend your arms

108a PULLEY LIFT (LEVEL 1)

Core stability is dependent on good spine control, and so true core-stability exercises involve keeping your spine still while working your arms and lower body. If you find Level 1 of this exercise too hard to begin with, try kneeling on both legs rather than just one. Gradually work through the levels as you master the technique.

Begin with your arms straight and fully extended

Bend your left leg at a right angle

Keep your core engaged and your hips aligned

Keep the cable taut and at the same angle

1 With the pulley to your right, position yourself with your left knee up and bent at 90 degrees and your right knee on the floor. Keep your back straight and your shoulders and hips in line. Take hold of the pulley rope or handle with both arms, keeping your arms fully straight.

2 Pull the cable up and into your chest with both hands bending at your elbows, keeping the cable taut and close to your body.

3 Following the direction of the pull across your upper body, push up with your hands until your arms are straight and fully extended. Hold briefly at the top of the movement, return to the start position, and switch sides.

108b PULLEY LIFT (LEVEL 2)

Performing the lift standing up brings your leg muscles into play, in addition to those of your torso and shoulders. Your core is also being made to work harder, improving your strength and stability in that area.

Engage your core

Keep your shoulders straight

Keep your hips facing forward

Push downward through your feet

Maintain the angle of the cable

Extend your arms fully

1 Stand with the pulley to your right and your feet shoulder-width apart. With your back straight and your shoulders, hips, knees, and ankles aligned, grasp the pulley handle with both hands, on straight arms.

2 Pull the cable up and into your chest with both hands bending at your elbows, keeping the cable taut and close to your body.

3 Following the direction of the pull across your upper body, push up with your hands until your arms are straight and fully extended. Hold briefly at the top, return to the start position, and switch sides.

108c PULLEY LIFT (LEVEL 3)

This progression of the movement involves changing your leg position to the less stable scissors stance. This makes you work your core slightly harder in order to maintain your balance.

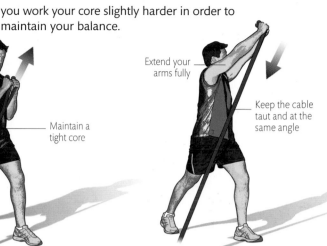

Stand with your left leg in front of your right, bending both knees slightly

Keep your shoulders straight

Keep your hips aligned

Maintain a tight core

Extend your arms fully

Keep the cable taut and at the same angle

1 Stand with the pulley to your right, with your legs in a split standing position and both knees slightly bent. Keep your back straight and your shoulders and hips in line. Take hold of the pulley rope or handle with both hands, keeping your arms fully straight.

2 Pull the cable up and into your chest with both hands, bending at your elbows and keeping the cable taut and close to your body.

3 Following the direction of the pull across your upper body, push up with your hands until your arms are straight and fully extended. Hold briefly at the top of the movement, return to the start position, and switch sides.

108d PULLEY LIFT (LEVEL 4)

The most complex version of the exercise requires good strength and stability in your core stabilizers. As with the previous levels, it builds strength and stability through your legs, torso, and shoulders, but by positioning yourself in a lunge position you place additional stress on your core, hip flexors, and gluteals.

Engage your core

Bend your left knee at a 90-degree angle

Keep your shoulders straight

Keep your hips facing forward

Press down with your left foot

Fully extend your arms

Keep the cable taut and at the same angle

1 Stand with the the pulley to your right and lunge forward with your left leg. Keep your back straight and your shoulders and hips in line. Take hold of the pulley with both hands, keeping your arms fully straight.

2 Pull the cable up and into your chest with both hands, bending at your elbows and keeping the cable taut and close to your body.

3 Following the direction of the pull across your body, push up with your hands until your arms are straight and fully extended. Hold briefly when you reach the top of the movement, then return to the start position. Switch sides.

109 HIP WIPER

This is a core-stability exercise that requires you to keep your pelvis still while moving one of your legs. It is a good exercise for your lower back and groin, and for the rehabilitation of sacroiliac joint instability, under your therapist's guidance. You will need a partner to help you.

1 Lie on your back with your arms spread wide and both legs in the air. Have your partner hold one of your legs to aid your stability.

Your partner holds your legs steady

Press your palms flat against the floor

2 Slowly lower your left leg to the side as far as you can, ensuring that your shoulder does not lift off the floor. Slowly return to the start position. Complete the set and switch legs.

Lower your leg as far as your pelvis allows

Keep your shoulders and arms flat on the floor

PROGRESSION—LEVELS 2 AND 3

Like most exercises, there are higher levels of difficulty to work through as you progress. For level 2, perform the exercise as above, but without a partner holding your stationary leg. For level 3, keep both your feet together and rotate them to alternate sides. For each movement, make sure that you control your pelvis and keep your shoulders and arms flat on the floor throughout the exercise.

Keep your legs straight and in line

Keep your shoulders and arms flat

Keep your feet together

110 MCKENZIE EXTENSION

This exercise helps ease aches in your lower back, such as those caused by sitting for long periods of time. It is particularly useful if you have been diagnosed with back conditions such as a slipped disk (»p.60), or if you have been suffering from disk-related sciatica (»p.60).

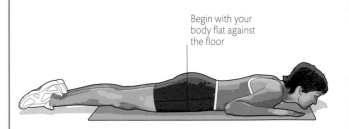

Begin with your body flat against the floor

1 Lie face down, with your hands flat on the floor and level with your shoulders, as though you are about to perform a push-up (»p.228).

Keep your legs straight

Keep your movement slow and controlled

2 Pressing your hips against the floor, push your upper torso upward with your arms, lifting your head and shoulders up as high as you can, relaxing your lower back, and breathing out. Pause and use your arms to lower your torso back to the start position.

VARIATION

If your injury means that one side of your back is more painful than the other, there is a useful variation of this exercise you can perform to help your condition. While you are lying face down on your stomach, as in Step 1, shift your legs towards your painful side and extend your upper torso upwards. Doing this will encourage your disc bulge to reverse and the disc to move back to its correct position.

111a EXTENSION HOLD (LEVEL 1)

This exercise helps balance your trunk by conditioning your lower-back muscles, which work opposite your abs. A strong trunk provides protection against back injury and will be a mainstay in the rehabilitation of any back or pelvic injury. You will need a partner to assist you with this exercise.

Rest your hands on the floor

Come to a straight back position but don't overextend

Keep your knees straight

1 Lie on a Swiss ball, positioning it under your midsection. Let your arms reach down to the floor, keeping your elbows slightly bent. Have your partner hold your ankles to keep your feet touching the floor for stability.

2 Keeping your legs straight, slowly lift yourself up into a straight back position. Hold for 8 seconds, then lower yourself down and rest for 2 seconds. Repeat for the required number of repetitions.

111b EXTENSION HOLD (LEVEL 2)

This next level of difficulty works your back further by making you engage more of your core and lower back.

Face the floor with your head, neck, and spine in line

1 Lie on a Swiss ball and position it lower down your body, so that it is now under your hips. Stretch your arms to the floor, and get your partner to hold your ankles.

Keep your spine neutral and your core engaged

2 Keeping your legs straight and your back flat, slowly lift your upper torso, taking care not to overextend. Hold for 8 seconds at the top of the movement, then lower yourself down to the start position for 2 seconds, and repeat for the required number of repetitions.

111c EXTENSION HOLD (LEVEL 3)

This variation necessitates that you control the rotation of your body and maintain a strong, aligned back.

Keep your legs straight throughout

1 Lie with a Swiss ball positioned under your hips and hold a dumbbell in your left hand. Rest your arms on the floor with your elbows bent. Get your partner to hold your ankles.

Raise the dumbbell off the ground

2 With your legs and back straight, lift your torso, squeezing your shoulder blades together and lifting your arms evenly until they are perpendicular to your body. Hold for 8 seconds, return to the start position, and rest for 2 seconds. Complete the set and repeat with the weight in your right hand.

112 BRIDGE

This exercise activates your gluteal muscles and back extensors. It is an important stabilizing movement for rehabilitation if you have suffered a back (»p.60), sacroiliac joint (»p.62), groin (»pp.104–07), or hamstring (»p.108) injury. There are a wide number of potential variations, making it a very versatile exercise.

VARIATION

This exercise can be varied by bending your knees further, or putting your feet on a Swiss ball. This adds a level of instability, making your core stabilizers work harder.

Keep your feet flat on the ground

Place your arms flat on the floor

Keep your knees in line with your shoulders

Maintain a straight back, and don't allow it to sag

1 Lie on your back with your knees bent at right angles and your feet flat on the floor, hip-width apart. Keep your arms at your sides, with your palms facing down.

2 Engaging your core, slowly lift your buttocks off the floor until your body is in a straight line from your knees to your shoulders. Pause at the top, then reverse the movement to return to the starting position.

113 SINGLE-LEG BRIDGE

A development of the bridge (see above), this exercise is useful for working your gluteals, or hip extensors, and the muscles of your core. Because you are performing it on one leg, it forces you to control the rotation and tilt of your pelvis. It is important to make sure that you keep your hips level throughout.

Ensure that your hips are straight

Keep your head and spine aligned

Keep your hips fixed and do not twist

Engage your abdominals

1 Lie on your back with your knees bent at 90 degrees, foot hip-width apart, and your hands down by your sides. Keeping your right foot flat on the floor, and your arms by your sides, raise your left knee up toward your torso until your thighs are at right angles.

2 Engaging the muscles of your abdomen and lower back, lift your buttocks until your hips are fully extended and your body is in a straight line from your lower knee to your shoulders. Hold this position, then reverse the movement to return to the starting position. Repeat with your other leg.

114 HORIZONTAL PULL

This useful exercise works the muscles of your upper back and arms, particularly your biceps, and also strengthens your grip. It is an essential movement for anyone wanting to strengthen the spine because it engages a large number of spinal muscles and the abdominals. To begin with, you may find it easier to perform it with your back on a bench.

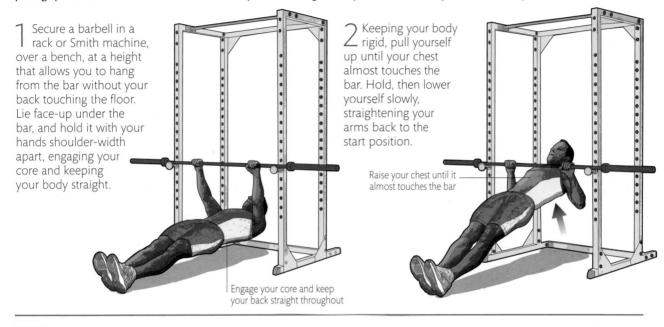

1 Secure a barbell in a rack or Smith machine, over a bench, at a height that allows you to hang from the bar without your back touching the floor. Lie face-up under the bar, and hold it with your hands shoulder-width apart, engaging your core and keeping your body straight.

2 Keeping your body rigid, pull yourself up until your chest almost touches the bar. Hold, then lower yourself slowly, straightening your arms back to the start position.

Raise your chest until it almost touches the bar

Engage your core and keep your back straight throughout

115 PILATES REFORMER

A very effective addition to your rehabilitation, the pilates reformer is a machine that is commonly used by physical therapists to help with a range of injuries, especially those that affect your back. It exercises your whole body and the difficulty of movements can be increased gradually. Your physical therapist will instruct you on the correct technique and exercises, depending on your condition and level of rehabilitation. The main exercise shown here is just one example of a basic, commonly-used movement, the variation is one of a more advanced level.

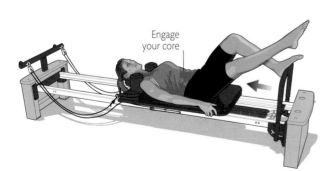

Engage your core

1 Lie on your back on the reformer with your neck held in place and your right leg extended and raised. Bend your left leg to 90 degrees with your foot on the end of the machine. Using your quads, hamstrings, and calf, push with your left leg, while stabilizing your pelvis and your right hip. Return to the start position, complete the set, and switch legs.

VARIATION

Sit upright on the reformer with your feet held in place and your knees bent at a 45-degree angle. Keeping your spine and shoulders stable, grasp the handles with your arms bent at a right angle and hold. Perform the movement for the desired number of repetitions, then rest.

Keep your back straight and your core tight

116 POWER CLEAN

Although technically difficult, this exercise is a fantastic all-round strength-builder. It can be used to rehabilitate any injury, and also makes an excellent warm-up exercise.

Keep your shoulders over the bar for as long as possible

Keep the bar close to your body

Start to drop your elbows when your shoulders reach their highest point

Drive up with your legs

Let the bar touch the tops of your thighs

Push off with the balls of your feet

1 Squat with your feet hip-width apart under the bar and your hips higher than your knees. Grip the barbell overhand, with hands just wider than shoulder-width apart.

2 Raise the bar above your knees. Push in your hips while driving up hard with your legs to give the weight momentum.

3 Forcefully extend your hips, knees, and ankles, keeping the bar close to your body. Shrug your shoulders upward hard.

117 PUSH PRESS

This is a good warm-up exercise with light weights, and is great for building all-round strength when you use a heavily loaded barbell.

Hold the bar at shoulder level

Lift the bar to a position in line with your feet

Lock out your elbows at the top of the movement

Keep your trunk upright and do not arch your back

Keep your core muscles engaged

Maintain a strong core to stabilize your body

1 Load up your barbell. Place your feet hip-width apart, bend your knees, and use an overhand grip to lift the bar onto your shoulders. Dip into a shallow squat.

2 As you reach the shallow squat position, dip down then explosively extend your legs and hips, pressing the bar up until you stand tall. Hold the bar overhead, keeping your arms locked-out and body strong.

3 Bend your knees and lower the bar under control. Rest the bar on your shoulders, and repeat the move until you finish the set.

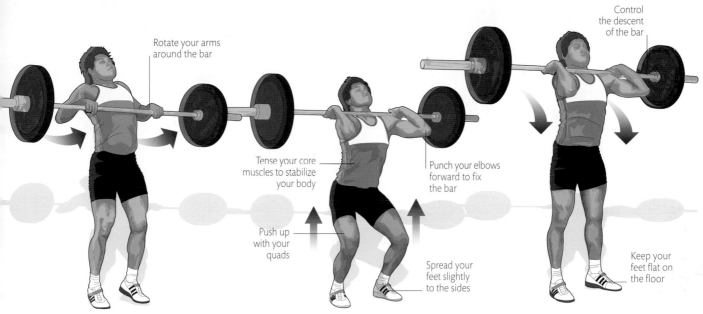

Rotate your arms around the bar

Tense your core muscles to stabilize your body

Punch your elbows forward to fix the bar

Push up with your quads

Spread your feet slightly to the sides

Control the descent of the bar

Keep your feet flat on the floor

4 When you reach full extension, lower your body under the bar, and drop and rotate your elbows downward and forward.

5 Flex your hips and knees into a semi-squat and catch the bar on the top of your shoulders. Stand up straight by extending your legs.

6 Keeping your back flat, let the weight down under control to your thighs, before returning the bar to the floor.

118 BARBELL JUMP SQUAT

Your entire body works hard in this dynamic movement that develops leg strength and balance. Make sure you execute the movement in a Smith machine to ensure safety and control.

Engage your core

Keep your elbows under the bar

Explode vertically from the squat

1 Hold a barbell across your upper back. Position your feet just wider than shoulder-width apart and plant your heels firmly on the floor.

2 Lower yourself into a quarter squat, bending at your knees and easing your hips back. Keeping your chest high, look straight ahead.

3 Explode upward from the squat with your legs—this should lift you off the floor. Cushion your landing by bending your knees and easing your hips back slightly. Repeat Steps 2 and 3, as required.

STATIC-STRETCHING EXERCISES

Static stretches are an important aspect of injury prevention and are also useful in recovery from injury. Static stretches should be performed after you have exercised; using them before may reduce your capacity to release power, and does little to reduce your chances of injury. You should always aim to balance both sides of your body.

119 SCARF STRETCH

This easy and effective stretch works the muscles around your shoulder joint. It is especially useful for weightlifters and those engaged in throwing events.

1 Stand with your feet hip-width apart, legs slightly bent. Bring your left arm across your body with your elbow slightly bent. Hold your left arm in at the elbow with your right hand until you feel the muscles working in the back of your shoulder. Relax and repeat with your right arm.

120 UPPER-BACK STRETCH

This easy stretch specifically mobilizes the muscles in your upper back, making it useful across a range of sports, particularly those that involve throwing.

Push your arms forward, feeling the stretch in your upper back

1 Interlock your fingers, palms facing out. Bring your hands to chest level and extend your arms, lock out your elbows, and push your shoulders forward.

121 LAT STRETCH

Specifically targeting the latissimus dorsi muscles, this stretch is useful for a number of sports, including weightlifting, rowing, and field athletics.

Feel the stretch in your lats

Keep a slight bend in your knees

1 Stand facing an upright support that will take your weight. Grip the support with both hands and lean back, bending your knees. Push with your legs and pull with your arms.

122 PEC STRETCH

This stretch targets the pectoral muscles of your upper chest, easing any tightness and increasing flexibility. It is also helpful if you train for sports that involve throwing.

Keep your chest out

Feel the stretch here

Rest your free hand on your hip

1 Stand sideways to a solid vertical support. Rest one arm behind the upright support, keeping your upper arm in line with your shoulder. Rock your body gently forward until you can feel the stretch in your chest.

123 ITB STRETCH

The iliotibial band (ITB) is a band of connective tissue that runs down the outside of your thigh. Runners, hikers, gymnasts, and dancers should perform this stretch regularly to help prevent inflammation of the area—iliotibial band syndrome (»p.132)—which is a common cause of pain.

Feel the stretch in the outside of your rear leg

Bring your front leg across

1 Stand upright with your feet hip-width apart. Bring one leg across the other while raising your opposite arm above your head for balance. Repeat on the other side.

124 PIRIFORMIS STRETCH

This seated stretch is more advanced than the ITB stretch (see left) because you need greater flexibility in your hip joint to perform it correctly. It is also a useful exercise for runners, hikers, gymnasts, and dancers, in preventing or easing iliotibial band syndrome (»p.132).

1 Sit on the floor with your legs extended. Bend one leg and cross it over your extended leg so that your foot is flat on the floor. Supporting yourself with one arm, reach over with your free hand and gently press on the outside of your knee until you can feel the stretch in your ITB.

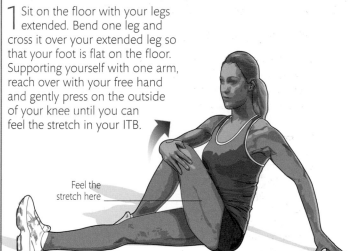

Feel the stretch here

125 3-POINT QUAD STRETCH

The purpose of this stretch is to work the quadricep muscles on the front of your upper thigh and promote flexibility at your knee joint. Relatively simple to perform, it is useful following any type of leg workout.

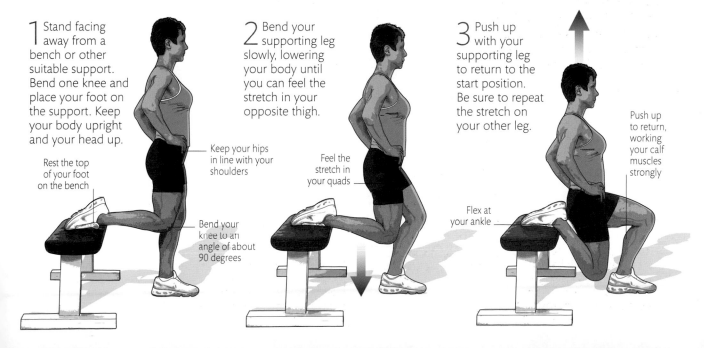

1 Stand facing away from a bench or other suitable support. Bend one knee and place your foot on the support. Keep your body upright and your head up.

Rest the top of your foot on the bench

Keep your hips in line with your shoulders

Bend your knee to an angle of about 90 degrees

2 Bend your supporting leg slowly, lowering your body until you can feel the stretch in your opposite thigh.

Feel the stretch in your quads

3 Push up with your supporting leg to return to the start position. Be sure to repeat the stretch on your other leg.

Push up to return, working your calf muscles strongly

Flex at your ankle

126 HAMSTRING STRETCH 1

Any activity that involves repeated knee flexion, such as running or bicycling, for example, can cause tightness in your hamstrings. This stretch helps you protect this vulnerable area.

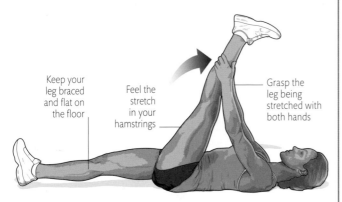

Keep your leg braced and flat on the floor

Feel the stretch in your hamstrings

Grasp the leg being stretched with both hands

1 Lie on your back with your legs extended. Lift each leg in turn, keeping your knee braced and the toes pulled back toward your body. If you are very flexible, try extending the stretch a little by pulling back on your leg.

127 HAMSTRING STRETCH 2

This is a simple general-purpose stretch that works all the muscles in your hamstrings, relieving the tightness that can stress your lower back. Stretch slowly and avoid "bouncing" at full extension.

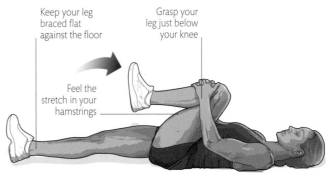

Keep your leg braced flat against the floor

Grasp your leg just below your knee

Feel the stretch in your hamstrings

1 Lie on your back with your legs extended. Bend your left knee. Pull gently on your left leg, bringing your knee toward your chest until you feel the stretch. Keep the back of your head on the floor. Relax and repeat with your right leg.

128 ADDUCTOR STRETCH 1

Stretching your adductor or groin muscles is key to maintaining hip flexibility for many sports.

Keep your body upright

Feel the stretch in your adductors

1 Keep your body upright and put your hands on your hips. Bend your left leg so that your left knee is over your left foot, your right leg is extended, and your right foot is flat. Rock gently to the side. Relax and switch legs.

129 ADDUCTOR STRETCH 2

This version of the adductor stretch works more on the short adductors. It is easy to perform and can be carried out anywhere.

Feel the stretch in your adductors

1 Sit on the floor and take a firm hold of the tops of your feet. Bring your legs in close to your body, pressing the soles of your feet together. Push your knees gently down towards the floor as far as you can, and hold.

130 CALF STRETCH

Tight calf muscles are more prone to injury during explosive movements like sprinting, so this easy stretch for your lower legs is a must if you are a runner.

Feel the stretch in your calf muscles

Extend your leg, pushing your heel into the floor

1 From a standing position, press your hands against a wall and take a good step backward, keeping your feet hip-width apart. Bend your left leg forward, ensuring you keep your knee over your foot. Repeat with your right leg.

131 STANDING GLUTE

This stretch uses a table to work the deep muscles of your gluteals, along with your iliotibial band.

1 Rest the outside of your left leg on a tabletop, bending at your knee, so your right leg is extended and your right foot is up on tiptoe. Tilt your pelvis forward until you feel the stretch in your left buttock. Hold, relax, and repeat with your right leg.

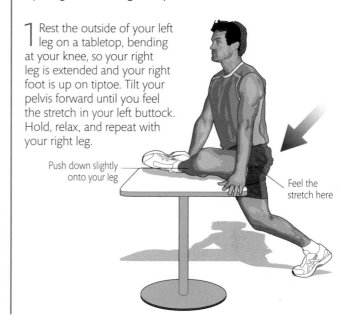

Push down slightly onto your leg

Feel the stretch here

132 KNEE-TO-WALL STRETCH

This is often used by physical therapists to gauge your ankle range of motion (dorsiflexion). Both sides are compared at the start of injury and then remeasured to track recovery.

1 Stand facing a wall with your left leg in front of your right. Keeping your heel flat, bend your left knee; if it touches the wall shift your foot back and repeat. When your heel starts to rise, measure the distance between your toe and the wall. Switch legs.

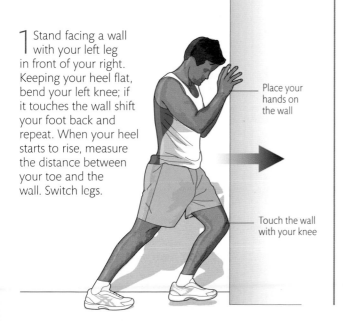

Place your hands on the wall

Touch the wall with your knee

133 QUAD STRETCH

This stretch works the muscles at the front of your thigh that enable you to straighten your knee. Because this stretch is performed in a standing position, it emphasizes good posture and balance.

Keep your head forward and your spine neutral

Tilt your pelvis back slightly

1 Stand with your back to a firm table. Place your left foot on the table and, keeping your legs parallel, tilt your pelvis back slightly so you can feel the stretch in the front of your left thigh. Hold, lower, and repeat with your right leg.

134 STRIDE STRETCH

This is a great stretch for your legs and hips, which can often tighten up, especially after sitting for long periods.

During the movement, ensure that you keep both of your hips pointing forward to prevent imbalance.

Look straight ahead

Straighten your back

Lean forward at your pelvis

Keep your feet flat

Keep your arms roughly in line with each other

Keep your hips aligned

Keep your knee bent

1 Step up onto a high box or bench with your right foot, and lean forward at your pelvis, keeping your back and left leg straight, both feet flat, and your hands by your sides.

2 Stretch out your arms at a right angle to your body and twist your torso, turning your head as you do so. Pause and return to the start position. Complete your set and repeat with your left leg.

135 LANCELOT STRETCH

This is a useful stretch if you suffer from a stiff lumbar spine because it stretches your hip flexors and, in particular, your

psoas muscle. Your psoas muscle is directly attached to your spine and it is important to keep it flexible.

1 Stand with your feet shoulder-width apart and your hands on your hips. Lunge forward with your left leg, bending both legs so that your right knee and the top of your right foot are touching the floor. Keep your spine neutral and look straight ahead.

Look straight ahead

Bend your leg so that your knee is at a right angle

2 Bring your arms together above your head, palms touching, your right arm in front of your left. Reach upward, rotating your pelvis backward. Pause and return to the start position. Complete the set and switch sides.

Feel the stretch in your torso as you reach upward

Squeeze your gluteals

136 SLEEPER STRETCH

Many people neglect the stretching of their posterior capsule (the back of the shoulder). It is very important to maintain adequate flexibility in this area to prevent shoulder problems, especially shoulder impingement (»p.72). This simple yet effective stretch targets your posterior capsule, and you should aim for equal mobility on both sides.

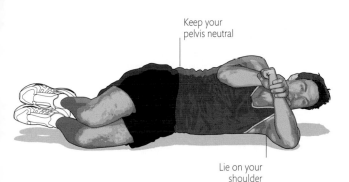

Keep your pelvis neutral

Lie on your shoulder

1 Lie on your left side with your head supported on a cushion and your left arm extended in front of you so that it is level with your collarbone. Your left forearm should point straight up toward the ceiling.

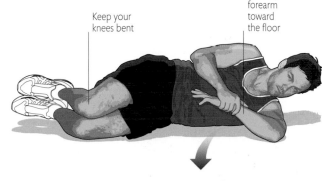

Keep your knees bent

Rotate your forearm toward the floor

2 Grab your left wrist with your right hand and slowly rotate your left arm toward the floor. You should be aiming to get your forearm flat on the ground. Hold for 20–30 seconds and then return to your start position before switching sides.

137 ICING OF QUADRICEPS

If you play a contact or collision sport then you are likely to have had a dead leg (»p.110). When this occurs it is important to ice your quadriceps while keeping your knee flexed as far as you can manage. This will help your recovery.

1 Strap the ice pack to your injured muscle and keep it in place with your knee bent for at least 20 minutes. Repeat twice every 1–2 hours for the first 48–72 hours, depending on the severity of your injury.

Use your arms for extra support

Bend your knee as far as possible

138 GOLF BALL FOOT MASSAGE

Using a golf ball to massage the sole of your foot is a good way to self-treat plantar fasciitis (»p.160). Start gently and gradually increase the pressure.

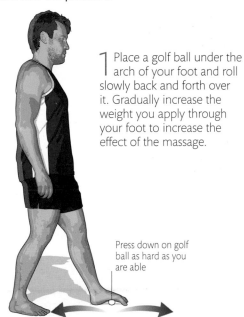

1 Place a golf ball under the arch of your foot and roll slowly back and forth over it. Gradually increase the weight you apply through your foot to increase the effect of the massage.

Press down on golf ball as hard as you are able

PROPRIOCEPTION EXERCISES

"Proprioception" is the name for the signals that your joints, tendons, ligaments, and muscles send to your brain to provide it with information about the position of your joints, and the direction and pressure of your movements. These exercises work to improve your balance, coordination, and agility, and often involve full-body movement.

139 SINGLE-LEG STAND

This exercise is a good starting point for developing your balance and proprioception in a weight-bearing position. You need to master this before moving on to more difficult exercises.

PROGRESSION

Once you can confidently perform a single-leg stand on a stable surface, try balancing on an Airex mat, wobble board (as shown here), and a BOSU board to make it harder.

Maintain a strong core

Keep the knee of your standing leg firm but not locked

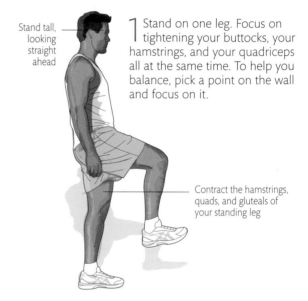

Stand tall, looking straight ahead

1 Stand on one leg. Focus on tightening your buttocks, your hamstrings, and your quadriceps all at the same time. To help you balance, pick a point on the wall and focus on it.

Contract the hamstrings, quads, and gluteals of your standing leg

140 JUMP AND STICK

Jumping is an essential skill to practise after any lower-limb injury, and it requires strength and power in your legs. You must master both takeoff and landing because each ability is equally important for athletic performance.

1 Stand with your feet shoulder-width apart. Take a moment to visualize how you are going to take off and where you are going to land.

Bend your knees to prepare

2 Bend through the hips, knees, and ankles, and push hard off the ground with both feet, swinging your arms to help propel yourself through the air.

Use your arms to help you drive forward

3 Land firmly on one foot, keeping both knees bent. You can vary the exercise by jumping and landing on both feet, or hopping off and landing on one foot.

Keep your left leg off the ground

Land firmly, taking your weight on your right leg

141 FOUR-POINT KNEEL

This exercise is good for improving your balance, and also works your hips, upper back, shoulders, and core. It is particularly useful in shoulder, groin, and lower-back pain rehabilitation. Begin with a wobble board and, as your strength and balance improves, progress through to Level 2 of the movement. Once you have mastered that, work through Levels 1–3 using a Swiss ball (see right).

Keep your neck, spine, and head in line and look down

Engage your core

Keep your chest high

1 Kneel with your feet hip-width apart. Place your left hand on a wobble board and extend your right arm up, keeping it in line with your torso, and support your body weight on your left arm and knees. Hold this position, relax, and swap arms.

PROGRESSION—WOBBLE BOARD LEVEL 2

Kneel on all fours, your feet hip-width apart and your left hand on a wobble board. In one smooth movement, extend your left leg out straight behind you and reach your right arm out in front. Support your weight on your left arm, hold, and switch arms.

Engage your core and keep your torso stable

Stretch through your leg and point your toes

Keep your chest high

PROGRESSION—SWISS BALL LEVELS 1–3

Level 1: Kneel with your toes tucked under and the Swiss ball at arm's length in front of you. Lean forward at your hip, extending your right hand to rest on the ball. Supporting your weight on your knees and your right hand, hold, and relax, before switching hands.

Keep your right shoulder relaxed

Engage your core

Level 2: Kneel with your feet slightly apart and the Swiss ball in front of you. Lean forward to rest both your hands on the ball, then raise your whole body up into a plank, supporting your weight on your arms and toes. Hold, then relax.

Keep your spine neutral and in line with your head

Engage your core

Level 3: Position the Swiss ball in front of you and kneel forward to rest both your hands on the ball. Raise your body up into a plank, then place your left hand on your hip. Support your weight with your right arm and toes. Hold, then relax, before switching arms.

Engage your core

142 FOOT CLOCK DRILL

The foot clock drill, hand clock drill, and multi-directional lunge work on your proprioception around your hip, knee, and ankle. They are perfect for any lower-limb injury or after surgery.

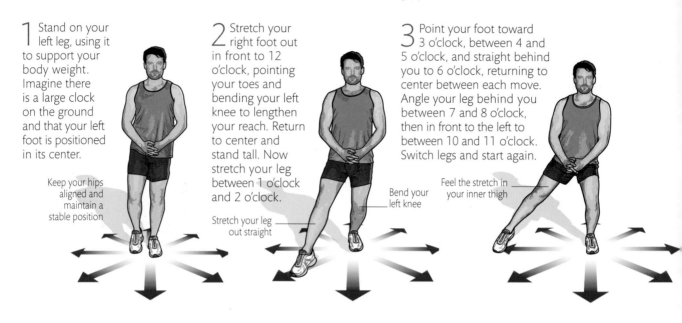

1 Stand on your left leg, using it to support your body weight. Imagine there is a large clock on the ground and that your left foot is positioned in its center.

Keep your hips aligned and maintain a stable position

2 Stretch your right foot out in front to 12 o'clock, pointing your toes and bending your left knee to lengthen your reach. Return to center and stand tall. Now stretch your leg between 1 o'clock and 2 o'clock.

Stretch your leg out straight

3 Point your foot toward 3 o'clock, between 4 and 5 o'clock, and straight behind you to 6 o'clock, returning to center between each move. Angle your leg behind you between 7 and 8 o'clock, then in front to the left to between 10 and 11 o'clock. Switch legs and start again.

Bend your left knee

Feel the stretch in your inner thigh

143 HAND CLOCK DRILL

This is a variation of the foot clock drill (see above) and requires slightly more control and balance. It is a terrific drill for any lower-limb injury because it involves skill, control, balance, and coordination.

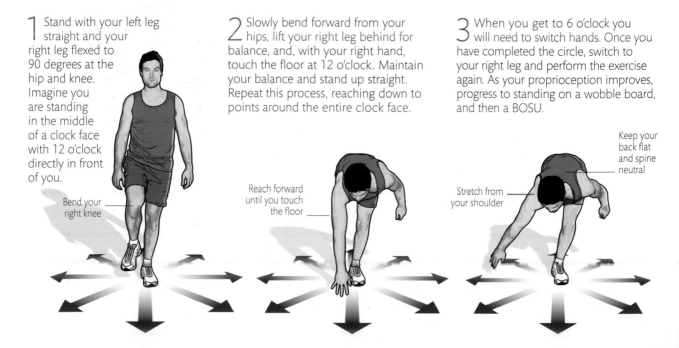

1 Stand with your left leg straight and your right leg flexed to 90 degrees at the hip and knee. Imagine you are standing in the middle of a clock face with 12 o'clock directly in front of you.

Bend your right knee

2 Slowly bend forward from your hips, lift your right leg behind for balance, and, with your right hand, touch the floor at 12 o'clock. Maintain your balance and stand up straight. Repeat this process, reaching down to points around the entire clock face.

Reach forward until you touch the floor

3 When you get to 6 o'clock you will need to switch hands. Once you have completed the circle, switch to your right leg and perform the exercise again. As your proprioception improves, progress to standing on a wobble board, and then a BOSU.

Keep your back flat and spine neutral

Stretch from your shoulder

144 MULTIDIRECTIONAL LUNGE

This exercise presents even more of a challenge in terms of coordination and flexibility. It requires full range of motion in the lower limbs, so, if you are recovering from injury, check you are sufficiently rehabilitated before attempting it.

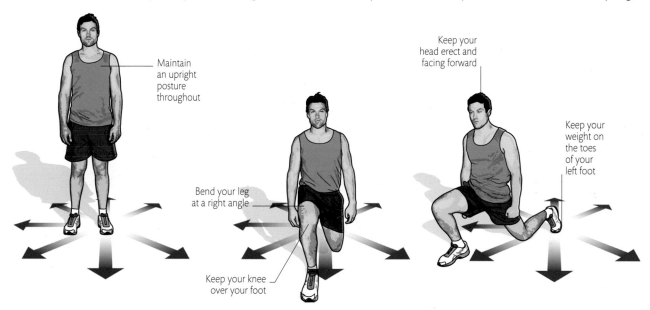

Maintain an upright posture throughout

Bend your leg at a right angle

Keep your knee over your foot

Keep your head erect and facing forward

Keep your weight on the toes of your left foot

1 Stand with your feet shoulder-width apart and your arms by your sides. Imagine that your left foot is placed in the center of a clock face.

2 Keep your left foot in place and lunge forward with your right foot to 12 o'clock. Pause then return to the center position after each lunge.

3 Lunge at an angle between 1 and 2 o'clock, then sideways to 3, then move your right leg behind to between 4 and 5. Lunge straight behind to 6.

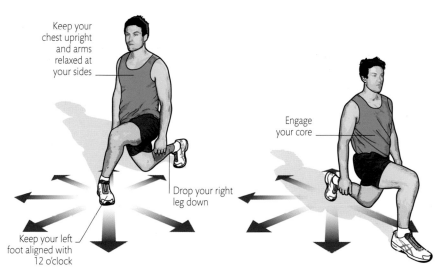

Keep your chest upright and arms relaxed at your sides

Keep your left foot aligned with 12 o'clock

Drop your right leg down

Engage your core

4 Hook your right leg behind your body, almost in a curtsey, and lunge backward to between 7 and 8 o'clock, then return to the center position.

5 Lunge forward to the left, angling your foot between 10 and 11. Return to the center position and swap legs.

PROGRESSION

Once you have completed the drill on one leg, switch legs and work your way around the clock face as described here. Note that you will not be reaching toward 9 o'clock during the multidirectional lunge. As your proprioception improves, you can move on to performing the exercise standing on a wobble board, and a BOSU.

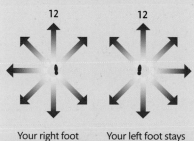

Your right foot stays in the center of the clock face

Your left foot stays in the center of the clock face

145 STEP-UP AND HOLD

This excellent functional exercise also improves your coordination and proprioception. It works the main muscles of your leg—your quads, hamstrings, and gluteals—and places stress on your core to keep your body stable.

Take a deep breath before starting the exercise

Use your trailing leg as little as possible during the step up

Keep your knee in line with your toes

Stand tall

1 Facing your step or bench, make sure it is high enough to allow an angle of 90 degrees at your knee joint.

2 Drive your body up, putting your weight onto your right leg and pushing down with your right heel.

3 Still supporting your weight on your right leg, bring your left leg up high until your knee is in line with your hips.

Swing your left arm back and right arm forward

Contract your right gluteal, hamstrings, and quadriceps

Your left knee makes a 90-degree angle at the top of the movement

Minimize any side-to-side movement

4 Bring your left leg down in one smooth movement, swinging your arms to aid your motion and balance.

5 Step down with your left leg, keeping your body upright and strong. Finish the set and switch legs.

VARIATION

When you have mastered this exercise, use a step or bench with a greater height. You will need even more power to drive your body upward, so remember to push down with your right heel and to use your right thigh and gluteal muscles to lift your left leg up and through. Another option is to step onto an unstable surface, such as a BOSU or wobbleboard.

146 SCAPULAR CLOCK

Gaining control of your scapula (shoulder blade) is crucial to recovery after any shoulder surgery. This exercise increases the movement, control, and strength of your shoulder joint.

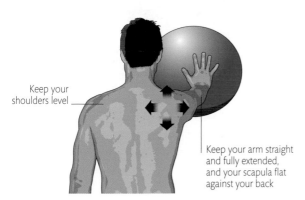

Keep your shoulders level

Keep your arm straight and fully extended, and your scapula flat against your back

1 Stand facing a wall. With a straight arm, hold a Swiss ball against a wall with the palm of your hand. Imagine a clock face drawn on your shoulder and move your shoulder up to the 12 o'clock position, before rotating to 3 o'clock, 6 o'clock, and 9 o'clock, and return to 12 o'clock to make a full circle. The ball should not move. Change arms and repeat.

147 SCAPULAR CIRCLE

This variation on the scapular clock (see left) increases your shoulder control. In this version you roll the Swiss ball in small circles.

Keep your scapula flat against your back

Keep the Swiss ball pressed against the wall

1 Stand facing a wall with your left hand on your hip and your right arm straight out in front of you. Press the Swiss ball gently against the wall with the palm of your right hand. Keeping your right arm straight, roll the ball around in small circles by moving your shoulder clockwise and then counterclockwise. Repeat with your left arm.

148 SCAPULAR CROSS

This second variation on the scapular clock (see above left) helps increase your shoulder control. It can be used in combination with the scapular circle exercise (see above right).

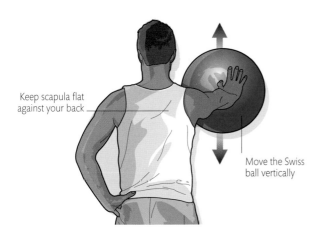

Keep scapula flat against your back

Move the Swiss ball vertically

1 Stand facing a wall with your left hand on your hip and your right arm straight out in front of you. Gently hold a Swiss ball against the wall with the palm of your right hand. Keeping your arm straight, raise and lower your shoulder to move the ball up and down in a straight line.

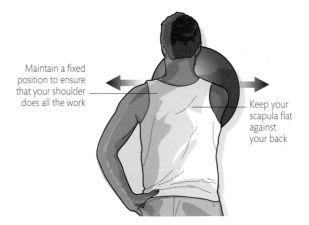

Maintain a fixed position to ensure that your shoulder does all the work

Keep your scapula flat against your back

2 Keeping your right arm straight, now use your shoulder to move the ball from side to side as though drawing a cross. Repeat both movements with your left arm.

149a WALK-JOG DRILL

After any lower-limb injury you should build up your speed, distance, and duration gradually. This is a useful drill to develop your movement from a comfortable walking pace to running. Ensure that your progress is monitored by your physiotherapist, and always warm up beforehand to minimize your risk of muscle strain.

1 Begin on a treadmill set to a 1 percent incline at a comfortable walking pace for 10 minutes. Provided you do not feel any pain, swelling, or loss of range of motion in your affected joint, increase the time by 3–5 minutes for each subsequent session, at the same incline and speed. Once you have reached 20 minutes without pain, swelling, or loss of range of motion, reduce the time to 10 minutes again, and increase your speed by 10 percent, still at a 1 percent incline. Repeat until you reach a full jogging speed. Perform one session on the treadmill at this speed for 10 minutes. If you still feel no problems, then begin a walk-run drill outside (see table right).

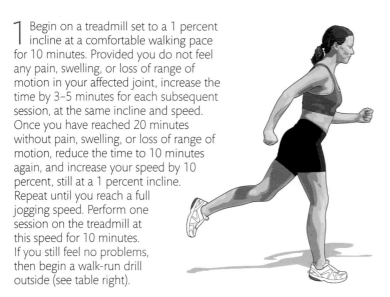

PROGRESSION – WALK-RUN DRILL

Session	Walk	Run
1–2	4.5 mins	0.5 mins
3–4	4 mins	1 min
5–6	3.5 mins	1.5 mins
7–8	3 mins	2 mins
9–10	2.5 mins	2.5 mins
11–12	2 mins	3 mins
13–14	1.5 mins	3.5 mins
15–16	1 min	4 mins
17–18	0.5 mins	4.5 mins

Each session should feel relatively comfortable. If you cannot complete a session because of pain, go back three sessions and start again from there. Do not try to run through pain. Once you have completed Session 18 pain-free, you can begin 30 minutes of running at a comfortable pace.

149b SPRINT DRILL

Running drills are an excellent way to improve your speed, mobility, and fitness, as they require quick bursts of energy and good control. This drill can be done over a range of distances and times, so speak to your physiotherapist or trainer about your sporting requirements. Warm up before the drill to minimize the risk of muscle strain.

1 Starting at cone A, run for 16 ft (5 m) toward cone B, building up speed so that you are at full sprint by the time you pass it. Keep sprinting for a further 82 ft (25 m) until you reach cone C, and decelerate for the last 16 ft (5 m) toward cone D. Rest as required, then turn and perform the drill in the opposite direction.

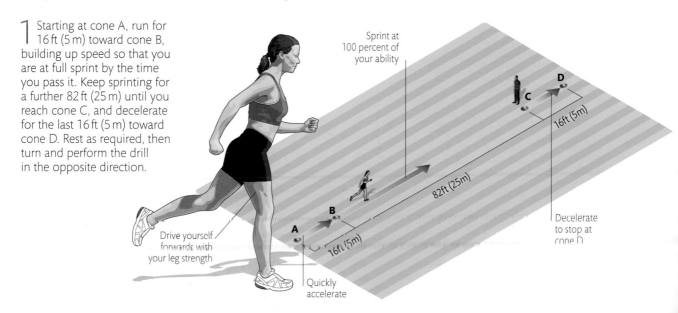

Sprint at 100 percent of your ability

16ft (5m)

82ft (25m)

Decelerate to stop at cone D

Drive yourself forwards with your leg strength

16ft (5m)

Quickly accelerate

149c FIGURE-EIGHT DRILL

This drill requires speed, spatial awareness, and quick turns —gaining confidence in cutting and turning is crucial to safe return to play after any leg injury. This drill is particularly suitable for sports that involve sudden changes of direction, such as rugby, soccer, and tennis. You will need to adapt the distances to your chosen sport.

1 Starting at cone A, sprint forward for 33 ft (10 m) to touch cone B. Turn and sprint 16 ft (5 m) to touch cone C. Turn at cone C, sprint forward 33 ft (10 m) to touch cone D, then turn and sprint the final 16 ft (5 m) to touch cone A. Rest and repeat as required.

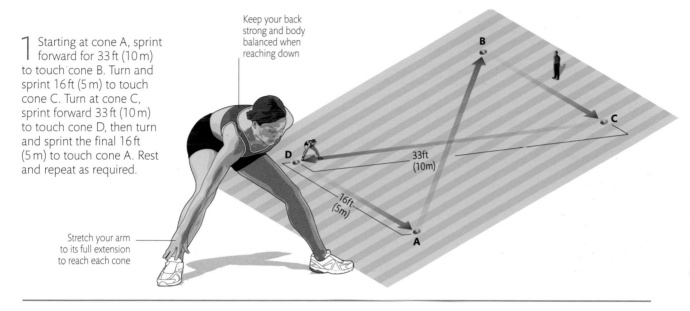

Keep your back strong and body balanced when reaching down

Stretch your arm to its full extension to reach each cone

33ft (10m)

16ft (5m)

149d SHUTTLE-RUN DRILL

Another test of agility, this basic running exercise involves only sprinting and turning. While it is a simple drill, it is good for building up stamina and general fitness, making it useful for every kind of sport. As with the other drills, it is easily adapted to other distances relevant to your chosen sport.

1 Starting at cone A, sprint 33 ft (10 m) to cone B, then turn and sprint 33 ft (10 m) to cone C. Turn at cone C and sprint 33 ft (10 m) to cone D, and so on until you reach cone I. Rest and repeat as required.

Use your arms to maintain balance and increase speed

Touch your foot to each cone

33 ft (10m)

66ft (20m)

PLYOMETRIC EXERCISES

Plyometric exercises are based on a range of movements that work to increase your speed, power, and flexibility, and are ideal for the vast majority of sports. The exercises **often involve stretching and contracting your muscles to build a combination of strength, responsiveness, and explosive power in your body.**

150 WALKING POP-UP

A low-level plyometric exercise, this movement is often used at the start of rehabilitation of foot and ankle injuries. Working your calves, ankles, and feet, it helps you develop strength and control in your hip, knee, and ankle.

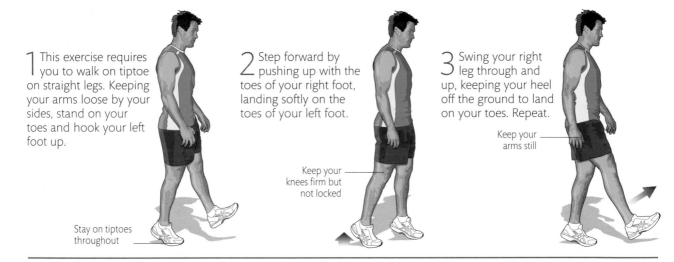

1 This exercise requires you to walk on tiptoe on straight legs. Keeping your arms loose by your sides, stand on your toes and hook your left foot up.

Stay on tiptoes throughout

2 Step forward by pushing up with the toes of your right foot, landing softly on the toes of your left foot.

Keep your knees firm but not locked

3 Swing your right leg through and up, keeping your heel off the ground to land on your toes. Repeat.

Keep your arms still

151 A-WALK

This functional drill gets you thinking about the mechanics of running, and involves exaggerated movements. Start slowly and speed up as you improve.

1 Engaging your core, raise your left knee as high as you can and swing your right arm up, hand balled in a loose fist.

Keep your feet flat on the ground

2 Step forward with your left leg under control and bring your right arm down. Raise your right knee and left arm and move forward. Repeat as required.

Keep your supporting leg straight

VARIATION

To vary the exercise, you can perform the movement with a skipping motion rather than one based on walking. Spring off the ground, raising your knees as high as you can, and swing your arms loosely.

152 STRAIGHT-LEG CIRCLES-IN

This plyometric drill works your calf muscles and Achilles tendons, while also beginning to engage the rotation of your hips. Again, as you improve you can increase the speed at which you perform the drill.

Keep your knees soft

Swing your leg out

Use your arms for balance

Engage your thigh muscles

1 Imagine a straight line. Stand with both feet on the line, your right leg behind you.

2 Walk forward by swinging your right foot out and then inward in a circular motion, and back to the line.

3 Step off with the toes of your left foot, swinging your left leg outward at your hip joint

4 Bring your left leg inward, returning your foot to the central line. Continue.

153 STRAIGHT-LEG CIRCLES-OUT

This variation on the straight-leg circles-in exercise (see above) requires you to swing your legs in an outward, rather than inward, arc. As with the straight-leg circles-in, you should aim to increase your speed as you improve.

1 Imagine two parallel lines in front of you.

2 Move forward by swinging your left leg inward and then outward, landing your left foot on the left parallel line.

3 Flex your right leg, swinging it in toward you.

4 Bring your right leg outward and onto the right parallel line to finish the move. Repeat.

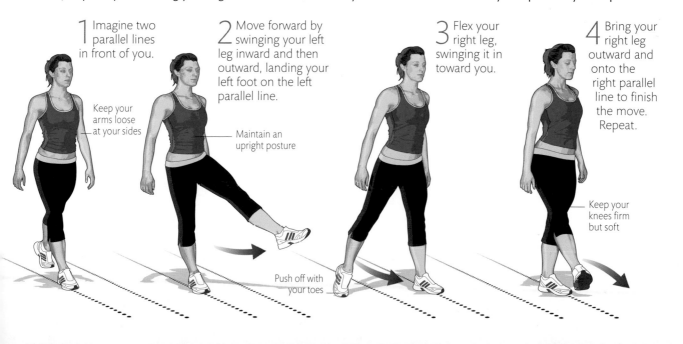

Keep your arms loose at your sides

Maintain an upright posture

Push off with your toes

Keep your knees firm but soft

154 STRAIGHT-LEG SCRATCH

This exercise is similar to the walking pop-up (»p.254), the key difference being that your movements are more pronounced with a longer stride and a greater swing of your arms. Speed up your movements as you improve.

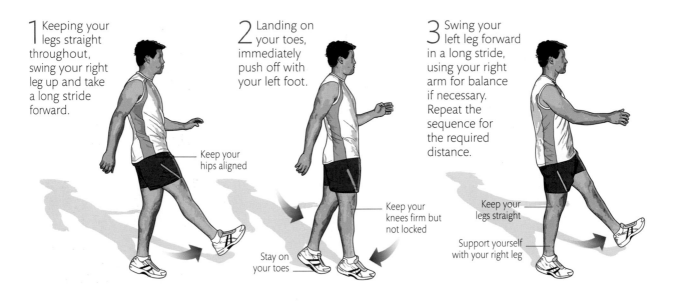

1 Keeping your legs straight throughout, swing your right leg up and take a long stride forward.

Keep your hips aligned

2 Landing on your toes, immediately push off with your left foot.

Keep your knees firm but not locked

Stay on your toes

3 Swing your left leg forward in a long stride, using your right arm for balance if necessary. Repeat the sequence for the required distance.

Keep your legs straight

Support yourself with your right leg

155 FORWARD-AND-BACK FLOOR JUMP

Once you have mastered taking off and landing with singular jumps and hops—see the jump and stick (»p.246)—you can progress to repetitive jumps and hops. This skill is essential for demonstrating that your legs can generate the necessary power to push off the ground, and that they are strong enough to take impact.

Bend your knees to prepare

Keep your feet together

Bend at the hips

Use your arms for balance and momentum

Keep your knees soft

1 Mark a line on the ground and stand behind it with your feet shoulder-width apart.

2 Bending through your hips, knees, and ankles, push off the ground with force to jump to the other side of the line, swinging your arms to aid your momentum.

3 Hit the ground in front of the line, and immediately jump back behind the line to the start position. Repeat. Once confident, try hopping, alternating your legs in takeoff and landing.

156 SIDEWAYS FLOOR JUMP

Learning to jump and hop sideways requires control and power along with balance and confidence. This basic skill is essential for demonstrating that your legs can take impact and also generate the necessary power to push off in a lateral direction. As you improve, you may start to jump and hop sideways over hurdles and boxes.

Bend your knees to prepare

Tuck your feet together

Land firmly on both feet

Take the impact evenly in both legs

1 Mark a line on the ground. Stand to the side of the line with your feet shoulder-width apart.

2 Bend through your hips, knees, and ankles and push off the ground toward the other side of the line.

3 When you hit the ground on the other side, immediately jump back over the line to the start position.

157 FORWARD-AND-BACK HURDLE JUMP

This exercise is based on the same action as the forward-and-back floor jump (see opposite), but increases the level of difficulty by requiring you to jump over a hurdle or a box. As you improve, start hopping instead of jumping.

Use your arms to aid the movement

Press your feet together

Disperse the impact through your hips

Land firmly on both feet

1 Place a hurdle in front of you, checking that the bar is set to a suitable height. Stand behind it with your feet shoulder-width apart.

2 Bending through your hips, knees, and ankles, push hard off the ground to jump over the hurdle.

3 Keeping your legs stiff but bent, land safely on the other side and immediately spring off the ground again, jumping back over the hurdle to the start position. Repeat.

158 SIDEWAYS HURDLE JUMP

This exercise is great for developing the power in your legs. It should only be performed once you feel comfortable performing sideways floor jumps (»p.257). Start with a small hurdle and gradually increase the height as you progress.

1 Stand to one side of a hurdle with your feet roughly shoulder-width apart and your knees bent slightly.

2 Push off the floor with force, bending through your hips, knees, and ankles, and jump sideways over the hurdle.

Tuck your knees up

Press your feet together

Bend your knees in preparation

3 When you land, immediately jump sideways over the hurdle the other way. Continue to jump back and forth over the hurdle as many times as required.

Land on stiff, bent knees

159 BOX JUMP-UP

This versatile exercise offers an effective workout for your lower body, and calls for a good amount of explosive power in your legs. Start with a low box, and increase the height as your power and confidence improve.

1 Stand facing the box with your arms by your sides and your knees bent.

2 Push off the floor with force and jump up onto the box.

3 Land on the box, using your arms to steady yourself. Hold briefly at the end of the movement and jump back to the start position.

Bend at your hips to prepare

Stand with your feet shoulder-width apart

Swing your arms for momentum

Land on stiff, bent knees

160 BOX JUMP-DOWN

This drill requires good strength in your quadriceps and hamstrings in order to control your knees. It is an advanced exercise that you should only attempt once you can perform box jump-ups (see opposite) without pain.

1 Stand on a high box with your feet shoulder-width apart and your arms hanging loose by your sides.

Bend your knees before the jump

2 Push up off the box, bending through your hips, knees, and ankles.

Swing your arms forward to aid your momentum

3 Land on the floor, keeping your knees soft and using your arms to balance yourself. Return to the start position.

Land on stiff, bent knees

Keep your feet firm on the ground when you land

161 BOUNDING

This advanced exercise helps improve your explosive power and acceleration, making it good for sports that require sudden bursts of speed or activity. It requires high levels of control and whole-body coordination.

Swing your arms for momentum

Raise your knee in an exaggerated stride

Push off from the ball of your foot

Land on your toes

1 Mark out a start and a finish line. From a standing start, lean your weight forward onto your left foot, swinging your left arm backward and your right arm forward.

2 Swing your right leg forward with power and push up as high as you can with your knee, bringing your left arm forward and your right arm backward at the same time.

3 Land on the toes of your right foot and push through with your left leg. Continue the movement for the required distance, bounding from leg to leg.

TESTING EXERCISES

Testing exercises are a useful means of monitoring the rate of your recovery and the development of your power, speed, reach, range of motion, balance, and proprioception during the rehabilitation process. They enable your physical therapist to assess your progress and identify areas for improvement.

162 HORIZONTAL JUMP

This test aims to measure the power in your legs by seeing how far forward you can jump. By holding your hands behind your back, you ensure that your legs do all the work—but be careful not to lose your balance. This test is useful when measuring recovery from a leg, ankle, or foot injury.

Keep your body upright

1 Stand with your feet hip-width apart and your knees slightly bent. Clasp your hands behind your back and keep them there for the duration of the test.

Plant your feet firmly on the ground

2 Drive off the ground, using your leg strength alone to propel you forward as far as you can go.

Swing your legs through to drive your body forward

3 Land on both feet and "stick" to the ground, moving no farther. Measure the distance traveled.

Land with slightly bent knees

163 VERTICAL JUMP

Like the horizontal jump (see above), this test assesses the power in your legs, working in unison, by measuring how high you can jump off the ground.

1 Take a firm stance with your feet hip-width apart and your core muscles engaged.

Bend your knees to prepare

2 Spring straight up, stretching your dominant hand as high as you can to help you lift off the ground.

Reach your arm up to its full extension

Use both legs equally to push off the ground

3 Land on both feet, bending your knees and dispersing the impact through your hips.

Land firmly and keep your legs soft

164 SINGLE HORIZONTAL HOP

Similar to the horizontal jump (see opposite), this test requires you to hop on one leg instead of jumping on both. It enables you to measure the power in each of your legs separately in order to make a useful comparison.

Keep your hands behind your back throughout

Keep upright and strong through your torso to keep your balance

Engage your core muscles

Bend your knee at a right angle

"Stick" to the ground

1 Stand on your left leg and bend your right leg up off the ground. Clasp your hands behind your back throughout.

2 Push hard off the ground with your left foot, and use the power in your left leg to hop forward as far as you can go.

3 Land on your left foot, keeping your knee firm but not locked and your right leg off the ground. Measure the distance traveled. Switch legs.

165 SINGLE VERTICAL HOP

This test is a variation on the vertical jump (see opposite), the difference being that here you are hopping rather than jumping up, enabling you to assess each leg in isolation rather than working together. It measures the power in the hopping leg, and also offers a good indication as to your coordination and balance.

1 Stand on your left leg and raise your right leg off the ground. Hang your arms by your sides and maintain a strong, upright posture.

2 Spring up vertically, using all the power in your left leg. Reach your right arm as high as it will go.

Stretch your arm up to gain extra height

3 Land firmly on your left foot, keeping your right foot off the ground. Repeat the test with your right leg.

Feel the movement in the back of your left leg

Keep your hips aligned

Bend your left knee slightly to prepare

166 ADAPTED CROSS-OVER HOP

This test assesses multiple skills in your legs such as agility, pain tolerance, and balance, and allows you to compare your left and right legs. It is useful for anyone recovering from a lower-limb injury or a surgical procedure. Test each leg three times, comparing either the best or the average effort from each, aiming for a 10% side-to-side difference.

1 Draw two parallel lines 8 in (20 cm) apart. Position yourself to the left of the left-hand line (A), standing on your left foot, with your right leg bent behind you off the ground. Ensuring that you land on your left foot each time, hop diagonally forward as far as you can to the right of the right-hand line (B). Without pausing, hop diagonally forward as far as you can to the left of the left-hand line (C), and then immediately again to the right of the right-hand line (D). Without pausing, hop diagonally to the left once more (E). On your final landing, remain stationary. Ask your partner to measure the distance from where your toes started to where they finished. Repeat the test on your right foot, starting from the right of the right-hand line.

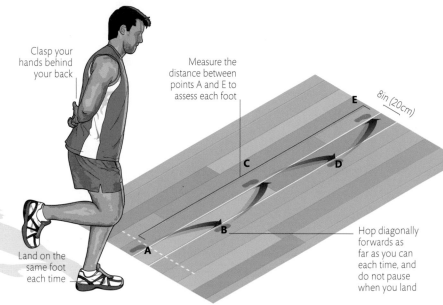

Clasp your hands behind your back

Measure the distance between points A and E to assess each foot

8 in (20 cm)

E

C

D

B

A

Land on the same foot each time

Hop diagonally forwards as far as you can each time, and do not pause when you land

---

167 TRIPLE HOP

This simple maneuver gauges your ability to produce enough power to hop repetitively, and also tests your confidence, pain threshold, shock absorption, and proprioception. The aim is to see how far you can go in three hops, while your therapist will be able to compare the performance of your left and right legs.

Clasp your hands behind your back

Keep your back straight

Push off your foot as soon as you land

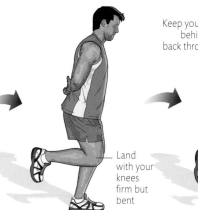

Land with your knees firm but bent

Keep your hands behind your back throughout

Land firmly on your final hop

1 Stand on your left foot with your toes touching a line perpendicular to your feet. Clasp your hands behind your back.

2 Hop forward as far as you can. Complete two more hops in quick succession.

3 Without pausing, hop forward again as far as you can, and then again for your third and final hop.

4 Land firmly after your third hop and do not move. Mark the distance and repeat the hops with your right foot.

168 T-TEST

This useful test can help you assess your recovery from an injury, and is a good method to measure your control, proprioception, confidence, power, and speed. It can also be used as a "T-drill" in the same way as the other speed drills featured in the book (**»pp.252–53**), varying the distances involved, as required.

1 Starting at cone A, run forward for 100 ft (30 m) to touch cone B. Side-step to your left for 16 ft (5 m) to touch cone C. Side-step to your right for 33 ft (10 m) to touch cone D. Side-step to your left 16 ft (5 m) to touch cone B. Then run 100 ft (30 m) backward from cone B to return to cone A. Rest and repeat as required. Record the time it takes you to complete the "T."

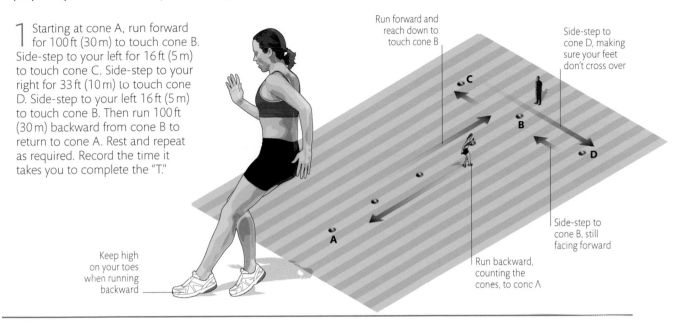

Run forward and reach down to touch cone B

Side-step to cone D, making sure your feet don't cross over

Keep high on your toes when running backward

Side-step to cone B, still facing forward

Run backward, counting the cones, to cone A

169 ISOKINETIC MACHINE TEST

Isokinetic machines provide objective, detailed statistics about the performance of your muscles in isolation, and can help your physical therapist assess your shoulder, hip, knee, or ankle, at an isokinetic speed (meaning it will not allow the limb being tested to move faster than the parameters set). It is useful for providing objective data for long-term injuries and can also be used to identify weaknesses or imbalances by comparing your left and right sides. If weakness or imbalances are identified, the machine can be used to work on them, alongside functional rehabilitation training (a technique known as an integrated rehabilitation). To ensure safety and accuracy, you should only use the machine under the guidance of your physical therapist.

1 Your physical therapist will instruct you on the correct techniques, along with the specific number of repetitions, sets, and speeds required. These will depend on your injury, the affected body part, and which stage you have reached in your rehabilitation. This will ensure that you use the machine safely and that the information it provides is accurate, helping your physical therapist direct your rehabilitation program and monitor your progress.

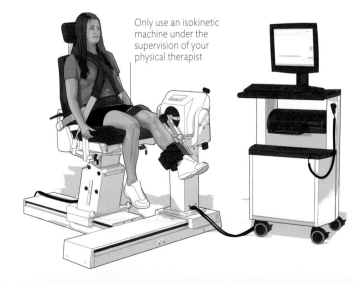

Only use an isokinetic machine under the supervision of your physical therapist

GLOSSARY

Abductor A muscle that functions to pull a limb away from your body.

Achilles tendon A long *tendon* in your body that attaches your calf muscles to your heel bone.

Active range of motion During rehabilitation, the movements you are able to make yourself using muscle strength, as opposed to your *passive range of motion*.

Acute Happening quickly or lasting for a short time.

Adductor A muscle that functions to pull a limb toward your body.

Aerobic A process that requires oxygen. Aerobic *metabolism* occurs during long-duration, low-intensity exercises, such as long-distance running and swimming.

Alternating grip A grip on a bar in which one palm faces toward your body, the other away. This grip prevents a loaded bar from rolling in your hands and is recommended when working with very heavy weights.

Anaerobic A process that takes place without oxygen. Anaerobic *metabolism* occurs during short-duration, high-intensity exercises, such as weight lifting and sprinting.

Analgesic medication Used to relieve or reduce pain, this can be applied topically or administered by tablet or injection. Different medications have different functions, for example reducing pain by reducing inflammation, but all produce the result of limiting your experience of pain in the body.

Antagonistic muscles Muscles that are arranged in pairs to carry out flexion and extension of a joint; for example, one muscle of the pair contracts to move a limb in one direction, and the other contracts to move it in the opposite direction.

Anterior The front part or surface, as opposed to *posterior*.

Barbell A type of *free weight* made up of a bar with weights at both ends, which is long enough for you to hold with at least a shoulder width grip. The weights may be permanently fixed or removable.

Baseline scores Measurements taken at the beginning of a process of training or physical therapy; these provide a control against which to judge levels of improvement.

Biceps Any muscle that has two *heads* or origins, but commonly used as shorthand for the biceps brachii, which is located on your upper arm.

Bone density The amount of bone tissue in a given volume of bone.

Bursa A sac of fluid found around most joints of the body. It reduces friction, allowing joints to move freely. The plural of bursa is bursae.

Bursitis Inflammation of the *bursa*, making movement of the joint to which it is attached difficult and painful.

Cable pulley machine A resistance training machine in which various attachments, such as a bar, handle, or rope, can be linked to weights by a cable. Force is transferred via a pulley or system of pulleys. These machines are designed to provide continual resistance throughout the full range of motion of the exercise.

Cardiac muscle A type of involuntary muscle found in the walls of your heart.

Chronic Persists for a long time.

Clean In weight lifting, a single explosive movement used to lift the weight to shoulder height.

Cool-down A period after completion of your main training session that includes activities such as slow jogging, walking, and stretching of your major muscle groups. It is designed to help return your body to its preexercise state.

Core The central part of the body, mainly the stomach and lower back muscles, but also including the pelvis, chest, and upper back.

Corticosteroids Hormones applied via injection, cream, or tablets, for example to reduce inflammation.

CT scan Stands for X-ray Computed Tomography. This type of scan builds a 3D picture of the body by taking two images and putting them together digitally.

Dislocation Usually caused by a blow to a joint, which then becomes detached from its setting.

Displaced fracture An injury where the two parts of a broken bone have pulled away from each other.

Drill Practice version of a skill required in sport, usually repeated.

Dumbbell A type of *free weight* made up of a short bar with a weight at each end. It can be lifted with one hand.

Dynamic exercise Any activity in which your joints and muscles are moving.

Erector A muscle that raises a body part.

Explosive power The maximum power you have, applied in a short burst.

Extensor A muscle that works to increase the angle at a joint—for example straightening your elbow. It usually works in tandem with a *flexor*.

Fracture A break in a bone, ranging from minor cracks to serious breaks into separate fragments.

Flexor A muscle that works to decrease the angle at a joint—for example bending your elbow. It usually works in tandem with an *extensor*.

Form The posture or stance used when performing exercises. Good or proper form makes the exercise more effective and helps prevent injury.

Free weight A weight—usually a *barbell* or *dumbbell*—not tethered to a cable or machine.

Head (of a muscle) The point of origin of a muscle.

Hernia Occurs when an organ protrudes through the wall of, for example, the muscle that holds it.

Hook grip A method of holding a barbell where the fingers cover the thumb, which helps maintain control of the weight.

Impingement Pain resulting from rubbing between the tendons of the rotator cuff in the shoulder, often caused by inflammation forcing them against each other.

Isometric A form of training in which your muscles work but do not contract significantly, such as when pushing against an immovable object.

Isotonic A form of training in which your muscles work against a constant resistance, so that the muscles contract while the resistance remains the same.

ITB (Iliotibial Band) A tough group of fibers running along the outside of your thigh that primarily works as a stabilizer during running.

Lactic acid A waste product of *anaerobic* respiration. It accumulates in your muscles during intense exercise and is involved in the chemical processes that cause muscular cramp.

Lateral Positioned toward the outside of your body or a part of your body. Movement in the lateral plane refers to a side-to-side movement.

Ligament A tough and fibrous connective tissue that connects your bones together at your joints.

Medicine ball A weighted ball for use in *plyometric* weight training. It can help to build explosive power.

Metabolism The sum of all your body's chemical processes; it comprises anabolism (building up compounds) and catabolism (breaking down compounds).

Mineral Any one of many inorganic (noncarbon-based) elements that are essential for normal body function and that must be included in your diet.

Mobility exercise An exercise that helps you maximize the ease of use of your joints, or helps a physical therapist assess your level of rehabilitation.

MRI (Magnetic Resonance Imaging) A type of scan that reads the molecular structure of the body to form an image to aid diagnoses.

Neutral spine The position of the spine that is considered to be good posture. In this posture, the spine is not completely straight, but has slight curves in its upper and lower regions. It is the strongest and most balanced position for the spine and needs to be maintained in many exercises.

One-rep max The maximum amount of weight that you can lift in a single *repetition* for a specific weight-based exercise.

Osteoarthritis A degenerative disease in which the body suffers a loss of cartilage, leading to stiff, painful joints.

Passive range of motion The movements a physical therapist or helper is able to make with parts of your body while fully supporting the weight of the body parts.

Plyometrics Exercises that aim to improve the speed and power of movements by training muscles to contract more quickly and powerfully.

Posterior The back part or surface, as opposed to *anterior*.

Power The amount of force produced by a body movement in a given time—a combination of strength and speed.

Preexhaustion A form of training in which you carry out a single joint exercise before a heavy compound movement for that body part, thereby stressing the target muscle before you start to work it properly.

Proprioception The term used to describe the signals originating from joints, tendons, ligaments, and muscles that is sent to the brain to provide information about joint position, direction, and pressure.

Quadriceps Any muscle with four heads, but commonly used to describe the large muscle at the front of your thigh.

Range of motion (ROM) A term used in physical therapy, this is the movements a particular joint is capable of in every direction. Limited ROM means that you are unable to use your joint as normal.

Regimen A regulated course of exercise and diet designed to produce a predetermined result.

Rehabilitation The process of recovering fully from an injury, often with the assistance of professionals.

Repetition (rep) One complete movement of a particular exercise, from start to finish and back.

Resistance training Any type of training in which your muscles work against resistance; the resistance may be provided by a weight, an elastic or rubber band, or your own body weight.

Rest interval The pause between *sets* of an exercise that allows muscle recovery.

Rotator cuff The four muscles—the supraspinatus, infraspinatus, teres minor, and subscapularis—and their associated *tendons* that hold your humerus (the long bone of your upper arm) in place in your shoulder joint and enable your arm to rotate. Rotator cuff injuries are common in sports that involve throwing motions.

Rupture A major tear in a muscle, tendon, or ligament. Organs can protrude through muscle ruptures, producing *hernias*.

Set A specific number of *repetitions*.

Shoulder girdle The ring of bones (actually an incomplete ring) at your shoulder that provides an attachment point for the many muscles that allow your shoulder and elbow joints to move.

Skeletal muscle Also called striated muscle, this type of muscle is attached to your skeleton and is under voluntary control. Contracting your skeletal muscle allows you to move your body under control.

Slide-board A smooth board with adjustable bumpers at either end.

Smith machine A common piece of gym equipment made up of a *barbell* constrained within sets of parallel steel rails that allow the motion of the bar only in a limited vertical direction.

Smooth muscle A type of muscle found in the walls of all the hollow organs of your body which is not under voluntary control.

Spotter A training partner who assists you with a lift, providing encouragement and physical support if necessary, for example intervening if you are about to fail the lift.

Sprain An injury sustained by a *ligament* that is overstretched or torn.

Stabilizers The muscles that help you to keep your balance while you are working a particular muscle. Sit-ups, for example, primarily work the stomach muscles but other muscles are also working to stabilize you.

Static exercise An exercise in which you hold one position—for example, pushing against an immovable object.

Strain An injury to muscle fibers caused by overstretching.

Strength training A form of *resistance training* in which your aim is to build the strength of your *skeletal muscle*.

Subluxation Partial dislocation of a joint.

Swiss ball A large, inflatable rubber ball used to promote stability during exercise. Also known as an exercise ball.

Tear A rip in, for example, a muscle.

Tendinopathy Painful *tendons*, often resulting from overuse while doing repetitive actions.

Tendon A type of connective tissue that joins your muscles to your bones, thereby transmitting the force of muscle contraction to your bones.

Thoracic Relating to the chest area.

Triceps Any muscle with three *heads*, but commonly used as shorthand for the triceps brachii, which extends your elbow.

Undisplaced fracture An injury in which cracks may form in the bone but the parts of the bone do not separate.

VISA-P (Victorian Institute of Sport Assessment patellar score) A measure of patellar fitness based on a questionnaire.

Warm-up A series of low-intensity exercises that prepares your body for a workout by moderately stimulating your heart, lungs, and muscles. These normally involve a combination of *dynamic exercises* and low-intensity cardiovascular work.

Wobble board Circular in shape with a flat top and hemispherical underside, this piece of equipment is used to promote good balance, and to improve the stability of your *core*.

INDEX

ACKNOWLEDGMENTS

ABOUT THE CONTRIBUTORS

Dr. Ian Beasley is Head of Medical Services for the English Football Association, and the senior England soccer team. He has worked for a number of soccer clubs in all the senior English divisions, and at major tournaments, such as the Olympic and Commonwealth Games. He is based in London, England.

Dr. Colin Crosby is Medical Director of the Department of Sports and Exercise Medicine at The Garden Hospital, London, England, and Treasurer and Past President of the Sports and Exercise Section of The Royal Society of Medicine.

Dr. Geoff Davies is a Wales-based Sports Physician who provides clinical services to both the NHS and the UK Ministry of Defence. He is also Sports Physician to the Cardiff Blues and Wales Under-18 rugby union teams.

Prof. Lennard Funk is an Orthopedic Surgeon at Wrightington Hospital, Lancashire, England, and Professor at Salford University, England. He lectures widely on shoulder surgery, sports injuries, and medical informatics.

Dr. Peter Gerbino is a Fellow of the American Academy of Orthopedic Surgeons. He is a team physician for the US figure-skating team and has provided medical care for many other top US athletes. He is based in Monterey, California.

Dr. Joanne Larkin is a Specialist Registrar trainee in Sports and Exercise Medicine (London Deanery), undertaking an MSc in SEM at Bath University, England.

Dr. Ritan Mehta is a Registrar on the Specialist Training program in Sports and Exercise Medicine in London, England, and Club Doctor for Barnet Football Club. He is also a general practitioner with a special interest in Musculoskeletal Medicine and Rheumatology.

Dr. James Noake is a Specialist Registrar trainee in Sports and Exercise Medicine (London Deanery), and gained an MSc SEM in 2006/07.

Dr. Gary O'Driscoll is Club Doctor for Arsenal Football Club. He was also Doctor to the Ireland rugby union team and the last two British Lions rugby union tour.

Filippo Spiezia is a fourth-year resident in Trauma and Orthopedic Surgery at Università Campus Bio-Medico, Rome, Italy. He has a special interest in Sports Trauma.

Dr. Richard Weiler is a Specialist Registrar in Sports and Exercise Medicine at Imperial College Healthcare NHS Trust, Charing Cross Hospital, London, England. He also works with the England soccer and British Paralympic teams.

Chris Lendrum is a practicing physical therapist at Kensington Physiotherapy, London, England, with interests in shoulder and spinal rehabilitation. A Member of the UK Chartered Society of Physiotherapists, he also holds a diploma in Personal Training and Sports Massage.

The publisher and consultant editors would also like to thank the following individuals for their contributions: **Dr. Jane Dunbar; Dr. Eric N. Dubrow; Dr. Graham Jackson; Dr. David Lloyd; Dr. Kalpesh Parmar; Mr. Ron McCulloch; Dr. Richard Smith; Mr. Andy Williams; Graham Anderson; and Paula Coates.**

PUBLISHER'S ACKNOWLEDGMENTS

Many thanks to the following people and organizations for their generous help in producing this book.

For modelling: Scott Tindal; Mary Paternoster; Gareth Jones; Sam Bias Ferrar; Chris Chea; Michelle Grey; Anouska Hipperson; Sean Newton; Caroline Pearce; Rufus Shosman; and William Smith.

For use of facilities: Fit Club, Wymondham, Norfolk, England; Jackie Waite and the staff at Woking Leisure Center & Pool in the Park, England; and Karen Pearce and the staff at Fenner's Fitness Suite at the University of Cambridge, England.

For additional material and assistance: Derek Groves; Glen Thurgood; Len Williams; the British Weightlifting Association (BWLA); Hannah Bowen; Cressida Tuson; Ruth O'Rourke-Jones; Constance Novis; Heather Jones; Jemima Dunne; and Mary Allen.

Many thanks to all the illustrators who worked so hard throughout the project: Philip Wilson; Debbie Maizels; Mark Walker; Mike Garland; Darren R. Awuah; Debajyoti Dutta; Richard Tibbitts (Antbits Illustration); Jon Rogers, Phil Gamble; and Joanna Cameron. Thank you also to Margaret McCormack for indexing.

PICTURE CREDITS

Thank you to the following agencies and individuals for their kind permission to use their photographs as reference:
Getty: 002-003c; 048-049c
Biodex Medical Systems, Inc.: 263b (photo courtesy of Biodex Medical Systems, Inc.)

SAFETY INFORMATION

All physical activity involves some risk of injury. Participants must therefore take all reasonable care during their training, and on the field of play. Any individual who is intending to start a new sporting activity or exercise program should always seek professional medical advice before they begin. Any treatment or rehabilitation program should always be carried out under the guidance of the appropriate professionals. Users of this book should not consider the information it contains as a substitute for the advice of medical professionals and accredited physical therapists.

The publishers of this book, and its contributors, are confident that the exercises described herein, when performed correctly, with gradual increases in resistance and proper supervision, are safe. However, readers of this book must ensure that the equipment and facilities they use are fit for purpose, and they should adhere to safety guidelines at all times. They should also ensure that supervisors have adequate insurance and relevant, up-to-date accreditations and qualifications, including emergency first aid.

The publishers, medical consultants, consultant editors, and contributing authors of this publication take no responsibility for injury to persons or property consequent on embarking upon the exercises and treatments described herein.